Gender, Sex, and Sexuality in Musical Theatre

Gender, Sex, and Sexuality in Musical Theatre

He/She/They Could Have Danced All Night

EDITED AND CURATED BY

Kelly Kessler

Bristol, UK / Chicago, USA

First published in the UK in 2023 by
Intellect, The Mill, Parnall Road, Fishponds, Bristol, BS16 3JG, UK

First published in the USA in 2023 by
Intellect, The University of Chicago Press, 1427 E. 60th Street, Chicago, IL 60637, USA

Copyright © 2023 Intellect Ltd

All rights reserved. No part of this publication may be reproduced, stored in a retrieval system, or transmitted, in any form or by any means, electronic, mechanical, photocopying, recording, or otherwise, without written permission.

A catalogue record for this book is available from the British Library.

Copy editor: MPS Limited
Cover designer: Aleksandra Szumlas
Cover image: Royer Bockus and Tatiana Wechsler in Rodgers and Hammerstein's *Oklahoma!*, directed by Bill Rauch, Oregon Shakespeare Festival, 2018. Photo by Mark Holthusen.
Production manager: Debora Nicosia
Typesetter: MPS Limited

Hardback ISBN 978-1-78938-619-6
ePDF ISBN 978-1-78938-620-2
ePUB ISBN 978-1-78938-621-9

To find out about all our publications, please visit our website. There you can subscribe to our e-newsletter, browse or download our current catalogue and buy any titles that are in print.

www.intellectbooks.com

This is a peer-reviewed publication.

*To the queer kids and gender outcasts
who found their adolescent homes in the musical.
I was you (and still am).*

Contents

List of Figures   xi
Acknowledgements   xiii
Introduction: Belting Away at Binaries   xv
  Kelly Kessler

PART 1: EXPLORING AND EXPLODING THE GENDER BINARY ON THE MUSICAL STAGE   1

1. The Radio City Rockettes and the Making of a Sisterhood   3
   Adrienne Gibbons Oehlers
2. *Billy Elliot the Musical*: Visual Representations of Working-Class Masculinity and the All-Singing, All-Dancing Bo[d]y   16
   George Rodosthenous
3. *Hamilton*'s Women   36
   Stacy Wolf
4. Rewriting the American West: Black Feminist (Re)Vision in *Bella: An American Tall Tale*   53
   Jordan Ealey
5. A-List Drag Queens, Accidental Drag Kings and Illegible Gender Rebels: (Mis)Representations of Trans Experience in Contemporary Musicals   72
   Janet Werther

PART 2: EMBODYING AND EXPLOITING SEX AND SEXUALITY ON AND OFF BROADWAY   95

6. Chorus Boys: Words, Music and Queerness (*c.*1900–36)   97
   David Haldane Lawrence

7. Emancipation or Exploitation? Gender Liberation and Adult Musicals in 1970s New York ... 112
   Elizabeth L. Wollman
8. A Substitute for Love: The Performance of Sex in *Spring Awakening* ... 144
   Bryan M. Vandevender
9. If You Were Gay, That'd Be Okay: Marketing LGBTQ+ Musicals from *La Cage* to *The Prom* ... 155
   Ryan Donovan

PART 3: DIVAS DON'T CARE ABOUT NOBODY'S RULES ... 175

10. Embracing Excess: The Queer Feminist Power of Musical Theatre Diva Roles ... 177
    Michelle Dvoskin
11. Stepping Out of Line: (Re)Claiming the Diva for the Dancers of Broadway ... 190
    Dustyn Martincich
12. Diva Relations in *The Color Purple*, the 2015 Broadway Revival ... 205
    Deborah Paredez
13. How Can the Small Screen Contain Her? Television, Genre and the Twenty-First-Century Broadway Diva Onslaught ... 226
    Kelly Kessler

PART 4: ONSTAGE, OFFSTAGE AND ONLINE: GENDER AND SEXUALITY IN PERSONAL AND PROFESSIONAL MUSICAL PRACTICE ... 247

14. The Queerness of *Copla*: Musical Hope for the Spanish LGBTQ ... 249
    Alejandro Postigo
15. Queering Brechtian Feminism: Breaking Down Gender Binaries in Musical Theatre Pedagogical Performance Practices ... 268
    Sherrill Gow
16. For Progress or Profit: The Possibilities and Limitations of Playing with Gender in Twenty-First-Century Musical Theatre ... 283
    Stephanie Lim

17. The Right to See and Not Be Seen: South Korean Musicals and   301
    Young Feminist Activism
    Jiyoon Jung

Notes on Contributors   319

Figures

2.1: George Maguire as Billy Elliot dancing (Victoria Palace, 2005). Photo: David Scheinmann. — 20

2.2: Haydn Gwynne as Mrs Wilkinson and company dancing (Victoria Palace, 2005). Photo: David Scheinmann. — 23

2.3: George Maguire as Billy Elliot dancing against the police (Victoria Palace, 2005). Photo: David Scheinmann. — 27

4.1: Bella (Ashley D. Kelley) harnesses the possibilities of her embodied power in a confrontation with Bonny Jonny Rakehell (Kevin Massey). In this scene, her booty becomes the source of her strength rather than an object to be sexualized by men (*Bella: An American Tall Tale*, courtesy of Joan Marcus). — 64

4.2: Evoking the power of black feminist collectivity and the continued empowerment of black women rooted in their communities, The Spirit of the Booty (Natasha Yvette Williams), Bella's ancestor and protector, appears to help Bella discover her inner strength (*Bella: An American Tall Tale*, courtesy of Joan Marcus). — 65

5.1: After the relationship between Reagan (Erin Markey) and companion Irish Cream (Becca Blackwell) turns aggressive and then awkwardly amorous, Reagan croons into the microphone while sporting the 'kiss' bestowed by Cream, a dashing horse/boat (*A Ride on the Irish Cream*. Photograph courtesy of Erin Markey). — 87

5.2: The at times complicated legibility of queer, non-binary and trans identity and desire comes to the stage as Reagan (Erin Markey) screams while horse/boat Irish Cream (Becca Blackwell) wraps their hooves around their femme companion (*A Ride on the Irish Cream*. Photograph courtesy of Erin Markey). — 88

9.1:	This heteronormatively-framed advertisement for *La Cage aux Folles* celebrating original star Gene Barry's return to the production appeared in the *New York Times* on 12 January 1986.	159
9.2:	Unlike its print campaign, *Fun Home*'s social media connected the show's message to queer-linked contemporary events, as seen in this Instagram post on the day the US Supreme Court made equal marriage the law. Image from *Fun Home*'s Instagram account, 26 June 2015, USA.	167
12.1:	*The Color Purple* original Broadway musical poster (2005). Artist Unknown. TMG – The Marketing Group.	210
12.2 and 12.3:	*The Color Purple* Broadway musical revival posters (2015, 2016). Photographer Unknown. Type A Marketing.	211
13.1:	Angela Lansbury's lovable Jessica Fletcher made *Murder She Wrote* an audience favorite, thrusting the Broadway diva's iconic Mama Rose, Mame and Mrs Lovett into the rearview mirror (*TV Guide* advertisement, 27 October–2 November 1984).	230
13.2:	The millennial trend of producing one-off musical episodes of fictional television shows created a perfect opportunity for crossover actresses like *Spamalot* Tony-winner Sara Ramirez to show off her diva chops. Here she blows out 'The Story' to the comatose version of her character in *Grey's Anatomy*'s (2011, Episode 'Song Beneath the Song').	240
14.1:	*The Copla Musical*'s protagonist La Gitana drawing inspiration from the Spanish *folklórica*'s gypsy features (*The Copla Musical*. Photograph courtesy of Alejandro Postigo).	262
16.1:	Heralding the ideological impact of its gender-bent casting and narrative reworking, the Oregon Shakespeare Festival posted the heartfelt sentiments of one of its *Oklahoma!* cast members on its Twitter feed, 17 July 2020, US.	293

Acknowledgements

I would like to thank the folks at Intellect for approaching me with this project and allowing me the opportunity to help contribute to the ever-growing body of scholarly work drawing together the inherent links between gender, sex and sexuality and the musical across stages and screens. *Gender, Sex, and Sexuality in Musical Theatre: He/She/They Could Have Danced All Night* provided me with a wonderful opportunity to comb over and revel in over a decade's worth of material published in *Studies in Musical Theatre* and (re)discover so much work that had been produced by my colleagues across the field of musical theatre studies. Huge thanks to Jessica Lovett for reaching out to me and working with me throughout. Also, thanks to the copyeditors at Intellect and all of the folks on the backend that made this project come to fruition.

I would also like to give a huge shout out to all of the original *Studies in Musical Theatre* contributors for their willingness to share their works in this volume, as well as George Burrows and Dominic Symonds for making the journal what it became. I love the idea of giving people's work a second life, as so many articles become lost in the jungle of journal databases. Tremendous thanks to my contributors who created new works for this collection: Ryan Donovan, Jordan Ealey, Stephanie Lim, Alejandro Postigo and Janet Werther. This project came to all of you during the crazy-times that were the COVID-19-shutdown of 2020, something that made everyone's already complicated life even more unruly. I cannot express my gratitude enough for each of you powering through to complete works that truly added amazing breadth to the existing essays. Also, thanks to Bryan Vandevender for being another set of eyes when I simply couldn't wrap my head around things and Elizabeth L. Wollman for her repeated advice and constant willingness to be a sounding board. (I owe you both drinks.) As an interloper from film and television studies, I consider myself incredibly lucky to have snuck into the world of musical theatre studies and found such amazing colleagues. You all know who you are.

And finally, thank you to my friends and family and everyone who put up with me and my overwhelmedness as I pulled through to the completion of this project during the COVID-19-era. As one of the many things I had agreed to do before the world imploded, this was a struggle at times. Far too many pieces of quarantine candy and far too many COVID-19-shutdown chips were eaten while trying to work while also homeschooling quarantined twins. High five to Katy Maher for keeping me sane with virtual support and shared snark. (I'd say hugs, but she knows I have personal space issues.) Huge kudos to my wife Elizabeth for deftly appearing as if she was listening to me when I was rambling about the project and for keeping the kids intact when I disappeared. Her ability to survive me is constantly baffling. In the words of Richard Rodgers through the mouth of *The Sound of Music*'s filmic Maria (in a song I love despite its overall lack of popularity): 'Nothing comes from nothing. Nothing ever could. So somewhere in my youth or childhood. I must have done something ... something good'.

Introduction:
Belting Away at Binaries

Kelly Kessler

When I was 11, my parents took me to the St. Louis Municipal Opera Theatre, also known as 'The MUNY' – the United States' largest outdoor musical theatre – to see Lynn Redgrave star alongside Michael Kermoyan in Rodgers and Hammerstein's *The King and I*. As I sat drenched in Midwestern humidity alongside 11 thousand other dedicated fans, watching and listening as the British star of stage and screen tamed the arrogant Siamese ruler while teaching him to dance, I learned just what passion was. Watching them whip each other into some kind of erotically energetic polka-waltz frenzy, dress hoops and silken trousers careening around the proscenium-bound ballroom, my preteen-self knew what romance and sensuality were supposed to look like. Summer after summer, a perfect synthesis of heartland heat and musicalized desire taught me the secrets of gender, sex and sexuality. I learned just as much about who I should be from watching *Hee Haw* honey Misty Rowe and National Football League Hall of Famer Joe Namath cavort in *Li'l Abner* as I had from whispers on the school bus and salacious made-for-tv movies.

    Although in retrospect it seems I may have been having an unwittingly queered voyeuristic love affair with a whirling Ms. Redgrave, critics and fans alike often mistake theatrical song and dance as evoking a sweeping sense of simplicity, heteronormativity and traditionalism. For me, nothing drives home the cultural misunderstanding of the genre's sexual and relational proclivities like my own mother's frequent insistence that my young niece and nephew and I watch the Clint Eastwood-Lee Marvin cinematic transfer of Paddy Chayefsky's *Paint Your Wagon* (1969) because it struck her as a 'sweet movie'. In her memory, good old-fashioned singing and dancing – matched with the power of an assumed hegemonic embrace of social norms – far outweighed the whoremongering, rampant alcoholism, wife-selling and what appears to be narratively sanctioned polyamory.

    Although certainly times have changed – as have the stories being musicalized and televised – gender and sexuality still find themselves embedded in the heart of tales being told through and about musical theatre. So, that's why we're here.

Over a span of four sections and seventeen authors, *Gender, Sex, and Sexuality in Musical Theatre: He/She/They Could Have Danced All Night* digs into a cultural site many critics and historians have framed as one of the most culturally conservative, traditional forms of theatre. This collection sets out to accomplish two simultaneous tasks: breathe new life into a series of articles published over a nearly fifteen-year span in *Studies in Musical Theatre*, and assemble a much-needed and accessible collection of established and emergent scholars wrestling with gender, sex and sexuality across methodologies, time periods, identities and nations.

To date, scholarly attention to these issues within musical theatre has been restricted mainly to single-subject books like Stacy Wolf's *A Problem Like Maria* (2002), scattered journal articles like David Savran's '"You've Got That Thing": Cole Porter, Stephen Sondheim, and the Erotics of the List Song' (2012) or passing reference in more canonical texts like Raymond Knapp's *The American Musical and the Formation of National Identity* (2005). Surely such works have helped establish the field of musical theatre studies; in fact, the influence of Wolf and Knapp will be seen all over the texts included herein. Although *Gender, Sex, and Sexuality in Musical Theatre: He/She/They Could Have Danced All Night* by no means presents a comprehensive or final say on the matter, the collection provides a broad gander at musical theatre across a range of intersecting lenses: race, nation, form, dance, casting, marketing, pedagogy, industry, platform-specificity, stardom, politics and so on. Gender and desire have been at the heart of the genre from inception, whether because 'birds and bees' (and 'educated fleas') were doing it, a farm girl simply couldn't 'say no', or one's 'tits and ass' were preventing them from landing a gig. This collection seeks to display the genre's breadth, as well as to demonstrate the growth and expanse of the ever-burgeoning sub-discipline of musical theatre studies.

As early as 1972, at least one historian – pre-dating the establishment of the musical theatre discipline by some two decades – was framing American musical theatre as a form driven by *love*. Sure, this romanticized analytical contextualization of the form was concurrent with Broadway pushing *against* more socially reconcilable narratives with an influx of sexually and politically charged productions like *Cabaret* (1966), *Hair* (1967) and *Oh! Calcutta!* (1969), but nonetheless, historians were freezing the form in over-simplified notions of heteronormative romance. It was 1972, the same year Stephen Schartz's existential *Pippin* took home the Tony for Best Musical and Robert Morse snatched Best Actor for rocking a dress and falling backward into a geriatric queer romance in Jule Styne and Bob Merrill's *Sugar*, that the composer and conductor-turned theater historian Lehman Engel identified *romance* – the heteronormative kind – as a central driver of musical theatre. The television and Broadway veteran's aforementioned seminal work, *Words with Music: Creating the Broadway Musical Libretto*, placed *romance* alongside five other characteristics he identified as the musicals 'outer form': feeling, lyrics and particularization, music and comedy (Engel 2006: 71). It would ultimately take until the late nineties and early 2000s for musical theatre as a scholarly discipline to really turn its attentions to the study of identity.

Scholars from my first academic home, film studies, published a wave of scholarship blending gender and the musical genre, starting in the late 1970s and moving on through the 1980s. Richard Dyer's 'Entertainment and Utopia' (1977), Thomas Schatz's *Hollywood Genres* (1981), Jane Feuer's *The Hollywood Musical* (1982) and Rick Altman's *The American Film Musical* (1987) all touched on various ways in which film norms, narrative structure, choreography, cinematography and gendered and bodily performances continually came together to project a cinematic form awash with hegemonic tales and heteronormative reconciliation – even if only through the magic of narrative gymnastics and cinematic wizardry.

By the 1990s and early 2000s, media scholars specializing in queer and gender studies – including Steve Neale ('Masculinity as Spectacle' [1983]), Alexander Doty (*Flaming Classics: Queering the Film Cannon* [2000]), Brett Farmer (*Spectacular Passions: Cinema, Fantasy, Gay Male Spectatorship* [2000]) and Steven Cohan (*Incongruous Entertainment: Camp, Cultural Value, and the MGM Musical* [2005]) – were exploring the intersections of queer reception, stardom, camp, bodily display, narrative form and cinematography in hopes of challenging the hetero-feminine framing of the foundational film genre. Although films often presented boy-meets-girl plots and storylines, scholars began exploring the ideological and affective implications of men's bodies engaging in musical performance, the queer meaning of Judy Garland's diegetic and real-world struggles and the queer pleasures of visual and performative excess within the musical genre.

All of these works influenced my 2010 book, *Destabilizing the Hollywood Musical: Music, Masculinity, and Mayhem*, and help me frame its exploration of how shifts in cinematic form, cultural norms, industrial practices and performance styles led to a spate of movie musicals undermining or decentring the hegemonic masculinity and heteronormative relationships which had formed the core of the genre. Certainly, films like *Phantom of the Paradise* (1974), *The Rocky Horror Picture Show* (1975), *Tommy* (1975), *Bugsy Malone* (1976) and *Cannibal! The Musical* (1993) took film – and gender studies – in new directions. But by the late 1990s, musical theatre studies, too, had begun to cohere as a subdiscipline, and to focus on identity and the ideological underpinnings of the musical stage.

In her overview of the disciplinary development of musical theatre studies, Elizabeth L. Wollman addresses the slow-to-start establishment of a dedicated space for the study of musical theatre within the academy. Whether because of the delegitimization of the middlebrow theatrical form by the academy or the ephemerality of its focus, musical theatre remained on the outskirts of academia – or subsumed by other disciplines – until at least the 1990s (Wollman 2021). In the last two years of the 1900s, both literary/film scholar DA Miller and theatre artist/scholar John M. Clum published landmark works addressing the intersections of queer reception, queer and homophobic narrative and gay culture: *Place for Us: Essay on the Broadway Musical* (1998) and *Something for the Boys: Musical Theatre and Gay Culture* (1999), respectively. Reclaiming the musical for gay men – both artists and fans – who had both driven the industry and been mocked for their reverence of it, Clum and Miller uncloseted the musical, delved into its textual and extratextual sexualities, and prompted other musical theater scholars to investigate and unpack aspects of the gendered, sexual and counter-hegemonic underpinnings of the art form.

Through the first two decades of the twenty-first century, publications like Stacy Wolf's *A Problem Like Maria: Gender and Sexuality in the American Musical* (2002) and *Changed for Good: A Feminist History of the Broadway Musical* (2011), Bud Coleman and Judith Sebasta's anthology *Women in Musical Theatre* (2008) and Elizabeth L. Wollman's *Hard Times: The Adult Musical in 1970s New York City* (2012) helped establish a powerful wing of musical theatre studies dedicated to historical, performative, formal, industrial and interpretive studies of gender, sex and sexuality. The journal *Studies in Musical Theatre*, established in 2005 by British musical theatre scholars Dominic Symonds and George Burrows, has helped foster a vibrant community of scholars invested in the academic study of musical theatre. This collection tips its hat to the work of that journal.

Design of collection

When Intellect contacted me about searching the archives of *Studies in Musical Theatre* to curate an anthology focusing on gender, sex and sexuality, I found myself confronted with a multi-part challenge: how to narrow down the nearly fifty articles that had run in the journal and engaged with one of those broad topics; how to organize the collection thematically within such a huge subject; and how to make the contributor list and subjects covered more inclusive. Addressing all three challenges forced me to leave an array of valuable articles from past *Studies in Musical Theatre* issues on the cutting room floor, articles by such prolific musicologists, cultural historians and artist/scholars as Jessica Sternfeld, George Burrows, Jessica Hillman-McCord, Julianne Lindberg, Maya Cantu and many others. As much as these scholars helped strengthen and inform the subdiscipline, I nevertheless ended up choosing pieces that I believe speak to larger issues around performance, story structure, production, reception or pedagogy.

During my dive into the journal's annals, I noticed a dearth of work by scholars living outside the US and UK, by queer scholars and scholars of color writing about

INTRODUCTION

their own communities, and by scholars engaging with trans or non-binary inclusion within musical theatre texts or larger industrial practices. Adding five new pieces to an already strong list of *Studies in Musical Theatre* articles, I sought to chip away at some of these omissions. While more diversity and inclusivity could certainly exist within the collection, new pieces on Spanish musical theatre performance and fandom; historicity and musical stories told through Black female authorship, gender-flipped; non-binary; and trans narratives, and the negotiated marketing of queerness on Broadway provide a solid start in diversifying scholarly voices and addressing some more contemporary musical productions, approaches and challenges.

The collection unfolds through four separate, overlapping sections: 'Exploring and Exploding the Gender Binary on the Musical Stage' takes a glance at gendered norms, expectations, and rebellion; 'Embodying and Exploiting Sex and Sexuality On and Off Broadway' focuses on musicalized sex and sexualized productions and performers; 'Divas Don't Care About Nobody's Rules' looks at gendered excess and iconography; and 'Onstage, Offstage and Online: Gender and Sexuality in Personal and Professional Musical Practice' traces the synthesis of gendered and sexual politics and theatrical practice. Although many of the essays bridge these larger subject areas, each one also adds to the bigger picture, which tracks musical theatre's shifting floor of ideological engagement.

Part 1: Exploring and exploding the gender binary on the musical stage

This first section negotiates various takes on codified notions of the gender binary. Rejecting any notion that musical theatre has frozen hegemonic gender norms into sonic and performative amber, the first five essays provide a look at the form through historically conservative performances of leggy Rockette femininity, *Billy Elliot*'s intersections of feminized dance and working class masculinity, contemporary struggles to articulate women's voices in *Hamilton* and *Bella: An American Tall Tale*, and the struggle for legible and marketable trans inclusivity in the contemporary musical landscape.

Performer, former-Rockette and musical theatre scholar Adrienne Gibbons Oehlers presents 'The Radio City Rockettes and the Making of a Sisterhood', a dichotomous look at the theatrical chorus girl via strictures of the Broadway-adjacent dance troupe. Since their pre-Depression Era beginnings, the high-kickers appeared as 'wholesome family entertainment', sidestepping (or kicking) the sexual stigma of Broadway chorus girls and ladies of vaudeville. Oehlers explores the Rockettes' magical synthesis of flesh and good clean fun through decades of racial and body-based homogeneity and contractual wholesomeness. Perhaps more than any other performers or performances discussed in this collection, the Rockettes *are* idealized femininity – at least per the good folks at Radio City.

Next, director and theatre researcher George Rodosthenous zeroes in on masculinity and strict codes of cis-hetero male performance in his essay '*Billy Elliot the Musical*: Visual Representations of Working-Class Masculinity and the All-Singing, All-Dancing Bo[d]y'. Rather than dismantling working class masculinity or framing dance as a means to explode hegemonic notions of straight masculinity, Rodosthenous highlights varying ways in which *Billy Elliot* reinforces working-class masculine norms of work, strength and self-discipline while creating a fissure allowing Billy's passions for dance, self-expression and individuality to come to fruition without taking on a queer veneer.

Both Stacy Wolf and Jordan Ealey place their sights on musicals' historiographically problematic tendency to handcuff women – and particularly women of color – into narrow or underdeveloped roles. In '*Hamilton*'s Women', the musical theatre historian and queer feminist scholar Wolf challenges Lin-Manuel Miranda's international phenomenon for relegating the show's three main female characters to the sidelines and into the well-worn roles of muse, wife and whore. Focusing on the show's musical stylings, the narrative positioning of Angelica, Eliza and Maria, and those three characters' fleeting articulations of feminist power, Wolf highlights Miranda's unwillingness to take the same liberties with historical realities of women as he does with men, as well as his belated, arguably hollow empowerment of Eliza as *author* in the final moments of the show.

In a piece written specifically for this collection, Ealey – a theatre scholar specializing in Black theatre and Black feminism – critiques the scarcity of Black women and more specifically Black women's diegetic authorship in the musical's telling and selling of histories. Addressing the simultaneous erasure of women and empowered Black bodies in stories of the American West, Ealey's 'Rewriting the American West: Black Feminist (Re)Vision in *Bella: An American Tall Tale*' engages Saidiya V. Hartman's Black feminist methodology and her encouragement of an imaginative form of historical storytelling. Shedding the restraints of *Hamilton*'s official history, *Bella* recounts a story of the American West through foregrounded exaggeration, communal storytelling and the gendered supernatural power of Black women's bodies and booties.

Section one concludes with queer performer/scholar Janet Werther's 'A-List Drag Queens, Accidental Drag Kings and Illegible Gender Rebels: (Mis)Representations of Trans Experience Through Body and Song'. Resisting unrestrained and uncritical celebration of the relative proliferation of trans and non-binary musicals through the 2010s, Werther explores the hits and misses of contemporary musical theatre's forays into trans inclusion. Focusing on a trio of shows from the mid-to-late teens – *Head Over Heels, A Ride on the Irish Cream* and *Southern*

Comfort – Werther delineates common pitfalls associated with trans-inclusive narratives and gendered notions and physical restrictions associated with singing voices; the conflation of nonbinary and trans experiences/bodies in casting; a general unwillingness to consider the advantages of rescoring to suit varied gender non-conforming vocal qualities; and the potentialities of queer, non-binary and trans world-making when artists are willing to go all-in on depicting trans and non-binary stories. The Rockettes' homogeneity be damned! Werther deftly wrestles with the struggles of and personal and relational need for effective and nuanced trans inclusivity within the world of musical theatre.

Part 2: Embodying and exploiting sex and sexuality on and off Broadway

Although queerness, particularly that constructed through gay artists and fans, has been connotatively linked to the musical for the better part of the last century, the genre itself commonly obscured sex across the spectrum, and either closeted or marginalized queer figures within its narratives. This second section highlights both the strained relationship between the musical, queer identities and storytelling, and those times when overt sexual permissiveness crept onto the musical stage to overpower what scholars like Engel (2006) and Knapp (2005) identify as the more romantic impulses of the form.

The work of the late theatre scholar David Haldane Lawrence considers the chorus girl's queer counterpart in 'Chorus Boys: Words, Music and Queerness (*c*.1900–36)'. Drawing on conflicting documented accounts and surveys from the early twentieth century, as well as later published works chronicling queer New York and London, Lawrence digs into historical assumptions linking theatricality, masculinity and homosexuality. Although acknowledging a dearth of archival content from which to work, he provides an exploration of the transition from the more debonair 'dancing gentlemen' of the 1920s to the effeminized and infantilized 'dancing boys' of Noel Coward's *Words and Music*. In addition to providing a historical framework for the chorus boy's long-sensed sexual proclivities, the chapter reaches into a 1933 article penned by retired chorus boy Cyril Butcher for a full-throated 'defense' of his comrades via their butch side-gigs as soldiers, pugilists and tennis champs.

Jumping ahead nearly four decades into an era and that flaunted its sexual inclinations, musical theatre historian Elizabeth L. Wollman foregrounds the narrative, performative and interpretive battles between revolutionary and exploitative impulses within highly sexualized Off-Off-, Off- and Broadway musicals of the late 1960s and early 1970s. 'Emancipation or Exploitation? Gender Liberation and Adult Musicals in 1970s New York' highlights this connotative tension through critical interrogation of personal interviews with cast members and creatives, exploration of popular press reviews, and analyses of librettos and vocal, choreographic and simulated-sex performance. Zeroing in on largely overlooked shows like *Let My People Come* and *Mod Donna*, Wollman considers how the historically conservative space of musical theatre coalesced with experimental theatre and the Gay Rights and Second Wave Feminist Movements to create polysemic musicals that managed to blend heterosexism, homophobia, misogyny and (at times) revolutionary feminist and queer expression.

Dramaturg, director and theatre historian Bryan Vandevender's 'A Substitute for Love: The Performance of Sex in *Spring Awakening*' continues to poke at the occasionally uncomfortable or uncommon blending of the musical and sex with a look at teen sexuality as depicted in the Duncan Sheik/Steven Sater Tony-winner. Pushing back on the notion that romantic *love*, not *sex*, undergirds the form's dramatic action, Vandevender's chapter details how *Spring Awakening*'s rock beats and choreographic lexicon of masturbation and mutual desire fuse to evoke a Foucaultian sense of sexual repression and transgression. Like Wollman, Vandevender highlights the musical's willingness to push at boundaries by imbuing the narrative with hetero-male sexual desire and sexualized performance, while simultaneously relegating female and queer agency and longing to the margins.

This section's last chapter asks readers to consider not the *telling* but the *selling* of theatre, and the ways economics and assumptions about audiences can drive the business of Broadway. Echoing Wollman's charges of musical exploitation in the 1970s, theatre scholar Ryan Donovan's new piece 'If You Were Gay, That'd Be Okay: Marketing LGBTQ Musicals from *La Cage* to *The Prom*' traverses a rhetorical path from problematically closeted, ambiguously marketed queer musicals to fleeting moments when shows let their pride flags fly on their marquees and social media streams. In wrapping up this section, Donovan drives home the economic conservatism of this connotatively queer artform left to scramble after traditionalist tourist dollars.

Part 3: Divas don't care about nobody's rules

And then on come the divas. Deviating – or diva-iating – from the three other sections, this portion of the collection draws attention to a singular, iconic figure. Exactly what defines a diva remains somewhat elusive: Selling or singing power? Temperament? Narrative positioning? Rejection or inflation of feminine norms? Or perhaps all of the above?

INTRODUCTION

Wayne Kostenbaum's *The Queen's Throat: Opera, Homosexuality and the Mystery of Desire* (1993) arguably launched contemporary diva studies. His diva destabilized the very core of personal performance, unsettling 'the world's gendered ground by making femaleness seem at once powerful and artificial' and mastering the 'art of anger' and 'will to power' (1993: 90). Since Kostenbaum published this book, diva studies have broadened across disciplines, with scholars like Clum and Susan J. Leonardi and Rebecca A. Pope (*The Diva's Mouth: Body, Voice, and Prima Donna Politics* [1996]), as well as entire issues of the feminist media studies journal *Camera Obscura* (2007 and 2008) and *Studies in Musical Theatre* (2018) dedicated to exploring the icon on and off-screen. Although the figure remains elusive, this section contributes to the furthering of a nuanced framework for the consideration of Broadway's divas.

Musical theatre scholar Michele Dvoskin's 'Embracing Excess: The Queer Feminist Power of Musical Theatre Diva Roles' works to establish a much-needed language for discussing the musical theatre diva. The influence of her piece radiates through the other three pieces in this section. Differentiating between what she terms 'diva characters' and 'diva roles', she teases apart the gendered politics, narrative placement and performance of *Hairspray*'s diegetic diva Motormouth Maybelle, *Gypsy*'s iconic Mama Rose and *Memphis*'s Felicia, whom Dvoskin terms a *diminished*, or sidelined, diva. She further underscores the parallelism of divadom and the gender outlaw. Drawing on the scholarship of Doty, Wolf and Clum, Dvoskin highlights the figure's embrace of gendered excess and queerness as the diva shatters an assortment of cultural contracts.

Although they all embrace frameworks laid out by Dvoskin, the three other diva-driven authors migrate to disciplines less travelled by the Broadway diva: dance studies, Black womanist theory and television studies. Dancer, choreographer and scholar Dustyn Martincich forges new ground in dance and diva studies with 'Stepping Out of Line: (Re)Claiming the Diva for the Dancers of Broadway'. In this chapter, Martincich constructs an argument for lending the appellation to dancers as well as singers. As she unsettles the body/voice hierarchy that commonly drives diva discourse, and disrupts the more gendered choreographer/muse trope saddling dancers, Martincich turns to the legacies of Gwen Verdon, Chita Rivera and Donna McKechnie to claim the dancer's rightful spot alongside more traditional Broadway diva singers.

Focusing on an industry often critiqued for its reliance on whiteness the cultural critic and professor of ethnic studies Deborah Paredez projects the diva through intersecting lenses of race, industry and performance. Focusing on one of Broadway's few predominantly Black-cast musicals to land a Tony nomination for Best Musical in the early twenty-first century, 'Diva Relations in *The Color Purple* 2015 Broadway Revival' breaks through the Great White Way's wall of hegemonic whiteness. Through a critical synthesis of ethnic, feminist and performance studies, Paredez evokes Alice Walker's womanist vision and the construct of the blues diva to build a nuanced study of how *The Color Purple* revival featured, staged and marketed an uncommon triumvirate of divas.

To wrap up this rumination on the diva, I pull focus away from the live stage and turn instead to the small screen. As I argue in my book *Broadway in the Box*, television has both embraced the musical – through televised musical re-stagings, Broadway stars making guest appearances and musical divas like Carol Channing and Barbra Streisand landing their own variety specials – and simultaneously struggled to make space for the performative excess often accompanying the musical diva. My own 'How Can the Small Screen Contain Her? Television, Genre and the Twenty-First-Century Broadway Diva Onslaught' considers the ways generic, geographic, economic and technological shifts within the television industry created a perfect storm, expanding the small screen to accommodate the diva power of Elaine Stritch, Liza Minnelli, Patti LuPone and their diva sisters.

Part 4: Onstage, offstage and online: Gender and sexuality in personal and professional musical practice

This final section interrogates the direct interplay between personal and professional *practice* and the scholarship of musical theatre. As Oehlers, Werther and Donovan all assert elsewhere in this collection, professional practices like casting, contracts and marketing play an integral part in determining how and through whom audiences experience the art of musical theatre. Who was cast? Why? How was the show altered to fit the new cast (or was it)? How was casting announced? How are audiences *using* texts? From a group of musicologists and musical theatre scholars – all of whom have varying connections to the world of theatre production and practice – these final essays anchor the performance and presentation of gender and sexuality more closely to the personal acts of performers, politicians, directors and fans.

Alejandro Postigo, the theatre artist/researcher and creator/star of the *The Copla Musical*, blends a historical and ideological recuperation of Spanish folkloric tradition with a critical analysis of his own performance of national and sexual identity. Postigo's 'The Queerness of *Copla*: Musical Hope for the Spanish LGBTQ' centres on the country's most musical theatre-adjacent entertainment form, one not widely studied or performed outside its native Spain. In his essay, Postigo highlights *copla*'s temporal and stylistic indebtedness to American Tin Pan Alley. He then traces Spain's melodramatic musical form from its pre-Franco heyday of excess and its subsequent appropriation and propagandization by the fascist Francoist regime, to its early closeted and later fulsome embrace by the Spanish gay male community. Postigo provides a glimpse into Franco-era performance and queer persecution, and considers the ways contemporary writer-performers like himself blend musical styles to enact an ideologically complex synthesis of personal, historical and political storytelling.

Both Sherrill Gow and Stephanie Lim use their professional practice to interrogate the personal, political and economic complexities of attempted destabilizations of restrictive gender binaries. Gow's 'Queering Brechtian Feminism: Breaking Down Gender Binaries in Musical Theatre Pedagogical Performance Practices' hearkens back to Werther's query regarding the potentialities of mounting both trans-inclusive and popularly legible musical theatre. Drawing on her own direction of a London-based post-graduate production of *Pippin* in which the titular role was portrayed by a trans man, Gow argues that the rehearsal space can function as an ideal locale for student theatre artists to blend practice with critical pedagogy. Gow explains how her production emerged through a larger Brechtian-feminist process of uncovering and foregrounding gendered stereotypes, ones on which Stephen Schwartz's *Pippin* – and much musical theatre – had been built.

Lim's 'For Progress or Profit: The Possibilities and Limitations of Playing with Gender in 21st Century Musical Theatre' steps beyond the more experimental space of Gow's academic theatre to shine light on the uneven effects of playing with gender in high-priced commercial theatre. Despite what can seem like a virtue-signalling hoopla driven by high profile, gender-flipped revivals and tours of *Pippin, Once on This Island, Company, Oklahoma!* and others, Lim challenges the overall efficacy of gender-flipped casting. With eyes toward stardom, economics and dramaturgy, the dramaturg and musical theatre scholar employs the terminology of cosplay – crossplay and gender-bending – to break down the 'why', 'who' and 'who cares', of gender-flipping. From 'drag-as-gimmick' and high-profile stunt-casting of trans stars M. J. Rodriguez (*Pose* to *Little Shop of Horrors*) and Laverne Cox (*Orange is the New Black* to Fox's *Rocky Horror* remake) to productions that gender-flip leads (*Company*), reposition the sexuality of romantic couples (*Oklahoma!*) or insert trans bodies or characters into established cis roles, gender play has become a go-to trope as art wrestles with cultural shifts and brushes up against the economic limits of pushing toward inclusivity. Lim challenges assumption regarding progressivity and inclusivity in her broad look at the popular phenomenon.

As this collection heads toward its conclusion, it turns to examine the intersections of musical theatre and the virtual space. In a world newly estranged from the once-impenetrable ephemerality of theatre, online platforms not only allow for the sharing of recorded live performances but also the connecting of fans who revel in such performances. Musical theatre scholar Jiyoon Jung's 'The Right to

See and Not Be Seen: South Korean Musicals and Young Feminist Activism' moves away from professional practice to consider the personal and political. Drawing on her fieldwork in South Korea, Jung positions musical theatre as a feminist safe space for young Korean women. The overwhelmingly female audience of Korean musical theatre subverts the constraints of patriarchal society through the homosocial and voyeuristic enactment of the female gaze; a rejection of restrictive norms of femininity and an embrace of an aggressive sense of debate via anonymized online fan sites; and incognito #MeToo-adjacent #WithYou protests sparked by fan forum chatter. Through an analysis of this hat trick of safe spaces, Jung reveals the regional specificity and personal power of female musical fandom.

Curtain up

Gender, Sex, and Sexuality in Musical Theatre: He/She/They Could Have Danced All Night brings together the romance, love and lust encompassing the musical genre. The following essays take on gendered icons of the chorus boy, chorus girl, Rockette and diva, while teasing apart various ways industrial practices, narrative stylings and political movements construct and disrupt notions of musicalized gender and sexuality to form variant and nuanced lenses through which to consider the genre's foundational romantic framework. Surely today's musical fans have been presented with something much more scandalous and nuanced than my tween love affair with Lynn Redgrave via Rodgers and Hammerstein, but as the essays to follow illustrate, the musical theatre form has pushed and continues to push the same erotically and ideologically charged buttons that once made me dream Ms Redgrave would teach me, too, to dance.

REFERENCES

Altman, R. (1987), *The American Film Musical*, Bloomington and Indianapolis: Indiana University Press.

Clum, J. (1999), *Something for the Boys: Musical Theater and Gay Culture*, New York: St. Martin's Press.

Cohan, S. (2005), *Incongruous Entertainment: Camp, Cultural Value, and the MGM Musical*, Durham: Duke University Press.

Coleman, B. and Sebasta, J. (2008), *Women in Musical Theatre*, Jefferson: McFarland and Company.

Doty, A. (2000), *Flaming Classics: Queering the Film Cannon*, New York and London: Routledge.

Doty, A. (2007), 'Fabulous! Divas, Part 1', *Camera Obscura*, 65:22, p. 2.

Doty, A. (2008), 'The diva issue strikes back', *Camera Obscura*, 67:23, p. 1.

Dyer, R. (1992), 'Entertainment and Utopia', in R. Dyer (ed.), *Only Entertainment*, New York: Routledge.

Engel, L. (2006), *Words with Music: Creating the Broadway Music Libretto* (rev. H. Kissel), New York: Applause Cinema and Theatre.

Farmer, B. (2000), *Spectacular Passions: Cinema, Fantasy, Gay Male Spectatorship*, Durham: Duke University Press.

Feuer, J. (1982), *The Hollywood Musical*, Indianapolis and Bloomington: Indiana University Press.

Kessler, K. (2010), *Destabilizing the Hollywood Musical: Music, Masculinity, and Mayhem*, London: Palgrave-Macmillan.

Knapp, R. (2005), *The American Musical and the Performance of Personal Identity*, Princeton: Princeton University Press.

Koestenbaum, W. (1993), *The Queen's Throat: Opera, Homosexuality, and the Mystery of Desire*, New York: Poseidon Press.

Leonardi, S. J. and Pope, R. A. (1996), *The Diva's Mouth: Body, Voice, and Prima Donna Politics*, New Brunswick: Rutgers University Press.

Miller, D. A. (1998), *Place for Us: Essay on the Broadway Musical in the 1950s*, New York: Oxford University Press.

Neale, S. (1983), 'Masculinity as spectacle', *Screen*, 24:6, pp. 2–17.

Savran, D. (2012), ' "You've Got That Thing": Cole Porter, Stephen Sondheim, and the Erotics of the List Song', *Theatre Journal*, 64:4, pp. 533–48.

Schatz, T. (1981), *Hollywood Genres: Formulas, Filmmaking, and the Studio System*, Philadelphia: Temple University Press.

Wolf, S. (2002), *A Problem Like Maria: Gender and Sexuality in the American Musical*, Ann Arbor: University of Michigan Press.

Wolf, S. (2011), *Changed for Good: A Feminist History of the Broadway Musical*, Oxford: Oxford University Press.

Wollman, E. L. (2012), *Hard Times: The Adult Musical in 1970s New York City*, London and New York: Oxford University Press.

Wollman, E. L. (2021), 'Musical theater studies: A critical view of the discipline's history and development in the United States and United Kingdom', *Music Research Annual*, 2: 2021.

PART 1

EXPLORING AND EXPLODING THE GENDER BINARY ON THE MUSICAL STAGE

1

The Radio City Rockettes and the Making of a Sisterhood

Adrienne Gibbons Oehlers

The Radio City Rockettes are a self-proclaimed sisterhood and are repeatedly quoted as such in memoirs, performance reviews and press publications. Although dancers for the Rockettes have had to submit to stringent requirements for physicality, personality and uniformity, Rockette alumnae can be quick to wax poetic on their years in the line. In this essay, I investigate the meaning and the making of such a sisterhood by looking at how a 'community of practice' is created through the structure of the company and the shared labour involved in precision dance (Wenger 1998). Understanding the bonds between the dancers is important in discerning why the Radio City Rockettes have long been viewed as wholesome family entertainment, at least when compared to their racier counterpart – the showgirl. I will examine how the Rockette identity has been developed from multiple points of departure, both onstage and off, not only looking at how their group dynamic was shaped through dance, but also recognizing its formation through the stable workplace and practices of Radio City Music Hall. I will also explore the ways in which this identity is viewed differently from other more sexualized dance companies that were performing concurrently.[1]

In her discussion of 'communities of practice', Wenger delineates the three core components of practice – mutual engagement, joint enterprise and shared repertoire – that contribute to the creation of a community (1998: 227–28). Each element is apparent in how the Rockettes labour together with a shared expectation of performance. These three modes, all essential factors in community formation, are amplified for the Radio City Rockettes because of the intensity of their time together. If, as Wenger asserts, communities are strengthened by shared sensibilities and routines that are experienced over time, then the Rockettes' self-identification as a type of sisterhood has been heightened by the feedback loop of 'participation' and 'reification', or the acts of partaking in multiple group endeavours, as well as creating a history and memories with the company (1998: 55, 61).

Both 'sisterhood' and 'community' are words that suggest solidarity and a shared commitment to a common purpose. While I am not suggesting that the Rockette experience was without friction or a lack of cohesion, the Rockettes' overall success and image depended on the communication of this idea of communal affection to the public. Whether or not the dancers were as agreeably synthesized as they were purported to be, they successfully carried an appearance of group harmony to both the press and the audience. Their demeanour is remarked on by many critics, such as Doris Hering, who in 1952 noticed their 'surprisingly unjaded smiles' and the way 'they resemble a row of guileless school girls' (1952: 47). Through their common goal of performing exactly in unison while suppressing any vestige of individuality, each Rockette *appears* to connect to the group both physically and in spirit. While all the women may not have felt this deep sense of kinship, their job required them to present a sisterly relationship to the audience, and this 'joint enterprise', thinking back to Wenger, in turn fostered a kind of true solidarity.

Beyond the showgirl

Originally one of the few permanent places for women to have a dance career (albeit only for those who fit certain requirements), Radio City offered a job that relied heavily on each dancer's exposed body and physical beauty. As the instrument of dance is the body itself, it is impossible to avoid talking about the physicality of bodies on the stage. Women onstage have a long history of being linked to prostitution and sex, from can-can dancers whose high kicks displayed their underwear or 'often no knickers at all' to chorus girls who used sex to supplement their incomes or social standings to burlesque dancers who traded in titillation from the safe distance of the stage.[2] In her study of the Ziegfeld Girl, Linda Mizejewski explored how chorus girls were both 'marginalized [...] and centralized', appearing onstage as a 'popular, nonthreatening challenge to traditional ideas about female modesty and the place of women outside the home' (1999: 187). Despite their leggy appeal, the Rockettes viewed themselves and were considered by others to be wholesome family entertainment, as critic Walter Terry noted in 1940, concurring that they exhibited a 'high plane of variety, good taste, and healthy spectacle' (1978: 62). This perception of the dancers as modest and 'healthy' was a projection of sexuality deemed suitable by Radio City executives, who wished the women to symbolize American values of virtuosity and optimism.

In 1978, critic Anna Kisselgoff recognized the demarcation between the Rockettes and other dancers of the time, remarking on the former's 1930s innocence and a 'firm idea of what the Rockettes are not. [...] They are not chorus girls, chorines or showgirls. They are so different that they have, among themselves, always been the same. They are the Rockettes' (1978: 15). Created in 1925 by founder Russell Markert in Missouri, the Rockettes found a permanent home in Radio City Music Hall in 1932 and remained under Markert's leadership until his retirement in 1971. As one of many all-female dance groups that were choreographed and directed by men, and one for whom a particular body type was imperative to being hired, the Rockettes are nonetheless usually excluded from discussions of 'leg shows' from the same time period, neither causing scandal or titillation with their semi-clad dancers. It is of special note that although the extravagant costuming of the Rockettes is similar in many ways to those of the showgirl – tight fitting leotards adorned with sequins and baubles, nude legs and high heels – the Rockette dancer differs in her lack of sex appeal.

Certainly, in form and figure, the Rockette has much in common with the showgirl, but several factors coalesce to create their becoming-yet-not-licentious stage presence. To begin with, the female precision dancer is deconstructed in a way that puts the emphasis on the unified whole, or Kracauer's 'mass ornament' ([1963] 1995: 78). While Kracauer's view of precision dance as a frightening production line of capitalism was not endorsed by the dance critics who wrote glowingly of the Rockettes' appeal, they often echoed his estimation of the 'asexual athleticism' he found in that style of dance (Donald 2007: 50). The nature of the choreography itself is the second determinant as, in order for dance to be coordinated between 36 women, the movements must be clean, sharp and strong. Moreover, Rockette stage pictures were created for the purpose of revealing a geometric pattern rather than individual physiques.[3] In contrast to a showgirl, a Rockette's job did not include graceful walks along the stage to display costumes. The primary jobs of the precision dancer (to dance as a unit) and the showgirl (to display the body) are not equivalent. Nonetheless, nothing stopped certain patrons from questionable gazes or voyeuristic spectatorship. And yet their 'pistol-leg action' – bare as their legs were – more often evoked comparison to the synchronized athletic manoeuvres of a collegiate rowing team than the slinky appeal of a burlesque performer (Hering 1952: 47).

The Rockettes have remained iconic and beloved, even if primarily as a throwback to an earlier era. The popularity of the Radio City Rockettes hit a low in the 1970s, with attendance continually waning and critics complaining that the show had declined to performing kitsch, or as Ada Louise Huxtable pointedly commented, 'Radio City is the Madame Tussaud of the entertainment world [...] a fossilized anachronism devoted to a myth of family entertainment' (1978: n.pag.).

Yet, when it seemed imminent that the doors would permanently close and Radio City would be demolished, people in the community came together and insisted that both be saved. Although the image of the Rockettes plummeted from an exemplar of modernism to the epitome of nostalgia, the reputation of the dancers themselves remained unblemished and the job's cachet persisted within dance circles.

All for one and one for all

The marketing surrounding the dancers was tightly regulated and contributed to propagating this Panglossian sisterhood. Individual Rockettes rarely spoke to the press and those who did completed publicity training, in which they were coached on the required buzz words and quote-worthy sound bites. Radio City has always doggedly controlled its publicity, and throughout the years, reporters have mentioned the inability to speak with individual Rockettes. In 1976, journalist Paul Leavin was told it was 'not professional' to interview one of the dancers, and in 2005 writer Mary Beth McCauley noted that 'management likes to keep certain things tucked up as tight and unseen as a line dancer's hair', specifically talking about the reticence over salaries and weight requirements (Leavin 1976: 69; McCauley 2005: 20). Rarely allowed to be interviewed, the women were not marketed as individuals, in sharp contrast to the practice of Florenz Ziegfeld, who continually singled out his females for profile pieces in the articles or photo ops for local events. Markert kept his name and his dancers' names out of the public eye. This held intact yet another barrier which kept audiences from personifying the Rockettes, whose names were not even listed in the programmes. They did not attend outside social events; management often used a private apartment created within RCMH for entertaining within their own walls.

In keeping the Rockettes from appearing as individual women in the public eye, the administration continually maintained a generic profile for their dancers and propagated their philosophical ideals through the Rockettes as embodiments of wholesome family values. As a result of Markert's value system and the management's commitment to mainstream popularity, the Rockettes' image reflected hard work and industry as well as an innocence that contrasted to the 'come-hither appeal of the individual chorus girl' found on other stages (Kisselgoff 1978: 15). In 1977, John Lahr wrote that 'the Rockettes don't bump and wiggle like the big girls on Broadway. Watching them is like watching your sister dance in the living room after dinner' (1977: 84). That they did not embody an overtly sexualized figure was a conscious choice by Markert, and one that aligned with the management's philosophy outlined when they built Radio City.

Over the past twenty years (or so), management has tried to reinvigorate the relevance of the dance troupe through more contemporary marketing practices and production values. In 2016, the Rockettes made newspaper headlines over their required participation at the presidential inauguration of Donald Trump. Initially speaking privately through her Instagram account, Rockette Phoebe Pearl wrote words of dismay about this planned appearance, which were then picked up by celebrity blogger Perez Hilton. Quickly going viral, Rockettes and management alike were thrust into the public eye as to whether or not each individual dancer would be allowed to choose to perform for the incoming president, who had been under scrutiny for objectifying women. As Katie Rogers and Gia Kourlas of the *New York Times* realized, this polarizing argument 'has reignited sensitivities within the corps that they are seen as beauty pageant contestants more than skilled performers' as well as calling attention to the unspoken reality that a Rockette should not publicly disapprove of her employer (2017: C1). Pearl's unauthorized opinion divulged via social media brought to light the practice that individual dancers were neither allowed to voice their beliefs independently of the packaged script, nor do anything that failed to toe the party line. Outside of the criticism unleashed on Radio City and the Rockettes over their Trump appearance, the dissenting opinions exposed a rift in the seemingly unified company, which was contrary to the administration's goal of presenting the dancers as a team and not as individuals. In today's post-feminist environment, such a marketing practice appears manipulative and dated. While a community between the women had been formed in dance rehearsals, backstage and onstage, the picture of the dancers and their employers working in utopian harmony was more realistically a marketing illusion.

On the line

Despite the demands for conformity, the term 'sisterhood' appears prevalently throughout the history of the Rockettes. Looking at how this Rockette community has been created through the process of labour and the construction of a shared identity helps to illustrate the power of social formation and explain the pull of Rockette affiliation. In her book, Wenger explains how mutual engagement creates a sense of belonging and a sense of ownership over identity, which I point to as contributing to the devotion within the Rockette alumnae. The Rockettes have been bound together through their collective exertion in rehearsals and performance, which is magnified due to the nature and demands of precision dance.

Every year, hundreds of young dancers descend on Radio City Music Hall for the chance to be seen by the director of the *Radio City Christmas Spectacular* at the annual audition for the Rockettes. The audition requirements today for a Radio City Rockette read as follows:

> [Dancers] must be between 5'6" and 5'10 1/2" and must demonstrate proficiency in tap, jazz, ballet, and modern dance. They need to display a radiant energy that will shine across the footlights to their audience. Rockettes must also be able to sing, and of course, perform those eye-high kicks.
>
> (Porto 2006: 13)

Dancers are first lined up and measured to see if they are truly within the height requirements before being allowed to dance a single step. These open auditions continue many of the strict guidelines set by Markert, who developed them during their first years as 'The Sixteen Missouri Rockets' in 1925. By their opening at Radio City in 1932, the renamed 'Radio City Rockettes' had expanded to a line of 36 women to span the enormous 10,000-square-foot 'Great Stage' of Radio City Music Hall.

With Markert at the helm, the audition protocol included a strict height requirement: his first 'girls' were required to be between 5'5" and 5'8".[4] In the Rockettes' line-up, the tallest women always danced in the centre with the other dancers tapering down in height on either end, creating the illusion of equal height through spacing. Each woman was trained to kick to her own eye level, which added to the appearance of uniform height and a uniform kick line. Passing the first rounds of auditions meant meeting Markert's vision of beauty and form, this more subjective requirement as important to him as the dance itself. Certainly, we must acknowledge that a uniform look during the origins of the Rockettes in the 1920s and 1930s included racial homogeneity. Racial integration among dancers on a commercial stage was not acceptable or expected. However, the Radio City Rockettes were shockingly slow to integrate their line, as the first black Rockette was not hired until 1987. As late as 1982, incoming director Violet Holmes was highly criticized when she defended the all-white line, citing artistic reasons, '[o]ne or two black girls in the line would definitely distract. You would lose the whole look of precision, which is the hallmark of the Rockettes' (Lambert 1987: 1, 27). This preference for an unbroken line of colour says much about how whiteness was the first requirement for the Rockettes sisterhood and about the hegemonic racism inbred in dance, and more generally about our culture's definitions of ideal images and beauty.

Before acknowledging the unique job opportunities that were offered at Radio City, it must first be said that like many dance companies, the Rockettes had no room for the unacceptable body, including the non-white but also those who did not fit other physical requirements. While unskilled but beautiful dancers were not accepted, or were told to go home and work on their weak areas of dance, those 'too ugly or too fat [were] sent on their way' (Mason 1934). Although being 'typed out' is still a practice in auditions, the overtness of the early twenties' shoptalk feels jarring today. Ironically, this weeding out of the 'unsuitable' – whether due to appearance, skill or attitude – meant that those who were hired as Rockettes fit within the specific parameters set by Markert and Radio City and that they shared this first and important bond, forging the beginnings of their community: an in-group created by the exclusion of others.

The structure of the Rockettes differs from most other dance companies in several ways, the primary deviation being that there is no formal hierarchy among the dancers. Unlike a ballet company, where dancers work in the corps de ballet in the hopes of one day moving into the roles of featured soloist or principal dancer, there is only one position with precision dancers: on the line. Each individual's spot in the line is determined by height, not by talent or beauty, and the positions change depending on the heights of the women in the company. This lack of upward mobility created a structure of power with the appearance of equality, helping to cultivate an 'all for one and one for all' mentality.

Creating a community through practice tethered the members together through a shared purpose, in this case, the objective of a consummate performance. Since the dancers were dependent upon each other for this success, participating in this professional aim gave value to their cohesion. As they held each other accountable, the Rockettes were mutually engaged, each sharing the responsibility of performing to the standards of the group. This pressure, plus the ability to execute the choreography at the required level and the subsequent sense of achievement after each show, continued to interlace the disparate women into a group – a sisterhood – who became united through the toil of rehearsals and the rewards of performance.

Learning the style of precision dance took place in a boot camp-like environment, quite similar to today's Rockettes, with many hours spent in 'exacting and strenuous' rehearsals (Anon. 1928). Taught by the dance director himself, a new recruit was coached to dance in an identical style to the 35 women who surrounded her. As in other dance companies, the director was assisted by several dance captains, who continued to give the new recruit individual instruction, extra drilling and extensive notes on her errors. In his rehearsal room, Markert did not hold dance class, but directly moved towards creating a single working unit, as auditions had already made sure that incoming dancers were well versed in tap and ballet vocabulary. The continual drilling of team performance intensified a dancer's ability to simultaneously concentrate on her own motion while also focusing the movement of the group, until doing both was second nature or 'a kind of sixth sense' (Anon. 1928). The dancer's peripheral vision was a key component to staying in sync. To stay in a straight line with military precision, dancers were instructed to 'guide right', which entailed lining up with the person to their right side using peripheral awareness while facing straight ahead. However, when a line was pivoting, every dancer turned her head in the same direction. Each dancer looked over her shoulder, guided by the chest of the person two dancers from herself. In this way, the overall effect of each individual dancer was invisibly tied to the group as a whole, working together in the 'joint enterprise' of unison choreography (Wenger 1998: 228).

Although the Rockettes dance together in unison, each dancer stands on her own. Even so, it is easy to only see the company as a geometric shape and forget the individuals who make up the line. The 'rookies' depended upon and were subsequently guided through their first performances by the veteran dancers on either side. Sometimes a slight nudge or soft whisper would alert the new dancer to a tiny misstep. Often un-noted is that fact that the Rockettes do not put any weight on their neighbouring dancers. Each woman stands in line, using the sensory experience of her body touching others to assist in the cohesion of movement, but not as a support for her own balance. If a new Rockette leans or presses on the dancer to either side of her, she is sure to be dressed down either by that senior Rockette, or by the dance captain. Other than 'kicking out' – kicking out of sync or in error – there is no greater faux pas than not supporting your own weight and movement (Lahr 1977: 83). These strict expectations in the rehearsal room and onstage developed the Rockettes' shared discipline, shaped further by the practice of privileging the group over the individual.

Even without an apparent ranking on the stage, however, inevitably a pecking order appeared backstage. New hires were given a spot in the dressing room in one of the far 'alleys' or rows of dressing room tables. As they became more senior, they would move up to more desirable locations (Love 1980: 20). With no promotions for which to compete, Rockettes still had an informal and less overt hierarchy based on which dancers had been there the longest. Belle Koblenz, a Rockette from 1966 to 1970, recounted the importance of the five-year anniversary, and of an unspoken attitude among the girls that this was when you became a 'real' Rockette (Koblenz 2016). Clearly, seniority was a factor backstage, but the senior dancers also had an investment in nurturing the new Rockettes. There was no small amount of pressure for a new recruit to perform well in her debut, and her fellow Rockettes – who had spent a large amount of rehearsal time 'putting in' the new dancer – had an investment in her success as well. Every time a new dancer joined the company, the dancers would be shifted to place her height correctly into the line-up, which could cause any number of veteran Rockettes to need to learn new spacing. Dancing as a Rockette in the early years was a coveted job: prestigious, well-paid and long-lasting, and there were many hopefuls waiting in the wings to audition for the rare spots that opened. Women who made it in the door worked hard to stay there; a dancer who could not fit in generally did not make it past her first two weeks of rehearsal (Mason 1934).

Discipline, dedication and denial

While the publicity surrounding the Rockettes is as shiny as their sequinned costumes, no one denies the amount of work, hours and commitment required by the job. Love, a Rockette in the 1960s, recounts many heart-warming stories in her memoir *Thirty Thousand Kicks: What's It Like to be a Rockette?*, but she also claims her days at Radio City were ones of 'discipline, dedication and denial' (1980: 8). She gives a detailed account of working as a full-time Rockette, which, in the days of year-round employment, meant working seven days a week for four weeks before getting a week off. In the late 1970s, Radio City Music Hall moved away from the daily movie/show format, with the final movie *The Promise* on 25 April 1979, and began to close for weeks at a time. The Rockettes were then hired for compressed seasons to perform in the Easter and Christmas shows. Although some Rockettes worked on small productions or promotions throughout the year, year-round employment came to an end.

In the years leading up to this change of schedule in 1979, each day could be as long as thirteen hours with up to four shows a day, rehearsals for the next new show, and costume fittings. In a format begun by famed show business and radio entrepreneur Samuel 'Roxy' Rothafel, each performance included a movie and a lavish stage show, featuring a number by the Rockettes that changed with every new movie, most of which ran for a week. During the 28-day stretch until the week of vacation, the usual routine was to have rehearsals as early as 7 a.m. and to work until the last show finished at around 10.30 p.m. While there were breaks during the day, the dancers would use many of the amenities within Radio City, which had been created as a 'livable city unto itself' (Francisco 1979: 69).The building included a dormitory, a cafeteria and a backstage medical clinic with a trained nurse in addition to their dressing rooms.

The women spent their waking hours inside the Great Hall, with little time for a life outside of Radio City. Acknowledging the challenges of their lifestyle, former Rockettes are also well aware of the prestige and advantages that came with working at Radio City. From the first, being a Rockette has been a highly desirable position: at $55 a week in 1928, the job of a Radio City Rockette during the Great Depression years included stability and a good salary, one that was the highest income for chorus dancers (Mason 1934). Even a famed Ziegfeld Girl dancing in the *Follies* had an average salary of $35 or $40 a week in 1924 (Spitzer 1924). By contrast, the average female office worker later in the 1920s was paid $27.57 per week (Breckinridge 1933: 181–82). Although the salary and longevity of the job offered a comfortable standard of living, the social mobility experienced by other dancers who took advantage of offers by 'stage-door Johnnys' was not seemingly a part of the Rockette experience. A Rockette for eleven years from 1959 to 1970, Patty DeCarlo Grantham claimed her days were 'as wholesome as a Doris Day movie', in part because the dancers had little to no time for a social life outside of her hours at RCMH (Hoffman 2015). Considering their rigorous schedule, it makes sense that their social hours were also wrapped up in their work community.

A Rockette's life included many components that were unusual and specific to this lifestyle. The extreme hours required in their work week – the onstage hours, rehearsal hours and downtime spent at Radio City – created a close-knit community. The women physically shared intimate space, whether socially lounging over a meal, changing in their dressing rooms or dancing in close proximity. Paramount in precision dance is the continual awareness of unifying one's own movement with the group, and this mindset, which created a feeling of solidarity onstage, often continued off the stage. The sense of unison that was moulded in the practice of precision dance fostered the offstage bonding between the Rockettes, which in turn strengthened the desire and ability to perform as one. The dynamics of this insular dance community carried into their offstage reputations, as the wholesome aspect of their onstage personas became realized, and perhaps prized, in the Rockettes' own lifestyles.

Conclusion

The strict requirements of shape, beauty and uniformity could have caused RCMH to be a very prescriptive or repressive place to work. However, among the few opportunities available for young women dancers, Radio City stood out for its stability and respectability. Working as a Rockette had cachet and acquiring the reputation that went along with the Rockette job was an additional asset to a work life that was all-encompassing. As Dorothy Rompalske summed up in 1992, '[a] steady paycheck in an unstable occupation, a chance to perform on one of the world's greatest stages, and the opportunity to be part of a uniquely American institution all combine[d] to make the job an appealing one' (1992: 22).

Radio City management, whose mission was to create wholesome family entertainment for a new mainstream market, offered safety, independence and remuneration for talented dancers who fit the specifications. Physically linked together on the stage as well as spending long hours training, performing and sharing backstage and dressing room space, these dancers experienced an intimate connection with each other on-and offstage. The shared labour created a kind of kinship – 36 synchronized dancers whose community was forged through their unison dancing, shared experiences and group mentality.

NOTES

1. During my own career as a professional dancer, I was a Radio City Rockette in *The Radio City Christmas Spectacular* during two seasons (1998 and 1999), although both contracts were outside of New York City. This experience, paired with my historical and theoretical inquiry, has shaped my questions throughout this project.
2. For a lengthy history of the association between dance and sex, see *Dance, Sex, and Gender: Signs of Identity, Dominance, Defiance, and Desire* by Judith Lynne Hanna. Ramsay Burt also discusses the tie between prostitution and dance in *Alien Bodies* (1998: 47–53).
3. The Ziegfeld Girls, while no longer associated with the bump-and-grind sexuality of burlesque, nonetheless were presented as explicitly sexualized, both on- and offstage. For further discussion, see Miller's 'Glorifying the American girl: Adapting an icon' in *The Adaption of History: Essays on Ways of Telling the Past* (2013) as well as Mizejewski's *Ziegfeld Girl: Image and Icon in Culture and Cinema* (1999). Tableaux vivants were a well-known tool to allow semi-nude women to be displayed on stage, because in many locales, various states of undress were allowed on stage only if the performers were not moving.
4. Whether truly teenage girls or older women, dancers have historically and currently been referred to as *girls* instead of women. Alongside famous dancing groups such as the Gaiety Girls, the Ziegfeld Girls and the Tiller Girls; the terms chorus girl, showgirl and dancing girl are common generic terms, which are still in use today but do not actually connote age.

REFERENCES

Allen, Robert C. (1991), *Horrible Prettiness: Burlesque and American Culture*, Chapel Hill: University of North Carolina Press.

Anon. (1928), 'Selecting girls for Roxyettes offers problem', *Herald Tribune*, clipping, 29 April, Scrapbooks, Rockettes Collection, Jerome Lawrence and Robert E. Lee Theatre Research Institute, Ohio State University Libraries, Box 1, vol. 1.

Breckinridge, Sophonisba P. (1933), *Women in the Twentieth Century: A Study of Their Political, Social and Economic Activities*, New York: McGraw-Hill.

Burt, Ramsay (1998), *Alien Bodies: Representations of Modernity, 'Race' and Nation in Early Modern Dance*, London: Routledge.

Donald, James (2007), 'Kracauer and the dancing girls', *New Formations*, 61, pp. 49–63.

Dudden, Faye E. (1994), *Women in the American Theatre, Actresses, Audiences 1790-1870*, New Haven: Yale University Press.

Erdman, Andrew L. (2004), *Blue Vaudeville: Sex, Morals and the Mass Marketing of Amusement, 1895–1991*, Jefferson: McFarland & Company, Inc.

Francisco, Charles (1979), *The Radio City Music Hall: An Affectionate History of the World's Greatest Theater*, New York: EP Dutton.

Hanna, Judith Lynne (1998), *Dance, Sex and Gender: Signs of Identity, Dominance, Defiance, and Desire*, Chicago: University of Chicago Press.

Hering, Doris (1952), 'The Rockettes: Pin point perfectionists', *Theatre Arts*, 36:5, May, p. 47, clipping, Rockettes, Miscellaneous manuscripts, Special Collections, Library for the Performing Arts, New York Public Library, Folder 1.

Hoffman, Barbara (2015), 'Former Rockettes reveal life behind the scenes – including a flirty Richard Nixon', *New York Post*, 5 December, https://nypost.com/2015/12/05/former-rockettes-reveal-life-behind-the-scenesincluding-a-flirty-richard-nixon. Accessed 6 January 2016.

Huxtable, Ada Louise (1978), 'Architecture view: Is it curtains for the music hall?', *New York Times*, 19 March, Section 2, p. 1.

Kisselgoff, Anna (1978), 'Precision dancing as art', *New York Times*, 2 April, p. 15.

Koblentz, Belle (2016), interview with Adrienne Oehlers, New York, 6 August.

Kracauer, Siegfried ([1963] 1995), 'The mass ornament', in T. Levin (ed.), *The Mass Ornament, Weimar Essays* (trans. T. Levin), Cambridge: Harvard University Press, pp. 75–88.

Lahr, John (1977), 'Fearful symmetry', *Harper's*, 255:1526, p. 83, http://nf4hr2ve4v.search.serialssolutions.com/docview/1301547131?accountid=9783. Accessed 16 March 2016.

Lambert, Bruce (1987), 'Rockettes and race: Barrier slips', *New York Times*, 26 December, pp. 1–27.

Leavin, Paul (1976), 'Twenty-one ways of looking at the Rockettes', *Eddy*, 8, Spring/Summer, pp. 69–79.

Love, Judith Anne (1980), *Thirty Thousand Kicks: What's It Like to Be a Rockette?*, Hicksville: Exposition Press.

Mason, Eve (1934), 'Backstage with the Roxyettes', *Entertainment*, 12 February, Scrapbooks, Rockettes Collection, Jerome Lawrence and Robert E. Lee Theatre Research Institute, Ohio State University Libraries, Box 2, Volume 3.

McCauley, Mary Beth (2005), 'Ninth from the left: One Rockette's holidays', *Christian Science Monitor*, 15 December, p. 20.

Miller, Cynthia J. (2013), 'Glorifying the American girl: Adapting an icon', in L. Raw and D. Tutan (eds), *The Adaptation of History: Essays on Ways of Telling the Past*, Jefferson: McFarland & Company, Inc., pp. 25–41.

Mizejewski, Linda (1999), *Ziegfeld Girl: Image and Icon in Culture and Cinema*, Durham: Duke University Press.

Porto, James (2006), *The Radio City Rockettes: A Dance through Time*, New York: HarperCollins.

Rogers, Katie and Kourlas, Gia (2017), 'Still kicking, but no longer silent', *New York Times*, 19 January, p. C1.

Rompalske, Dorothy (1992), 'Kick, and kick, and kick, and kick: Stay together, girls! The Rockettes' precision dancing has made them a legend', *Arts and Entertainment*, March, pp. 22–25, clipping, Rockettes (company), Miscellaneous manuscripts, Special Collections, Library for the Performing Arts, New York Public Library, Folder 1.

Spitzer, Marian (1924), 'The chorus lady, model 1924', *Saturday Evening Post*, 197:11, 13 September.

Straus, Rachel (2010), 'Russell Markert', *Dance Teacher Magazine*, 8 December, http://www.dance-teacher.com/2010/12/russell-markert/. Accessed 16, January 2016.

Terry, Walter (1978), *I Was There: Selected Dance Reviews and Articles: 1936–1976*, New York: Marcel Dekker, Inc.

Wenger, Etienne (1998), *Communities of Practice: Learning, Meaning and Identity*, Cambridge: Cambridge University Press.

Wershing, Susan (1982), 'Russell Markert: Father of precision dance', *Dance Teachers Now*, 4:6, pp. 28–29.

2

Billy Elliot the Musical: Visual Representations of Working-Class Masculinity and the All-Singing, All-Dancing Bo[d]y

George Rodosthenous

Introduction

This essay examines the visual representations of working-class masculinity portrayed in Stephen Daldry's stage musical adaptation of the film *Billy Elliot* (2000). After a brief discussion of the portrayal of the male ballet dancer in the dancing scene since the 1990s and the inherent voyeuristic inclinations of contemporary audiences, the analysis will focus on five aspects of male presence in *Billy Elliot the Musical* (2005). The dynamics of working-class masculinity will be contextualized within the framework of the family, the older female, the community, the self and the act of dancing itself. These aspects will be referenced using reviews of the musical version of the work and articles written on the film of *Billy Elliot*. The discussion will suggest also that the all-singing, all-dancing bo[d]y is transformed on stage from an ephemeral phenomenon to an iconic symbol of its age. However, have today's audiences conditioned their gendered gaze to allow for the male ballet dancer to dominate the contemporary stage? Or do we still control our social perceptions and cultural associations with out-of-date images of the past? Have popular perceptions about the male ballet dancer changed? Is there a birth of a new male dancer phenomenon?

Even if the nineteenth-century ballet became 'so concerned with the display of female bodies that male characters became almost an impossibility (or reduced to the kind of mime and choreographic support-work)' (Henson 2007: 5), the twentieth century had its notable exceptions with the charismatic Vaslav Nijinsky, the legendary Rudolf Nureyev (on stage), the athletic Gene Kelly, the suave Fred Astaire and the magnetic John Travolta (on stage and screen). If we examine the dance scene since the 1990s, we would observe that the male ballet dancer has been reinvented in the theatre canon.[1] Mathew Bourne is partly responsible for this new trend of presenting the male dancer on stage, with examples like his male *Swan Lake* (1995), which is also used at the end of the film version of *Billy Elliot*, and *The Car Man* (2000) changing the popular assumptions that ballet as a masculine activity is a suspect phenomenon. And this proves the point that male ballet is a much more complex activity than just that. Companies like DV8 and Lloyd Newson have blurred the boundaries between the classical male ballet dancer and the 'new' male dancer with works such as *Dead Dreams of Monochrome Men* (1989) and *Enter Achilles* (1995). These works eroticized, and homoeroticized, the male body giving it a new political status. Michael Clark and Wim Vandekeybus renegotiated masculinity and its positioning within the canon while other choreographers such as Javier de Frutos[2] have liberated the male body by exposing the dancers and himself with naked displays of unrestrained emotion.

The androgynous male ballet dancer has been replaced by strong muscular gymnasts who treat contemporary dance as a new form of sport and who are more than happy to display their muscles to their audiences. Spectacular shows by Cirque du Soleil and new musical extravaganzas such as *Stomp*, *Tap Dogs* and *Riverdance* have redefined the presence of the male on the stage. The stereotypical expectations of ballet (for example, the female body being the object of the spectator's desire) have now been reversed. Carlos Acosta of the Royal Ballet features in as many posters as his fellow ballerinas, while the sensual Joaquin Cortes continues to perform in sell-out houses all over the world.[3]

> Popular perceptions and attitudes like 'real boys don't go to dance classes', (Gard 2001: 213) are beginning to disappear. More boys are now dancing and through their dance they have managed to uplift the antimale dancer taboos. Henson writes that Billy Elliot's dance shows his transformation from boy to man, the struggle to achieve and the liberating power of artistic expression. [It] also communicate[s] a powerful view of male balletic dancing, a form of male performance prone to stereotype and misunderstanding. Billy is no 'sissy' […]: he is an innovator, an achiever, a sportsman.
> (Henson 2007: 1)

But how do the audiences react to changes in visual representations of masculinity? The voyeuristic tendencies of recent audiences (apparent in audience behaviours towards the so-called reality television such as the *Big Brother* phenomenon), together with a desire to come into closer, more direct contact with the dancer's flesh, have created new forms of performance, whether site-specific, or even one-to-one encounters. The body physicality of the 'new' male dancer signifies strength and physical presence that might have been associated with working-class ethics and manual labour in the past. Images of males dancing are being released from their homoerotic associations and invite new semiotic readings. Karen Henson notes on the audience–performer relationship: the audience now 'consumes with delight but distance, nuance but also desire and pleasure' (Henson 2007: 9).

Since the late 1990s, masculinity[4] started emerging as a major subject in academic discussions, works of art and stage productions. This revolution was also felt in films such as *Brassed Off* (1996) and *The Full Monty* (1997), which dealt with the alienation of the Northern male from his traditional habitat – the working-men's club and the brass band – and looked at life from a male perspective. The management of male energy (either by playing in bands or through stripping in the respective films mentioned above) is fully explored in *Billy Elliot the Musical* through aggressive dance sequences and moments of explosive percussive rigour.

Billy Elliot the Musical has enjoyed positive critical acclaim including Charles Spencer's verdict that it is 'the greatest musical yet', a work where 'there is rawness, a warm humour and a sheer humanity [...] that is worlds removed from the soulless slickness of most musicals' (Spencer 2005). The show portrays a masculine crisis in a coal-mining village in England in 1986 and explores family relationships in a most intricate and personal way. In that respect, dance comes into direct opposition with the working-class practices of the males of the mining community: it is ridiculed and equated with homosexuality. Cynthia Weber, however, insists that 'even though it might popularly be read otherwise, ballet [and in our case, dance] is not necessarily a queer space for men. [...] Billy thinks of dance as a male and masculine space' (Weber 2003). This essay will apply Weber's claim and use the musical version of *Billy Elliot* as its main case study for its findings.

Solidarity (of the community) and the male individual: Brothers fighting

[T]he musical [...] counterpoints Billy's personal triumph against the community's decline.

(Billington 2005)

Billy Elliot, a miner's son, is found amidst the confusion of daily struggles that involve the miners standing restlessly on picket lines at the colliery gates. The fighting tends to break out when the police attempt to escort strike-breaking miners into the pit. This is also a reflection of Billy's home working-class environment where his brother (also a miner) is fighting with his father on issues directly related to the strike. One of the main differences of the film version of *Billy Elliot* and its stage transfer is that, in the latter, there is more opportunity to explore issues of class and conflict through aesthetic imagery, thanks to Peter Darling's choreography[5] and Elton John's music. Benedict Nightingale comments that

> we get dances of police and miners that start in Keystone style but get more menacing with the introduction of batons and clubs, and end with a stupendous number in which the cops become a terrifying wall of riot shields against which Billy flutters and bangs like a distracted moth.
>
> (Nightingale 2005)

The stage becomes a platform to explore one of the main issues of Thatcherite Britain: the complete disempowerment of the workers' unions. The workers sing the song 'Solidarity' that reflects the traditional socialist chant 'The workers united shall never be defeated' – the fabled 'unity is strength' slogan of the trade union tradition:

> Solidarity, solidarity
> Solidarity for ever
> All for one and one for all
> We are proud to be working class.
>
> ('Solidarity', Hall 2005: 17)

The status quo that Billy is trying to overturn clashes with his desire to dance. This locks him out of the 'macho' male world of the miners and makes him different from the rest of the males. Billy wants to break out of this solidarity and hopes for the day when he will 'fly away'; even if this will make him an outcast, he will find a better tomorrow away from the 'stifling confines of the enclosed and embattled community' (Kirk 2002).

The binary of the community and the individual gains a new dimension that becomes confronted with an element of competition amongst the males of that working-class community. Billy and his brother are fighting for two different ideals: personal individuality and solidarity. Billy wants to break free; his brother fights to maintain the male traditions of colliery workers. Lancioni notes that 'the frustration and hopelessness of the striking coal miners of Durham County, England, are certainly real enough. A postindustrialized society is draining them of hope and self-respect' (Lancioni 2006: 726). This is felt rather explicitly with the failed strike actions of the workers and the gloomy fact that they are fighting

FIGURE 2.1: George Maguire as Billy Elliot dancing (Victoria Palace, 2005). Photo: David Scheinmann.

an already lost battle. In the first song, 'The Stars Look Down', there is a sense of a hymn, fighting the good fight against the forces of darkness. Lee Hall's lyrics reflect this:

> We will always stand together
> In the dark, right through the storm
> We will stand, shoulder to shoulder
> To keep us warm.
>
> ('The Stars Look Down', Hall 2005: 17)

The militaristic togetherness, with its possible homoerotic undertones, is also representative of the communities represented in Elia Kazan's film *On the Waterfront* (1954). Terry Malloy's fight against the system, the corruption of the Mafia, his determination to change the status quo and his insistent refusal to conform has clear parallels with Billy Elliot. Also, the relationship of the two brothers in *On the Waterfront* reflects, in a way, the narrative of Billy Elliot. Boxing is a prominent feature in both stories: in *On the Waterfront* Terry Malloy enjoyed a brief yet successful career as a boxer which was terminated after the interference of his brother who 'sold' the boxing match for money. This is evident from this classic exchange from the film:

> CHARLEY: Look, kid, I – how much you weigh, son? When you weighed one hundred and sixty-eight pounds you were beautiful. You coulda been another Billy Conn, and that skunk we got you for a manager, he brought you along too fast.
>
> TERRY: It wasn't him, Charley, it was you. Remember that night in the Garden you came down to my dressing room and you said, 'Kid, this ain't your night. We're going for the price on Wilson'. You remember that? 'This ain't your night'! My night! I coulda taken Wilson apart! So what happens? He gets the title shot outdoors on the ballpark and what do I get? A one-way ticket to Palooka-ville! You was my brother, Charley, you shoulda looked out for me a little bit. You shoulda taken care of me just a little bit so I wouldn't have to take them dives for the short-end money.
>
> CHARLEY: Oh, I had some bets down for you. You saw some money.
>
> TERRY: You don't understand. I coulda had class. I coulda been a contender. I coulda been somebody, instead of a bum, which is what I am, let's face it. It was you, Charley.
>
> (Schulberg 1954)

In *Billy Elliot* (paying homage to Kazan's film), this is reversed by the insistence of Billy's brother (and father) that Billy should take up boxing in his spare time, banning him from going to ballet classes. The strong masculine activity of boxing, which could potentially double as a self-defence exercise for young Billy, is one of the more accepted forms of recreation for young males, even in today's working-class societies. Muir reports that,

> though boxing has many detractors, who say it is dangerous and allows aggressive young men to display their tendencies to more devastating effect, [...] the home secretary [David Blunkett] said 'The discipline of amateur boxing training can give young people the chance to keep fit, learn sportsmanship and self-discipline and benefit from the support of a mentor in their boxing coach. It can also offer positive routes into training, education and employment, as many young people who are beginning to master the sport are finding. [...] Amateur boxing is an activity that more and more young people from deprived neighbourhoods are choosing to become involved in. While it may not have the associated glamour of some other sports it gives young people status and an opportunity to make something of their lives – and how can that be a bad thing?
>
> (Muir 2004)

Boxing requires focused energy and constant alertness; but so does dance. Billy sees dancing 'just like sport' and not 'prancing about like a fruit'. In this way, he is also trying to convince the members of his family (and his community) that dance is indeed a valid and acceptable activity. And by doing this, he celebrates his individuality by having secret dance classes and keeps his promise to his dead mother's request to 'always be' himself. James Leggott reminds us that,

> [i]nitially sceptical, Billy's father is eventually persuaded of his son's talent, no doubt intuiting how Billy is involved in the formation of a new model of new athleticism. As such, Billy's achievement is at once a subversion of patriarchal expectation, and also a project of reclamation on his father's behalf, a mission to devise a viable new expression of masculinity.
>
> (Leggott 2004: 171)

Billy chooses to free himself from the solidarity and ordinariness of his working-class male surroundings and find refuge in the ballet classes. Even if dance involves pain, emotional and physical strain, he challenges the conventionality of his own masculinity by self-improvement. His efforts are focused on getting the dance right. Alan Sinfield comments, on the other hand, on Billy's escape, saying that '[t]here is no prospect here of transforming the system. The struggle is to maintain it! Solidarity is important for consolation and respect. Billy Elliot escapes, largely because the system is already permeable' (Sinfield 2006: 169).

The absent mother and the female teacher: Dance as conversation

> The emotion always seems real and spontaneous, rather than cunningly manipulated to pull at the heartstrings. And there is anger as well as joy, bitter resentment as well as compassion, above all a sense of nagging grief. That grief is both personal and political. Young Billy Elliot is in mourning for his mother, who died two years before the show begins, haunted by her memory, and trapped in an oppressively masculine world that allows few displays of tenderness and affection.
>
> (Spencer 2005)

Having examined Billy's relationship with the other males of the family and their solidarity within the community, we will look at his relationship with the three older females of his life: the dance teacher Mrs Wilkinson (as mother-replacement), the absent mother and his grandmother.[6] After the death of Billy's mother, the only female in his family is the forgetful grandmother, until he meets the dance

FIGURE 2.2: Haydn Gwynne as Mrs Wilkinson and company dancing (Victoria Palace, 2005). Photo: David Scheinmann.

teacher Mrs Wilkinson. This dramaturgical device allows for the show's emotional qualities to be presented in an intimate way. What is significant here is that Billy has plenty of male role models in his family. The absent mother, though, allows the possibility of a special relationship with the dance teacher who is female.

The male-to-male boxing lesson tradition is replaced with Mrs Wilkinson who is also a mother-replacement figure. In this way, Billy can be more open about his feelings than he would otherwise be with a male teacher (or even his boxing instructor). Billy is also very direct and painfully harsh with her at times, proving that he has not had any experience in talking to females in a sensitive or tactful way. However, the dance teacher is the one who encourages him to develop his talent in dance, however, bizarre that sounds in the context of the society in which they live, and she is the one that has to face the opposition of Billy's father and brother.

This involvement with Billy's strongly patriarchal family environment elevates her relationship with Billy from a platonic one to a closer, family one. That reversal of roles creates a strong dynamic between the two and thus allows for a powerful female to qualify as a quasi-male equivalent within the community.

In Daldry's direction, the absent mother is represented through the letter that she left for Billy before she died. The letter, and consequently the song written for it ('Dear Billy [Mam's Letter]', first sung by Billy, then by Mrs Wilkinson and then as a duet between Mrs Wilkinson and the dead mother), creates a very moving encounter between Billy and his dance teacher. There are brief appearances of the mother figure from the 'kitchen door' and these illusionary moments for Billy become even more difficult for the audience when the mother figure disappears and in its place we just have a slightly shuffled curtain. Again, through the absent mother's letter and her advice to 'always be yourself' ('Dear Billy [Mam's Letter]', Hall 2005: 18), we witness Billy getting inspiration for his dance and through his dance, he converses with both the spirit of his *absent* mother and the guiding *present* Mrs Wilkinson.

The third female presence in Billy's life, his grandmother, is mostly used for comic effect and as a living reminder that men actually used to 'go dancing' in the old days ('We'd go Dancing', Hall 2005: 17). She repeatedly states that she loved dancing and keeps reminiscing about her dancing escapades with Billy's grandfather that provided them with a sense of freedom: 'we were free [...] from the people we had to be' ('We'd go Dancing', Hall 2005: 17). This functions as a connecting thread to Billy's desire to dance and links dance to personal freedom, but the grandmother is not in a mental state to develop or promote Billy's talent. The absent mother, the mother-replacement and the grandmother are all three interlinked with dance: through Billy's desire to dance, he converses with the female. According to Kirk,

> amid the aggression, there is also a kind of *muteness* [original emphasis] about this culture, it is inert: Billy's father seems unable to express emotions that are clearly damaging him, the grandmother has trouble putting together a single, coherent sentence and Billy's brother tends to resort to angry, helpless tirades or demands for silence from his brother.
>
> (Kirk 2002)

Dance becomes a catalyst for that conversation to take place and compensates for the harshness and muteness of his relationships with his family.

Dancing instead of ... boxing: Masculinity games in the working-class boxing club

> Choreographers are aware of the convention that, in order to represent masculinity, a dancer should look powerful [...] being 'extremely aggressive' is a way of reimposing control and thus evading objectification.
>
> (Burt 1995: 51)

The third aspect to be discussed is Billy's experience in the working-class masculine space of the boxing club. Traditionally, that space is used for the homosocial activity of sport, but Billy reinvents that to practise his dance moves. Billy makes a conscious and difficult decision to abandon his boxing lesson and take ballet classes instead. Like sport, dance requires self-discipline, strength and control that are characteristics of a good sportsman.

Hill observes that the boxing club is used as 'an aid to male bonding [and] is counterposed to the hitherto all-feminine world of the ballet class to which Billy becomes ineluctably drawn' (Hill 2004: 104), but 'there is little of its emphasis upon the reconstruction of the traditional homosocial community as the means to the recovery of male self-respect' (Hill 2004: 108).

But how can ballet dance be viewed as a muscular, masculine and athletic activity? Can the male ballet dancer be associated with Artaud's notion of a 'heart athlete' (Artaud 1999: 100)?[7] The 'new' male dancer refuses to be associated with the accusations of dance as an un-masculine activity and uses the aggressive element to affirm his power. And thus, the reality comes into direct conflict with fantasies of escapism from County Durham's grey setting. Kirk argues that

> sport, a traditional escape route for the working-class kid, is replaced by 'art': low culture substituted by high, and yet there is a definite sense that [the work] sets out to deconstruct this binary, as it sets out, too, to problematise ideas about masculinity and the 'male norm'.
>
> (Kirk 2002)

What is more, the presence of Michael (the effeminate best friend who cross-dresses and wears tutus) as the only other male youngster helps create a binary opposition between the two boys. The director Daldry and choreographer Darling take full advantage of this binary opposition in the show-stopper number 'Expressing Yourself' in Act 1. Darling juxtaposes Billy and Michael in a comic scene of cross-dressing. When this is repeated in Act 2 and displaced from Michael's bedroom to the boxing club, the two boys' activities are watched by their not-too-happy fathers. This dramaturgical device leads to a climactic moment of conflict where issues of sexuality inevitably need to be clarified between the boys and their fathers.

However, for the rest of the show, Billy's solo dance choreography involves more than formally studied ballet steps and incorporates everyday moves from his private movement vocabulary. Billy's anger and frustration create explosive solos that represent his inner desire for self-expression and challenge any accusations of being effeminized through dance. Maybe the replacement of boxing with dancing could have become a homosocial activity, if only his fellow dancers were ... heterosexual boys.

Daldry reports that his approach wanted to portray '[d]ance as action rather than as aesthetics; dance as conversation rather than as abstract; the kid expressing himself rather than the brilliance of the finished product' (Daldry 2000: 12). In the case of Billy, even though the boxing-ring option is abandoned, Darling's choreography still manages to keep an edgy and raw energy which is linked to a stereotypical athlete, rather than a traditional male ballet dancer. Henson claims that in the film version of *Billy Elliot*, 'Daldry and Bell communicate their sportsmanlike view of ballet' (Henson: 2007: 8). The stage version of *Billy Elliot* also sustains the elements of athleticism and sportsmanship in its choreography.[8] Daldry's *mise-en-scène* and its visual representations of masculinity have another direct link with Burt's observations that

> [t]he ways in which the male dancer's presence succeeds or fails in reinforcing male power is [sic] clearly central to an understanding of representations of masculinity in theatre dance. How spectators read dancers' presence is partly determined by visual cues.
>
> (Burt 1995: 50)

In the dance sequence where Billy is dancing against the police in the closing sequence of Act 1, the tap movement is amplified to serve as a percussive musical sound which is dominant and empowering for Billy. He is using movement to release his anger. Darling's choreography is full of pain and the representation of Billy's anger, highlighted with the blue and red lighting of Daldry's *mise-en-scène* (a Union Jack reference) and the smoke, symbolizing Billy's own revolution against the system and his personal clash against society and its norms. It is a male-to-male battle and it ends the first half with an outstanding exhibition of power and conviction.

This clash of masculinities suggests a strong conflict which releases male energy and proves Cynthia Weber's point that 'dance is commonly thought of as liberating, transformative, empowering, transgressive, and even as dangerous' (Weber 2003). The games of masculinity, both within and outside the working-class boxing club, aim for a personal and communal freedom: the freedom that will enable the men of this working-class community to express themselves through their profession, expertise and skill.

FIGURE 2.3: George Maguire as Billy Elliot dancing against the police (Victoria Palace, 2005). Photo: David Scheinmann.

The freedom of the dancing male: The 'flying' kid expressing himself

> This socialist musical becomes a lyrical celebration of self-expression set against, and deriving from, multiple expressions of grief: grief for Billy's dead mother, and for the strike's failure.
>
> (Macaulay 2005)

To reach his own personal freedom and deal with the grey surroundings of his working-class living environment, Billy has to accept and also justify to his family that dance is an alternative and a valid replacement for sport[9] (and the abandoned boxing lessons). Gard believes that 'the process of defining male rejection of dance as a "problem" for boys is indicative of a wider tendency to see the projection and cultivation of hegemonic masculine norms of behaviour as paramount' (Gard 2001: 214). This is partly one of the reasons why the dramatic tensions of *Billy Elliot* work on a purely psychological level: Billy's actions have consequences that are related not only to the immediate family, but also the community's attitudes towards dance. Gard continues by relating this attitude to dance as sport, but rejects the suggestion that

> any particular codified dance form [...] provides access to, or expression of, universal human needs or desires. [...] As a means for developing, composing, sequencing and evaluating movement skills, there is no clear-cut reason why one might not use dance as the medium of instruction instead of gymnastics, tennis, or, for that matter, football.
> (Gard 2001: 221)

I would disagree with part of his suggestion because dance does provide a physicalized expression of emotions and personal desires and could lead to a personal self-transformation. If the main virtue of sport is the release of energy in a 'healthy' competitive environment, then dance is enhancing this activity by its ability to do the above and also provide the liberating excitement of personal creative expression.

The 'paradox' of a male ballet dancer raises questions of sexuality, which cannot really be ignored in a small mining community. Gard believes that 'some dance forms offer a unique setting for explicitly addressing sexist and homophobic norms of bodily practice' (Gard 2001: 221). These diverse understandings of dance and the popular perceptions of the social construct of 'working-class masculinity' give the impression that there is still work to be done for ballet to be fully accepted as a non- suspect activity for males.

Billy's journey to freedom through self-expression could have a plethora of interlinked readings (the escape, rebirth, rags to riches, from shadow to light, etc.),[10] but Judith Lancioni chooses to read *Billy Elliot* as the fairytale of Cinderella. Lancioni maintains that there is a clear transformation here:

> Billy Elliot is Cinderella because, through the intervention of a chain-smoking fairy godmother, he is transformed from a gangly working-class kid, destined for the coal mines to a mature, self-assured ballet star. Instead of boxing gloves or a glass slipper, he dons ballet shoes, and in doing so he transforms not only himself, but his family's and his community's concept of masculinity as well.
> (Lancioni 2006: 710)

The journey for Billy is one of self-improvement and freedom. Dance is the medium for self-expression and change, where 'adolescent energy is transformed into athleticism' (Henson 2007: 1), and during that process, self-discovery is achieved. It would be helpful to note Sue Palmer's insistence that

> males are still born with the genetic encoding of Stone Age hunters. As they grow their bodies yearn to rehearse this masculine role: they need to run across fields,

clamber through the undergrowth, fashion tools and weapons, push boundaries, take risks. If they don't fulfil these needs, they are likely to suffer in terms of development: physically, emotionally, socially, cognitively.

(Palmer 2007)

It is evident that Lee Hall's lyrics demonstrate this desire for using dance as a symbol of escapism and personal development: pushing one's existing boundaries and linking it to the idea of 'flying' freely 'like a bird' (creating possible links to the ballet *Swan Lake*) ('Electricity', Hall 2005: 18).

The motif of 'flying' is first introduced in the only dream sequence of the show (just before the end of Act 1). Dream sequences (either as flash-backs or flash-forwards) interrupt the action and give an alternative 'what-if' scenario in the form of a fantasy-based vision. In our case, Billy is presented dancing under the guidance of an 'older self' figure. In this sequence, the platonic tutoring support he receives is changed from the female tutor (Mrs Wilkinson) to a male older self (brother-like) figure. The athletic–gymnastic imagery (with the use of the aerial rope work) is combined with finer subtler balletic moves and music from Tchaikovsky's ballet *Swan Lake*. The older dancer could also be said to double up as Billy's guardian angel (who is more experienced at 'flying') and new mentor. His aerial exploits (just like the other flying boy of the theatre, Peter Pan) focus the attention of the audience on Billy and not his surroundings. The action of 'flying' stresses his desire to move on to a new, more culturally vibrant environment and is possibly visually one of the few 'brighter' moments of the show. Billy is not avoiding manhood and the responsibilities of adulthood here: he is simply escaping and transforming his predestined fate.

The freedom of 'flying' and its association with dancing is developed even further during Billy's audition at the Royal Ballet School (in Act 2). When he is asked by a member of the interviewing panel 'What does it feel like when you are dancing?' Billy aptly responds:

Suddenly I'm flying, flying like a bird
Like electricity, electricity
Sparks inside of me
And I'm free, I'm free.

('Electricity', Hall 2005: 18)

Up to that point, Billy was singing what it meant to him to dance. But, suddenly he breaks into a spontaneous, improvised, self-expressive dance sequence. When words and music are not enough, then the movement is there to explicate inner desires. Darling's choreography (which is appropriated and adjusted to the different strengths of each Billy) has an acrobatic edge to it and makes it a muscular and dangerous activity. It is full of anger and quasi martial-arts qualities and expresses Billy's restlessness and affinity with dance. And at the end of it, he continues with the song, concluding that dance is indeed like electricity: the force that leads him to freedom. And this relates directly to my understanding of the concept of 'The British dream',[11] a term which needs urgently to be given a definition. 'The British dream' – in this case, the desire to do better than one's own parents, the forbidden desire to dream and the action of dreaming – is now finally permitted.

Tension(s) and release: Dance as action

We are capable of making lives for ourselves which are full of joy and self-expression [...]. We owe it to the next generation to create a world where it is possible for the Billy Elliots as yet unborn to have a chance to succeed and flourish rather than to be fed to the machine which grinds us into identical pieces only fit for consumption. If Billy Elliot conveys any message at all I hope it is that it is possible to fight back and resist and it is possible to move on without forgetting where you come from.

(Hall 2005: 3)

In order to complete our discussion, we need to address the issue of dance as an act of intervention. In what ways, can dance act as a medium for transformative change? The whole publicity around *Billy Elliot the Musical* and the 'Billy Elliot Academy' in Leeds (where the young performers are trained so that they may fulfil their dreams and perform on the West End stage) has created a new genre that could be possibly described as the 'athletic musical': a new genre which allows for the athletic body to be celebrated, admired and looked at purely for its strength, muscular energy and beauty.

All-singing, all-dancing bodies have always been a source of huge financial gain for show business producers and it is important that some of these gains are now being put back for developing, forming and training those young bodies in a gymnast-like academy. 'It costs thousands to train a new Billy Elliot – and there's no guarantee they'll get the part in the end [because] puberty is enemy number one' (John 2006). There are, of course, many psychological dangers involved and other day-to-day difficulties, but the reality is that a boy playing Billy is on a 'six-month contract; as well as performing two or three times a week he has to spend some nights at the theatre as cover for whoever is on stage' (John 2006). But still, the young performers in *Billy Elliot the Musical* would have experienced what most of us will never do, the opportunity to expose their talent in front of sold-out houses night after night. And that requires both tension(s) and release and the discipline of any athletic sport. The young Billy, through his dancing, has also managed to change the popular public perception that claims that 'real boys don't go to ballet classes' (Gard 2001: 213) to 'only real boys can dance like this'.

In *Billy Elliot the Musical*, the closing imagery of the miners going down the pit pays tribute to the closing imagery of Elia Kazan's *On the Waterfront*, where Marlon Brando's Terry Malloy assumes control of the docks. That personal success – the end of that struggle – is linked with Billy's entry to the Royal Ballet School and the positive connotations of that achievement.

> We will go as one
> The ground is empty
> And cold as hell
> But we all go together as we go.
>
> ('Once We Were Kings', Hall 2005: 18)

While the miners are singing, Billy leaves his village for London. This powerful moment gives us a visual representation of the double edge of masculinity. The working-class males with their strong muscular bodies earning their 'daily bread' by working closely together in difficult situations, and a young male leaving all of this behind to go and pursue a different kind of future: one where physical strength is desired and valued, but in an aesthetic way. While the miners 'all go together' to the ground that is 'cold as hell', Billy leaves, with his luggage, through the middleclass audience in the £60-per-seat stalls. This reverses the dynamic opening of the show, where solidarity and a collectiveness of masculine energy were viewed as the norm. Billy's transformation is now complete, empowering and transgressive. Dance with all its tension(s) has now released a forward-looking momentum which acted as a catalyst for the change in Billy's (and, in some respects, the community's) perceptions and understanding of reality.

Conclusion

The young male *enfants terribles* in *Billy Elliot the Musical* break the conventional gender roles of representing the bo[d]y on stage, upsetting the existing tradition of females performing the younger male roles. The audience's curiosity and amazement with the young talent, the new 'younger' audiences who flock to the Victoria Palace Theatre (and soon other theatres in Australia and the United States of America) remind us that there is a need to re-evaluate what we could/would like to expect from a night out at the theatre.

The athletic fireworks, the references to the circus and the inherent sadness linked to watching gymnasts perform, the obsessive attention to accuracy are all closely linked to the ritualistic invocations of an all-singing, all-dancing bo[d]y. And it is at this point that we can talk about the body not as an ephemeral object of manual labour and strength, but as a timeless work of art: movements of arms and legs that will live forever in the audience's imagination; bodies that will be admired and looked at, freely, on stage, even if what they are doing is not widely regarded to be as valuable as the practical physical action of manual labour.

Theatre is the space where this transformation is made possible by uniting the body *performing* on stage with the body *watching* from the stalls. Visual representations are the decisive pointers that, through the semiotics of the *mise-en-scène*, allow the audience to apply their own mapping and understanding of the work's text and subtexts and relate them to their own reality. *Billy Elliot the Musical* and its creative team managed to redefine the British musical theatrical scene and its insistent lack of new British work and to celebrate 'the British dream' through the all-singing, all-dancing bo[d]y, raising the bo[d]y's status to one of a role model for future generations.

NOTES

1. The scope of this study does not allow us to have a more extensive overview. On the other hand, there is a dearth of academic writing on the male dancer. Notable exceptions are Ramsay Burt's *The Male Dancer: Bodies, Spectacle, Sexualities* (1996) and Michael Gard's *Men Who Dance: Aesthetics, Athletics and the Art of Masculinity* (2006).
2. Award-winning choreographer Javier de Frutos (born in Venezuela in 1963) is currently the artistic director of Phoenix Dance Theatre. His recent work includes choreography for the musicals *Cabaret* (West End) and *Carousel* (Chichester).
3. The bestselling and most discussed show during the 2006–07 theatrical season in Athens (Greece) was Demetris Papaioannou's 2, a dance theatre extravaganza featuring 22 males.
4. This essay will not attempt to present the 'bo[d]y and masculinity' within a gender or sexuality framework. This has been explored by Mangan in *Staging Masculinities: History, Gender, Performance* (2003), Shilling in *The Body and Social Theory* (2003), Turner in *The Body and Society* (1996), Petersen in *Unmasking the Masculine: 'Men' and 'Identity' in a Sceptical Age* (1998), Watson in *Male Bodies: Health, Culture and Identity* (2000), Lehman in *Running Scared: Masculinity and the Representation of the Male Body* (1993), Middleton in *The Inward Gaze: Masculinity and Subjectivity in Modern Culture* (1992), *Men, Masculinity, and the Media* (1992) edited by Craig and others.
5. Peter Darling's choreography credits include the musicals: *The Lord of the Rings, Our House, Closer to Heaven, Merrily We Roll Along, Candide* and *Oh! What a Lovely War*.
6. The relationship with Mrs Wilkinson's daughter (and the other younger females) will not be analyzed here, since it creates new possibilities and comments further on Billy's sexuality. That could constitute an entirely new chapter for discussion.

7. In Artaud's 'Theatre of Cruelty', he suggests that

    > an actor is like a physical athlete, with this astonishing corollary; his affective organism is similar to the athlete's, being parallel to it like a double, although they do not act on the same level. The actor is a heart athlete.
    >
    > (Artaud 1999: 100)

8. Gard comments on a not dissimilar work, Magorian and Ormerod's picture book *Jump* (1992) that

    > the implied and taken-for-granted heterosexuality of male sport is reinforced [...] a boy can be both a sportsperson and a dancer, the reliance on this dichotomised view of physical movement simply reiterates that they embody dichotomised sexual meanings for many people.
    >
    > (Gard 2001: 217)

9. The *BBC News: Health* website supports this view by claiming that 'dance classes could be a good way to tackle childhood obesity [...] creative dance should be considered as an alternative to sport for children' ('Dance "could keep young healthy"' 2007).

10. There are other ways that this journey has been interpreted and it would be worthwhile to include another reading of *Billy Elliot's* narrative of escapism here. Thomas Kerkhoven reads *Billy Elliot* in 'Shiva on the Durham Coalfield: On the Pertinence of Hindu Myth to the film *Billy Elliot*' as a coming-of-age story:

    > Lee Hall's script under Daldry's direction portrays Billy's developing personality in particularly vivid imagery from fairy tales and biblical stories, and even more, from Hindu mythology. This mythology is brought to bear on Billy's coming of age by a creative magical realism. In fact, this psychological drama presents the passage of youth by a clever adaptation of a cycle of intricate Saiva (pertaining to the god Shiva) Hindu myths transplanted to modern day England. [...] Billy stands in the semblance of the god Shiva, supreme ascetic and master of eroticism, who appears in certain puranas (medieval tales) as 'boy by illusion' or 'young beggar, of perfect beauty' rather than as mature immortal. Shiva's developing relation to the goddess Parvati (Michael) and Billy's performance of Shiva's Tandava dance of regenerative destruction then provide an uncanny portrayal of Billy's coming of age.
    >
    > (Kerkhoven 2003)

11. Boris Johnson writes that

    > Americans all understand instinctively that they are equal citizens of the greatest country on earth, and they all have an equal chance of rising to the top of that country. That is the idea of America, the American dream; and we have been

comparatively hopeless at communicating any sense for the British dream, or the British idea.

(Johnson 2005)

REFERENCES

Artaud, A. (1999), *Collected Works, Volume 4* (trans. J. Calder), London: Calder & Boyars Ltd.

Billington, M. (2005), 'Billy Elliot', *The Guardian*, 12 May, http://arts.guardian.co.uk/reviews/story/0,,1482089,00.html. Accessed 26 November 2007.

Burt, R. (1995), *The Male Dancer: Bodies, Spectacle, Sexualities*, London: Routledge.

Daldry, S. (2000), 'Cosmic Dancer', *Sight and Sound*, 10, pp. 12–13.

'Dance "could keep young healthy"', *BBC News: Health*, http://news.bbc.co.uk/1/hi/health/6470815.stm. Accessed 21 March 2007.

Gard, M. (2001), 'Dancing around the "Problem" of Boys and Dance', *Discourse: Studies in the Cultural Politics of Education*, 22:2, pp. 213–25.

Hall, L. (2005), 'Adaptation', programme notes to *Billy Elliot The Musical* (original West End production, directed by Stephen Daldry).

Henson, K. (2007), 'Introduction: Divo worship', *Cambridge Opera Journal*, 19:1, pp. 1–9.

Hill, J. (2004), 'A working-class hero is something to be? Changing representations of class and masculinity in British cinema', in P. Powrie, A. Davies and B. Babington (eds), *The Trouble with Men: Masculinities in European and Hollywood Cinema*, London: Wallflower, pp. 100–09.

John, E. (2006), 'Billy and the kids', *The Guardian*, 10 May, http://arts.guardian.co.uk/features/story/0,,1771290,00.html. Accessed 26 November 2007.

Johnson, B. (2005), 'The British Dream: We must all speak the same language', *The Daily Telegraph*, 4 August, http://www.telegraph.co.uk/opinion/main.jhtml?xml=/opinion/2005/08/04/do0401.xml. Accessed 26 November 2007.

Kerkhoven, T. (2003), 'Shiva on the Durham Coalfield: On the pertinence of Hindu myth to the film *Billy Elliot*', *Journal of Religion and Popular Culture*, 4:1, http://www.usask.ca/relst/jrpc/art4-billyelliot-print.html. Accessed 19 January 2006.

Kirk, J. (2002), 'Changing the subject: Cultural studies and the demise of class', *Cultural Logic*, 5, http://www.clogic.eserver.org/2002/kirk.html. Accessed 19 October 2007.

Lancioni, J. (2006), 'Cinderella dances *Swan Lake*: Reading *Billy Elliot* as fairytale', *The Journal of Popular Culture*, 39:5, pp. 709–28.

Leggott, J. (2004), 'Like father?: Failing parents and angelic children in contemporary British Social Realist cinema', in P. Powrie, A. Davies and B. Babington (eds), *The Trouble with Men: Masculinities in European and Hollywood Cinema*, London: Wallflower, pp. 163–73.

Macaulay, A. (2005), '*Billy Elliot the Musical*, Victoria palace theatre', *The Financial Times*, 13 May, http://www.ft.com/cms/s/0/8e5f8046-c34d-11d9-abf1-00000e2511c8.html?nclickcheck=1. Accessed 26 November 2007.

Muir, H. (2004), 'Boxing lessons are good for you, Blunkett tells the poor', *The Guardian*, 27 September, http://www.guardian.co.uk/guardianpolitics/story/0,,1313291,00.html. Accessed 26 November 2007.

Nightingale, B. (2005), 'Billy Elliot', *The Times*, 12 May, http://entertainment.timesonline.co.uk/tol/artsandentertainment/article521505.ece. Accessed 26 November 2007.

Palmer, S. (2007), 'Boys must be boys – For all our sakes', *The Sunday Times*, 18 November, http://women.timesonline.co.uk/tol/lifeandstyle/women/thewaywelive/article2889307.ece. Accessed 26 November 2007.

Schulberg, B. (1954), *On the Waterfront*, USA: Horizon Pictures, http://www.imdb.com/title/tt0047296/quotes. Accessed 20 January 2006.

Sinfield, A. (2006), 'Boys, class and gender: From Billy Casper to Billy Elliot', *History Workshop Journal*, 62, pp. 166–71.

Spencer, C. (2005), 'Billy boy, this is the greatest musical yet', *The Daily Telegraph*, 12 May, http://www.telegraph.co.uk/arts/main.jhtml?xml=/arts/2005/05/12/btbilly12.xml&sSheet=/arts/2005/05/12/ixartright.html. Accessed 26 November 2007.

Weber, C. (2003), '"Oi, Dancing Boy!" Masculinity, sexuality, and youth in *Billy Elliot*', http://www.genders.org/g37/g37weber.html. Accessed 1 October 2006.

3

Hamilton's Women

Stacy Wolf

Introduction: Dissonant pleasures

Hamilton ends with Eliza's breath. The actor stands down centre stage, captured in a spotlight.[1] The ensemble sings in a soft call-and-response, 'Time, time, time' and 'Who lives, who dies, who tells your story?' ending in unison, on one note. Eliza looks up and out ... at the spirit of Hamilton? At the image of her own death? At a vision of the future beyond this time and place? It is a quiet moment at the end of a noisy, beat-driven, word-full, kinesthetically packed evening. She is still. The company is still. The actor playing Hamilton is still, after having led her by the hand to this place onstage.

The last moment of a musical is crucial, as it leaves the audience with an image that we are meant to hold in our minds as we think back over the whole evening and the story we have witnessed. Most musicals (though certainly not all) conclude with a rousing chorus and the celebration of a community (including Miranda and his collaborators Tommy Kail, Andy Blankenbuehler and Alex Lacamoire's first Broadway hit, *In the Heights*). But around five minutes before the end of *Hamilton*, the eponymous character dies in the prefigured duel with Burr, then Eliza takes over and narrates what she does with the rest of her life. She becomes an anti-slavery activist; she founds an orphanage; and most importantly, she solidifies the memory of Hamilton and his historical legacy. The lyrics are sung quietly, but the events are clear: she and Angelica gather his vast number of letters and organize his archive. They tell his story. Eliza, it seems, is the entire reason that we have been here.

To a degree, this final moment and sudden revelation that Eliza is Hamilton's biographer position her as the centre of the show. Her status as archivist and editor expands her role in the story itself – that of a wife. At the end, she is a historian herself, the one 'who tells his story'. Theatrically, it is a powerful final moment of self-reflexive historiography with a woman downstage centre. Nevertheless, the story she tells is his. This gesture cannot undo what the past 150 minutes have been about: men.

In this essay, I explore the women of *Hamilton*. My argument is simple: *Hamilton* puts women on the sidelines and relegates them to the most obvious and time-worn stereotypes. The musical's cleverness, its engaging music and vibrant energy, and its occasional nod to the societal constraints experienced by women seduce spectators into looking away from the demeaning representation of women. The show feels so cool, hip and yes, revolutionary (not to mention the against-all-odds frenzy to score a ticket) that critics, spectators and musical theatre students do not want to find fault with its politics, including its gender politics.[2]

My critique of *Hamilton* is not intended to diminish the importance of this musical in its remarkable retelling of US history, its radical use of rap and hip hop and its casting of actors of colour. Nor does it reduce my fandom of the show. Rather I want to embrace a divided regard for the musical, one admiring and disappointed, celebratory and critical. My larger goal is to (re)articulate paradox and contradiction as a viable critical stance, which feminist fans of popular culture frequently inhabit: that we can enjoy what we also critique, and that practicing such critique is itself pleasurable and compelling, in seeing, hearing and noting what mainstream critics often miss. Maybe it is time to reassert the importance of a conflicted feminist spectator of musicals specifically, which somehow still suffer from the 'it's only entertainment' syndrome. As well, musical theatre as a performance form compels what I have called 'kinesthetic spectatorship', an intense, affectual engagement borne of music and dance's infectiousness harnessed for storytelling. I read *Hamilton*, then, as offering what I will call 'dissonant pleasure': a feminist spectator's forceful love/hate relationship with a musical. This notion refuses a distinction between feeling and thinking because, in fact, a feminist assessment of a musical often starts with feeling, specifically that 'something's not quite right here' feeling. This interpretive position is neither about 'guilty pleasure' nor about ambivalence. To the contrary, 'dissonant pleasures' are strong feelings of admiration and fury – often both at the same time – during a given moment of performance.[3]

Hamilton's dissonant pleasures start from the fact that there are only four named women in the show (plus several women actors in the mostly gender-neutralized ensemble): the three Schuyler sisters, Angelica, Eliza and the youngest sister, Peggy, who only appears rarely, and Maria Reynolds (played by the same actor who plays Peggy). The women are introduced at the end of the opening number in which every character notes their relationship to Hamilton. The men sing, 'Me, I trusted him'; 'Me, I died for him'; 'We, we fought with him'. The three women, standing in a group on the upper level catwalk, intone together, 'Me, I loved him', and the section ends with Burr's 'And me, I'm the damn fool that shot him'. By having the women speak next to last, building to Burr's co-star role, the musical signals their relative importance. But it undercuts them as well. First, they are above the action, which is where they spend much of the show, not on the stage floor participating in the story, but watching it unfold from a distance. Second, they introduce themselves in a group of three, indistinguishable because they all 'loved him'. Except for Lafayette/Jefferson and Hercules/Madison, who sing together, each of the male characters has a separate relationship to Hamilton, but the women are lumped together and only exist to serve the romance plot(s) of the musical.[4]

The musically layered, visually kinetic and narratively packed powerful opening number also features a mixed-gender ensemble, who supplement the 144 words-per-minute storytelling with striking visual cues (see Libresco 2015). Their movement ranges from filling out stage pictures to pantomiming action, and, at various times, their function is literal or figurative, and always aesthetically dynamic. For the most part, the women and the men undertake the same movements and play bystanders, servants and soldiers. The multigendered ensemble, while of crucial importance in the musical, does not change the gender dynamics of the named characters' story.

'The bullet' that kills Hamilton, though, is embodied by a woman performer. In slow motion, she 'stops' Burr's bullet after he fires by placing her hand over the gun's muzzle, then mimes propelling it halfway across the stage. Finally she becomes the bullet herself, lifted horizontal by several ensemble members and carried towards Hamilton, until all of the actors seem to explode outward and freeze, each in a different, off-kilter pose.[5] This actor gets the chance to be the centre of this crucial moment, but she bears the unfortunate burden of playing the object that kills Hamilton.

Hamilton's historical source material, which has led numerous teachers (somewhat alarmingly) to teach the show as US history, might seem to validate the women's small roles, since the founding fathers were all men.[6] Though the show has sparked a welcome renewed interest in the American Revolution and the early days of this country, it is a piece of art, wrought from the creative energies of numerous collaborators, including Miranda, Kail, Lacamoire, Blankenbuehler, as well as Ron Chernow's biography, itself a representation of Hamilton's life. In Miranda and Jeremy McCarter's indispensible *Hamilton: The Revolution*, a coffee table book of the libretto, photos and essays on different aspects of the production, Miranda annotates the script with examples of where, why and how he took liberties with history and made things up. He offers examples of countless moments and scenes that did not happen as they are shown in the musical or did not happen at all. In an interview with Mark Binelli for *Rolling Stone*, Miranda speaks 'about the task of liberating history's most revered figures from their own legend' (Binelli 2016: 39). He emphasizes how the show is an artistic project, an adaptation of Chernow's biography and of the historical record, not history itself.

Moreover, the decision to tell this story in hip hop and a contemporary vocabulary with a cast of actors of colour removes the show from historically accurate storytelling. As Miranda writes, 'This is a story about America then, told by America now [...]. We want to eliminate any distance between a contemporary audience and this story' (Delman 2015). This musical is a riff on US history, which is precisely what gives it power. Shannon Walsh, in a review in *Theatre Journal*, observes that *Hamilton* 'use[s] American history to tell the story of people of color in the present day' (2016: 457). The musical is radical for Broadway in its use of performers of colour, of rap and blues music, and of a contemporary lingo. Our enthusiasm for the show might cause us to overlook a dynamic that is conservative and limiting for the female characters and for female performers. Moreover, *Hamilton*'s politically progressive elements only make the diminishment and stereotypical treatment of women all the more striking. 'History' becomes a distraction from what we are really experiencing: dissonant pleasure.

Meet 'The Schuyler Sisters'

After the opening segment, the sisters do not enter the action for a full fourteen minutes – a sign of their insignificance – but when they arrive, it is in an infectious and effervescent number. The catchy song is built on tight harmonies reminiscent of Destiny's Child (or for older audience members, the Pointer Sisters), girl groups whose sound is familiar and empowering for feminist spectators. Though the ensemble slightly ridicules them because, as Burr sings, 'There's nothing rich folks like more than going downtown slumming with the poor' and describes them as desirable solely because of their father's wealth, once they start to sing and command the stage, they are a force in candy-coloured satin ball gowns.

After we forget that almost 10 per cent of the show has gone by with no women characters, this number falls squarely on the 'pleasure' side. The song functions as their 'I Am/I Want' trio, articulating their collective excitement to be in New York City at this time and differentiating the brilliant Angelica from the sweet Eliza from the youngest (and ultimately forgettable) Peggy. Peggy's good girl lyrics, 'Daddy said to be home by sundown', allow Angelica to assert, 'Daddy doesn't need to know', and Eliza, 'Like I said, you're free to go', making it clear that they are disobeying their father's wishes by going out unescorted and at night. They are irrepressible, as they sing in a joyful circular, eighth-note-dominated melody, 'Look around, look around at how / Lucky we are to be alive right now!'. This motif becomes Eliza's theme, which she repeats several times in the show. They sing, 'History is happening in Manhattan and we / just happen to be in the greatest city in the / world!'. They are amazed and excited by the city, energetic and vibrant women who have nonetheless been sheltered.

The staging is visually engaging and kinetic, focused on the three women grouped and surrounded by the ensemble. To convey the sense of movement through the streets, the centre circular section of the stage revolves and a larger ring of stage space rotates in the same or the opposite direction, allowing actors to seem to move faster or slower in relation to other bodies. The women's choreography is fast and sharp, a combination of hip hop, Broadway jazz and gestures pantomimed and directly connected to the lyrics. The movement is at once visceral and communicative.

Though the number features the three women, Angelica dominates, and the song operates as her own 'I Am/I Want' song, too.[7] Angelica is described in the hip-hop-meets-Broadway casting call as 'a combination of Nicki Minaj and Desiree Armfeldt' (Miranda and McCarter 2016: 78), suggesting a powerful, sexy, articulate woman who suffers unrequited love. At one point, she steps downstage in an encounter with Burr, whose flirtations ('I'm a trust fund, baby, you can trust me') she promptly rejects and follows with a fast-paced demonstration of her intellectual prowess and political ambitions: 'I've been reading *Common Sense* by Thomas Paine. / So men say that I'm intense or I'm insane. / You want a revolution? I want a revelation / So listen to my declaration'. She is also self-aware, continuing, '"We hold these truths to be self-evident / That all men are created equal". / And when I meet Thomas Jefferson, / I'm'a compel him to include *women* in the / sequel!' with her sisters backing her. Miranda has often said that Angelica is the smartest character in the show (see Hillman 2016). Eliza, for her part, is seemingly not very bright – or at least not politically aware – as she sings, 'Angelica, remind me what we're looking for'.

The number's dramaturgical purpose is to introduce the three women, the New York City setting and the atmosphere of excited anticipation. But ideologically, this song also lets the audience know that *Hamilton* knows what it is doing with gender. In spite of being upper class, the sisters refuse to obey their father's instructions, and Angelica is smart but limited because she is a woman. In this way, the number allows *Hamilton* to barely squeak by the Bechdel–Wallace test, as there are at least two named female characters in *Hamilton*, and they talk about something other than a man – sort of.[8]

Performance wise, the number is irresistibly pleasurable. The female-dominated song is infectiously kinetic, tuneful, energetic, forceful and fun. Further, introducing Angelica as a politically savvy, perceptive intellectual opens a representational space not frequently embodied by a woman of colour. This number articulates the societal limitations on women but also hints that maybe the women will prevail. Unfortunately, that does not turn out to be the case.

Over the course of the musical, feminist spectators' pleasure in *Hamilton* morphs into dissonant pleasure.

Eliza in love and 'Helpless'

Somewhat predictably, the women do not reappear until the show turns from politics to romance – fifteen minutes later – in 'Helpless' and 'Satisfied', two linked numbers that tell the story of Hamilton and Eliza's courtship and wedding from each sister's point of view. More than the purely exhilarating 'Schuyler Sisters', this segment is complicated and contradictory, calling up dissonant pleasures. 'Helpless' functions as Eliza's 'I Am/I Want' song, as she announces herself, 'I have never been the type to try and grab the spotlight', and sets the scene: 'We were at a revel with some rebels on a hot night'. The R&B number quickly expresses her essential self: 'helpless', 'down for the count', 'look into your eyes [...] and I'm drownin' in 'em'. She sings beautifully about being helpless.

Eliza's casting call blurb – 'fiercely loyal, self-possessed, proud. Evolves from lovesick, wealthy young woman to the sole keeper of her late husband's legacy. Alicia Keys meets Elphaba; soprano'– highlights how she changes over the course of the show (*The Hamilton Mixtape* 2016). But this number finds her more passive than active at every turn, repeating how 'helpless' she feels. In the bouncy and infectious number, and backed by her sisters and the female ensemble as a doo-wop group, Eliza explains how she sights Alexander, falls for him instantly and confides the crush to Angelica, who introduces them to one another. Then Eliza receives letters from Alexander and waits anxiously while he asks her father's permission to marry her. The end rhymes, dominated by 'oo' sounds with an ornament on the last note of each line, underline her girly infatuation.

The waltz-inflected choreography is fantastic and features swirls and circles, from the rotating stage floor to the dizzy twirling of the women's layered skirts. The scene follows musical theatre's conventional romantic dance, during which the couple meets and instantly falls in love while dancing, such as Rodgers and Hammerstein's *Cinderella* and Bernstein and Sondheim's *West Side Story*, which Miranda claims as inspiration for this section of the show (Miranda and McCarter 2016: 71).

The song becomes a love duet when Hamilton interjects a short rap section. After Papa Schuyler approves the marriage, Alexander pulls Eliza aside and admits that he is poor and has nothing but 'a couple of college credits and my top notch brain'. The song echoes Beyoncé's 'Crazy in Love', in which Jay-Z sings a verse (Miranda and McCarter 2016: 68). (Ashanti and Ja Rule later sang a cover on the 2016 *Hamilton Mixtape*.) As Miranda and McCarter write, '"Helpless" doesn't riff on this tradition – it *is* this tradition [...] a sweet girl sings about the boy she loves, then the rough-around-the edges boy pops up to rap his reply' (2016: 69, original emphasis). This song, Miranda and McCarter explain, is meant to be their courtship song in musical theatre terms: 'The musical theater canon offers many ways to depict this courtship [that is, between two characters who are from opposite walks of life]: sweeping waltzes, soaring ballads, the conventions of stage romance' (2016 : 68). Like Nellie and Emile in 'Twin Soliloquies' in *South Pacific*, Eliza and Alexander never sing together in the song but rather offer alternate perspectives on their relationship. That they do not sing in unison or harmony but in different musical styles underlines their different views on the world.

Dramaturgically, this number is as effective as any in *Hamilton*. As McCarter writes, 'Lin uses the convention of a pop song to help a twenty-first-century audience understand eighteenth-century social distinctions. And he does it with the extreme concision that a theater song demands: A meeting, courtship, and a wedding flit by in four minutes of stage time' (Miranda and McCarter 2016: 69). Still, although this song features Eliza and is her big number – reinforced by the strong spotlight that follows her around the stage and places other actors in shadow – it concludes with the ensemble singing, 'In New York, you can be a new man', repeating phrases from the show's opening number. Unlike the typical musical theatre love duet of a balanced meeting between two principals, this song tells her story, but shifts to his in the last few lines. In the end, 'Helpless' causes dissonant pleasure: it is a terrifically enjoyable and engaging production number, but is, ultimately, about Alexander's rise up the social ladder through marriage and how Eliza exists to help build him up.

Angelica will never be 'Satisfied'

By the time Eliza sings her final 'Helpless', the scene is mid-wedding and Angelica offers her toast in 'Satisfied'. Like 'Helpless', this galvanizing number gives the woman voice, visibility and agency, and yet, in reality, confines her in the end to serve as Hamilton's helpmate. Angelica shouts, 'A toast to the groom! / To the bride! / From your sister [...] May you always / be satisfied', followed by a record-skipping reverb of Angelica's voice singing, 'I remember that night' repeatedly, and the ensemble re-performing the choreography from 'Helpless' backwards. The stage rotates and lighting effects explode in wide circles on the stage before shrinking to a dot and disappearing. Design, sound and movement all combine to make the action seem to move in reverse and the scene to 'rewind' to the night when Alexander meets Angelica and Eliza – the start of this affair.

In 'Satisfied', Angelica presents the meet-and-marry story from her point of view, reinforcing her characterization as a woman who is smart, self-possessed, sharply observant, loyal to her sister and trapped by her gender and class responsibilities. She stands centre stage and narrates how she and Alexander feel a fast, intense connection in their initial meeting, which the two performers then enact. He opens, 'You strike me as a woman who has never been satisfied', to which she replies as the upper-class woman she is, 'I'm sure I don't know what you mean. You forget yourself'. He comes back with 'You're like me. I'm never satisfied', and she quips, 'Is that right?'. They stand close to one another, noses almost touching, and the electricity is palpable. Miranda said, 'I thought a lot about Maria and Tony in *West Side Story*, when they first meet. You have eight lines to encapsulate love at first sight: Go. The challenge here is the same' (Miranda and McCarter 2016: 71).

Angelica is smitten, as she raps, 'So so so – / So this is what it feels like to match wits / With someone at your level! / What the hell is the catch? It's / The feeling of freedom, of seein' the light'. She is determined to 'take him far away from this place', but then hears and sees her 'helpless' sister, and quickly regains her keen logical view. She enunciates the three 'fundamental truths': that she needs to marry a rich man to maintain her family's class status ('Angelica and Alexander are equals in wit, but not in status, and she is well aware of her station and its demands', observes Michael Schulman in *The New Yorker* [Schulman 2015]), that he wants her because she is rich, and that her sister is in love with him but would sacrifice herself if she knew that Angelica loved him, too. Nonetheless, Angelica will always desire him. From there, she leads Hamilton across the room and introduces him to Eliza, repeating the same staging and delivery that the audience previously witnessed in 'Helpless'. By playing the same scene twice, the musical posits the women as temperamental opposites, though both obsessed and in love with the same man.

The number provides the audience with knowledge of Angelica's feelings, of her intelligence (that she expresses herself in complex rhymes and the fastest word delivery in the show), of her love for her sister and also of her agency, as she is the one to set up Eliza and Hamilton. Importantly, she ably communicates in the same competitive, athletic musical genre that the men use and that *Hamilton* values most: rap.[9]

Though Angelica's verse in 'The Schuyler Sisters' suggests she might be an active participant in the country's formation, after arranging the match between Alexander and her beautiful and vacuous sister, she does little else but pine for him for the rest of the show. At the end of the song, she sings, 'He will never be satisfied. I will never be satisfied', and the ensemble repeats, 'Be satisfied'. As Miranda writes, 'Funny thing about saying a word a lot: It starts to feel the opposite of what it means. With the world [the ensemble] singing "be satisfied", without the first half of the sentence, it feels like a perverse, tragic mantra' (Miranda and McCarter 2016: 85). Jessica Sternfeld calls this phenomenon 'the *Little Mermaid* problem', in which a female character is introduced as 'someone who wants to see the world but then falls in love with the first boy she sees, and then she nobly sacrifices herself for him' (Sternfeld 2017).

Like all of the women's numbers in the show, 'Satisfied' is a tour de force for the actor who plays a self-abnegating character – the quintessential dynamic of dissonant pleasure. From this point on, we only hear from Angelica briefly during Act 2's 'Take A Break', which, as Miranda says, 'is our only personal check-in with Hamilton's family in a politically heavy second act' (Miranda and McCarter 2016: 168). Later, Angelica urges him to negotiate with Jefferson, and she appears once more to support Eliza after Alexander publishes the Reynolds Pamphlet. (She also sings, 'It's Quiet Uptown', but as a neutral storyteller, not in character.)

In the end, Angelica gets very little stage time and simply does not have much to do in the musical. She plays the role of the muse, the supportive sister, the brainy equal of Hamilton who takes on no overt role in the country's formation. Though her intellectual prowess confounds stereotypes of women of colour, her helping role reinforces them. Angelica appears as a remarkable, powerful and potentially ground-breaking character but ultimately occupies a familiar gender stereotype.

Eliza the wife

Because Eliza is the wife – the musical's second predictable female stereotype – she gets more songs ('That Would Be Enough', 'Take a Break' and 'Burn') and more stage time than Angelica in the latter half of the show. Beautiful and loving, she raises their son to speak French and play the piano and exemplifies the cult of true womanhood.[10] Although the musical's eighteenth-century setting predates this nineteenth-century phenomenon, 'true womanhood' provides audiences with a readymade and familiar image of the docile, prim and proper wife. Dissonant pleasures abound: a woman of colour portrays a character type – the idealized wife and mother – typically embodied by a white actor, but that role limits Eliza's emotional activity to nagging, then suffering.

'That Would Be Enough', which takes place midway through Act 1, and 'Burn', which takes place midway through Act 2, form bookends for Eliza's reckoning with her husband's ambitions and her own domestic preoccupations, and she is fretful and vulnerable in both. In the former, Eliza sings, 'If you could let me inside your heart [...] And I could be enough / And we could be enough' and 'Let me be part of the narrative', which sets up 'Burn': 'I'm erasing myself from the narrative'. Miranda penned the end of the first song to give Eliza more agency, as he wrote, 'If she's "erasing herself from the narrative" in Act Two, she needs to be part of it in Act One' (Miranda and McCarter 2016: 110). The songs are musically and staging-wise unlike others in the show – aurally quiet and acoustic, with a more typical musical theatre sound, and visually quiet, too, with soft blue lighting, the actors sitting still, and a bench as the one set piece. Eliza's songs – the '"white" music of traditional Broadway', as Lyra D. Monteiro observes – contrast with *Hamilton*'s liveliest scenes, which are performed by the men in rap (Monteiro 2016: 91).[11] And her motif, 'that would be enough', which signifies passivity, is the exact opposite of Alexander and Angelica's restless, active 'never be satisfied'.

Between her two solos, Eliza's main objective – against all odds – is to domesticate Hamilton. She pesters him to pay more attention to their son, and she harangues him to leave work behind to 'run away with us for the summer / let's go upstate' with the family. Because he is passionately committed to the formation of the United States and insatiably ambitious about his legacy, her efforts seem not only futile but off base, a misreading of who he is and what he cares about. When Eliza reminds him that John Adams spends time with his family, Hamilton quips, 'John Adams doesn't / have a real job anyway'. (Meanwhile, he and Angelica carry on epistolary flirtations through this section of the musical.) The audience is in a conflicted position here. We later understand that Eliza is right: the fact that he stays in town without her leaves him exhausted and vulnerable to Maria's charms. One also might argue that his lack of attention to Phillip causes the boy to develop an exaggerated loyalty, which leads to the duel in which the youth is killed. But these dynamics are overshadowed by the larger (masculine, public and historical) subject of the show: politics. Whatever his domestic (and later, marital) failings, Hamilton rises up from nothing and builds America, the noblest job of all. Eliza, then, embodies the all-too-familiar and unfortunate role of the nagging wife.

Later in Act 2, Eliza becomes the sympathetic, long-suffering wife when she finds out about Hamilton's affair with Maria Reynolds that summer. In 'Burn', she wears a soft, flowing, white dress with an empire waist and a low-cut neckline, which makes her look vulnerable and open, in contrast to the protective, armour-like mint green satin gown with a rigid corset and bustle from 'The Schuyler Sisters'. She is humiliated by the announcement – by Hamilton's own pen – of his extended tryst and sings, 'In clearing your name you have ruined our lives', as the accompaniment builds from a soft and haunting arpeggio. As the only solo number in the show (i.e. the only song in which the single actor occupies that stage alone – except for King George's), 'Burn' calls up dissonant pleasure. On the one hand, Eliza gets a lovely song all to herself, with the focus on her, and the actor can display pathos. On the other hand, she is essentially deserted onstage, stuck there alone, out of context and unsupported by backup singers. Her singularity is especially striking when compared to other solo numbers that nonetheless get the ensemble's support, such as Burr's 'Wait for It'. Ironically, Eliza is as isolated in her numbers as the ridiculous and foppish King George, the show's running joke.

The purpose of 'Burn' is equal parts dramaturgical and characterological, as the song underlines the theme of historiography, the question of how history is written and by whom. 'Let future historians wonder / How Eliza reacted when you broke her heart', she sings, wresting her point of view into her own hands, but through erasure. By burning their letters, the evidence of her story, Eliza's agency is an act of negation. After their son dies, Eliza forgives Alexander.

For most of the musical, then, Eliza represents a stereotypical wife. After 'Helpless', all of her songs are quiet and pained. She adds an important musical texture to *Hamilton*, but it is less compelling than the beat-filled rap music, the non-stop rapid choreography and the driving energy of the men. In *Hamilton: The Revolution*, Miranda and McCarter note the theatrical difficulty of creating a character whose key trait is goodness: 'Eliza's warmth and vibrancy make her a remarkable woman, but they also make her a challenging character. "It's difficult to make pure goodness compelling", Ron [Chernow] said' (2016: 107). So goes dissonant pleasure.

Maria the seductress

The character Maria Reynolds, the other woman in the musical and in Hamilton's life, fills the stereotype of the seductress with attendant dissonant pleasure for the feminist spectator. Predictably, Maria sings a gorgeous, bluesy number, 'Say No to This', as her sole purpose in the show is to get Hamilton into her bed through a performance of her weakness. As Schulman observes, she 'isn't much more than an archetypal femme fatale – sort of a sultry Rihanna type' (Schulman 2015).

The number, which follows right on the heels of 'Take a Break' – Eliza and Angelica's failed attempt to persuade Alexander to 'go upstate' – is staged to appear as if Maria is encroaching on Alexander. He sits at his desk in a small pool of light, then the stage's outer ring rotates and three street lamps slide in, as does Maria herself, pre-set. Lit in dark shadows, a gelled light painting the stage floor red, the scene finds Maria in a red, low-cut satin dress, which at once contrasts and harmonizes with the green satin on Alexander's jacket. The song interweaves R&B – Maria's musical style – and softly tempered rap, the style in which Alexander relates the story. The ensemble participates as a Greek chorus throughout, urging him to 'Say no!' (Miranda and McCarter 2016: 174).[12] Maria sings 'Stay?' and 'Hey' on the flat sixth, which one fan commentator calls 'the sultriest of blue notes', 'irresistible to our dear Hamilton' (Anon. 2016c).

'Say No to This' is Maria's one appearance in the show, but it is narrated by Hamilton, who tells the story of their meeting and affair in the song.[13] Miranda explains, 'Hamilton's the only one who can narrate the song at this point in the story: It happened to him, in secret, and we don't know Maria or James Reynolds yet. So he does it' (Miranda and McCarter 2016: 176). Miranda's (weak) reasoning intensifies this irresistible number's dissonant pleasures, reminding us that this is Alexander's story, and we never know what Maria thinks and what she is feeling. Jasmine Cephas Jones, who originated the role of Maria and Peggy Schuyler says that 'what makes "Say No to This" interesting is the possibility that she's also falling in love with him […]. That's what makes the stakes so high' (quoted in Miranda and McCarter 2016: 175). But the song does not function to track her feelings. On the contrary, her role is narratively purposeful – to move his story forward.

Maria's appearance and social stature are the opposite of Eliza's: her low-cut, form-fitting red dress to Eliza's pale green gown with white fabric at the neck; Maria's hair long and flowing to Eliza's neat ponytail (or half-back ponytail); Maria's languid, undulating physicality to Eliza's perfectly straight posture; Maria's poverty to Eliza's wealth; Maria's blues to Eliza's Broadway ballad. Eliza represents the cult of true womanhood and Maria is the Jezebel – an already racialized type – but they are linked by the lyric 'this one's mine' and most of all, by being 'helpless'.

Unfortunately (for Hamilton and for the musical's gender politics), it is this matrimonial betrayal that brings him down. Even though all of the other men – Jefferson, Madison and, of course, Burr – hate him personally and politically, they cannot get rid of him until they follow the money trail of his affair. Hamilton is intellectually brilliant and politically dogged, able to withstand every pressure except the sexual appeal of a woman, which the musical portrays as understandable: he is alone in the city; he is exhausted; he knows he should 'say no to this'. The music is seductive to the audience, too, as we witness her pressing him, professing her desire and her need, her helplessness. 'While the show doesn't let Hamilton off the hook, he comes across more as a dupe than as an adulterer', writes Schulman (2015). Though the musical focuses on Hamilton's political miscalculation and his naiveté in believing that confessing the affair keeps him politically clean, this major plot device – Hamilton's destruction – is caused by a woman. But then, the show does not even give Maria the power of a villain, as she is ultimately the pawn in her husband's blackmail scheme. Again, this narrative is far too culturally familiar.

Hamilton's *historiographical finale*

In the end, then, the three women in the musical occupy the most conventional and stereotypical roles – muse, wife and whore – which is all the more troubling since *Hamilton* goes such a long way to dismantle stereotypes of race and masculinity. In his review in *The New Yorker*, Hilton Als called the musical a 'bromance' and found the female characters to be 'plot points in silk' (Als 2015). To be sure, the show is well aware of its gender problems, which it tries to resolve historiographically. In the finale, Eliza decides to 'put myself back in the narrative' and offers an account of her life, which continued for 50 years after Hamilton's death.[14] She becomes an activist, 'speak[ing] out against slavery' and founding 'the first private orphanage in New York City'. She and Angelica gather Hamilton's letters, and 'I try to make sense of your thousands of pages of writing', to write his story, to write *this* story. The self-reflexive musical ends with a commentary on the very writing of history, underlining the importance of the author. 'Who lives, who dies, who tells your story?' repeats the Company. In the end, *Hamilton* reveals, all of this exists because of Eliza, her efforts and her ability to write and to tell his life's narrative. She is the author.

The musical's last number is quiet and choir-like, and reuses Eliza's 'It Would Be Enough' theme. Her music ends the show and surprises an audience accustomed for the past two-and-a-half hours to seeing the women on the sidelines. On the one hand, it is a profound gesture of respect towards Eliza. But theatrically, it is too little too late. After a musical packed with nonstop movement, dramatic intensity, strong melodies and galvanizing rhythms, the song is narrowly focused and understated. Though appropriate for the show's conclusion, it cannot rescue Eliza, Angelica or Maria from their stereotypical roles.

Because *Hamilton* provides as much pleasure as dissonance, feminist spectators, critics, scholars and artists are energetically engaging with the work, from the gone-viral YouTube clip of '#Ham4Ham 1/3/16 with The Ladies of Hamilton' that features the women actors impersonating the male characters outside the theatre, to fan fiction, critical blogs and commentary (Anon. 2016a). Miranda has stated that he welcomes cross-gender casting when the rights are released for amateur productions, especially high school shows when 'no one's voice is set': 'I'm totally open to women playing founding fathers once this goes into the world. I can't wait to see kick-ass women Jeffersons and kickass [sic] women Hamiltons once this gets to schools' (Robbins 2015). In time, women in these roles will be sensational, but dissonant pleasures will remain, as cross-gender performance will also foreground how limited and stereotypical the female characters are in *Hamilton*. For consonant pleasures, we might have to wait for Miranda or another musical theatre firebrand to write a show about Michelle Obama.

ACKNOWLEDGEMENTS

My thanks to Jill Dolan for inviting me to write about *Hamilton* for her *Feminist Spectator* blog and for reading drafts of that (and this) essay. Some of these ideas were first published in Wolf (2016). Thanks to Wendy Belcher, Ryan Donovan, Alosha Grinenko, Ray Knapp, Zelda Knapp, Laura MacDonald, Jeff Magee, Danielle Nussbaum, Deborah Paredez, Doug Reside, Joshua Robinson, David Savran, Jessica Sternfeld, Tamsen Wolff, Liz Wollman and Morgan Woolsey, who read drafts and offered comments. The author also thanks Katie Welsh and Maddie Meyers for their excellent research assistance and the Princeton undergraduates in GSS 365 Fall 2016 for discussing these ideas with me. Finally, thanks to *Studies in Musical Theatre's* peer reviewers for their helpful comments and suggestions and Peter Kunze for his editorial diligence.

NOTES

1. I saw *Hamilton* with Phillipa Soo, who originated the role. As of this writing in May 2018, Lexi Lawson plays Eliza in the Broadway production. All quoted lyrics appear in *Hamilton the Revolution*, Hal Leonard Vocal Selections or online.
2. For a superb and complementary assessment of *Hamilton*, including a section on '*Hamilton*'s (more than questionable) feminism', see McMaster (2016). Also see the many thoughtful online responses that support McMaster's reading.
3. As noted, embracing a contradictory mode of reception was amply developed in feminist film and television studies – and cultural studies more generally – from the late 1980s onward. Scholars including Richard Dyer, Constance Penley, Janice Radway (on romance novels), E. Ann Kaplan, Mary Anne Doane, Julie D'Acci, Christine Gledhill and many others have articulated the complexities of feminist fandom of sexist or misogynist texts and enacted readings of 'dissonant pleasure'. See, for example, Gledhill (1988).
4. This reading focuses on the named female characters and what they do and how they function in the musical, but another feminist interpretation might consider, for example, how some spectators identify with characters across gender or derive pleasure from the male bodies onstage.
5. Discussion of 'the Bullet' (#thebullet) abounds on social media. See Anon. (2016b).
6. Women, of course, actively participated in America's formation, especially in the private sphere, and they fought in the Revolutionary War. See The Women's Project of New Jersey, Inc. 1990, http://www.njwomenshistory.org/about/. My thanks to Ferris Olin for sharing this resource with me.

7. Angelica was originally played by Renée Elise Goldsberry, who won Lucille Lortel, Drama Desk and Tony Awards for her performance. Mandy Gonzalez played the role as of this writing in May 2018.
8. Thanks to Zelda Knapp for the correct term for this feminist measurement tool.
9. John McWhorter writes, 'Rapping is, to an extent, sport. This works so well in *Hamilton* because the characters are men in competition' (2016: 52).
10. See Welter (1966).
11. Monteiro notes that Philippa Soo, though Chinese American, 'reads as white', 'while the eldest sister Angelica who sings in the more "black" genres of R&B and rap, is black (Renee Elise Goldsberry)' (2016: 91). As of this writing, Lexi Lawson 'reads' as darker than Mandy Gonzalez. It will be interesting to see how racial dynamics will change in future casting on Broadway and in other productions.
12. Apparently, Sondheim liked this song the most when he first heard the score – because of its stylistic variety.
13. She is onstage for 'The Reynold's Pamphlet' but has no lines.
14. Miranda notes that Kushner and Tesori's *Caroline, or Change* gave him the confidence to end the musical with 'somebody other than the protagonist' (Miranda and McCarter 2016: 280).

REFERENCES

Als, Hilton (2015), 'Boys in the Band: A musical about the founding fathers', *The New Yorker*, 9 March, http://www.newyorker.com/magazine/2015/03/09/boys-in-the-band. Accessed 15 February 2017.

Anon. (2016a), 'Ham4Ham 1/3/16 with The Ladies of *HAMILTON*', YouTube, https://www.youtube.com/watch?v=Tbfws-YZQu4. Accessed 15 February 2017.

Anon. (2016b), 'The federalist freestyle', 20 September, http://thefederalistfreestyle.tumblr.com/post/150698452182/the-bullet-an-ensemblemember-with-nothing-to. Accessed 26 September 2017.

Anon. (2016c), 'Sandwichenthusiast blog post on "Say No To This" thread', *Genius.com*, https://genius.com/7928534. Accessed 23 February 2017.

Binelli, Mark (2016), '*Hamilton* mania! Backstage at the cultural event of our time', *Rolling Stone*, 1 June, p. 39, https://www.rollingstone.com/music/features/hamilton-mania-backstage-at-the-cultural-event-of-ourtime-20160601. Accessed 27 May 2018.

Brantley, Ben (2015), 'In *Hamilton*, Javier Muñoz puts a different spin on the title role', *New York Times*, 30 November, https://www.nytimes.com/2015/12/01/theater/in-hamilton-javier-munoz-puts-a-different-spinon-the-title-role.html. Accessed 27 May 2018.

Delman, Edward (2015), 'How Lin-Manuel Miranda shapes history', *The Atlantic*, 29 September, https://www.theatlantic.com/entertainment/archive/2015/09/lin-manuel-miranda-hamilton/408019/. Accessed 9 October 2016.

Evans, Suzie (2016), 'The room where it happens', interview with Lin-Manuel Miranda, *American Theatre*, 15 September, pp. 24–31.

Gledhill, Christine (1988), 'Pleasurable negotiations', in E. D. Pribram (ed.), *Female Spectators: Looking at Film and Television*, New York: Verso, pp. 64–89.

Hillman, Kerrie (2016), 'Lin-Manuel Miranda on dirty politics and the founding fathers', *New Yorker Radio Hour*, 29 January, http://www.wnyc.org/story/lin-manuel-miranda-on-dirty-politics-and-the-founding-fathers/. Accessed 3 March 2018.

Kaufman, Joanne (2015), 'A night out with Renée Elise Goldsberry of *Hamilton*', *New York Times*, 9 October, http://www.nytimes.com/2015/10/11/fashion/a-night-out-with-renee-elise-goldsberry-ofhamilton.html?r=0. Accessed 8 March 2018.

Lampen, Claire (2015), '*Hamilton* musical is doing a national tour – Here's what we know about cities and tickets', *Arts.Mic*, 9 December, http://mic.com/articles/130002/hamilton-musical-is-doing-a-national-tour-here-swhat-we-know-about-cities-and-tickets#.iS7mctXHO. Accessed 8 March 2018.

Lampert-Greaux, Ellen (2015), 'Birth of a nation: Colonial lighting', *Live Design*, 6 October, http://livedesignonline.com/hamilton-broadway/birthnation-colonial-lighting. Accessed 8 March 2018.

Libresco, Leah (2015), '*Hamilton* is the very model of a modern fast-paced musical', *FiveThirtyEight*, 5 October, https://fivethirtyeight.com/features/hamilton-is-the-very-model-of-a-modern-fast-paced-musical/. Accessed 26 September 2017.

McMaster, James (2016), 'Why *Hamilton* is not the revolution you think it is', *HowlRound*, 23 February, http://howlround.com/why-hamilton-is-not-therevolution-you-think-it-is. Accessed 8 June 2017.

McNulty, Charles (2015), 'Critic's notebook: *Hamilton*'s revolutionary power is in its hip-hop musical numbers', *Los Angeles Times*, 4 November, http://www.latimes.com/entertainment/arts/la-ca-cm-hamilton-hip-hop-notebook-20151031-column.html. Accessed 8 March 2018.

McWhorter, John (2016), 'Will *Hamilton* save the musical? Don't wait for it', *American Theatre*, 16 March.

Miranda, Lin-Manuel (2016), *The Hamilton Mixtape*, http://atlanticrecords.com/HamiltonMusic/. Accessed 17 February 2017.

Miranda, Lin-Manuel and McCarter, Jeremy (2016), *Hamilton: The Revolution*, New York: Grand Central Publishing.

Monteiro, Lyra D. (2016), 'Race-conscious casting and the erasure of the black past in Lin-Manuel Miranda's *Hamilton*', *The Public Historian*, 38:1, February, pp. 89–98.

'Renee Elise Goldsberry' (2016), *Theater People Podcast with Renée Elise Goldsberry*, Episode 56, 4 January, https://www.acast.com/theaterpeople/renee-elise-goldsberry-episode-56. Accessed 21 April 2018.

Robbins, Caryn (2015), '*Hamilton*'s Lin-Manuel Miranda is "totally open" to women playing the founding fathers', *Broadway World*, 13 November, http://www.broadwayworld.

com/article/HAMILTONs-Lin-Manuel-Mirandais-Totally-Open-to-Women-Playing-The-Founding-Fathers-20151113. Accessed 15 February 2017.

Schulman, Michael (2015), 'The women of *Hamilton*', *The New Yorker*, 6 August, http://www.newyorker.com/culture/cultural-comment/thewomen-of-hamilton. Accessed 12 February 2017.

Sternfeld, Jessica (2017), discussion, Musical Theatre Forum, New York Public Library, 22 April.

The Women's Project of New Jersey, Inc. (1990), *Past and Promise: Lives of New Jersey Women*, Metuchen: Scarecrow Press.

Tishgart, Sierra (2016), 'Brian d'Arcy James, Jonathan Groff, and Andrew Rannells on playing *Hamilton* fan favorite King George II', *Vulture*, 14 January, http://www.vulture.com/2016/01/hamilton-king-georgebrian-darcy-james-jonathan-groff-andrew-rannells.html. Accessed 8 March 2018.

Tommasini, Anthony and Caramanica, Jon (2015), 'Exploring *Hamilton* and hip-hop steeped in Heritage', *New York Times*, 27 August, http://www.nytimes.com/2015/08/30/theater/exploring-hamilton-and-hip-hop-steepedin-heritage.html. Accessed 8 March 2018.

Walsh, Shannon (2016), '*Hamilton*: An American musical', *Theatre Journal*, 68:3, p. 457.

Welter, Barbara (1966), 'The cult of true womanhood: 1820–1860', *American Quarterly*, 18:2, pp. 151–74, http://xroads.virginia.edu/~DRBR2/welter.pdf. Accessed 4 July 2017.

Wolf, Stacy (2016), '*Hamilton*', *The Feminist Spectator*, 24 February, https://feministspectator.princeton.edu/2016/02/24/hamilton/. Accessed 3 March 2018.

4

Rewriting the American West: Black Feminist (Re)Vision in *Bella: An American Tall Tale*

Jordan Ealey

In 2017, Kirsten Childs's fourth musical, *Bella: An American Tall Tale* opened off-Broadway at Playwrights Horizons. Two of her other musicals, *Miracle Brothers* (2005) and *Funked Up Fairytales* (2007) had enjoyed modest success, with *Fairytales* having been extended during its original run at Barrington Stage Company in Pittsfield, Massachusetts (Hetrick 2007). But the premiere of *Bella* re-inserted Childs into the mainstream theatre lexicon. Originally premiering at Dallas Theatre Center on 22 September 2016, the musical debuted off-Broadway on 19 May 2017. Directed by acclaimed director-playwright, Robert O'Hara (*Bootcandy*, *Insurrection: Holding History*) and choreographed by Tony-nominated choreographer Camille A. Brown (*Choir Boy*), the Western musical centres on Bella, a plus sized woman of 'mythic proportions', who sets out to start over in the American West. Despite *New York Times* theatre critic Ben Brantley's slight that the piece 'collapses into inertia', the musical was a hit with audiences (2017) and continues Childs's dramaturgical methodology of satire and comedy, as she celebrates black women, body diversity, and a reclamation of people of colour in the Old West.

The field of cultural geography proves incredibly useful in exploring the intersection of black bodies and particularly those of women, the under-told African American history of the American West, and the intersection of the two. In her book *Demonic Grounds: Black Women and the Cartographies of Struggle*, cultural geographer Katherine McKittrick contends that poet Dionne Brand 'writes the land' (2006: ix). McKittrick's claim refutes the traditional, colonial understanding of a 'map', and, instead, mobilizes the idea that geography is not material, but *human*. Brand rejects the notion that she is bound to country or geography in any way that would signal individual ownership or imperial belonging. Both Brand and McKittrick provide a framework for black feminist conceptualizations of land and worldmaking. Building upon this idea, I argue that through *Bella*, Childs is similarly writing the land. She listens to what the land is telling her and writes of those histories that have been lost or erased through the practice of forgetting. Even Childs's author note reads: 'This American tall tale is a big-assed lie created to point out outrageous American home truths. So please, my dear actors, put your booty in it'. By drawing attention to her 'big-assed lie', Childs provides not only clever wordplay but also about a succinct critique of the 'outrageous' racial and ethnic one-sidedness of American history.

Like musical theatre, histories of the American West remain largely white, male, cisgender, heterosexual, and able-bodied, leaving little room for the region's varied and multivalent histories. Childs seeks to rectify this substantial dearth with *Bella*. In an interview with *American Theatre*, Childs highlights the ways in which popularized legends and retellings of the American West have obscured the legacies of the people of colour who were essential to that geographic region (Greenberg 2017). *Bella* circumvents this as it follows the journey of Isabella 'Bella' Patterson, 'a young [black] woman of late nineteenth century America', who leaves her home of Tupelo, Mississippi to escape her alleged crimes committed against a white man and sets out West to find her long lost love, the Buffalo Soldier. What ensues is a hilarious and irreverent journey full of Bella's mishaps, mistakes, and misgivings; but ultimately, the musical presents a compelling coming of age story through which a young black woman learns to love her heritage, her community, and herself for what they are. Notably, this kind of narrative is not one unfamiliar to Childs: her first Obie Award-winning musical, *The Bubbly Black Girl Sheds Her Chameleon Skin* similarly centres a young (bubbly) black girl who navigates the ills of racism, sexism and classism to find a truer and more complete version of herself. Childs's artistic investment in complicating what representation for black girls and women can look like in American musical theatre began with *Bubbly Black Girl* and continues through *Bella*.

In her most recent work, Childs takes her intervention a step further. *Bella* provides not simply an intervention into the world of *musical theatre* through its centring of a plus-size black woman, but also a portrait of the *American West* just as diverse and multivalent as its (often obscured) history. Thus, in this chapter, I contend that *Bella: An American Tall Tale* serves as a black feminist (re)vision of the history of the American West. I argue that Childs disrupts the hegemonic representation of Western American life as merely white opportunity, Indigenous erasure and black invisibility. I examine how the musical's intervention relies not just on its representational politics, but additionally on its *sonic* reconfigurations.

I situate *Bella: An American Tall Tale* in a tradition of black feminist historiography that focuses on corporeality and embodiment. Through this exploration, I suture black performance theory and black feminist theory together in order to read *Bella*'s focus on the black female body (as well as other bodies of colour) as a way to rethink how one constructs history, one that centres the voices of those on the margins.

Bella: An American Tall Tale imagines a racially heterogeneous West, one defying all convention of how the West has been hegemonically understood in musical theatre. Configurations of the West prove to be equally problematic when it comes to gender representation as it has been regarding race and ethnicity, as heroes of Western musicals tend to be (white) men. Childs's musical, therefore, challenges convention on multiple fronts by focusing on a black woman: a full-bodied, independent, black woman who writes the land through action and voice.

The shadow of Oklahoma!: *The American West in musical theatre*

Certainly Black women playwrights tackled and disrupted the presentation of a racially homogenous 'American West' prior to Childs. Pearl Cleage's *Flyin' West* (1996) tells the story of the late nineteenth-century all-black settlement of Nicodemus, Kansas; Aleshea Harris's spaghetti Western *Is God Is* (2018) features two black women as the protagonists; and Angelica Cheri's musical, *Gun and Powder* (2020), depicts two black women heading West to find opportunity and help their mother live a better life. Each of these stories connects its audience to a different way of imagining the West and the Western, asking them to *hear* it differently than it previously sounded in predominantly white and male Western tales. *Bella* fits into that incredible genealogy and arguably moves it forward by reconstructing and diversifying what was once one-dimensional, racially homogeneous American history through a process of speculation, imagination, and narrative play.

Films, television series, and history texts have produced a fraught concept of 'the West', geographically and ideologically; such texts have consistently separated the *Mid*west from technological advancement and simultaneously constructed it as possessing a homogeneous racial makeup. Performance studies scholar Stephanie Batiste writes: 'Imaginative and physical appropriations of the West, open space, and nature stand in as signifiers of cultural and material power' (2011: 27). In essence, the idea of the West in the collective American imaginary metaphorically represents America's imperial power: seemingly untouched, with empty land ready to be conquered. It ignores and obscures the genocidal violence inflicted upon the

Indigenous communities who had already been there or demonizes them to the point where the violence appears to be 'necessary' to protect the white, male colonial hero, as well as the presumed virtue of white women.

Over and over again, white masculinity has defined the West in the popular imagination: John Wayne Westerns, Western novels and television series like *Bonanza* and *Rawhide*. Broadway has also informed America's hegemonic framing of the West, perhaps most consistently through Rodgers and Hammerstein's *Oklahoma!*, premiering on Broadway in 1943, revived in 1951, 1953, 1980, 2003 and 2020, and emerging as a big-budget Hollywood musical in 1955, one which produced a double platinum soundtrack album that peaked at number one on the *Billboard* charts and remained on those charts for over a full year. From its arrival on the Broadway stage, *Oklahoma!* crystallized the American musical as a symbol of US nationalism and the American West as racially and culturally white. I argue that the cultural prominence of *Oklahoma!* subsequently silhouetted all future theatrical productions situated in the West, including *Bella*. Although Childs likely did not explicitly intend to challenge the project of *Oklahoma!*, *Bella* ultimately serves as a meaningful juxtaposition to *Oklahoma!*'s historical precedent. *Bella: An American Tall Tale* challenges the territory of *Oklahoma!* and its seemingly totalizing monopoly on musical theatre's staging of the American West as it opens up American theatre and American history for people, specifically women, of colour.

In his book, *The Great White Way: Race and the Broadway Musical*, musical theatre scholar Warren Hoffman pinpoints the musical's complicity in such problematic historical rewritings of the West (2014: 56). Touching on early musicals such as *Rose-Marie* (1924) and *Whoopee* (1928), Hoffman hones in on Broadway's most notorious 'Western' musical: *Oklahoma!* Based on Lynn Riggs's 1930 play *Green Grows the Lilacs*, the show narrates a typical 'love plot' where cowboy Curly and farmhand Jud vie for the affection of farm girl Laurey. On its surface, *Oklahoma!* appears as a simple love story with a compelling love triangle and satisfying ending. But its setting illuminates musical theatre's complex relationship with ideas of national identity and empire. Musicologist Raymond Knapp lays out the American musical's intimate tie to nationhood and contends that 'defining America' is the central theme embedded in the very form of the musical (2005: 7). Pointing to the show's backdrop of Indian territory being overtaken and turned into a 'civilized' Oklahoma, Hoffman argues that Curly and Laurey's marriage directly mirrors the cultural nationalism embedded within *Oklahoma!*'s narrative (2014: 57).

If in fact musical theatre tells the tale of American identity and nationhood, then *Oklahoma!*'s evasive and harmful racial and gender politics reveal a great deal about the marginalized position of people of marginalized racial and/or gender identities. Despite the fact that an author of Cherokee ancestry wrote the text upon which the musical was based, *Oklahoma!* lacks even a single identified Indigenous person throughout the duration of the show (Hoffman 2014: 61). Hoffman expertly reveals how the erasure and destruction of Indigenous history and culture lies at the very dramaturgy of the musical and how no critical mass of all-black or all-Asian American productions can fix the original show's stark lack of diverse representation. At its core, *Oklahoma!* only perpetuates the myth that the Midwest region was and remains as racially homogenous as musical theatre itself. Casting cannot fix the whiteness endemic to the musical theatre industry and yet, non-traditional and colour-blind casting practices continue to be the go-to solutions to calls for greater diversity and inclusion.

Oklahoma!, in addition to its issues regarding racial representation, produces troubling representations around gender. As black feminist scholar Kimberlé Crenshaw contends in her theorization of the unique ways that Black women experience structural oppression –via 'intersectionality' – the effects of sexism and racism cannot truly be considered apart from each other (1989: 140). Musicologist Susan C. Cook takes this intersectional approach in her discussion of *Oklahoma!*, paying attention to how race, gender, and class interlock to create troublesome representations. Examining the waltz through both sound and choreography, Cook reads the gender dynamics of *Oklahoma!* through both masculinity and femininity and how such gendered performances emerge through Curly and Laurey. Contending that Curly's dialect in dropping the 'g' in 'morning' reifies racialized discourses around language that date back to minstrelsy, Cook additionally argues that 'Oh, What a Beautiful Mornin' employs the waltz to evoke gender performativity, as well as class positionality. She writes: 'To dance, however, is to flirt with the body and the feminine, as social dance has historically, and especially in Anglo-America, been women's purview' (2009: 40). Cook examines the waltz as an upper-class dance that reifies patriarchal logics, rendering Curly as the male leader and Laurey as the female follower. Thus, when he enters, singing 'Beautiful Mornin', Cook contends that Curly's search for a waltz partner (ultimately Laurey) mobilizes 'the dance' of gender, or what dance scholar Susan Leigh Foster refers to as the choreography of gender (1998: 5). Additionally, Laurey's solo, 'Many a New Day', which comes towards the conclusion of the musical's first act, focuses solely on her ontological experience of womanhood through a romantic, heterosexual relationship – a further codifier of *Oklahoma!*'s narrow logics around heteronormativity and the gendered expectation that women are merely preoccupied with romantic relationships with men. At its core, *Oklahoma!* recapitulates existing, harmful hegemonic notions around gender, race, and nation.

Surely other musicals have broadened the ways in which women circulate in the cultural imaginary of the American West: *Annie Get Your Gun*, *Calamity Jane*, *The Unsinkable Molly Brown*, *Paint Your Wagon* and so on. Many continue to come up short in their articulations of gender, race, and ethnicity, often following patterns established by the musical format. Dorothy Fields, Herbert Fields and Irving Berlin's *Annie Get Your Gun* (1946), for example, dramatizes the life and times of real-life sharpshooter Annie Oakley. The title role was perhaps most notably played by Broadway luminary Ethel Merman in the show's Broadway premiere and later by Broadway diva Bernadette Peters and country music icon Reba McEntire in the show's 2001 revival. Despite Dorothy Fields's place on the creative team and a notoriously counterhegemonic female historical figure at the show's centre, *Annie Get Your Gun*, too, bends to gendered demands. Feminist musical theatre scholar Grace Barnes points out that Oakley 'deliberately loses the finale shoot out [...] because to demonstrate her real prowess would lose her the object of her affection, Frank Butler' (2015: 50). Hoffmann also notes the show's narrative reliance on the troublesome history of Wild West shows, conflating so-called 'stage Indians' with real-life Native individuals. Although he goes on to caution against readings that merely reduce the musical to its racial and ethnic representational issues, contending that the Native American characters in the show are not stereotyped, but actually represented sympathetically against 'truly unlikeable' white characters (2014: 69), I believe considering these representational problems to be an imperative.

Approaching the study of musical theatre through an intersectional lens highlights the ways in which race and gender – both within the form and embodied, lived experiences – are co-constitutive. Put another way, taking into full account the convergence of multiple identity categories and how they emerge in different bodies, especially in bodies of colour, leads to a more holistic and nuanced comprehension of how nonwhite people move through the world and the stage. This recognition is crucial for reading performances and texts by and about women of colour, especially black women, and essential to thinking through musical theatre's problematic history and politics via the black feminist intervention provided by Kirsten Childs through *Bella: An American Tall Tale*. I do not provide this critique and historicization of *Oklahoma!* to reduce Childs's artistry to a simple *response* to whiteness and patriarchy, but to convey the musical genre's much-needed *interruption* of the normative racial and gendered representations on the musical stage. With *Bella*, Childs produces more complex discourses around racialized and gendered subjectivity. The next section provides a close-reading (and a close-listening) of *Bella: An American Tall Tale*'s black feminist historiography, one achieved primarily through the thematic elements of storytelling, heritage, and community. Specifically, the next section focuses on how Childs employs black female embodiment and sound to provide a historiographic revision of previous historical and musical representations of the West.

Historical reconstruction: Wild imaginations and unexpected storytellers

As the story goes, Kirsten Childs's own reasoning for wanting to tell this story is just as wild and unexpected as the musical itself. In the liner notes for *Bella*, Childs recalls:

> I was walking down a New York street, on my way home to my apartment, when in front of me I spied a young African-American couple. The woman was tiny, with a well-proportioned hourglass figure and one of the biggest behinds I have ever seen on a human being. Every man that passed her stopped and turned and gazed admiringly and longingly at her backside. And when I say every man, I mean *every man* – poor, rich, black, white, Asian, Hispanic, young, old, gay, straight – if it was a carbon-based life form with XY chromosomes, apparently the laws of physics left it no option but to stop and marvel at that woman's booty. Hers was an allure not linked to straight hair or light skin, or any of America's tropes of so-called beauty, and she knocked those palookas over like so many tenpins.

What Childs describes in this musical's origin story is both an awe of the beauty of the young black woman she saw, as well as the reactions that woman received. Additionally, Childs, through an observation that the young woman's 'allure [was] not linked to straight hair or light skin, or any of America's tropes of so-called beauty' calls into question the twinned disadvantages that dark-skinned black women face from systems of white supremacy and colourism. Through a celebration of the beauty of dark-skinned black women and a questioning of Eurocentric, patriarchal formulations of beauty, Childs is already challenging, critiquing, and changing the musical theatre landscape right from the musical's inception and making clear whose stories she values.

The tall tale communicated through *Bella* begins not in New York, but with a girl on a train. More specifically, Isabella 'Bella' Patterson has boarded a train she hopes will change her life. Traveling from Mississippi to New Mexico, Bella is both running away from and toward something. From the start, she sings about history being 'a tall tale', as the title of the musical suggests. Both Bella and Childs urge the audience to think about history differently – not simply as something learned through traditional kinds of scholarship, but told through alternative modes: hyperbolic oral history, song, the voices of women, and the stories of people of colour. This particular tall tale method of storytelling and constructing history continues throughout the musical, animating a nearly metatheatrical understanding of Childs's artistic project of narrating, rewriting, and reimagining an alternative story of the West, one with a black woman 'with a large, voluptuous behind' at its center. As soon as its opening number begins, the show signals to Childs's reconstruction of the West; Bella, portrayed by the incredible Ashley D. Kelley in the Playwrights Horizons production and cast recording, opens the show by singing that the history told throughout the musical would be one more colourful than versions of American history previously presented.

Imagination and storytelling undergird *Bella*, as even the project of Childs's musical itself demonstrates a black feminist praxis. Bella and other *colourful* characters narrate their own tall tales. Although characters commonly tell their own stories through song in musical theatre, in *Bella*, such characters provide insight into various marginalized viewpoints not traditionally explored through the musical, especially ones depicting stories of the West. Childs' black authorship privileges black narratives from black perspectives, a feat unfortunately still quite rare in mainstream musical theatre. Her position as a black woman composer and librettist, as well as the specific intervention she makes with *Bella*, a musical featuring a black woman as the protagonist, should be celebrated. *Bella* critically diverges from the expected structure of the integrated book musical, making use of a less narratively driven story than canonical texts like *Oklahoma!* and instead focusing on Bella's interior journey through dialogue, lyrics, music, and movement. Black musical theatre scholar, composer and lyricist Masi Asare draws attention to Childs's innovative use of form in *Bella* and connects Childs's use of the revue to a longer history of black musical form going back to the Theatre Owners Booking Association (TOBA) that shepherded the African American vaudeville circuit of the early twentieth century. Asare employs this history to argue that the revue 'allows for a diverse range of characters, musical and dance styles, and perspectives'. She contends that the form underscores Bella's 'useful overactive imagination', one which – like the revue – allows the storyline some room to breathe and space for its comedic and political points to land. It formally rejects the notion that 'everybody must bend to the hierarchy of one tight storyline'. Thus, the revue, as a staple in African American musical theatre form, is both a creative innovation and a statement of self-definition. It rejects the linearity and positivism of a perfectly unified integrated book musical – one often championed in musical theatre creation – and presents the disjointed form as a recognition that black history in and of itself cannot be linearly constructed or perfectly unified. This type of breathing room, as Asare observes, facilitates the black feminist self-definition the character of Bella achieves at musical's end. It further allows Childs, as author of this black woman's story, room to seize the opportunity to challenge what is widely accepted as 'proper' musical theatre structure.

Standing on the shoulders of theatre and performance studies scholar Marta Effinger-Crichlow, author of *Staging Migrations Toward an American West: From Ida B. Wells to Rhodessa Jones*, I consider *Bella* to be an inherently spatial and geographic project that remakes the history and geography of the West. Effinger-Crichlow argues that:

> Black women's narratives have been forced to the background. When black women are excluded from the discourse of an American West, an abridged version of the western narrative is being offered. An inclusion of black women into a western narrative ultimately makes the narrative of the West more complex.
>
> (2014: 5)

Here she underscores the idea that a (re)vision of the American West that centres black women troubles the homogeneity dominant in the American consciousness. Effinger-Crichlow's observation underscores Childs's project of transforming and diversifying cultural representations of the West. By having Bella's body and voice drive the narration, Childs emphasizes the importance of privileging black women's perspectives in producing their own histories. This practice certainly has theatrical precedent. Cleage previously used such power of narrativity in *Flyin' West*, putting black women in charge of their own narratives to remake the frontier in which those characters circulate. Each of the black women has her own way of telling her own story: Sophie, the gun-toting firecracker, speaks her mind and shares her dream of owning her own land and taking care of her family; the loving, bookish Fannie writes down every story she hears from her sisters to ensure the preservation of their narratives; and Miss Leah, the matriarch, recalls the tales from her long and storied life, promising to share them with her new granddaughter at play's end. This type of storytelling serves as a powerful tool, particularly salient for black women who have historically found themselves silenced and/or erased.

Historian Hayden White argues that narrativity and reality co-create a robust historiographic method(ology), problematizing traditional historical research's preoccupation with 'the real'. He writes, 'The reality which lends itself to narrative representation is the conflict between desire, on the one side, and the law, on the other' (1980: 16). Thus, an antagonistic and dialectical relationship exists between narrativity and reality, one where each side fights for historiographic significance. Put another way, White contends that historians' longing for a *good story* directly conflicts with the alleged 'truth' of the archive. Refuting the very basis of this tension, black and feminist (and most importantly, black feminist) historians and researchers have argued that historians should be questioning reality itself. Cultural historian Saidiya V. Hartman's analytic of 'critical fabulation' – which is both a black feminist methodology and a reading praxis of using archival sources to imagine what the documents *cannot* and *do not* say – implores historians to consider the ethics of historiographic research (2008). It positions historical storytelling as a reflection of one's own ethical investment, moving away from the historian as a distant, objective, cold observer into a subjective and intimate witness. Thus, critical fabulation requires imagination on the part of the scholar or historian, as it challenges the assumed neutrality of archival documents and urges a creative approach to telling untold stories in history.

In *Bella: An American Tall Tale,* Bella, as the narrator of her own story, embodies this subjective and intimate witness to a marginalized history, as Childs embodies the role of the imaginative historian. As both the first figure present and first character introduced in the musical, Bella captures the attention of onlookers instantly. Immediately upon boarding the train, she meets Nathaniel, a porter, who takes notice of her fancy clothes. Bella, however, slips up in their conversation, inadvertently revealing her tenuous relationship with 'facts' and introducing herself as 'Isabella Patterson' when her ticket provides the surname of 'Johnson'. As Nathaniel points out this mistake, Isabella attempts to cover it up:

BELLA: […] I'm Isabella Johnson. I got a wild imagination, you see, and sometimes I just like to make up things, like names. But that's my real name right there, Miss Isabella Jenkins.
NATHANIEL: Johnson.
BELLA: Johnson.

This comedic exchange undoubtedly establishes an important aspect of Bella's character; she likes to make up stories with her 'wild imagination'. Her penchant for making up stories and the use of the word 'wild' to describe what happens inside of her head signals to the employing of a critical politics of imagination, one embedded in black feminist methodology and especially relevant in narrating black feminist history.

Black feminist historiography requires imaginative ways of 'doing' history, a doing that performance methodology illuminates expertly. Hershini Bhana Young frames black performance as 'a methodology that can animate, suture together, and disrupt disciplinary investments in writing black histories' (2019: 4). This act creates a kind of black feminist storytelling through black performance methodology; Bella and *Bella* not only embody, enact, and narrate history, but through a highly fraught, contested, and problematized area of black women's bodies: the booty. 'The Spirit of the Booty', a spiritual entity that rests in Bella's most recognized body part, propels forth a narrative of embodied history. Black women's booties have been the subject of international attention for centuries, arguably beginning with the capture and subjugation of Saartjie Baartman. Baartman, an enslaved black woman, was paraded around Europe in an exhibition from 1810 to 1815. Known as the 'Hottentot Venus', Baartman's body was spectacularized for white audiences and spectators, and it seems that even today she cannot rest, as her legacy continues to haunt black women's performance cultures centuries after her death.[1] Black feminist scholar Janell Hobson argues that black women's beauty lies in their booties, 'signify[ing] sexual excess', as a result of the historical framing of the Hottentot Venus (Hobson 2018: 108; Young 2019).[2] White, patriarchal culture often problematically categorizes Black women's bodies (and especially their booties) as excessive, taking up too much too much space.[3]

'One Ass to Another', The Spirit of the Booty's debut song, may overtly perpetuate the historical precedent regarding the excess associated with black women's booties, but Bella's characterization had already animated Hobson's claim. Her first song, and in fact the first number of the musical itself, declares Bella a 'Big Booty Tupelo Girl', immediately cementing an intimate and seemingly permanent link between her identity and her booty. And while we are invited to gaze upon her body (and her booty), the reveal of the Spirit of the Booty imbues the booty with powerful, magical, and supernatural qualities. In other words, Childs characterizes the booty as having spiritual significance, moving it from simply Bella's most objectified body part to an animated source of her strength. Bella's most important character moments feature the Spirit of the Booty. In fact, her major conflict revolves around her being 'wanted' for attacking her white employer, Bonny Johnny Rakehell. Bella insists that her side of the story provides a clearer view of what happened – despite the titular character's tendency to exaggerate and embellish her stories – and Childs turns this on its head, as Bella reveals that Rakehell *was* attacked, just not by Bella, but by her booty (Figure 4.1).

The Spirit of the Booty appears when Bella needs her most. After a violent confrontation with Johnny, Bella swears she will report him for all of his crimes against her and her family. In response Johnny queries, 'And who's gonna believe your tragic tale?' The Spirit of the Booty responds. 'I will', and continues: 'It is I, your ancestor, the Itty Bitty Gal. On a ship of misery, from far across the sea I have come here to tell you that that man is talking out of his ass. And now it is time for you to talk out of yours'.

Bella, through the Spirit of the Booty, does not *talk*, but rather sings. As the song begins, the Spirit of the Booty sings a melodic, virtuosic sound. A chorus of women join her, physically and aurally embodying her 'female body parts' and visually signifying female empowerment. Although this investment in the biologically female body limits the bounds of what constitutes 'woman', particularly as queer theorists and feminist thinkers have rightfully pushed for a reconsideration

FIGURE 4.1: Bella (Ashley D. Kelley) harnesses the possibilities of her embodied power in a confrontation with Bonny Jonny Rakehell (Kevin Massey). In this scene, her booty becomes the source of her strength rather than an object to be sexualized by men (*Bella: An American Tall Tale*, courtesy of Joan Marcus).

of the links between biology and gender, the Spirit of the Booty provides powerful images and sounds to evoke a chorus of ancestors. The global African diaspora's ancestral connection runs deep and *Bella* animates that profundity. As the Spirit of the Booty belts her powerful R&B-infused song, supported by the flowered chorus of women around her, ones Childs's stage directions describe as channelling 'the rage of Bella's brutalized and raped female ancestors', Childs reinscribes the booty not simply with beauty or sexual(ized) excess, but magic and strength (Figure 4.2). An embodied narration erupts (quite literally) from Bella's booty, not a narration that fragments and subjugates, but one that challenges, disrupts, and takes hold of Bella's own liberation. For Bella, the booty *is* history, collectivity, and community, connecting her to her historically marginalized ancestors who continue to protect her from beyond. By placing this community within the musical, Childs reasserts the value of a community that is not traditionally represented or empowered within the 'official' historical record. Through this, Childs demonstrates the importance of *subjectivity* in telling history. The booty connects Bella with her ancestors and, I speculate, black women who encounter this musical.

Childs underscores how black feminist historiography disrupts traditional structures of time, as the past, present, and future of the booty converge, illustrating the power of black feminist collectivity.

As the narrator of her own tall tale, Bella embodies the black feminist project of self-definition, one Patricia Hill Collins argues has the power to 'question not only what has been said about African American women but the credibility

FIGURE 4.2: Evoking the power of black feminist collectivity and the continued empowerment of black women rooted in their communities, The Spirit of the Booty (Natasha Yvette Williams), Bella's ancestor and protector, appears to help Bella discover her inner strength (*Bella: An American Tall Tale*, courtesy of Joan Marcus).

and intentions of those possessing the power to define', leading black women to 'clearly reject the assumption that those in positions granting them the authority to interpret our reality are entitled to do so' (2000: 114). Through her own elaborately constructed stories, Bella denies anyone else the opportunity to define her; she defines herself and, with the help of the ancestral chorus, the journey of black women. The chorus of ancestors, in fact, guides her and ideally the audience to better understand the importance of telling one's own story, disrupt temporal limitations, and connect one's experience to a greater form of community.

Repopulating the West: Bella's *colourful cast of characters*

A theme of self-definition significantly underpins *Bella*, evidenced by the show's extended and multicultural cast of characters who narrate their own histories. Although – and perhaps because – it becomes progressively clear that many of these characters exist in a blurry space between the 'real' and products of Bella's dreams and tall tales, they further complicate the project of writing a nuanced and diverse history while providing self-actualization through vocal performance and individualized storytelling. Ida Lou Simpson, the second character Bella encounters on her train journey, underscores the tragedy of being black in America, particularly in the nineteenth century. Ida Lou and her baby Matthew are on an important journey of their own. She and her fellow 'Exodusters', had turned their backs on the South with hopes of achieving land-ownership in Kansas, a state which had been admitted to the Union as a free state. But Ida brought with her a too familiar story. She details the tragic story of her husband, after whom her baby has been named:

> The day they strung him up, and invited their friends and neighbors and children out on a bright noonday picnic to watch. My Matthew was guilty of three crimes. The crime of bein' uppity. The crime of believein' in the United States Constitution. And the crime of thinkin' that, for the South, the war would ever be over.

At the time this play is taking place (1877), the legal institution of slavery has been abolished, but the brutality against black people has not ended. This crime against her husband occurs because of 'bein' uppity' and for daring to take hold of the citizenship black people were denied due to slavery.

Perhaps further challenging codified notions of history, Childs bases many of her characters on actual historical figures, some better known than others. Ida Lou's character resembles that of the real-life journalist and activist Ida B.

Wells, whose groundbreaking investigation of lynching brought a national spotlight to these horror-filled crimes (Brooks 2006: 57). In addition to her significant journalistic career, Wells created a pamphlet where she urged African Americans to flee the Southern horrors of lynching and move West, particularly to Kansas (Effinger-Crichlow 2014: 20). In this urging, she encouraged black self-determination and ownership as a way towards freedom and citizenship. With the character of Ida Lou, Childs draws upon Wells's histories, allowing them to be transformed in this fictionalized version. Ida Lou's song, 'Kansas Boun' furthers the show's articulation of black self-determination, as she convinces Bella that the West, free from the violence of the South, provides a better place geographically for black people. The song's sonic motif, a violin, sounds throughout the entire number. The intrusive violin duels with the other instruments and its beautiful thrashing cuts through them, forcing attention to the complex aural mixture of beauty and pain. This combination presents an uneven sound reflective of the unevenness of what 'freedom' means for black people after the abolition of slavery and the struggle that lies ahead for them in this country. Strikingly, Ida Lou's emphasis on believing in the Constitution and an idealized version of American democracy that *includes* black people came crashing down when her husband was lynched for daring to believe that he too was an American citizen. For Ida Lou, moving to Kansas and the pursuit of 'freedom' through the self-sufficiency associated with land-ownership provides her a path to this liberated future, highly fraught as it might be. The song – delightfully errant, inchoate and defiant – cannot easily be defined in terms of genre. Blending an acoustic traditionally 'Western' sound with hints of gospel and blues, Ida Lou's dream of Kansas escapes categorization.

When Ida Lou sings of Kansas, she sings of a promise, a promise that her people can be safe and comfortable, away from white violence. Ida Lou, portrayed in the original cast recording by Marinda Anderson, sings with a clear voice and vision. Anderson pronounces each of Ida's words clearly, without much decoration in her vocal style. Such clarity requires great skill on the part of the performer, but also reveals an important character trait about Ida Lou. Like her real-life counterpart, black feminist visionary Ida B. Wells, she is strong and unwavering in her move toward Kansas. Once they arrive, Ida Lou and the other 'Exodusters' – a group arguably erased from many popular retellings of the post-Civil War era – set out to begin anew.

Although certainly foregrounding the presence of black Americans in the West and Midwest, *Bella* arguably repeats one of the same erasures as *Oklahoma!*, with no Indigenous characters represented onstage. So, when the characters arrive in Kansas, seemingly untouched land waits for them, not territory which had been stolen by white settlers. Rebuking the unapologetic erasure of Indigenous people in musicals like *Oklahoma!*, however, Childs has the train's porter Nathaniel relay to Bella the unethical and horrific nature of settling and colonizing land, regardless of the settler's race. Surely more needs to be done to rectify the Indigenous erasure in musical theatre of the West, but Childs – if didactically – foregrounds the problematic legacies of both the West and musical theatre, encouraging her audiences to question history and generic form.

The complex, intersectional project of *Bella* further explores links between gender and race through the characters of Diego Moreno, a Mexican cowboy, and Tommie Haw, a Chinese cowboy. These two characters introduce themselves through their own songs and present different views of exactly *who* can occupy the position of cowboy; not just *Oklahoma!*'s Curly or any number of white cinematic or theatrical rugged white men of the West. Through Diego Moreno's sultry love song, 'Quien Fuera Luna', he attempts to romance and charm Bella. During this number, Diego and a minor character, Miss Cabbagestalk, dance what Childs's script notes refer to as 'a pas de deux of Afro-Mexican ecstasy'. 'Quien Fuera Luna' mixes traditional Mexican musical stylings with country and R&B to demonstrate the complex demographic intermixing which had been present in the American West but underexplored in existing musical theatre scholarship and production. When Bella encounters Tommie Haw, a character based on archival research Childs had conducted on Asian-Americans in the Rocky Mountain region, she exclaims that Chinese cowboys cannot and do not exist. He quickly corrects her through his song 'Tommie Haw', presented in a traditional, classic country style of music – one reminiscent of the 1950s. Through her choice of sonic genre and Tommie's Southern accent, Childs leads her audience to rethink who can be considered 'country' and, even further, who can be and who has been a cowboy – the traditional white, American hero.[4] Through her reconstruction of the West in the American musical theatre, Childs disrupts the very *sound* of the region through her musical score.

Bella and the rest of the colourful cast of characters illustrate the significance of self-narration. Childs aims to reclaim the underexplored history of people of colour in the American West and achieves this through character-driven songs and the blurring of real and imagined. Her characters fashion themselves through salient musical styles and self-narration: Bella tells her story and clears her rightful name; Ida Lou reveals how black people can find self-determination settling in the West; and Diego Luna and Tommie Haw embrace hybrid musical forms as they broaden the American cowboy to include men of colour. Eschewing the objectivity often idealized by historians, Childs embraces Hartman's notion of critical fabulation through a historiographic path of subjectivity and self-determination. She imagines an expansion of the archive. At the same time, the musical presents a black feminist historiographic intervention into the musical theatre form as *Bella: An American Tall Tale* creates a powerful connectivity among those who are most marginalized in history, democratizing storytelling as an important tool for women and people of colour.

Black women defying America through musical theatre

If, as Raymond Knapp contends, a project of 'defining America' thematically underpins the American musical, then perhaps '*defying* America' thematically links black women's musical theatre. In both the musical theatre industry and scholarly investigations of the form, little attention has been given to black women as cultural innovators, particularly in their roles as composers, lyricists, librettists and directors. Black women librettists and composers such as Pauline Hopkins (*Slaves' Escape; or, The Underground Railroad*), Shirley Graham Du Bois (*Tom Tom: An Epic of Music and the Negro*), Micki Grant (*Don't Bother Me, I Can't Cope*), Vinnette Carroll (*Your Arms Too Short to Box With God*), Regina Taylor (*Crowns*), Jackie Taylor (*Legends: The Musical*), Angelica Cheri (*Gun & Powder*) and Kirsten Childs seldom find producers, on the Broadway or the regional circuit, willing to provide the intellectual and artistic space commonly offered to their white and/or male counterparts. Oftentimes, even in dedicated histories of Broadway, black musical theatre remains marginal and within that, black women find themselves excluded. Childs pushes back against these omissions. With *Bella: An American Tall Tale*, she challenges the erasure of black women and people of colour from the writing and writings of historical record; she listens to the land and writes with its sounds and its diversity of voices, defying history (and America) along the way, and reminding us, too, to put our booties in it.

NOTES

1. For example, there are still fascinations with black women's bodies with celebrity singer Beyoncé Knowles-Carter singing about her 'Sarah Bartman hips' in her song 'Black Effect' and the countless articles that compared rapper Nicki Minaj to Bartman after the release of her cover for her song, 'Anaconda', in which she is crouched down looking back at the camera, donning a thong that shows her bare naked butt.
2. Also, see Hershini Bhana Young's *Illegible Will* for her chapter on Baartman.
3. See: Nicole Fleetwood's concept of 'excess flesh', beautifully articulated in her manuscript, *Troubling Vision: Performance, Blackness, and Visuality*.
4. For more information on the complex history of Chinese cowboys and the American West, Frank Chin's play *The Chickencoop Chinaman* illustrates it unfailingly.

REFERENCES

Anon. (2017), 'Bella: An American tall tale', *Playwrights Horizons*, https://www.playwrightshorizons.org/shows/plays/bella/. Accessed 1 March 2019.

Asare, Masi (2017), '10 reasons you should go see Kirsten Childs's *Bella: An American Tall Tale*', https://masiasare.com/blogs/blog/posts/10-reasons-you-should-go-see-kirsten-childs-s-bella-an-american-tall-tale. Accessed 8 August 2021.

Barnes, Grace (2015), *Her Turn on the Stage: The Role of Women in Musical Theatre*, Jefferson: McFarland & Company Publishers.

Batiste, Stephanie (2011), *Darkening Mirrors: Imperial Representation in Depression-Era African American Performance*, Durham: Duke University Press.

Bhana Young, Hershini (2019), *Illegible Will: Coercive Spectacles of Labor in South Africa and the Diaspora*, Durham: Duke University Press.

Brantley, Ben (2017), 'Review: In *Bella,* an indomitable hero goes west', *New York Times*, 12 June, https://www.nytimes.com/2017/06/12/theater/bella-an-american-tall-tale-review.html. Accessed 20 July 2020.

Brooks, Daphne (2006), *Bodies in Dissent: Spectacular Performances of Race and Freedom, 1850–1910*, Durham: Duke University Press.

Catanese, Brandi Wilkins (2011), *The Problem of the [Color]blind: Racial Transgression and Politics of Black Performance*, Ann Arbor: University of Michigan Press.

Childs, Kirsten (2019a), 'Track-by-track breakdown: Kirsten Childs on the wild ride of *Bella: An American Tale*', *Playbill*, 15 February, https://www.playbill.com/article/track-by-track-breakdown-kirsten-childs-on-the-wild-ride-of-bella-an-american-tale. Accessed 8 August 2021.

Childs, Kirsten (2019b), *Bella: An American Tall Tale*, New York: Concord Theatricals.

Collins, Patricia Hill (2000), *Black Feminist Thought: Knowledge, Consciousness, and the Politics of Empowerment*, New York: Routledge & CRC Press.

Cook, Susan C. (2009), 'Pretty like the girl: Gender, race, and *Oklahoma!*', *Contemporary Theatre Review*, 19:1, pp. 35–47.

Crenshaw, Kimberlé (1989), 'Demarginalizing the intersection of race and sex: A black feminist critique of antidiscrimination doctrine, feminist theory, and antiracist politics', *University of Chicago Legal Forum*, 1:0, pp. 139–67.

Effinger-Crichlow, Marta (2014), *Staging Migrations Toward An American West: From Ida B. Wells to Rhodessa Jones*, Boulder: University Press of Colorado.

Fleetwood, Nicole (2011), *Troubling Vision: Performance, Visuality, and Blackness*, Chicago: University of Chicago Press.

Foster, Susan (1998), 'Choreographies of gender', *Signs* 24:1, pp. 1–33.

Gallella, Donatella (2015), 'Redefining America, arena stage, and territory folks in a multiracial *Oklahoma!*', *Theatre Journal*, 67:2, pp. 213–33.

Greenberg, Shoshana (2017), 'Kirsten Childs thinks big', 15 May, *American Theatre*, https://www.americantheatre.org/2017/05/15/kirsten-childs-thinks-big/. Accessed 25 July 2020.

Hartman, Saidiya V. (2008), 'Venus in two acts', *Small Axe*, 12:2, pp. 1–14.

Hetrick, Adam (2007), 'Kirsten Childs' *Funked Up Fairytales* extends at Barrington stage', *Playbill*, 8 August, https://www.playbill.com/article/kirsten-childs-funked-up-fairy-tales-extends-at-barrington-stage-com-142867. Accessed 23 July 2020.

Hobson, Janell (2018), 'Remnants of Venus: Signifying black beauty and sexuality', *WSQ: Women's Studies Quarterly*, 46:1, pp. 105–20.

Hoffman, Warren (2014), *The Great White Way: Race and the Broadway Musical*, New Brunswick: Rutgers University Press.

Knapp, Raymond (2005), *The American Musical and the Formation of National Identity*, Princeton: Princeton University Press.

McKittrick, Katherine (2006), *Demonic Grounds: Black Women and the Cartographies of Struggle*, Ann Arbor: University of Michigan Press.

Pao, Angela (2010), *No Safe Spaces: Re-Casting Race, Ethnicity, and Nationality in American Theater*, Ann Arbor: University of Michigan Press.

Parks, Suzan-Lori (1995), 'Possession', in S. Parks (ed.), *The America Play and Other Works*, New York: Theatre Communications Group.

White, Hayden (1980), 'The value of narrativity in the representation of reality', *Critical Inquiry* 7:1, pp. 5–27.

5

A-List Drag Queens, Accidental Drag Kings and Illegible Gender Rebels: (Mis)Representations of Trans Experience in Contemporary Musicals

Janet Werther

During the second decade of the twenty-first century, various plays and musicals, both mainstream and experimental, have been lauded for their transgender storylines and, in particular, their use of transgender actors. In the last half-decade, shows like *Head Over Heels* (Oregon Shakespeare Festival, 2015 and Broadway, 2018), *Southern Comfort* (The Public Theatre, 2016) and *A Ride on The Irish Cream* (Abrons Arts Center, 2016) have staged trans visibility for a range of LGBTQ+ and cisgender heterosexual audiences. Despite this increased stage presence, not all trans representations benefit trans communities or even present fundamentally accurate representations of trans lives. Rather, these musicalizations of trans experience have been highly uneven. Intentional or merely inept misrepresentations of trans characters in live performance can perpetuate misunderstandings on the part of well-intentioned cisgender audience members and would-be trans allies, further compounding or obscuring the frequent violence and indignities faced by trans folks in daily life.

Jack Halberstam argues that scholars should not

> approach the visual materials documenting trans* life with a moral framework that leads only to adjudication; instead, we are better served by considering the formal methods by which trans* experience can be represented and the benefits and liabilities therein.
>
> (2018: 85)

In this essay, I analyze *Head Over Heels*, *Southern Comfort* and *A Ride on the Irish Cream* for the benefits and liabilities of their particular transgender representations, further highlighting the broader pitfalls and promises of the musical theatre genre for transgender performance. I consider whether it would even be possible to create trans representation on musical theatre stages that would simultaneously affirm trans peoples' experiences, legibly educate cis audiences about trans realities, and be commercially viable enough to grace mainstream stages. What would the enabling conditions of such a production be?

Trans-inclusive casting contributes to what trans historian Susan Stryker has called a transgender 'tipping point', an exponential increase in mainstream trans visibility in the twenty-first century. Popular television shows, reality TV stars, and even children's books have contributed to this recent explosion of transgender representation.[1] Yet this so-called 'trans tipping point' did not happen suddenly; it is predicated on 'the cumulative consequence of decades of activism' (2017: loc. 2836). Stryker describes this trajectory of representational progress as 'more like the fulcrum of a teeter-totter, tipping backward as well as forward' (loc. 2836). Alongside the aforementioned entertainment forms, news stories about transphobic violence contribute to mainstream trans visibility and legibility, albeit in negative ways. Since at least the mid twentieth century and despite transgender activism within and outside the theatre industry, shows with trans performers and storylines remain few and far between. Parsing trans-inclusive casting practices, not just trans narratives, enables us to consider whether or not the mere presence of trans actors is a sufficient condition for adequately communicating trans experience on stage. Producers, playwrights and directors must work to create and make available accurate and empathetic representations of trans experiences. Doing so will help educate cis-normative viewers about the oppressed minority status of trans populations, and may even reduce transphobia by encouraging positive familiarity amongst cisgender audiences.

All staged in New York between 2016 and 2018, *Head Over Heels*, *Southern Comfort* and *A Ride on the Irish Cream* take important steps toward the enactment of trans inclusive musical theatre, albeit at-times fraught ones. The most mainstream of the three and having run at Broadway's Hudson Theatre for 36 previews and 164 performances, *Head Over Heels* took the important step of putting a trans actor center stage in a Broadway production. Based on the sixteenth century prose poem *The Arcadia* by Sir Philip Sidney, the show uses music of The Go-Gos to tell the story of a kingdom that risks annihilation if it cannot become less tethered to ossified and arbitrary traditions. Carnivalesque queerness suffuses every aspect of the plot: a transgender actress performed the non-binary oracle Pythio; princess Pamela and her handmaid Mopsa share a lesbian awakening; the younger princess Cleophila has an illicit affair with her impoverished cross-dressing lover Musidorus; and a bisexual love triangle ensnares the king, queen, and the cross-dressed interloper.

Nonetheless, and perhaps not surprisingly for a commercial Broadway production, the show makes key errors with regard to trans experience. Two years before *Head Over Heels* premiered on Broadway, *Southern Comfort* made important inroads for trans performance in musical theatre Off-Broadway at The Public Theatre. Based on the eponymous 2001 film, *Southern Comfort* showcases a tight knit trans community in rural Georgia, centering on Robert Eads, a middle-aged trans man dying of ovarian cancer. Despite its narrative challenges to biological essentialism and a highly publicized open call for trans actors, *Southern Comfort*'s casting ultimately reinforced normative biomedical imperatives. Finally, the trans-led absurdism of Off-Off Broadway's *A Ride on the Irish Cream* starkly contrasts with the aforementioned and more mainstream efforts. Throughout its three-year development period, the show became increasingly untethered to narrative closure. One press release described the show as:

> a relationship between Reagan (Markey), a vainglorious self-made girl, and Irish Cream (Becca Blackwell), her family's pontoon boat/horse. They are in love, but when their relationship is tested by dust ruffles, sex for money, severe T-storms, and a secret cellar, the only way to stay together is to remember all the parts of themselves their bodies tried to forget.
>
> (Anon. 2016)

Co-created by two non-binary performers, the cabaret musical demonstrates the power of trans authorship in creating 'authentic' expressions of trans experience and queer intimacy. Nonetheless what *A Ride on the Irish Cream* gains in 'authenticity', it loses in accessibility. All three shows, through their varied associations with commercialism and narrative traditionalism, wrestle with what it means to project virtuosity and authenticity in the contemporary trans musical.

Queer theory, trans experience

If gender is a copy without an original, as Judith Butler has long asserted, then appeals to an authentic 'truth' of gender are inherently suspect and the very notion of 'authenticity' loaded, particularly for LGBTQ+ individuals ([1990] 2006). I invoke 'authenticity' not to ossify perceptions of what 'trans' *is* or *means* but to demand that depictions of trans life be produced in alignment with the material realities of trans experiences beyond the footlights. In *The Feminist Spectator as Critic*, Jill Dolan outlines a materialist feminist praxis focused 'on the construction of ideology in social formations influenced by gender, race, class, and categories of sexual preference' as a way of understanding systemic power relations – relations that are yet 'capable of change' ([1988] 2012: 16). In other words, according to

Dolan, feminist analysis should focus on the lived conditions of women and on how womanhood is itself a lived condition impacted by other intersections of privilege or oppression. By focusing on the impacts of trans casting and staged representation for lived trans experience, I insist on a materialist *trans*feminist critique in alignment with Dolan's praxis.

Structural cissexism, society's often unexamined privileging of individuals whose genders align with the sex they were assigned at birth, often factors into these trans misrepresentations. Trans artists often find themselves excluded throughout the creative and producing processes. In many such cases, cisgender directors bring in trans actors to perform cis-written roles in hopes they will lend cis-led trans storylines a *veneer* of authenticity. Subsequently these trans actors, hungry for roles within a casting system that reflects the structural transphobia of our society, feel compelled to express gratitude even when the depictions directors expect them to showcase are problematic or inaccurate. After all, a trans actor has been cast in the trans role instead of, as is more commonly the case, a cisgender actor. Trans activist and performer Julia Serano calls this exploitative phenomenon – 'where gender-variant people are used as a device to bring conventional notions about maleness and femaleness into question' – *ungendering* (2007: 195–96). In such cases, trans characters solve problems or create opportunities for cisgender people, while playwrights fail to imbue those same trans characters with their own complexities. These ungendered trans characters, narratively resolving the problems of more normative characters, enable audiences to feel virtuous for simply for attending a show with trans representation. I do not contend that musicals or other theatre productions *intend* to exploit trans actors and communities. However, when a show profits from a liberal and seemingly progressive use of trans actors and narratives while inaccurately representing trans experience – and marginalizing or exoticizing trans bodies and voices in the process – it is difficult to ignore the *fact* of exploitation. Impact matters more than intent.

As part of one of the most mainstream theatre genres, trans-inclusive musicals contribute to the trans 'tipping point' by increasing trans representation in general and by making trans virtuosity more visible in particular. Yet despite the form's increasing engagement with transgender narratives and moderate strides toward trans-inclusive casting, trans artists seldom find themselves at the helm of these projects: creating, producing, or directing. Critiques of limited trans inclusion need not diminish the importance of trans stories and characters in mainstream theatre. Efforts towards trans visibility are important for transgender and cisgender audiences alike. Trans people are part of our world and should be represented accordingly. These gains must be taken seriously, and directors and producers should be commended for casting trans actors in trans roles. Nonetheless, when trans representations go awry the 'teeter-totter' of progress tips backward – both onstage and off. Beyond exploitative ungendering, theatrical misrepresentation can result in confusion, distrust of trans people's self-declared realities and the pain of misrecognition felt by trans audiences. Not confined to the liminal time and space of the theatre, these misunderstandings and negative affects infiltrate daily life, creating a negative feedback loop between our inherently transphobic society and well-intentioned theatrical productions that nonetheless continue to centre cisgender perspectives.

Despite the very real risks of misrepresentation, theatre has the potential to richly communicate the material and affective realities of trans experience. The live co-presence of audiences and the actors' bodies produces theatre's unique capacity to intervene in audience perceptions of those 'other' than themselves. Beyond – and because of – its mainstream appeal, musical theatre has a uniquely important role to play in trans performance praxis. The genre's dynamic use of song and dance creates a unique opportunity to showcase embodied trans virtuosity. Queer theatre critic and scholar Alisa Solomon suggests that theatre's liveness presents a particularly queer problem. She posits that the presence of bodies in all their 'sweating, spitting specificity' alienates well-heeled, normative audience members, even offending the social order (Solomon 2002: 9). This direct confrontation between performer and viewer becomes particularly crucial when the actor's body is non-normative, in this case transgender. Yet, as Ryan Donovan acknowledges, 'the casting of Broadway musicals reproduces aesthetic values from the dominant culture', reinforcing established hierarchies as to which bodies are valuable or disposable, superior or inferior (2019: 1). Although Donovan refers specifically to 'fat' actresses, his analysis can be aptly applied to a range of stigmatized bodies, including trans bodies.

Musicals, as commercial enterprises, are not inherently progressive. Commercial theatre works within a liberal framework that upholds, while seeking to expand, the limits of the social order rather than disrupting or overturning it. Trans-focused musicals nonetheless dramatize trans experience beyond the level of mere narrative, allowing social disruption – or trans liberation – through trans embodiment. Virtuosic performance can either include trans people as experts – viscerally demonstrating the materiality of trans experiences – or structurally exclude them. Theatrical uses of virtuosic song and dance can either *reproduce* the values of the dominant culture, profiting from trans inclusion while failing to disrupt cis-normativity, or they can *offend* the social order. When an otherwise stigmatized body performs virtuosically, the performer asks the audience to value that body – and the person it belongs to – in a new way. When a narrative further celebrates that character, it encourages audiences to celebrate those characters and performers. When a production further employs trans artists as full-fledged collaborators, rather than marginalizing them within the creative process, true progress becomes possible. Audiences and reviewers praise shows for casting trans actors because such a practice *seems* to fulfill a promise that these actors, and by extension trans people writ large, will be seen, valued, empathized with and celebrated. Yet merely showcasing trans performers in supporting roles, or in roles that exoticize or distance them from the staged community, cannot make up for a production's narrative failures or for music and dance scores with embedded transphobia. For trans representation in musicals to fulfill its progressive promise, trans people must be empowered as fully realized creative voices at every stage in the development process.

Trans representation falls Head Over Heels

Head Over Heels was first produced at the Oregon Shakespeare Festival in 2015 with a cis woman (Michele Mais) as the (otherwise unnamed) Oracle of Delphi (Scott 2015). By the time the show arrived on Broadway, the Oracle – now named Pythio – had been re-worked as a non-binary AFAB (assigned female at birth) character and positioned as the ostensible star of the show, and the role had been cast to be performed by out Black trans woman and former *RuPaul's Drag Race* contestant Peppermint. Indeed, Broadway marketing for *Head Over Heels* relied heavily on the appeal of seeing a well-known drag queen live on stage. Playbill.com, Broadway World and even NBC News promoted the show with various versions of 'Peppermint Is Turning Broadway on Its Head' (Carley 2018; see also McPhee 2018; Robbins 2018; Kacala 2018). Capitalizing on Peppermint's allure as an out transgender drag performer became a significant part of *Head Over Heels'* marketing strategy, appealing to excited neophyte allies whose only framework for queer performance was mainstream, televised drag. The campaign's desire to hail trans and queer audiences seemed secondary at best.

Although the production's 'shoehorning' of music by The Go-Gos into a plot based on Sidney's *The Arcadia* was almost universally panned by critics (Isherwood 2015; Paulson 2017; Brantley 2018; Evans 2018), even vitriolic reviews acknowledged the significance of Peppermint's star turn. Ben Brantley wrote a review so transphobic – intentionally misgendering the oracle Pythio ('her – I mean them') and scoffing at the show's attempted deconstruction of the gender binary – that he later issued a formal apology, and the *New York Times* re-wrote portions of his original review. Yet even Brantley's malicious criticism acknowledged Peppermint as 'the first transgender woman to create a principal role on Broadway', an important and historic first (Brantley 2018; NYTimes Communications 2018).

The first trans woman starring as a principal on Broadway *should* be a celebratory moment for trans artists and allies. Yet, the show fell short of its presumably progressive goals in various ways. First, Pythio remains separated from the rest of the cast for most of the narrative. As an oracle Pythio is powerful, respected, even revered, yet they are not part of the Arcadian community. Although set apart as 'special' and magical, the narrative nonetheless *others* Pythio, even if gesturing toward their reintegration within the community at the show's conclusion. The embodied storytelling of *Head Over Heels* thus reinforces the othering of trans and non-binary individuals within normative cisgender society. Second, by casting Peppermint as Pythio, the show presents the ostensibly AFAB non-binary character through a binary (AMAB) trans woman.

Next, Peppermint's racial identity further problematizes the 'set apart' nature of her role, leading Pythio to resemble the two dimensional 'magical negro' which has long plagued both stage and screen. According to David Ikard, such 'magical negroes function ideologically as sidekicks, good luck charms, spiritual forces, and the like whose raison d'être in white redemption narratives is to support/heal/enlighten/inspire the white character(s) in crisis' (2017: 161). Peppermint's Pythio aptly fits this trope as their prophecy forces the Arcadians to journey beyond their heteronormative and gender binary comfort zones, accepting the queerness in themselves and others as the price of salvation. Most significantly, Pythio's white cisgender husband – who earlier had banished Pythio after they expressed their true non-binary identity in the wake of their daughter Mopsa's birth – vows to accept Pythio in the fullness of their gendered complexity. Although this belated acceptance back into the community goes some way toward rectifying their separation from society at large, the character's reintegration serves as only a coda, pasted to the conclusion of the play's broader narrative. Further, having the only Black trans woman on stage serve as a foil for the personal growth of a white cis man reifies her/their (Peppermint's/Pythio's) role as a transgender magical negro 'other'.

Additionally, casting Pythio with a trans actress does not adequately compensate for the plot point wherein a lowly shepherd (Musidorus), lover of princess Philoclea, infiltrates the community disguised in Amazon drag as Cleophilia to secretly woo and win the young princess. Though Philoclea knows of Cleophilia's true male identity before they make love, the subplot nonetheless reinforces transphobic anxieties about trans women in women's spaces – such as bathrooms – and fears that trans inclusion merely provides an opportunity for disguised cisgender men to sexually violate cisgender women and girls. Musidorus's tongue-in-cheek admission that he 'should like to keep around' his womanly alter-ego provides less of a nod to contemporary notions of gender fluidity than an attempt to obscure the transphobic elements of the Musidorus/Cleophilia subplot (Whitty et al. 2018: 100). In a world where state and local governments pass anti-trans bathroom bills to keep trans people from using public accommodations and where national governments have rescinded protections for trans youth, the Musidorus/Cleophilia plot reinforces transphobic fears about trans women as male interlopers, regardless of the show's attempt to complicate Musidorus's deceptive cross-dressing.

Finally, casting a transgender woman as the AFAB non-binary oracle misrecognizes Pythio's trans experience with negative implications for recognition and medical access in the off-stage world. Not all trans and non-binary people experience life or embodiment in the same way, and those diverse experiences are not interchangeable. Pythio has a uterus. They gave birth to Mopsa. Since *Head Over Heels* invokes contemporary understandings of sex and gender (somewhat anachronistically), this character would have been assigned female at birth and should be on a transmasculine spectrum (i.e. moving *from* 'female' toward a non-binary existence that is likely – though not necessarily – more masculine than 'woman' is often presumed to be). Peppermint, by contrast, is a trans woman. She was *not* assigned female at birth and could be described as 'MTF' (male to female) because of the binary nature of her own transfeminine identification.

Understandably, many trans people want to eliminate language that centers birth-assigned sex, such as FTM/MTF (female to male/male to female) or even AFAB/AMAB because those acronyms reassert the individual's (mis)assigned sex rather than their true and/or chosen gender. Yet in the context of theatrical representation, failure to consider the directionalities of transition can have damaging repercussions. By casting a trans woman to play a transmasculine non-binary character, *Head Over Heels* potentially, although perhaps inadvertently, confuses the public understanding of trans experience and anatomy. This common confusion can have negative healthcare repercussions. For example, transfeminine people need prostate care and transmasculine people need gynecological care. At risk of reifying a certain kind of biological essentialism, Peppermint does not have a uterus. I would never claim that an individual's biology or sexual morphology does – or should – determine their gender or what fictional roles they can perform. As a non-binary femme who recently gave birth, however, it is important to me that the very few gestational trans and non-binary characters in mainstream performance accurately depict those of us who live these experiences. Fidelity in representational embodiment matters here precisely because important reproductive medical realities are at stake.

Certainly, trans actors – like cisgender actors – *should* be allowed to perform roles that do not directly correlate with their own gendered experiences. Yet, as art historian Kobena Mercer has articulated with regard to the 'burden of representation' for Black artists,

> when artists are positioned on the margins of the institutional spaces of cultural production, they are burdened with the impossible task of speaking as

'representatives', in that they are widely expected to 'speak for' the marginalized communities from which they come.

(1994: 235)

Although race and gender cannot be conflated, in the context of marginalized representation, trans performers of various racial and ethnic backgrounds must also contend with such burdens of representation. As trans playwright MJ Kaufman puts it: 'the bodies we see onstage make our experiences visible. For invisible people, like trans and gender nonconforming people, it is necessary that we use ourselves to tell our stories' (2013). As mainstream theatre, including Broadway musicals, increasingly scripts trans characters, trans representation has the opportunity to reach new and unfamiliar publics. Such productions must not, through their casting practices, mirror the actions of well-meaning and high-profile cisgender allies who misspeak and thus reinforce misunderstandings regarding trans anatomy and medical care.[2]

The whimsical fictions of stories like *Head Over Heels* can never be fully divorced from their real-world impacts. Without an exponential proliferation of trans roles performed by trans actors *and* trans artists in positions of institutional power and authority, trans performers will continue to bear these particular burdens of representation whenever they appear on stage.

Transgender drag in Southern Comfort

Southern Comfort invokes traditional drag aesthetics more consistently than *Head Over Heels*' Cleophilia subplot. Drag epitomizes the depiction of *Southern Comfort*'s main character Robert Eads, only without a classic drag 'reveal'. Cisgender actress Annette O'Toole performs the out transgender man Robert – patriarch of a tight knit trans community – in drag. In addition, and despite The Public Theater's groundbreaking call for trans performers, two more of the five trans characters in the six-person cast were played by cisgender actors. Only Sam, a burly trans man (played by Donnie Cancicotto) and Carly (played by Aneesh Sheth), were cast with trans actors. Carly, the trans female girlfriend of the more narratively significant character Jackson, was also the only person of color on stage.

In November of 2015, The Public Theater issued an open call specifically for trans actors. This incredibly uncommon decision seemed to signal The Public's desire for inclusivity (Clement 2015), but the lack of detail provided in that call retrospectively underscores the show's tertiary commitment to such trans inclusivity. The *Southern Comfort* call read, in part: 'The Public Theater has encouraged transgender artists to contact the casting department' (2015).

Although the explicit hailing of trans artists made this call unique, the open call failed to mention the number of trans actors sought or any other standard details of the genre including age, vocal part, or character descriptions. In total, 130 transgender actors submitted resumes and materials (Tran 2016). In December, The Public announced the production's full cast, with only two of five trans characters, both minor, played by trans performers. Many trans actors and allies were frustrated with this ratio, including genderqueer theatre artist Frankie Edelhart who penned an open letter to The Public, which included more than three hundred other signatories. The open letter addressed the institution's failure to deeply invest in the work of trans artists (Edelhart 2015) and led to The Public holding a March 7 'Public Forum' town hall event addressing *Southern Comfort*'s transgender representation and asserting the organization's intended commitment to trans inclusivity. At the town hall event Edelhart, who had been in private communication with The Public since the open letter's circulation, delivered a prepared statement, which they later published (2016). While commending The Public for 'receiving the message' that the production's casting choices were insufficient and even offensive, Edelhart also exhorted The Public Theatre to 'start putting trans artists first' by, for example, producing plays by trans writers (2016). Some other trans artists and audiences, however, were simply pleased to see any progress at all. As performer Becca Blackwell noted at the time, 'there's more [trans representation and casting] because there was like none' (Tran 2016). *Southern Comfort* was, after all, one of only five NYC shows with trans actors playing trans characters in 2016, a marked *increase* from previous years.

Problems with the cis-cast trans roles in *Southern Comfort*, however, were not merely mathematical. Kaufman asserts that 'a trans body can do very important visual and physical work for communicating gender identity' (2013). O'Toole as Robert, Jeff McCarthy as Lola and even Jeffrey Kuhn as Jackson inherently cannot perform this trans labor as cisgender actors in trans roles. O'Toole as Robert visually and narratively reinforces negative stereotypes about transgender people as 'failed' or partial imitations of cisgender norms. Having transitioned long ago, Robert serves as the *Southern Comfort* community's glue and should emerge as the confident mentor of others within that community. Instead, the show represents Robert's trans experience only superficially in body and voice and the book presents him as the only character who fails to develop or change throughout the play, merely serving as a backdrop or prop for the development of others. The narrative arc of his illness catalyzes changes in and for others but Robert's character appears set, even ossified. The show problematically re-enacts a lack of dimensionality through O'Toole's drag as merely a 'play of surfaces' to paraphrase Judith Butler's foundational theorization ([1990] 2006: 185).[3] Drag fails here as an adequate representational tool for narrativizing Robert's life and death outside the binary imperative, instead reinforcing simplistic binaries: his life as a non-woman and his death as a failed man.

O'Toole's Robert wears black jeans, cowboy boots, flannel, a large cowboy hat, and a large belt buckle across her belly. Robert's attire reflects a common sartorial style within his peer group of poor, white, southern, rural men, but O'Toole's costume also epitomizes a comic drag king style that pillories such masculine iconography. The Public Theater's urbane audience in downtown Manhattan seem less likely to associate this style with actual rural southern men than with drag night at the dyke bar. When O'Toole struts onstage at the top of the show – her breasts taped down but still visible under her black t-shirt, her false goatee meticulously applied – the crowd immediately cheers. They applaud a drag king, not a trans man. Furthermore, the use of cross-dressing here imposes a regressive form of what queer scholar Elizabeth Freemen has called 'temporal drag' (Freeman 2010). It freezes Robert's embodiment at the *earliest* stages of transition, contradicting the hard-won, non-binary manhood he purportedly embodies. Whereas Robert has taken testosterone for a decade at this point, O'Toole never has. Whereas Robert grows facial hair, O'Toole's glued-on goatee communicates 'costume'. Whereas Robert has had top surgery, O'Toole's bound breasts are still visible beneath her flannel.

More troublingly, casting cisgender actors to originate the roles of trans characters in new musicals ensures that composers will embed cissexism within the very score of the play. Hormones, especially testosterone, deeply and irrevocably impact the voice. Casting cisgender actors to originate trans – especially transmasculine – roles creates an inherent incompatibility between songs written for cisgender voices in drag performance and hormonally modified trans voices. Such musicalized cissexism dramaturgically buttresses *Southern Comfort*'s other narrative shortcomings.[4] Throughout the musical O'Toole attempts to masculinize the quality of her voice, a challenge having not taken the hormones that would have materially altered her vocal presentation. The superficial layering of an artificially masculine timbre on her soprano merely highlights the disjuncture between O'Toole's voice and a man's. In Robert's song 'Barbara', O'Toole sings out without imitating masculine color, as a male chorus member stands in as Robert's longed for but apparently unachievable male voice. A pun from 'Barbara', that childhood 'truly was a drag', encapsulates the song's focus on the surface trappings of gender: clothes, playthings. The shadow duet reinforces the superficiality of these visual markers, omitting the material effects of testosterone on transmasculine voices. Robert's hormone therapy would have permanently changed and lowered his voice.

The trope of the shadow duet functions somewhat more effectively in the case of Lola Cola (McCarthy), Robert's lover, who is quite new to her own transition.

In her first song, 'Bird', Lola performs a moving expression of dysphoria. While not all trans people feel dysphoric, this friction between how one is perceived by others (most of the world sees Lola as a man) and how one perceives or imagines oneself (she imagines a bright soprano voice instead of her resonant baritone) comes through in the shadow duet as a uniquely trans musical experience. A female chorus member sings in unison alongside Lola but an octave higher. Lola's voice cracks periodically, straining to reach the notes she would rather sing but never quite can. Later in the play, however, McCarthy uses a crystalline falsetto. This use of the actor's natural falsetto demonstrates Lola's burgeoning sense of comfort in her own womanly skin. Unlike Robert, Lola Cola experiences growth as she begins her transition.

Casting a cisgender man as Lola has more potential for producing empathy in the audience than casting Robert in drag does. The show presents the close-knit community as initially suspicious of Lola due to the disjuncture between who she *is* and who she *appears to be*. Jackson dismisses Lola because she has not yet transitioned socially or begun taking hormones. He questions what he calls 'Lola's commitment to Lola', comparing her unfavorably to drag queens. Whoever plays Lola must be able to pass as male in business situations. By narrative necessity, she must appear un-'believable' at first. In the end, however, Lola remains by Robert's side. She thus proves her commitment to herself, to Robert, and to the community. This dramatic unfolding encourages the audience to accept Lola's transfeminine identity because of her commitment to Robert and her care for him at the end of his life. The aural shift to an apparent ease in her falsetto voice supports this character development, confirming sonically what has become clear narratively. Robert does not receive the opportunity for such growth within *Southern Comfort*'s script or score, and O'Toole's sartorial and vocal drag anchor his characterization to, at best, a nascent pre-transition transmasculinity. In other words, O'Toole fails to adequately represent Robert's status as a long out, hormonally transitioned trans man, while the show simultaneously fails to provide his character with any opportunity for development.

In their embodiments and stage movements, trans actors Aneesh Sheth as Carly and Donnie Canciotto as Sam stand out, even in minor roles. 'Walk the Walk' appears during the Southern Comfort trans conference, where Carly leads a workshop on feminine movement for other trans women. Carly twirls across the stage and struts her stuff, posing as if on a catwalk. The other performers watch in awe. Even Melanie, Sam's cisgender wife, works to mimic Carly's poise and sensuality. By demonstrating norms of feminine embodiment as a learned set of behaviors Carly's number deconstructs biological essentialism while affirming her position as a skilled expert. A cisgender woman in the role of Carly would reinforce naturalized (cisgender) femininity while the song purports to empower trans women and denaturalize the feminine. A cisgender man in drag as Carly would at best demonstrate virtuosity and confidence in cross-gender performance while conflating transgender embodiment with cis drag queen performances. At worst a cisgender man in drag, if the performer were not virtuosic, would reinforce transphobic fears of trans women as 'grotesque' pretenders to femininity. A trans woman who lacked Sheth's confidence and virtuosity could unwittingly reinforce those same transphobic fears. But a confident, virtuosic trans performer like Sheth uses her practiced grace to wow the audience. Carly's skillful performance of femininity also enables her to 'pass' in the real, transphobic world outside the supportive microcosm of the conference. This virtuosity will hopefully insulate Carly/Sheth from the ubiquitous violence that trans women of color face daily offstage. In other words, the visible subtext of 'Walk the Walk' is safety. Sheth woos the audience and, in exchange, wields a social power often withheld from women like herself.

Sam's most striking embodied moment comes on the heels of a stressful visit with his parents, one made in hopes of securing a loan for Robert's medical expenses and to help save his home. Back at the Southern Comfort trans conference, Sam's wife Melanie straightens his tie, resting her hands on his chest. Sam quickly jumps back as if assaulted. Melanie, confused, remarks that Sam's top surgery scars have long since healed. Indeed, physical scars sometimes heal more quickly than invisible scars. When Sam leaves to visit his family of origin, he shaves his beard in full view of the audience. Though Sam tries to psych himself up for the encounter, ringing the doorbell with a bouquet of gas station flowers and a smile on his smooth-shaven face, the audience can easily presume that the visit will include deadnaming and misgendering, if not full-scale rejection. The trauma of allowing his family to read him as female metaphorically opens up old wounds for Sam, ones which manifest physically. This extremely brief moment brings with it an exceptional affective power. The subtlety and depth of Canciotto's physicality as Sam presents a realness borne of his specific transgender experience. By contrast, O'Toole has been coached into Robert's masculine performance. Walking and standing with legs spread apart and taking long strides, O'Toole projects a stylized physical demeanor not unlike Mary Martin as Peter Pan.

Fundamental problems exist for trans-supportive future casting when developing a musical score with cisgender actors in trans roles. A 2019 production of *Southern Comfort* in Chicago cast all trans roles with trans actors, and much of the music needed to be transposed. The show's composer laudably agreed to the transpositions, but the results were 'substantially different than the original versions', illustrating the cissexism of the original score (Reszel 2019). In the Chicago production even the songs for Sam and Carly were transposed to better accommodate the particular trans voices of that production and the actors' various relationships to medical transition. Musical Director Robert Ollis noted that, 'every person has a different range' (Reszel 2019). Differential use of hormone therapies enlarges these inherent differences, which are further exacerbated by the dysphoria and anxiety that trans folks may experience when envoicing a character in a musical. For musical theatre to adequately accommodate trans voices, musical scores may need to remain radically open. Bruce Kirle has celebrated the 'innate incompleteness' of musical theatre as each production's casting and audience reception creates a show anew (2005: 1). In particular, Kirle attends to performers' unique styles and to the socially, temporally, and geographically situated nature of audience responses. He suggests that 'the privileging of the closed text is inextricably linked with the idea of definitive performance' (10), but argues that performance can go against the grain of a show's text, subverting the creators' original intent (118–19).

Changes in casting, *mise-en-scène* and performance approach are more common and more easily approved (and funded) than alterations to libretti and/or song substitutions. In professional musical theatre, it remains particularly uncommon for productions to transpose an original score purely for casting purposes, thus enabling actors of various vocal ranges to take on any roles they choose. Instead, casting calls typically list the vocal part sought for each role based on the original (purportedly closed) score. While Kirle uses examples of textual revision to illustrate his thesis on the malleability of musicals, his focus remains primarily on performance. Kirle does not detail the cost of literally re-writing musicals for revival. Whereas most musicals (outside Jerome Robbins' oeuvre) are re-choreographed for each new production, it remains far less common to repeatedly transpose a show's score. Yet doing so would open myriad opportunities for trans performers. How far are writers and directors willing to go to accommodate trans actors seeking their places on the musical theatre stage? How much are producers willing to budget for trans inclusivity?

Alternate crossings: A Ride on the Irish Cream

The musical cabaret *A Ride on the Irish Cream* arguably presents trans narratives less problematically than the two aforementioned texts. While still utilizing tropes of *crossing*, unlike most trans narratives, it does so outside of gender altogether. Creator/performer Erin Markey's dramaturgical strategies – playfulness, fantasy, absurdism and unintelligibility – develop an embodied trans aesthetic that steps beyond the confines of realism. *A Ride on the Irish Cream* (literally) crosses a horse with a boat creating a fantastical, previously unimagined creature that is neither a horse nor a boat but somehow both. Trans performer Becca Blackwell embodies Irish Cream, the horse/boat, with their trademark swagger and bravado.

A Ride on the Irish Cream 'drags' not only gender but reality and all its determinate norms. Positioning itself outside the regulative system of gender, and thus outside of realism, Markey relieves *Irish Cream* of the onus of representation while still privileging transgender embodiments and intimacies.

Both Becca Blackwell's and Markey's performances emerge as transgender and non-binary not merely due to the non-binary trans genders of the performers but also due to the unstable character mashups that the two enact: Blackwell as a horse/boat and Markey as the heroine Reagan, Reagan's villainous friend Nino, and at times even themself, Markey.[5] Likely appealing more to an audience of queer gender rebels and experimental performance aficionados than the tourist Broadway crowd, *A Ride on the Irish Cream* befuddled the uninitiated. Charles Isherwood asked in his *New York Times* review, 'How on earth can you be both simultaneously', ostensibly referring to Blackwell's pontoon boat/horse character, not their own non-binary gender (Isherwood 2016). Yet Blackwell's own transgender embodiment confused Isherwood just as much as the anti-binary pontoon boat/horse character they represented, and the slippages – between performer and character, horse and boat, non-binary trans person and horse/boat – exacerbated this confusion. Isherwood's writing continued to fumble linguistically around Blackwell's gender throughout the review, despite Blackwell having announced their personal pronouns in the show's program. The reviewer seems equally baffled by Markey's use of 'bizarre' language and what he perceived as a lack of clear narrative as he is with Blackwell's non-binary embodiment. The show emerges as utterly incomprehensible for Isherwood, whose writing re-performs the unstable anxiety of *unknowing* that *A Ride on the Irish Cream* produces in him.

Our linguistic intelligibility within gender systems regulates the very livability of human life (Butler [1990] 2006; Butler 2004). 'How does one access a language outside of and in contradistinction to the governing codes that currently determine human definition, such that it gives rise to new meanings, forms of life, and genres of being', asks trans historiographer C. Riley Snorton (2017: 183)? Markey's wholesale refusal of the normative gender system in *A Ride on the Irish Cream* – both textually and personally – thus directly confronts the limits of language, leaving the show's signposts for intelligibility extremely limited.

Relying on the sensate universe of childhood, Markey creates a distinctly femme world. Irish Cream and Reagan consider embarking on a search for jewels in the woods. Later they have an explosive argument about a hidden angel Irish Cream discovered but did not disclose. These fantastical images, discussed by the characters as if they are mundane, likely provide the most accessibility to viewers who grew up with 'girly' imaginative play. Through their exploits Markey and Blackwell do not merely evoke child's play but also fumble to articulate adult queer intimacies. An aggressive standoff turns clumsily amorous. Instead of having

Irish Cream offer Reagan a kiss, Blackwell sticks a large sticker with pursed lips onto Markey's forehead (Figure 5.1). In return, Markey awkwardly presses their forehead – with the sticker – onto Blackwell's butt, 'kissing' their partner's ass. Adding to the play's ebullient confusion, songs that humorously memorialize mortifying scenes from Markey's actual youth and young adulthood intersperse throughout the play's bizarre fictions. More directly narrative than the non-musical scenes, these songs intersect only obliquely with the un-closed 'plot' of the Reagan/Irish Cream/Nino story. If, as Snorton suggests, 'The task of writing invention is beset with difficulties, surrounded and beseeched by failure' (183), then Markey's 'failure' to reach Isherwood (and others like him) should be easily anticipated as they invent new queer and trans ways of being through the cabaret musical.

Markey's capacity to completely upend the norms that undergird our systems of language, knowability and subjectivity rises as the greatest strength of their work. *A Ride on the Irish Cream* refuses to conform to a world that obscures and oppresses non-binary gender and queer sexuality; the resulting performance is itself an act of queer and transgender worldmaking. In its absurdity, the show performs a 'truer' truth of experience. Unlike traditional perceptions of cross-dressing and drag, crossing here *reveals* rather than obscures (Figure 5.2). Irish Cream is neither a horse dressed up as a boat nor a boat performing a horse impersonation. As a horse/boat Irish Cream

FIGURE 5.1: After the relationship between Reagan (Erin Markey) and companion Irish Cream (Becca Blackwell) turns aggressive and then awkwardly amorous, Reagan croons into the microphone while sporting the 'kiss' bestowed by Cream, a dashing horse/boat (*A Ride on the Irish Cream*. Photograph courtesy of Erin Markey).

FIGURE 5.2: The at times complicated legibility of queer, non-binary and trans identity and desire comes to the stage as Reagan (Erin Markey) screams while horse/boat Irish Cream (Becca Blackwell) wraps their hooves around their femme companion (*A Ride on the Irish Cream*. Photograph courtesy of Erin Markey).

demonstrates certain commonalities of horses and boats – they are large and good for riding on – while invoking certain incommensurable qualities of horses and boats: it is the horsiness of Cream that makes them warm and animate. Displaced from their human host onto the horse/boat character, these qualities and experiences emerge as affectively *true* if not literally *real* in their evocation of non-binary experience.

In an alternative expression of non-binary trans experience, Markey performs both the story's heroine Reagan and Reagan's best friend/nemesis Nino. While Reagan appears as a 'normal' pre-adolescent girl, Nino takes shape as sometimes anxious, sometimes jealous, sometimes sneaky and conniving. Nino strokes Reagan's ego, manipulates and temporarily abandons her, flirts with Irish Cream and ultimately helps rescue Reagan from the chaos that Nino alone kickstarted. All the while Nino communicates in a soundscape of high-pitched mumbles and non-word sounds. By taking on both characters without even a costume change, Markey demonstrates a kind of non-binary both/and experience of selfhood different from Irish Cream's. Instead of the *both*-ness of Irish Cream as a pontoon boat/horse, Markey's Reagan/Nino expresses fluidity. Markey exists sometimes as Reagan, sometimes Nino, and sometimes as themself singing directly to the audience about their true childhood experiences.

Although one of its greatest strengths, this capacity for worldmaking is also, perhaps, the greatest limitation of *A Ride on the Irish Cream*. The linguistic and performative annihilation of norms that undergird the world as we know it – leading to revelation for some and utter unintelligibility for many others – do not combine to form a recipe for packed theatre houses. This is the limitation of Markey's dramaturgy. As their work continues to develop a strong subcultural audience of young queer artists in New York City, their anti-narrative absurdism and whimsical language can create a wedge between 'insider' audiences and the uninitiated, audiences for whom the radical genderqueer bedrock of Markey's theatrical worlds seems foreign, even alien. Those not accustomed to questioning the very foundations of social norms will likely not find it comforting to sit in a theatre for 90 minutes feeling totally unmoored, especially surrounded by others who seem unbothered and positively gleeful. If one believes, however, that art should comfort the afflicted and afflict the comfortable, as the saying goes, then *A Ride on the Irish Cream* undoubtedly fulfills its role as art.

Conclusion

At the start of this essay, I asked if it was even possible to create the kinds of trans representation on musical theatre stages that would simultaneously affirm trans experiences, legibly educate cis audiences, and be commercially viable. None of these examples do all three. I have utilized Markey and Blackwell's collaboration on *A Ride on the Irish Cream* as a successful example of trans affirmation, yet this bizarre little musical revels in its opacity; it was never intended for mainstream audiences. *A Ride on the Irish Cream* does not educate cis-normative audiences so much as provide affirmation for non-binary, trans and other gender non-conforming folks who find reflections of themselves and their queer loves in the fantastical world of the show. Inverting the sense of alienation that queer and trans people experience within the dominant (cis- and hetero-normative) culture, Markey's show may alienate people who have *not* grown up gender crossed or fluid in a 'girly' wonderland.

A Ride on the Irish Cream and other social inversions for the stage certainly hold value. Experimental aesthetic practices, particularly those derived from a collaborative ethic that empowers marginalized performers to have full ownership as co-creators of their work, have value. Mainstream accessibility is also valuable. Reaching a large audience has power, particularly when minoritized representation is on the line. *Head Over Heels* made history by casting a transgender woman in a leading role. Broadway advertising often shies away from groundbreaking queer representation, as in 2015 when *Fun Home* promoted itself as 'not just a new musical, a new kind of musical' rather than featuring its butch lesbian protagonist in press materials. In 2018, *Head Over Heels* aggressively promoted Peppermint's role and the historic nature of her casting. Did the press blitz around trans casting in the musical seek to drive sales? Of course. Despite my critiques of the production, the promotional choice to lean into the excitement surrounding Peppermint's ground-breaking participation demonstrated the production team's pride in their casting selection. We must recognize the value in highly visible cultural products publicly modeling pride in affiliation with Black trans women, particularly in a society which continues to disproportionately murder trans people, most often Black and Latinx trans women (Anon. 2020).

Those of us invested in transgender representation cannot merely abandon the mainstream because profit motives complicate efforts. Without the mainstream we forfeit larger audiences (who could become trans allies) and with them opportunities to highlight and compensate trans virtuosity. Mainstream productions like *Head Over Heels* and *Southern Comfort* should be commended for attending to trans stories and casting trans performers, but we must do better. The materials and techniques of musical theatre must be used in service of resonant enactments of trans experience. Including trans people at all stages of development can help ensure that trans-inclusive productions are appropriately cast, that their representations are relevant to and reflective of (historic or contemporary) trans realities and that the trans people on stage are not exploited or 'ungendered'. If the 2019 Chicago production of *Southern Comfort* can become a model – however laborious – for making musical theatre more responsive to trans voices, that will be an enormous and crucial legacy. To embrace trans inclusivity, producers, directors and composers must practice flexibility, for example allowing a show's score to be perpetually re-written and casting high-profile roles with trans actors, rather than simply employing transgender dramaturgs or publicists for damage control once criticisms have already been lodged by local community members.

We need *more* trans representations. 2016 was a banner year for trans performance in New York City, with only five shows, two of them musicals, centering on trans experience and casting trans actors (Tran 2015). When a dearth of trans representations appear across productions, members of the community and allies will scrutinize relevant productions and excoriate them for their failures, however good their intentions. With adequate representation, however, the burden of representation for each production decreases. With adequate representation a show could say *one* thing without having to know and show *everything* (Mercer 1994: 258–85). Trans communities starve for representation, affirmation and most of all safety. Here's to a future full of musicals that develop trans allyship, a future in which gender fluidity (and horse/boats) won't seem quite so strange.

NOTES

1. Contemporary trans representations in pop culture include TV shows like *Pose*, *Supergirl* and *Orange is the New Black*, celebrities like Caitlyn Jenner and Chaz Bono, and children's books like *I am Jazz* (based on the childhood experiences of trans teen reality star Jazz Jennings).
2. Former Democratic presidential candidate Julián Castro mistakenly said that 'trans females' deserve access to abortion alongside cisgender women, later clarifying that he meant AFAB trans people (McCaskill 2019). Such mistakes still happen amongst staunch allies, with sometimes violent consequences.
3. As Elizabeth Freeman notes in *Time Binds: Queer Temporalities, Queer Histories*, Butler turned 'from a theory of performativity based on the play of surfaces' to a more temporally situated notion of the self as an aggregation of past selves with the publication of *The Psychic Life of Power* in 1997 (2010: 63–64).
4. Unlike most musical theatre casting breakdowns, casting calls for *Southern Comfort* do not tend to list the vocal part of each character. Robert Ollis, Musical Director for the 2019 production in Chicago, has confirmed that O'Toole's songs were written for a soprano voice (Reszel 2019).
5. Markey was not out as trans and non-binary in 2016, but they have since come out as such on social media and use they/them pronouns. Blackwell also uses they/them pronouns and did so at the time of the performance, which was noted in their performer bio in the show's program.

REFERENCES

Anon. (2016), 'Erin Markey – *A Ride on the Irish Cream*', *New York Performance Artists Collective*, http://www.nypac.org/2016/markey/. Accessed 18 December 2020.

Anon. (2020), 'Murders of transgender people in 2020 surpasses total for last year in just seven months', *National Center for Transgender Equality*, https://transequality.org/blog/murders-of-transgender-people-in-2020-surpasses-total-for-last-year-in-just-seven-months. Accessed 6 December 2020.

Brantley, Ben (2018), 'Review: Ye Olde Go-Go's Songs Hit the Renaissance in *Head Over Heels*', *New York Times*, 26 July, p. C1, https://www.nytimes.com/2018/07/26/theater/head-over-heels-broadway-review-go-gos.html. Accessed 24 November 2020.

Butler, Judith (2004), *Undoing Gender*, New York: Routledge.

Butler, Judith ([1990] 2006), *Gender Trouble: Feminism and the Subversion of Identity*, New York: Routledge.

Carley, Brennan (2018), 'Peppermint Is Turning Broadway on Its Head', *GQ*, 6 September, https://www.gq.com/story/peppermint-is-turning-broadway-on-its-head. Accessed 24 November 2020.

Caruso, Thomas (dir.) (2016), *Southern Comfort*, The Public Theater, Anspacher Theater, New York, 23 February–27 March.

Clement, Olivia (2015), 'Public theater seeking transgender actors for newly announced *Southern Comfort* musical', *Playbill*, 5 November, https://www.playbill.com/article/public-theater-seeking-transgender-actors-for-newly-announced-southern-comfort-musical-com-370323. Accessed 1 October 2020.

Dolan, Jill ([1988] 2012), *The Feminist Spectator as Critic*, 2nd ed., Ann Arbor: The University of Michigan Press.

Donovan, Ryan (2019), '"Must Be Heavyset": Casting women, fat stigma, and Broadway bodies', *The Journal of American Drama and Theatre*, 31:3, pp. 1–17, https://academicworks.cuny.edu/gcpubs/539/. Accessed 1 October 2020.

Edelhart, Frankie (Taylor) (2015), 'An open letter to the public theater', https://docs.google.com/document/d/1V9uJrZkGQLIerRm83UF-z8QoUXZefExFQgD3AT89Acc/edit. Accessed 10 January 2021.

Edelhart, Frankie (Taylor) (2016), 'WHO COMES FIRST: A speech given at the public theater's town hall meeting on gender identity, representation, and theatre', *Medium*, 15 March, https://medium.com/@TheConduit/who-comes-first-a-speech-given-at-the-public-theater-s-town-hall-meeting-on-gender-identity-d654c2fbaa7a. Accessed 10 January 2021.

Evans, Greg (2018) '*Head Over Heels* Review: The Go-Go's Musical That Isn't', *Deadline*, 26 July, https://deadline.com/2018/07/head-over-heels-broadway-review-go-gos-musical-belinda-carlisle-our-lips-are-sealed-1202433387/. Accessed 1 October 2020.

Fein, Jordan (dir.) (2016) *A Ride on the Irish Cream*, E. Markey, Performed by Becca Blackwell, Erin Markey, Ian Axness, Chenda Cope, Mike Marcinowski and Emily Bate, Abrons Arts Center, New York, 13 January–6 February.

Freeman, Elizabeth (2010), *Time Binds: Queer Temporalities, Queer Histories*, Durham: Duke University Press.

Halberstam, Jack (2018), *Trans**, Oakland: University of California Press.

Ikard, David (2017), *Lovable Racists, Magical Negroes, and White Messiahs*, Chicago: The University of Chicago Press.

Isherwood, Charles (2015), 'Review: In *Head Over Heels*, Jukebox Musical Meets Elizabethan Romance', *New York Times*, 17 August, p. C1, https://nyti.ms/1IY4Cga. Accessed 1 October 2020.

Isherwood, Charles (2016), 'Review: *A Ride on the Irish Cream*, Erin Markey's Tale of an Odd Affair', *New York Times*, 22 January, C3, http://nyti.ms/1OMbfD8. Accessed 1 October 2020.

Kacala, Alexander (2018), '*Drag Race* star Peppermint on Broadway debut: "It's a dream come true"', *NBC News*, 13 August, https://www.nbcnews.com/feature/nbc-out/drag-race-star-peppermint-broadway-debut-it-s-dream-come-n900276. Accessed 1 October 2020.

Kaufman, MJ (2013), 'Don't Call me Ma'am: On the politics of trans casting', *HowlRound*, 29 September, https://howlround.com/dont-call-me-maam. Accessed 1 October 2020.

Kirle, Bruce (2005), *Unfinished Show Business: Broadway Musicals as Works-in-Progress*, Carbondale: Southern Illinois University Press.

Mayer, Michael (dir.) (2018–19), *Head Over Heels*, J. Whitty and J. Magruder, Ambassador Theatre Group, Hudson Theatre, New York, 26 July–6 January.

McCaskill, Nolan D. (2019), 'What Castro meant when he said trans women need access to abortions', *Politico*, 27 June, https://www.politico.com/story/2019/06/27/julian-castro-debate-abortion-1385950. Accessed 24 November 2020.

McPhee, Ryan (2018), '*RuPaul's Drag Race* Star Peppermint Will Make Her Broadway Debut in Go Go's Musical *Head Over Heels*', *Playbill.com*, 29 January, https://www.playbill.com/article/rupauls-drag-race-star-peppermint-will-make-her-broadway-debut-in-go-gos-musical-head-over-heels. Accessed 1 October 2020.

Mercer, Kobena (1994), *Welcome to the Jungle*, New York: Routledge.

NYTimes Communications (2018), 'Here is Ben Brantley's response to the conversation surrounding his review of *Head Over Heels* https://nyti.ms/2NP9xat. We are updating the review to reflect some of our readers' concerns now', Twitter, 27 July, https://twitter.com/NYTimesPR/status/1022864714525749248. Accessed 6 December 2020.

Paulson, Michael (2017), '*Head Over Heels* sets sights on Broadway, After San Francisco', *New York Times*, 12 December, p. C3, https://nyti.ms/2l91Zqd. Accessed 1 October 2020.

Reszel, Barry (2019), 'The authenticity of Pride Films & Plays' *Southern Comfort* may just make humans better', *Chicagoland Musical Theatre*, 7 March, https://www.chicagoland-musicaltheatre.com/the-authenticity-of-pride-films-plays-southern-comfort-may-just-make-humans-better/. Accessed 1 October 2020.

Robbins, Caryn (2018), 'Debut of the Month: We're Mad About Her! Peppermint Makes Her Broadway Debut in *HEAD OVER HEELS*', *Broadway World*, 24 September, https://www.broadwayworld.com/article/Debut-of-the-Month-Were-Mad-About-Her-Peppermint-Makes-Her-Broadway-Debut-in-HEAD-OVER-HEELS-20180924. Accessed 1 October 2020.

Scott, Aaron (2015), 'Tony-Winning Playwright Mashes-Up The Go-Go's with Arcadia', *Oregon Public Broadcasting*, 27 June, https://www.opb.org/radio/programs/state-of-wonder/article/the-oregon-shakespeare-festival-mashes-up-the-go-gos-with-old-arcadia/. Accessed 1 October 2020.

Serano, Julia (2007), *Whipping Girl: A Transsexual Woman On Sexism and the Scapegoating of Femininity*, Berkeley: Seal Press.

Snorton, C. Riley (2017), *Black on Both Sides: A Racial History of Trans Identity*, Minneapolis: The University of Minnesota Press.

Solomon, Alisa (2002), 'Great sparkles of lust: Homophobia and the antitheatrical tradition', in A. Solomon and F. Minwalla (eds), *The Queerest Art: Essays on Lesbian and Gay Theatre*, New York: New York University Press, pp. 9–20.

Stryker, Susan (2017), *Transgender History*, 2nd ed., New York: Seal Press.

Tran, Diep (2016), 'Trending Now: The Trans* Experience', *American Theatre*, 4 February, https://www.americantheatre.org/2016/02/04/trending-now-the-trans-experience/. Accessed 24 November 2020.

Whitty, Jeff, James, MacGruder and The Go-Go's (2018), *Head Over Heels: A New Musical*, Perusal Script, *Broadway Licensing*, https://broadwaylicensing.com/shows/head-over-heels-copy/. Accessed 21 December 2020.

PART 2

EMBODYING AND EXPLOITING SEX AND SEXUALITY ON AND OFF BROADWAY

6

Chorus Boys: Words, Music and Queerness (c.1900–36)

David Haldane Lawrence

The chorus boy in early twentieth-century musical comedy

The musical comedy phenomenon of the late nineteenth and early twentieth centuries was largely masculine driven. Male impresarios like C. B. Cochran, André Charlot and George Edwardes promoted shows that featured an abundance of femininity, while emphasizing heterosexual codes of behaviour. Librettos, lyrics and music were largely written by men, and the aim was to please a heterosexual audience. Plots involving topical subjects such as department stores and fashion appealed to the interests of women, while their male companions liked to gaze at youthful female bodies on the stage (Platt 2004: 106). It is hardly surprising that chorus boys played a subsidiary role in this feminine predominance – particularly as managers were inclined to engage girls for their good looks, while ignoring the physical attributes of their male colleagues. Writing around 1900, the playwright and journalist George R. Sims maintained that 'chorus gentlemen are engaged more quickly than the ladies'. This was because 'Their appearance is not studied as closely by the management as that of the fair sex. If a man has a good voice he may be short or tall, plain or handsome' (Sims 1900: 48).

This attitude was to change. During the 1920s, there was an increasing American influence on West End musical comedy and revue. Its hedonistic promotion of youth, fun and romance meant a demand for a slicker, better-looking chorus (Walsh and Platt 2003: 76); this applied as much to boys as to girls. Nevertheless an overt emphasis on femininity remained, and fewer chorus boys were engaged than chorus girls. A survey of the cast lists of musical comedies produced from 1900 to 1930 reveals that from 20 to 30 girls could be employed in a chorus, while men average at about twelve. For instance, the popular

American musical comedy *No, No, Nanette* (Irving Caesar, Otto Harbach and Vincent Youmens, Palace, 1925) employed twenty chorus girls and ten boys ('The London Palace Boys and Girls').[1] Of course, the number of chorus men employed accorded with the requirements of the show and could vary considerably. Noel Coward's *Bitter Sweet*, when presented at His Majesty's in 1929, had 26 men in the chorus against 33 girls (Ganzl 1986: 315–17). As we shall later see, the First World War further reduced the numbers of men employed in musical comedy choruses.

Although fewer men were employed in the chorus, they were useful as a frame for femininity. In production numbers ranks of 'boys' surrounded and supported the female star giving her the central focus. Their archetypal outfit of top hat and tails suggested the suave and sophisticated 'man-about-town'. Dressed as mirror images of affluent male patrons attending their shows, the 'chorus gentlemen' in early twentieth-century revue and musical comedy assisted in the display of femininity for the 'male gaze'. For instance, in *The Earl and the Girl* (Ivan Caryll and Seymour Hicks, Adelphi, 1903) chorus men pushed girls seated on swings wreathed with garlands of electric lights out from the stage and over the heads of the audience, undoubtedly to the delight of gentlemen in the stalls and dress circle (Platt 2004: 36). The blatant advancement of female sexuality by upper-class males is also apparent in Lionel Monckton and Howard Talbot's *The Arcadians* (Shaftesbury, 1909). A chorus of 'young men-about-town in evening dress' positively encourage the gaze of men in the audience when they introduce: 'the dear little girls/ Sweet Arcadian peaches and pearls/ Dainty maids, all blushes and curls/ To flirt and tease and banter!' (Monckton and Talbot 1909: 142–43).

By the 1920s, the role of the chorus boy had become more involved and active. This was largely due to the influence of imported American musicals, and more especially the popularity, beginning in the previous decade, of energetic social dances such as 'rags' and foxtrots. The sedate 'chorus gentleman' was now usually labelled as a 'chorus boy', suggesting a youthful, vigorous appearance. He became more integrated with the plot, and was inclined to offer advice, matrimonial or otherwise, to the emancipated post-First World War woman. These musicals had contemporary settings, usually in a well-to-do upper-class milieu, while the male (often gay) chorus members emulated fresh-faced young men found at fashionable house parties. For instance, a line-up of ten 'bachelors' in the highly successful American import of *No, No, Nanette* by Vincent Youmans (Palace, 1925) gives marital counselling to Lucille and her errant husband Billy (Mander and Mitchinson 1969: Plate 40). In *Mercenary Mary* (London Hippodrome, 1925), chorus boys encourage the heroine to become as mercenary as 'all the men' (Mander and Mitchinson 1969: Plate 41).

Noel Coward's Words and Music: *The chorus boy in revue*

Despite the relative prominence of the male chorus in American 'song and dance musicals', it was the girls who received the bulk of media publicity. Dozens of articles and photographs of female chorus members appeared in newspapers and magazines, while comparatively less attention was paid to their male counterparts. Even when Noel Coward featured a line-up of eighteen 'Dancing Boys' in his revue for C. B. Cochran, *Words and Music* (Adelphi, 1932), more publicity was given to Cochran's inevitable 'Young Ladies' – whose name suggested a demureness that belied their erotic subjection to the male gaze. This was despite Coward's showcasing of the male chorus in routines where they danced on their own, without female partners. Particularly innovative was his use of the male and female choruses at the opening of the show. Instead of the curtain rising on the 'Dancing Boys' as adjutants to a bevy of Cochran's 'Young Ladies', Coward began the revue with two production numbers introducing each line-up separately. He did away with an opening number featuring boys and girls together. This separation of the male and female choruses diminished, to a certain extent, Cochran's usual emphasis on femininity. The first section introduced the 'Young Ladies' in their dressing room. Their appearance was rapidly followed by a highly energetic routine for the 'Dancing Boys'. The *Punch* reviewer noted that Coward

> conscious perhaps that we should see less of Mr. Cochran's Young Ladies than usual, shows us as much as possible of them in their dressing room, following this by a mass introduction of eighteen Dancing Boys in one of the most successful individual scenes of the revue.
>
> (Anon. 1932a: 358)

Meanwhile the *Dancing Times* saw the Dancing Boys' routine as the 'male counterpart' to the Young Ladies' preceding number (G., G. E. 1932: 349). Attention was focused exclusively on a group of dancing boys, and their efforts earned them acclaim unusual for male chorus members. According to *The Times*, it was 'a brilliantly decorative opening' and the audience cheered 'before the opening chorus was spent. The cause of this early enthusiasm was not as you would reasonably expect, Mr. Cochran's Young Ladies but his Young Gentlemen' (Anon. 1932b: 8). The energetic 'Dancing Boys' created a sensational effect in their number. Full evening dress was discarded and they wore only black trousers and white shirts. According to the *Dancing Times*, 'the omission of the jackets from the men's evening dress' retained 'the balance' of the grey tones in the setting. While they danced 'ground flood lights, threw triple shadows of varying strength on to the gauzes and hangings' (G., G. E. 1932: 349). The dancing of the boys inspired an ecstatic outburst from *The Times* critic: 'Round about the stage; round went the young gentlemen, leaping and glissading in an excess of terpsichorean relativity' (Anon.1932b: 8). *Punch* described the effect with less verbal exuberance:

> Dancing with, across and against the movement of the revolving stage, their shadows thrown, enlarging and dimming on the plain muslin-curtained background in a brilliant kaleidoscopic pattern – a startlingly beautiful effect which won an unmistakably spontaneous tribute from us all.
>
> (Anon. 1932a: 358)

The 'Dancing Boys' had another number on their own in *Words and Music*. As German prisoners, they performed a Tyrolean dance in the skit 'Journeys End', which managed to combine lampoons of R. C. Sherriff's anti-war drama of that name, together with the vogue for 'kitsch' Teutonic musicals such as *White Horse Inn* (Ralph Benatsky, Hans Mueller and Irving Caesar, Coliseum, 1931). But the 'Dancing Boys''s most memorable contribution remained the shadow dance sequence at the opening of the show. They inspired other 'boy' routines in revue. For instance, *Stop Press* (Noel Gay et al., Adelphi, 1935) featured 'The London Boys'. Needless to say, more publicity was given to the 'Hollywood Girls', who also appeared in the show, than to the 'Boys'.[2]

Boys and girls together: The working life of the chorus boy

Coward's division of the male and female choruses into separate entities for the opening number of *Words and Music* could also be viewed as a reflection of backstage sexual segregation. Although chorus boys partnered girls on the stage, the sexes tended to be kept apart behind the scenes. Victorian anxieties about theatrical morality still prevailed. The morality and sobriety of performers was a prime concern and discipline had to be strict if high performance standards were to be maintained. In most theatres and companies, the chorus was subject to fairly strict rules. For the sake of respectability male and female dressing rooms were generally located on opposite sides of the stage. On tour chorus boys and girls, as well as principals, faced further sexual segregation. In trains they travelled in single-sex carriages (Coleman 1885: 27). On tour, they were lodged in separate 'digs'. According to one ex-chorus member, if a boy and a girl wanted to be together, they would sometimes give false house numbers such as 58 and 58A to the stage manager, pretending one place was two (Vicinus 1979: 366). It was essential for major companies to maintain an outwardly respectable appearance, especially as musical comedy performers could, sometimes justifiably, arouse suspicion of immorality. While the morality of chorus girls was a constant anxiety, rules for men could be just as rigid. These were mainly concerned with matters such as drinking, gambling or sexual misconduct. Men in theatre companies, including members of the chorus, were supposed to be examples of chastity and sobriety. Managers were anxious to prevent any hint of scandal and often made a great effort to portray their companies as models of middle-class morality.

Despite their backstage separation, the careers of chorus boys paralleled those of their chorus girl partners. Both sexes shared the ups and downs of theatrical life. They experienced the drudgery of waiting in agents' offices, and attendance at crowded and competitive auditions. In the Depression years of the early 1930s, 'anything of up to a thousand applicants' could be found waiting to audition for 'a vacancy of perhaps ten men' (Butcher 1933: 36). Physical attributes were as important as the ability to sing and dance: if the applicant's 'dancing, singing and appearance' was up to 'the requisite standard' and if he (or she) pleased 'the management's eye' they would be engaged. Rejection meant joining 'another thousand applicants at another audition' (Butcher 1933: 36). If engaged, a West End chorus man earned around £3 to £4 per week. This was more than was paid to his female counterparts, despite the greater emphasis placed on their performance onstage. An ex-chorus boy, interviewed by Martha Vicinus in 1979, began his career on £4 per week, while chorus girls in the company received about £2 (Vicinus 1979: 366). This could be seen as a reflection of more universal gendered pay differentials. Even so, the chorus boy's wage was low when compared with the amounts received by those higher up the scale. Furthermore managements made encroachments into male salaries, low or high. For instance, in the early 1930s, the sum of one shilling and seven pence was deducted for insurance from an Adelphi chorus boy's wage of £4 per week (Butcher 1933: 36). A chorus boy or girl also had to agree to 'any clause which the management may see fit to put into a contract' (Butcher 1933: 36); this could include a 'no play, no pay' clause, which meant that if a performer was ill his or her salary was stopped for the performances missed. A doctor's certificate had to be produced on return to the company. But if a chorus boy or girl could not afford medical advice there was the risk of being dismissed (Butcher 1933: 37). It is no wonder that chorus boys often felt that they were 'underpaid, overworked and unappreciated' – despite earning more than girls in the chorus (Butcher 1933: 36).

Chorus boys came from varied social backgrounds. According to Cyril Butcher, the male Adelphi chorus contained 'as democratic a class of young men as it would be possible to find'. The 'proverbial peasant' worked alongside the 'proverbial belted earl' (Butcher 1933: 37). Since the 1890s, there had been an influx of middle to upper-class performers in the theatre. So far as chorus boys were concerned, there was the possibility that upper-class gay members found a safe haven in a profession that was considered to be below their station. Also, the mixing of classes observable within the gay milieu was more than likely to have been reflected in the different social backgrounds of theatrical employees.

More important than social differences was a youthful appearance. Chorus members, both male and female, were required to be 'full of pep', and a good performer had to be able to act, dance and sing. For a show to be successful, discipline was as essential as it was for more 'serious' branches of theatre such as opera and ballet. Keeping up appearances was very important when seeing agents or attending auditions, and a considerable amount of a chorus boy or girl's low income was spent on the purchase and upkeep of clothes (Halling and Lister 1908: 442).

Hours for the chorus could be extremely long and demanding. Stamina was required, particularly when having to rehearse or perform under difficult circumstances. In most theatres, rehearsals started at 10 a.m., but sometimes a chorus boy would have to attend the tailor an hour earlier, at 9 a.m., for a costume fitting (Butcher 1933: 37). Rehearsals lasted until 1 p.m., with occasional five minute breaks. There was an hour for lunch. Work carried on 'from two till six and seven till eleven or midnight' (Butcher 1933: 37). A chorus boy or girl could spend nearly the whole day in the theatre rehearsing and performing. The strain of performing in the chorus was 'terrific'. Only those who were 'perfectly healthy' could 'last the run of a show' (Butcher 1933: 36). They needed to be 'fit' to keep up with the physical demands of performing in the chorus. Tap dancing was, from the experience of Cyril Butcher, 'the most strenuous exercise in the world' (Butcher 1933: 37). In spite of 'the apparent ease and slickness to the onlooker', obtaining the desired effect in a routine could be 'tiring' and 'exhausting' (Butcher 1933: 36). Butcher claimed total concentration was required when working 'especially when, as often happens, we have to play small parts as well' (Butcher 1933: 37). Otherwise there was very little room for individuality. The chorus was under the control of the 'dance producer' (or choreographer). He 'carefully set' the movements and the chorus had to do 'exactly as [they were] told' (Butcher 1933: 36). An observer at the *Words and Music* rehearsals noticed how an 'exact action' was demonstrated 'again and again' by the choreographer until the boys of the chorus could 'do it right themselves' (Fawcett 1932: 4).

In 1924, the *Era* brought attention to the conditions in some theatres presenting twice-nightly revues. Artists complained of cold in the wings. Often there was no hot water to remove grease paint. Sometimes 20–30 people had to wash themselves in the same room. Many chorus boys and girls employed in lower scale theatres were forced to survive on starvation wages (Anon. 1924: 8). Even in the most prestigious of West End theatres, 'the chorus man, being the most lowly of creatures', usually had to share a communal dressing room on 'the topmost floor of the building'. According to Butcher, to reach their dressing room in the Adelphi Theatre, chorus boys 'had to climb seven storeys every time' they changed; this was despite the fact that in a revue they may have fourteen or more changes of costume 'some of them in less than five minutes' (Butcher 1933: 37). To have to rush up and down stairs to and from their dressing room, as well as making quick costume changes, would have added extra strain to a chorus boy's performing life; he would have needed a great deal of stamina to put up with these conditions.

As well as bad working conditions, musical comedy chorus work was surrounded by uncertainty, and there was the constant fear of unemployment. But this did not prevent a large turnover in the chorus. Several musical comedy stars began their careers as chorus members, and they considered it to be important training for a stage career. Writing in the *Era,* the well-known musical comedy actress, Binnie Hale, stated that the chorus was 'the best way to begin' (Hale 1924: 11). It taught a young aspirant stage presence and how to sing, dance and walk on stage. The practical experience offered by chorus work could be better training than attending a stage school. Touring in the chorus of a West End production was considered to give a beginner self-assurance. Another musical star maintained that you could not afford to be slack on tour as provincial audiences were 'often stricter than London audiences' (Barbour 1924: 9). More importantly, as a chorus member, you were under the eye of the management, which was always on the lookout for talent. There was the chance of being given a line to say, or a small part 'which you had to be good enough to fill, otherwise back into the chorus' (Barbour 1924: 9). A few who had luck and talent could rise from the chorus to stardom; while countless others never made it, or fell by the wayside. In many cases, it was the effeminacy of the male chorus members, more than their talent, which prevented them from furthering their careers and landing leading roles. Thus some became drag artists in variety or cabaret (Chauncey 1994: 315).

The chorus boy and assumptions of queerness

Like their counterparts in the world of ballet, chorus boys were subjected to what Michael Gard has termed an 'assumption of homosexuality'. Men dancing on the stage aroused anxieties regarding the 'feminisation' of masculinity; their choreographed movements seemed to oppose 'normal' male physical attitudes, in particular those relating to sport (Gard c. 2006: 42–43). The same criteria could be applied to boys singing and dancing in musical comedy and revue choruses. They had an androgynous appeal that was disturbing to the 'normal' male gaze. This aroused accusations and suspicions of degeneracy and homosexuality.

There were, however, a large number of gay men in musical comedy and revue choruses. Many were attracted by the glamour and escapism of the musical stage. Also, during an era of prejudice and legal repression, the theatre could offer some form of protection from outside hostility. As early as 1897, John Addington Symonds noted the attraction of a theatrical career for 'inverts' (Ellis and Symonds 1897: 124). He also speculated on same-sex desire among chorus girls, who, 'cooped-up' together in crowded dressing rooms with a wait of 'perhaps two hours between performances', are given every opportunity for the expression of lesbian sentiments (Ellis and Symonds 1897: 83–84). There does not appear to be any such psychosexual record regarding groups of 'inverted' chorus boys. However, there are occasional police records and medical reports regarding individuals (see Houlbrook 2005: 131–32; Chauncey 1994: 281). Lack of evidence regarding queer chorus boys is possibly because of the silence surrounding the question of male homosexuality in the late nineteenth and early twentieth centuries, particularly with regard to its presence in the theatre (Burt 2007: 28–29).

Nevertheless, it is easy to imagine chorus boys crowded together in the close proximity of the dressing room, where they dressed and undressed, put on wigs and make-up and shared in gossip. The dressing room could be a very busy place, particularly for revue, where a number of rapid costume changes were required. While there may have been same-sex relationships between young men in the chorus, there was more likely to have been an element of male prostitution. In 1908, the pseudonymous Xavier Mayne claimed that prostitution was 'by no means rare among the more mercenary Adonises of the theatre' and that 'young actors often profit by the passions of rich male admirers' (Mayne 1908: 399). Doubtless some chorus boys were not averse to accepting gifts and favours from managers or gentlemen in the audience, particularly if they wanted to further their careers.

With so many chorus boys reputed to be gay, the theatrical milieu could be seen as a microcosm of the queer world. Chorus boys, after performances or between engagements, were supposed to be part of the gay 'underworld' outside the theatre – that of queer bars, pubs, clubs, cafes and parties. In the 1920s and 1930s, a gay clientele frequented venues such as the Criterion in Piccadilly, the Fitzroy Tavern, the Trocadero Long Bar and the Tea Kettle in Wardour Street (Houlbrook 2005: 69). This would undoubtedly have included a number of young men who performed in the theatre. In these clubs and bars, some wore make-up (discreetly applied) just as they had for the stage. Like other 'queans' of the period they referred to each other in feminized terms, as 'she' or 'her'; or gave each other female nicknames appropriate to their character or behaviour; or even feminized their own names (Houlbrook 2005: 142). The theatre was also a source for the gay slang known as 'palare'. This was a patois distinctive to British gay men, and it allowed for defiant and outlandish conversation at a time of legal and social repression. Undoubtedly the banter of this 'gayspeak' was shared between queer chorus boys in West End and provincial dressing rooms.[3]

Because of their theatricality, chorus boys did not usually need to wear a mask of normality like gay men involved with the 'real' world. Occasionally problems, such as a gay chorus boy being arrested for immoral conduct, could arise. This was not difficult in an era when gay sex was punishable and homosexual activity came under suspicion. Matt Houlbrook, in his book *Queer London* (2005), cites the case of a London chorus boy who was prosecuted for holding queer parties in his Fitzroy Square basement flat over the winter of 1926–27 (Houlbrook 2005: 132–33). Undoubtedly there were similar cases, but it is also probable that many of those arrested gave false names and occupations or were protected by the enclosed world of the theatre. The presence of so many chorus boys who were 'bent' could also create a problem for girls, who may have been seeking husbands or boyfriends from within the company. Apart from those unattainable because of their sexual orientation, others were too busy trying to advance their careers and avoided close relationships, unless they were useful on the ladder to success. But not all chorus boys were gay or ambitious and heterosexual relationships were sometimes formed with girls from the cast (Vicinus 1979: 368).

Although not every chorus boy was queer, to the general public, they were seen to represent sexual deviance and outlandish behaviour. Even the term 'boy' with its suggestion of youth, hinted at a pederastic appeal. Like male ballet dancers, chorus boys were associated with homosexual effeminacy. The costumes they had to wear and the movements they were obliged to perform often confirmed this impression. Appearances as sailors or Canadian Mounties had gay connotations, while exotic costumes and make-up could make them appear androgynous or effeminate.[4] Notions of queerness were abetted to a certain extent by the specific promotion of the male chorus line in revue, with labels such as 'The Dancing Boys' or 'The London Boys'. In fact, a suggestion of homophobia could be discerned in reviews of the 'Dancing Boys' appearing in Coward's *Words and Music*. The *Empire News* wrote that the 'Dancing Boys have amused us without offending our masculinity' (B., F. M. 1932: 2). *The Times* found the name 'Dancing Boys' a 'trifle alarming' (Anon. 1932b: 8). Meanwhile Alan Bott, writing in the *Tatler*, referred to them as 'the nicely named Dancing Boys' (Bott 1932: 22). A masculine appearance on stage depended to a great extent on choreography and the way the chorus boys were presented. According to Butcher, if the movements of the male chorus appeared effeminate it was 'the fault of the producer'. At the conclusion of *Words and Music*, 'everybody congratulated Mr Cochran on the masculinity of the chorus gentlemen'. But 'the same set of boys in somebody else's hands might have had exactly the opposite effect' (Butcher 1933: 36).

Defending the 'Chorus Gentlemen'

The chorus boy was popularly viewed as being 'dissipated, weak and effeminate'. Butcher in his article on 'Chorus Gentlemen' retaliated against this notion:

> I am sick to death of this continued and almost proverbial attack on our morals and our virility. Let me admit at once that I know several chorus boys who *are* effeminate and even one or two who are dissipated, but these types are to be found in all walks of life, including the non-theatrical world that professes to despise us so much.
> (Butcher 1933: 36, original emphasis)

He claimed that chorus boys 'as a class' were 'a quiet living, healthy, hardworking, uncomplaining set of fellows' (Butcher 1933: 36). After a long, hard day's work in the theatre, the chorus boy 'barely manages to catch the last train or bus home' to the suburbs (Butcher 1933: 37). He would have been too exhausted to participate in a queer nightlife. Yet many chorus boys lived close to the West End, in flats and rooms, in areas such as Fitzrovia or Oxford Street (Houlbrook 2005: 116, 131). These locations were not only adjacent to the theatres where they worked, but were also close to central London's gay bars and clubs. Such bars and clubs could provide a useful venue, not only for meeting other queer men but also for catching up on theatrical gossip and, more importantly, news of auditions and employment possibilities.

In his article, Butcher goes to great pains to prove the non-effeminacy of the chorus boy. He deliberately equates him with 'normal' masculinity and describes his activities in terms that could be applicable to a sportsman. Butcher's chorus boy practises his dance routines as a perspiring example of masculine exertion. His rehearsal gear consists not only of a pair of 'tap shoes', but of 'manly' apparel such as 'an old pair of flannels' and a cricket shirt (Butcher 1933: 37). After practicing, 'His face is red with exertions and is covered with sweat, and not with the powder and cosmetics as some seemingly well-informed sneerers would suggest' (Butcher 1933: 37). Butcher is also anxious to exemplify the ultra-masculine achievements of his fellow 'Dancing Boys'. The youngest member of the line-up was a 'Public Schools tennis champion', while at least one member had served in the Great War (Butcher 1933: 37). Meanwhile the assistant choreographer was a boxer before embarking on a theatrical career (Butcher 1933: 118). None of this suggests the weakness and dissipation popularly associated with the chorus boy. Yet while Butcher takes such great pains to proclaim the 'masculinity' of the male chorus, he is not wholly convincing. His overt emphasis seems a rather obvious 'cover-up' for a prevalence of effeminacy. At the same time, there was the need for protection during an era when homosexuality was still regarded as being shameful – a 'condition' that was policed and medicalized. Furthermore, effeminacy on the stage brought derision, and discomforted those who considered themselves 'normal'.

The chorus boy in the Great War and its aftermath

An even greater challenge to the masculinity of the early twentieth century chorus boy was the call up for the Great War of 1914–18. The Military Service Bill called for the compulsory conscription of all able-bodied males aged between 18 and 41. This affected not only musical comedy but also all male employees in all branches of the theatre. Some male performers claimed exemption from military service. If they were not called up, or rejected for service, many vacated the theatre to work in munitions factories. Managers, not wishing to be seen as unpatriotic, encouraged their male staff to register for national service. Some theatres included recruiting notices in programmes, as well as declarations stating the military availability status of men in the cast. For instance the programme for the musical comedy *Vivien* at the Prince of Wales Theatre, Birmingham in 1915 declared that: 'Every Male Member of the Company has actually served at the Front, or has attested, or is ineligible for active service' (Collins 2004: 32). Statements such as these protected managements who might have been suspected of employing men who should have joined up. They also helped protect performers from the hostility directed towards those not in uniform.

Shortage of men affected musical comedy, as much as other branches of theatre that relied on chorus work, particularly opera. In 1916, the *Era* complained of the impossibility of getting tenors and basses for musical comedy choruses (Anon. 1916a: 13). The phenomenally successful musical *Chu Chin Chow* (Oscar Asche and Frederic Norton, His Majesty's Theatre, 1916) had an entirely female chorus when it opened in London the same year (Ganzl 1986: 48–50). There was also the fear, especially in the music hall, of American artists being imported to take the place of British performers who had been called up (Anon. 1916: 13). Many of the remaining male performers were elderly, and the lack of youthful, zestful chorus boys threw greater emphasis on the chorus girl. Sometimes girls dressed as boys replaced the male chorus. Several of Cochran's wartime revues featured male impersonation by female chorus members.[5] Despite the lack of young men on the stage, there was a demand for a light, bright musical theatre offering a temporary escape from the war. By 1919, *The Stage Year Book* was able to exclaim that revue and musical comedy 'were never more alive' (Baughan 1919: 5). This was partly because, due to the shortage of men, West End theatres tended to present musical comedies and revues where they could use even more women in the chorus. These shows, with their abundance of pretty girls, were highly popular with battleweary soldiers home on leave.

After the armistice, soldiers returning from the war and unable to find other employment occasionally joined musical comedy companies as 'chorus men'. This was much to the annoyance of those 'who had spent their entire lives in the profession' and could not get work. Managements advertised for ex-servicemen to join the chorus and greatly underpaid them because they received a pension. On 11 March 1920, the *Evening News* published an interview with a former major in the Guards who was now employed in a musical comedy chorus. He received £4 per week for eight shows, with the promise of a 'real part next month'. The theatre manager claimed that he 'would like to have more of our type for the chorus'. He thought that ex-servicemen were 'more natural on stage than the ordinary chorus men' (Anon. 1920a: 4); this remark seems to be directed toward effeminacy. Being supplanted by 'manly' yet inexperienced ex-servicemen provided another grievance for maligned chorus boys, as it restricted opportunities for engagements.

Chorus boys in drag and the question of a 'gay allure'

A group of returning soldiers also made appearances on stage in drag. This was a company known as Les Rouges et Noirs and all were soldiers who had been on active service in France. They toured with the all-male 'revusical vaudeville' entitled *Splinters*, an outstanding feature of which was 'the talented corps de ballet composed of soldiers who have seen service in the trenches' (Mander and Mitchinson 1971: Plate 75). The universal appeal of this cross-dressed troupe may be gauged from the *Stage* review of their performance at a matinee at the London Coliseum in November 1920, when the audience consisted of 'numerous parties of children' which emphasized 'the family character of the house'. The performance was considered 'bright and cheerful throughout' with its 'feminine impersonation at a high level' (Anon. 1920b: 12). The Les Rouges et Noirs company lasted until the 1930s, mainly playing to ex-servicemen drawn to their performances through a sense of nostalgia.

Chorus boys dressed up as chorus girls in all-male revues negated the heterosexual promotion of female sexuality on the mainstream musical stage. No matter how innocent the material used in revues such as *Splinters*, chorus boys partnering other men dressed as pretty women undoubtedly introduced a homosexual undercurrent. Which brings us to the question of the allure of chorus boys. Heterosexual men may have enjoyed viewing lots of pretty girls, but it was 'problematic and conflictual' for them to enjoy looking at other men dancing on the stage (Burt 1995: 12). This does not rule out, however, an alternative, clandestine 'homosexual gaze' from closeted queer men, or even outrageous queans, who are likely to have been part of a mixed-sex audience.

Conclusion

Not only was the early twentieth century chorus boy subservient to a highly promoted femininity on the stage, but he was also subjected to anti-gay social attitudes and prejudices. Whether he was gay or straight he was popularly assumed to be a queer man. This assumption was accompanied by the outward denial of homosexuality in the theatre. The outrageous and feminized behaviour, camp mannerisms and a specific undercover language of a coterie of chorus boys, could therefore be seen as a rebellion against the subjugation and prejudicial attitudes of the status quo. Furthermore, the effeminacy and outrageousness of many chorus boys brought them the attention often denied in their subsidiary onstage capacity. However, there were moments when the chorus boy came into his own, as demonstrated by the 'Dancing Boys' routine in Noel Coward's revue *Words and Music*. By all accounts, Coward's innovative routine seems to point toward future developments, particularly in the American musical: the emergence of a more dominant and positive role for the male chorus, with the performative projection of energy, virility and assertiveness. The image of the limp-wristed, dissolute chorus boy has been left far behind, although an 'assumption of queerness' still lingers on in the case of singing and dancing men.

NOTES

1. From the Palace Theatre programme in the V&A Theatre Collections.
2. See cuttings in the 'Adelphi Theatre 1933–1935' file: V&A Theatre Collection.
3. See Houlbrook (2005: 152) and Cook (2007: 31 [illustration], 157); also interview with John Alcock, Hall-Carpenter Oral History Project, National Sound Archive C456/03/02.
4. For instance, in the Persian ballet costumes designed by the great Parisian couturier Paul Poiret, worn by the male chorus in Andrè Charlot's revue *Eight Pence a Mile* (Alhambra, 1913); see Moore (2005: 42 [illustration]).
5. For example, in *Pell Mell* (Fred Thompson, Morris Harvey and Nat Ayer, Ambassadors, 1915), chorus girls appeared dressed as young men about town (*Play Pictorial* 1915: 165, 27, 86); in *More (Odds and Ends)* (Harry Grattan and Edward Jones, Ambassadors,

1915) girls impersonating male 'cocodes' partnered other girls dressed as 'cocodettes' (*Play Pictorial* 1915: 165, 27, 91).

REFERENCES

Anon. (1916), 'Percentage or patriotism?', *Era*, 24 May, p. 13.

Anon. (1916a), 'How to carry on?', *Era*, 31 May, p. 13.

Anon. (1920a), 'The new chorus man', *Evening News*, 11 March, p. 4.

Anon. (1920b), 'The variety stage: The London coliseum', *Stage*, 4 November, p. 12.

Anon. (1924), 'Theatrical employees' grievances: Mass meeting at Liverpool', *Era*, 20 February, p. 8.

Anon. (1932a), 'At the play: *Words and music* (Adelphi)', *Punch*, 28 September, pp. 358–59.

Anon. (1932b), 'Mr. Coward's Revue: *Words and Music* at the Adelphi', *The Times*, 17 September, p. 8.

B., F. M. (1932), 'Coward's castor oil bottle: A Cure for all our conceits', *Empire News*, 28 August, p. 2.

Barbour, J. (1924), 'The importance of chorus training: Theatrical ladder should be climbed rung by rung', *Era*, 12 March, p. 9.

Baughan, E. A. (1919), 'Drama of the year: Revues and musical comedies', *Stage Year Book*, p. 5.

Bott, A. (1932), 'Entertainments à la Carte: Mr. Coward's Annual', *Tatler*, 5 October, pp. 22-23, xxvi.

Burt, R. ([1995] 2007), *The Male Dancer: Bodies, Spectacle, Sexualities*, London and New York: Routledge.

Butcher, C. (1933), 'Chorus gentlemen', *Britannia and Eve*, 29 April, pp. 36, 37, 118.

Chauncey, G. (1994), *Gay New York*, London: Flamingo/ HarperCollins.

Coleman, J. (1885), 'The social status of the actor', *National Review*, 5, March, pp. 20–28.

Collins, L. J. (2004), *Theatre at War 1914–18*, Oldham: Jade.

Cook, M. (ed.) (2007), *A Gay History of Britain: Love and Sex Between Men Since the Middle Ages*, Oxford and Westport: Greenwood.

Ellis, H. and Symonds, J. A. (1897), *Studies in the Psychology of Sex: Volume I, Sexual Inversion*, London: Wilson and Macmillan.

Fawcett, L. (1932), 'Words, music and Coward', *Manchester Evening Chronicle*, 27 August, p. 4.

G., G. E. (1932), 'Notes on Décor: *Words and Music* – and Decoration', *Dancing Times*, December, pp. 349–353.

Ganzl, K. (1986), *The British Musical Theatre, Volume II 1915–1984*, London: Macmillan.

Gard, M. (c. 2006), *Men Who Dance*, New York and Oxford: Peter Lang.

Hale, B. (1924), 'The chorus as a training ground: An Irishman's letter of love and a reply', *Era*, 16 January, p. 11.

Halling, D. and Lister, C. (1908), 'A minimum wage for actors', *Socialist Review*, August, pp. 441–51.

Houlbrook, M. (2005), *Queer London: Perils and Pleasures in the Sexual Metropolis 1918–1957*, Chicago and London: University of Chicago Press.

Mander, R. and Mitchinson, J. (1969), *Musical Comedy: A Story in Pictures*, London: Peter Davies.

Mander, R. and Mitchinson, J. (1971), *Revue: A Story in Pictures*, London: Peter Davies.

Mayne, X. (a.k.a. Edward Irenaeus Prime-Stevenson) (1908), *The Intersexes: a History of Similisexualism as a Problem in Social Life*, Naples: privately printed.

Monckton, L. and Talbot, H. (1909), *The Arcadians: A Fantastic Musical Play in Three Acts*, London: Chappell.

Moore, J. R. (2005), *André Charlot: The Genius of Intimate Revue* (ed. N. Jefferson), Carolina and London: McFarland.

Platt, L. (2004), *Musical Comedy on the West End Stage 1890–1939*, Basingstoke: Palgrave Macmillan.

Sims, G. R. (1900), *Without the Limelight: Theatrical Life As It Is*, London: Chatto and Windus.

Vicinus, M. (1979), '"Happy Times … If You Can Stand It": Women entertainers during the interwar years in England', *Theatre Journal*, 31:3, pp. 357–69.

Walsh, D. and Platt, L. (2003), *Music Theater and American Culture*, Westport and London: Praeger.

7

Emancipation or Exploitation? Gender Liberation and Adult Musicals in 1970s New York

Elizabeth L. Wollman

The sexual revolution was built on equal measures of hypocrisy and honesty, equality and exploitation. Indeed, the individual strands contain mixed motivations and ideological charges. Even the most heartfelt or best intentions did not always work out for the good when put into practice by mere humans with physical and psychological frailties.

(Bailey 1994: 257–58)

A curious legacy of the 1960s sexual revolution was the 'adult' musical, a number of which cropped up in New York City, occasionally on and especially off- and off-off-Broadway, through the 1970s. Adult musicals generally distinguished themselves from other types of musical in their reliance on strong sexual content in the form of any or all of the following: full-frontal nudity; simulated sexual activity; and frequent sexually suggestive or explicit dialogue, musical numbers or dance numbers. With few exceptions, representatives of the subgenre were reviled by theatre critics, who alternately attacked them either for going too far in the direction of hardcore pornography or, conversely, of being so preachy about contemporary sexuality that they were not erotic enough. Some theatre producers worried that at their most explicit, adult musicals were not terribly distinct from the live sex shows and pornographic films that had begun to proliferate in Times Square by the late 1960s. Nevertheless, adult musicals appealed to other producers – especially young, up-and-coming ones – because they were surprisingly easy to cast with young, eager unknowns, were usually cheap to stage, and, of course, were not difficult to costume. And even the ones that earned the nastiest reviews usually made money. Clearly, spectators were more interested in the nudity and simulated sex that these musicals promised than they were in what critics thought about their orchestrations, scenic design or dramatic flow.

Few adult musicals were published or recorded before they closed. The subgenre as a whole dwindled significantly by the early 1980s as the social and political climate grew more conservative, and seems to have gone entirely out of fashion by mid-decade, when fears surrounding the AIDS epidemic subdued free sexual expression. Virtually no scholarly work exists on adult musicals; historians and journalists who mention them at all tend to emphasize their dated music and subject matter, amateur production values, or the seemingly mercenary desires of producers to capitalize on the American public's fascination with sex at a time when sexual mores were shifting dramatically across the country.[1] Yet while they have been dismissed as trifles that collectively amounted to the musical-theatre equivalent of streaking – a forgettable fad befitting a silly decade – adult musicals represent aspects of 1970s American culture at their messiest and most confused, and thus perhaps at their most honest. These musicals reflect the country's rapidly changing, often contradictory attitudes about gender and sexuality at a time when the sexual revolution had given way to the gay and women's liberation movements.

Beginnings

Aesthetically speaking, the adult musical owes much to burlesque for its bawdy subject matter and its structure. While a few adult musicals – for example the 1970 off-Broadway production *Stag Movie* – featured full-length plots, most were written in revue form, in which songs, skits and dances were loosely thematically interconnected. Yet the adult musical is most closely connected with the overarching aesthetics and idealism of the off-off-Broadway experimental theatre of the 1960s.

At a physical and philosophical distance from the Great White Way, off-off-Broadway inhabited roughly the same geographical area as its immediate predecessor, the off-Broadway realm, but was freer in terms of its organization and objectives.[2] The movement began in the late 1950s in reaction to off-Broadway's increasing commercialism, and thus stretched even further than off-Broadway had in terms of scope and experimentation (Kauffmann 1979: 37). In its heyday in the 1960s, off-off-Broadway was populated by individuals and collectives devoted to developing artistically challenging work in alternative, non-commercial spaces. Practitioners pondered potential roles for the theatre in a tumultuous nation; many off-off-Broadway companies devoted themselves to using theatre as a tool for socio-political change by blending political and aesthetic radicalism, pushing the boundaries of what was deemed theatrically appropriate, and encouraging audiences to engage directly with – and thereby become part of – performances (Banham 1995: 647). While Broadway entered something of a creative standstill in the 1960s, off-off-Broadway was invigorated by the anti-war movement and the counterculture, and exerted unprecedented stylistic influence on the theatrical mainstream well into the 1970s.

When it opened at the Biltmore Theater on 29 April 1968, *Hair: The American Tribal Love-Rock Musical* broke ground as the first critically and commercially successful rock musical to land on Broadway. This musical served as a linchpin that linked the commercial potential of the theatrical mainstream with the experimentalism of off-off-Broadway; in this respect, its influence cannot be overemphasized. Featuring a book and lyrics by Open Theatre members Gerome Ragni and James Rado, and an innovative score by jazz and R&B musician Galt MacDermott, *Hair* was originally produced off-Broadway in 1967 as the inaugural production of Joseph Papp's Public Theatre. Recast by La MaMa director Tom O'Horgan for its move uptown to Broadway, *Hair* retained plenty of its rough-edged off-off-Broadway sensibility, including its disjunct structure, disregard of the traditional fourth wall, hodgepodge of left-leaning social and political messages, emphasis on communal experience both in rehearsal and performance, and use, in the first act finale, of male and female full-frontal nudity.[3]

Stage nudity remained relatively taboo both in the experimental and commercial realms through the early 1960s. This would begin to change when the Royal Shakespeare Company production of Peter Weiss' *The Persecution and Assassination of Marat as Performed by the Inmates of the Asylum of Charenton Under the Direction of the Marquis de Sade* (commonly known as *Marat/Sade*) opened to enthusiastic reviews at Broadway's Martin Beck Theatre on 27 December 1965. The production, directed by Peter Brook, created a mild sensation not only because it featured 'a realistic tableau of guillotined heads, buckets of [...] blood being poured down drains, [and] an actress using her long hair as a whip', but also because it allowed audiences a glimpse of the naked backside of Ian Richardson as Marat, as he emerged from a bathtub beneath the stage (Drutman 1966: 1).

Stage nudity became increasingly fashionable, especially off- and off-off-Broadway, among playwrights and directors interested in honest depictions of the human condition. Playwright Robert Patrick, an active member of the 1960s Caffe Cino scene, remembers, 'when we first started putting nudity into plays, it was in situations where people would be nude in real life. So when people were making love in my plays, I had them nude! Who makes love in armour?' (Patrick 2005). As off-off-Broadway continued to exert stylistic influence on the mainstream, nudity became a familiar, if still controversial, feature on both fringe and commercial stages by the turn of the decade, and arguably helped draw audiences to such plays as *The Prime of Miss Jean Brodie* (Broadway, 1968), *Scuba Duba* (off-Broadway, 1967) and *Tom Paine* (off-off-Broadway, 1968). The nude scene in *Hair*, then, was representative of the fringe's attempts to close the gap between audience and performers, and to use theatre as a tool with which to explore socially relevant subject matter, including that which – like sexuality – was traditionally considered taboo.

What helped set this particular nude scene apart from many of its experimental predecessors was its joyful quality. Writing in 1969, *New York Times* critic Walter Kerr lamented that 'in virtually all of our uninhibited plays, sex and nudity are associated with dirt, disease, bloodshed and death' and that 'the last thing any of these plays is is playful' (Kerr 1969: 26B). On the contrary, the nudity in *Hair*, which occurred at the Act 1 finale during the re-enactment of a human be-in, was intended merely as 'a beautiful comment about the young generation' (Ward 2002). The dimly-lit scene, which featured male and female cast members undulating happily beneath a sheer, flower-printed sheet, was an attempt at theatrical realism: hippies espoused the body beautiful, so why shouldn't actors playing hippies do the same? It also happened to be entirely celebratory, which likely added to its appeal.

Hair's extraordinary commercial success resulted in countless imitations, and thus more theatrical nudity, not only in straight plays but now, also, in musicals. By the end of the 1968–69 season, nudity had attained such faddishness, especially off- and off-off-Broadway, that critic Otis L. Guernsey, Jr, was prompted to gripe,

> This was a season [...] of experimentation with nakedness onstage, not so much on Broadway as in the smaller playhouses. Males and females in various combinations peeled, groped and pressed against one another. Very little came of it except publicity, and not much of that. There was hardly even a sense of shock. Theatrically speaking, the nudity and mimed fornication accomplished so little, at the cost of so much effort, that perhaps we have got *that* notion out of the way at last, once and for all.
>
> (Guernsey 1969: 3)

Of course, Guernsey was wrong. When it came to adult musicals, 1969 was just the beginning.

Oh! Calcutta!

The first adult musical, *Oh! Calcutta!*, opened off-Broadway on 17 June 1969. An 'erotic revue' devised for 'thinking voyeurs' (Tallmer 1969: n.pag.), *Oh!*

Calcutta! was the brainchild of esteemed theatre critic Kenneth Tynan, who solicited a number of writers he admired to 'dramatize their own sexual fantasies or observations on sexuality' (Tynan 1969: 1). The result was a collection of sketches contributed anonymously by writers and playwrights including Samuel Beckett, Sam Shepard, Leonard Melfi, Sherman Yellen, John Lennon and Tynan himself.

Oh! Calcutta! reflected off-off-Broadway's influence not only in showcasing playwrights like Shepard, Melfi and Beckett, but also in Tynan's interest in 'taboo' subject matter and his choice of director. Former Open Theatre associate Jacques Levy was enlisted to shape the songs and skits into an evening's entertainment. During the rehearsal period, Levy led the cast through a series of experimental exercises, including a number of encounter sessions designed to 'enable each actor to accept the fact of his own body and to work comfortably with his fellow actors – without clothes' (Dunbar 1969: 40). Musically speaking, *Oh! Calcutta!* took a nod from *Hair*'s contemporary sound: the score was composed and, with a few full-cast song-and-dance numbers as exceptions, performed by a rock trio called The Open Window, featuring Peter Schickele, pre-P.D.Q. Bach fame.

Despite these off-off-Broadway moorings, Tynan made clear his desire to attract a highbrow audience for *Oh! Calcutta!* 'It seemed to me a pity that eroticism in the theatre should be confined to burlesque houses and the sleazier sort of night club', he wrote (Tynan 1969: 1). 'Some time ago it occurred to me that there was no place for a civilized man to take a civilized woman to spend an evening of civilized erotic stimulation. We're trying to fill that gap with this show' (Karpel 1969: 40). The result, Tynan hoped, would be 'a few cuts above burlesque in intelligence and sophistication' (Tynan 1969: 1). Tynan's attempt to promote the show as 'an entertainment in the erotic area in the best possible taste' (Tynan 1969: 1) is evidenced in his choice of title, borrowed from a painting of the backside of a female nude by the artist Clovis Trouille named *Oh! Calcutta! Calcutta!* The title is a pun on the French '*Oh, quel cul t'as*', or roughly, 'What a nice ass you have!' (Rich 1989: C13).

To quash rumours that cast members would actually have sex onstage, thereby relegating *Oh! Calcutta!* to little more than a Times Square peepshow, producer Hilliard Elkins opened rehearsals to New York City officials and made himself available to hear their concerns. The creative team publicly emphasized the high calibre of the contributing writers, the professionalism of the actors and the many accomplishments of Tynan himself. The producers spared no expense on *Oh! Calcutta!*, which was clearly a commercial venture from inception. An old burlesque house, the Phoenix Theatre on Twelfth Street and Second Avenue, was refurbished and renamed the Eden for the production, which boasted state-of-the-art lighting and scenic design. All jokes about saving money on the costume budget notwithstanding, *Oh! Calcutta!* exceeded $100,000 in production costs, making it the most expensive show in off-Broadway history when it opened (Bunce 1969: 10).

While it is unclear whether all the attempts to position *Oh! Calcutta!* as highbrow entertainment helped sell more tickets than did the simple promise of nudity, it does seem to have aided the audition process. Original cast member Boni Enten remembers insisting on auditioning for the show, despite the concerns of her agent:

> I had read about *Oh! Calcutta!* and I knew who Kenneth Tynan was. I called my agent and said, 'I want to audition'. He said, 'Are you, *crazy*?' And I said, 'No, I want to audition'. So he got me the audition. Jacques Levy, the director, had done experimental theatre in New York. And the list of people involved as writers? I *knew* those people! I just had a feeling that this was going to *be* something.
>
> (Enten 2005)

Tynan's interest in 'elevating' his show above the then-low status of burlesque is clear in the finished product, which featured only a single sketch – 'Was It Good for You Too?' credited to humorist Dan Greenburg – that was clearly rooted in the burlesque tradition (Barrett 1973: 35). This Masters and Johnson send-up featured a Marx brothers-inspired medical team documenting the mating habits of male and female volunteers as madness erupts in the laboratory. A vast majority of the sketches, however, attempted more deeply-layered musings about sexuality. Topics included swinging, fetishism, sexual tensions between spouses, the emotional and physical brutalities of the singles' scene and the generation gap.

For its risqué subject matter and the amount of controversy it generated in the press during rehearsal and preview periods, *Oh! Calcutta!* struck most critics as more quaint than progressive when it opened. Few critics registered any moral outrage in reviewing the show, although James Davis of the *Daily News* attacked it as 'hard core pornography' that was at once 'dull' and 'disgustingly clinical' (Davis 1969: 74), and Emily Genauer for the *Post* called it

> a bitter, mocking, outrageous [...] sick but powerful social statement offering [...] every obscene word and gesture imaginable, an endless catalogue of impersonal sexual transactions and bottomless contempt for the human psyche, for sensibility, for sex and for life itself.
>
> (Genauer 1969: 14)

Yet most of the critics agreed that the show was too self-congratulatory and schoolboyishly silly to be truly erotic, or even consistently entertaining. '*Oh! Calcutta!*

is likely to disappoint different people in different ways, but disappointment is the order of the right [*sic*]', Clive Barnes wrote for the *New York Times*. 'I think I can recommend the show with any vigor only to people who are extraordinarily underprivileged, either socially, sexually, or emotionally. Now is your time to stand up and be counted' (Barnes 1969: 33).

As it turned out, an awful lot of people were so underprivileged. Despite the reviews, the show ran to full houses at the Eden until February 1971, when it moved uptown to Broadway's Belasco Theatre for another year and a half. An even more successful revival opened at the Edison Theatre on 47th Street a mere four years later. Playing to houses so packed with tourists that programmes were eventually offered in nine different languages, this production ran for thirteen years before closing in August 1989 (Reif 1983: 20).

Oh! Calcutta! does seem enormously conservative, especially in retrospect. The sketches, all of which were written by white men and performed by an all-white cast, depict nothing but white, heterosexual, middle-class concerns. Race and class issues did not seem to have crossed Tynan's mind in creating the show, and he explicitly forbade any gay subject matter with the blunt explanation that 'there's been enough of that around' (Ward 2002). His homophobia extended to the casting process: according to original cast member Raina Barrett, men who were openly gay or too effeminate for Tynan's taste were automatically refused roles (Barrett 1973: 13). The sole mention of homosexuality in *Oh! Calcutta!* is in passing: a single derogatory aside of 'weirdo' (Rich 1989: C14). Quite a few sketches reflected Tynan's own sexual preoccupations, however. These included Victorian attire, sadomasochism and the debasement of women by whipping, gagging and imprisoning in hanging baskets or nets.

Despite their different authors, most of the sketches are built on traditional gender stereotypes. In one sketch – 'Will Answer All Sincere Replies' by screenwriters David Newman and Robert Benton – a young couple nervously prepares for a visit by a slightly older couple of experienced swingers. The young wife makes it abundantly clear that she is unhappy with the arrangement, which was her husband's idea. Midway through the sketch, the young man prematurely ejaculates while dancing with the older woman and, mortified, slinks off to change. He returns to find that his wife has enthusiastically joined the swingers' lovemaking; as the sketch ends, he stands by limply (literally and figuratively), newly filled with self-doubt.

The punchline of this sketch relies on the element of surprise that occurs when traditional stereotypes – men as socially active and sexually predatory; women as emotionally and sexually passive – are subverted. The assumptions made here are typical of just about every sketch in *Oh! Calcutta!* In scene after scene, female characters are rendered as erotic appendages to the men, unless a punchline relies on undermining conventional perceptions.

Salvation, Stag Movie *and the rise of gender activism*

Despite its lacklustre reviews, *Oh! Calcutta!* was a hit at the box office and thus paved the way for more adult musicals, which began to crop up off- and off-off-Broadway by the turn of the decade. One of the first, *Salvation*, appeared briefly at the Village Gate in concert form in spring 1969 before reopening in September for an open-ended commercial run at the Jan Hus Theatre. This revue had music by Peter Link and a book and lyrics by C. C. Courtney, who would pursue separate careers in the theatre and music industries once their second effort, the rock musical *Earl of Ruston* (1971), closed on Broadway after a mere five performances. *Salvation* was performed by a cast of eight accompanied by a seven-piece rock band called Nobody Else, and featured nineteen songs, all of which purported to critique organized religion and celebrate the various social and political messages embraced by the counterculture. The revue ran for 239 performances and spawned a top-40 hit, '(If You Let Me Make Love to You Then) Why Can't I Touch You?' recorded by *Hair* alumnus Ronnie Dyson (Whitburn 2000: 205).

Due in part to its sparse set and loose staging (The Jan Hus was in the cavernous basement of an Upper East Side church), *Salvation* was judged almost entirely on the merits of its score and talent, both of which struck critics as uniformly impressive. Despite the fact that its budget was smaller than those of both *Oh! Calcutta!* and *Hair*, comparisons to both shows were inevitable, since the revue touched on similar themes and espoused similar messages. Like its predecessors, however, *Salvation*'s countercultural posturing and left-leaning politics concealed morals that were ultimately rather conservative: at the end, the cast concludes that in 'the quest for inner peace, perhaps religion' – or at the very least, spiritual reflection – 'still has more to offer than the various drugs and assorted kicks so prominent in the contemporary scene' (O'Connor 1969: 18). Or, as an anonymous review in *Time* put it, '*Salvation* [...] trades on the residual puritanism behind its ostensibly anti-puritan outlook. A people at ease with sexuality, and casually and thoroughly iconoclastic, would not pay good money to see an inept affirmation of a puerile paganism' (Anon. 1969: 78).

Such sentiments apply to most post-*Oh! Calcutta!* adult musicals, often despite their creators' best intentions. Because these shows were often developed and produced by young adults – many of whom were involved in the off-off-Broadway scene – most were at once less opulent and self-consciously highbrow, and at least somewhat more political, than *Oh! Calcutta!* Many adult musicals, inspired directly or indirectly by gay liberation, attempted to include aspects of gay life; several also attempted to address women's issues in ways that *Oh! Calcutta!* did not. Yet despite attempts to move beyond *Oh! Calcutta!*'s conservatism, most adult musicals ultimately reflected the most stubbornly traditional of gender roles – and stereotypes – both on stage and behind the scenes.

A case in point is *Stag Movie* (1971), which opened at the Gate Theatre on Tenth Street and Second Avenue, a stone's throw from the Eden, where *Oh! Calcutta!* was playing to packed houses. Written by David Newburge, a playwright and lyricist who later turned to writing erotica, *Stag Movie* was a spoof meant to capitalize on current theatre trends. Producer Richard R. Lingeman acknowledged that *Stag Movie* would feature 'nudity, simulated sex acts [...] four-letter words and all the rest. Which means, ideally, we'll have it both ways' (Lingeman 1971: 14).

The plot of *Stag Movie* focuses on a group of out-of-work actors who decide to pool their resources and make a musical porn film based on the stag reel known as 'The Grocery Boy'. Shooting, which takes place in a seedy motel near Kennedy Airport, is repeatedly interrupted by aeroplane noise, the mafia, the police and an elderly maid who wants a part in the film. Musical numbers, which were never recorded, were composed by Jacques Urbont; they included 'Get Your Rocks off Rock', 'Try a Trio', the romantic duet 'We Came Together' and a wistful ballad titled 'I Want More Out of Life Than This', sung by the lead female character, played by a then-unknown Adrienne Barbeau:

> As I do the dishes I dream of a rapist
> Who'd force me to do his desire.
> He'd grip me, he'd strip me, he might even whip me,
> He'd set my whole body on fire.
> But my handsome husband has sexual equipment
> That hasn't been used since his bris!
> I want more out of life than this!
>
> (Newburge 2006b)

Unlike *Oh! Calcutta!*, *Stag Movie* featured gay and lesbian characters and, as the lyrics above imply, ponder the possibility of female sexual desire, if not in the most progressive of ways. Nevertheless, in part because of its reliance on gender stereotypes – especially that of the mincing, effeminate gay man – *Stag Movie* became the target of the Gay Liberation Front, an activist group of gay men and lesbians that formed shortly after the 1969 Stonewall riots.

In a move that seems laughably naive in retrospect, the producers of *Stag Movie* had invited the Gay Liberation Front (GLF) to a critics' preview on 2 January 1971, in hopes that the musical would catch on with a gay audience. Ensconced in the balcony, approximately 30 GLF members began heckling almost as soon as *Stag Movie* began; the group grew increasingly agitated by the reliance on gay stereotypes and objected to the fact that the lead female character was completely naked for most of the show, while the male characters appeared naked more infrequently (Anon. 1971a). Heavy use of the word 'faggot' throughout the show didn't help matters much (Newburge 2006a).

The hissing, booing and catcalls – including chants like 'Sexist pigs!', 'Dirty old men!' and 'Raise your level of consciousness!' – built to such a degree that the actors eventually stopped trying to recite their lines. Some cast members attempted to maintain order, while others joined the melee and began shouting at the protesters from the stage until the police arrived to remove the protestors and allow to the musical to continue (Anon. 1971a).

In his review, Barnes admitted that while such disruptions are generally disrespectful, this one was 'a welcome diversion from the seemingly endless tedium' of *Stag Movie*, which he called 'dispiriting', 'dismal' and 'as erotic as cold mulligatawny soup laced with frozen porridge' (Barnes 1971: 39). Despite a near-universal critical drubbing, *Stag Movie* ran for several months due to a break on the theatre rental arranged by the producer, and word-of-mouth about the protests (Anon. 1971b). Of course, the nude Adrienne Barbeau – whose ample 'mammary equipment' caused many a critic to interrupt his review mid-scathe in order to blather blushingly and with something approaching genuine awe – probably also helped keep *Stag Movie* running longer than it might have otherwise (Lewis 1971: n.pag.).

Gay liberation and The Faggot

Bad musicals often incite vitriol in the press, and in this respect *Stag Movie* is not atypical. Yet the fact that *Oh! Calcutta!* – with all its advance publicity and ultimately traditional take on sexuality – escaped much in the way of social criticism while a mere two years later a low-budget spoof stocked with tired stereotypes would be the target not only of contempt in the press but of virulent protest speaks in part to the increase in gender activism that occurred in New York City and across the country between the late 1960s and the early 1970s. After all, *Oh! Calcutta!* opened a mere two weeks before the Stonewall riots erupted in Greenwich Village, and only nine months after the women's liberation movement unofficially launched during an organized protest at the 1968 Miss America Pageant in Atlantic City.

While gay activism existed long before the Stonewall riots erupted on 28 June 1969, the 1970s movement benefited greatly from the ideologies and practices of the New Left on which it was based, and also on its trajectory (Valocchi 2001: 451). Whereas pre-Stonewall activism was relatively covert, the riots sparked 'an entirely new kind of gay organization advocating radical social change' (Heidenry 1997: 102–03).[4] For example, the Gay Liberation Front – which, for all the ideological problems that would cause its demise in 1972, would survive long enough to disrupt the preview of *Stag Movie* in 1971 – was formed within weeks of the riots by seasoned members of the New Left (Valocchi 2001: 455–56).

Post-Stonewall gay activism quickly found a place in New York's theatre fringe, in part because there had already been a burgeoning gay theatre established there, most notably at the Caffe Cino. Largely credited as the cradle of modern gay theatre, the Cino opened in late 1958 and by the mid 1960s had become an influential off-off-Broadway scene. Stephen Bottoms writes,

> The Cino initially developed as a venue in which young writers, directors, and actors [...] could exercise their skills. Many of these artists fully intended to seek careers in the mainstream [...] but in the meantime they discovered that the Cino was [...] so free of commercial concerns that they could try out anything, even if this meant casually breaking rules of form and content that were sacrosanct in the professional theater. Moreover, the fact that the Cino's regular staff and customers were largely (though certainly not exclusively) gay, made them outsiders of another sort in relation to mainstream culture: though sexuality was by no means a defining theme in the Cino's hugely diverse range of work, there was an underlying awareness of difference [...] that facilitated the celebratory abandon with which Cino writers embraced the bizarre, the ridiculous, and the taboo.
>
> (Bottoms 2004: 39)

The free-spirited atmosphere allowed for the cultivation of an impressive number of gay playwrights including Doric Wilson, Robert Patrick, H. M. Koutoukas and Lanford Wilson.

By the time the Cino closed in 1968, various like-minded off-off-Broadway troupes had formed. Many of these companies – for example the Judson Poets' Theatre and the Playhouse of the Ridiculous – were devoted to the exploration of contemporary sexuality in general, and queer sensibilities in particular. While the gay theatre that developed in the 1960s and gained momentum through the 1970s was not, for the most part, 'militantly or aggressively political', the increased focus on various aspects of gay culture worked both to subvert traditional stereotypes and to expand them 'to revel in self-parody, a gesture of defiance' which was in itself seen as a political act (Bigsby 1985: 416–17). It is perhaps unsurprising, then, that with the exception of *Stag Movie*, most post-*Oh! Calcutta!* adult musicals approached gay male characters with increased maturity and sensitivity. This is especially the case since many adult musicals were off-off-Broadway productions in the first place, with creative teams often comprising gay men who were at least tangentially connected to the gay liberation movement.

In 1973, for example, *The Faggot*, which opened at the Judson Poets' Theatre, was enough of a commercial and critical success to justify a move to the larger Truck and Warehouse Theatre for an extended run. Written, composed and directed by Al Carmines, *The Faggot* was praised in the mainstream press as a 'tribute to personal sexual liberation' that satirized 'the pressures placed on individuals to deny their orientation' in song and sketch (Bottoms 2004: 359). The revue purported to reflect the lives of various gays and lesbians – including prominent figures like Oscar Wilde, Gertrude Stein and Alice B. Toklas – from different time periods. Original cast member David Summers argued that *The Faggot* was groundbreaking simply because it recognized the fact that homosexuality existed: 'Al Carmines runs the gamut from closet queens and hustlers to open love relationships. There are positive and negative statements, all made without tears' (Gustavson 1973).

While a curious few questioned why the number 'Art Song' – in which Catherine the Great sang in praise of bestiality – belonged in a revue about gay life, some of the depictions in *The Faggot* drew ire among gay activists.[5] As Bottoms points out, Carmines' attempts to 'underline the wrongs of societal oppression by stressing the consequently seedy, secretive nature of some gay lives' was easily misinterpreted, and *The Faggot* thus generated hot debate about the distinction between politics and art and the overall message of the revue (Bottoms 2004: 359–60). Infuriated by what he saw as the reinforcement of gay stereotypes, Martin Duberman wrote in the *New York Times* that *The Faggot*

> pretends to [be] a kaleidoscopic view of gay life. It insists on treating issues with serious implications for millions of people – and does so in terms of tinkly tunes, perky choreography and cartoon realities. In the process, it trivializes everything it touches – gay love or loneliness, fearful secrecies and open struggles, privatism and politics, problems of age and youth, monogamy and promiscuity, jealousy and devotion [...]. Seeing it, you'd have no idea that gay life in 1973 is in any way different from what it had been in the '50s – except in the absence of all authentic emotion [...]. With friends like *The Faggot*, the gay movement needs no enemies.
>
> (Duberman 1973: 4)

Carmines' open response maintained that politics should not influence creative vision:

> although I agree with Mr. Duberman's political position regarding gay liberation, in the case of *The Faggot* he is not dealing with a political position paper, but rather

with a personal, idiosyncratic, quirky, highly subjective theater piece [...]. I do not believe politics is art and I believe a confusion of those two human activities is a dangerous and ultimately catastrophic misunderstanding [...] as a political entity, I am committed to gay liberation [...]. As an artist, I am committed only to the absolute human truth as I see it. And that truth is far more complicated than any party line, however noble, could ever be.

(Carmines 1973: D12)

As the debate continued in the press and among activists, *The Faggot* ran at the Truck and Warehouse for 203 performances. Doric Wilson, the playwright and founder of the gay theatre company TOSOS (The Other Side of Silence), acknowledges that, while not without its problems, *The Faggot* struck him as more liberating than the more overtly political gay theatre typical of the time. '*The Faggot* meandered here and there and was amateur and was meant to be', he remembers. 'But you came away [...] feeling deeply moved. And very proud that you were gay. And a little taller' (Bottoms 2004: 361).

Women's liberation and Mod Donna

Like gay liberation, the second wave of feminism had roots in the socio-political movements of the 1960s. While many feminists broke away from the New Left due to its perceived institutional sexism, the women's movement nevertheless embraced its emphasis on 'personal experience over tradition and abstract knowledge', especially since, many feminists argued, 'theory and historiography had been based on norms and values shaped by oppressive ideologies' that the movement had been formed to combat (Canning 1993: 530–31). Also like gay liberation, the women's movement, which gained momentum through the 1970s, had a symbolic kick-off late in the 1960s, when the New York Radical Women held an anti-Miss America Pageant protest on the Boardwalk in Atlantic City on 7 September 1968 (Bailey 2004: 110–11). Yet although the off-off-Broadway scene benefited from the hard work and dedication of many women, the second wave of feminism did not affect either the fringe or commercial theatre as quickly or to the same degree as did gay liberation.

There are several reasons for this. In the first place, off-off-Broadway preceded both social movements, and developed at a time during which men – regardless of sexual orientation – were expected to be leaders, while women – also regardless of sexual orientation – were relegated to supporting roles. Thus, as the gay and women's liberation movements began, the gender imbalance off-off-Broadway largely emulated that of the dominant culture. There were, of course, exceptions: Ellen Stewart's leadership of La MaMa; the output of playwrights like Rochelle Owens, Maria Irene Fornés, Megan Terry and Adrienne Kennedy; and the Judson Poets' resolution to seek out and produce plays by women. Yet through the 1960s, most troupes focused on work written, directed and produced by men – which was not hard, since this constituted the vast majority of theatrical output at the time, anyway – and thus reflected the same patriarchal mindset inherent in the New Left and the counterculture (Bottoms 2004: 120).

For all their moorings in the fringe, then, it is unsurprising that even counter-culture-era musicals viewed as particularly groundbreaking would ultimately view sexuality in traditional ways. Gender stereotypes perpetuated in *Oh! Calcutta!*, for example, exist in *Hair* as well, despite that musical's liberal bent and 'revolutionary' status. Bottoms describes one plotline:

> Claude's friend Berger [...] resolves that, before going to war, Claude will get to [...] sleep with Sheila, a member of the tribe who is in love with Berger. Sheila is thus placed under enormous pressure, as Berger tries to persuade her that it is her duty as a member of the free-love community, whether or not she is attracted to Claude [...]. Sheila finally submits to sex with Claude, and Claude – appetite sated – goes poignantly off to war. *Hair* thus staged a bizarre variant on the age-old patriarchal right of men to use and trade women as if they are property.
>
> (Bottoms 2004: 212)

To date, astoundingly little in the way of oral or reception history about *Hair* makes any mention whatsoever of its sexism. Yet *Hair* neatly, if inadvertently, sums up problems inherent in the counterculture and the New Left, and by extension much of the 1960s off-off-Broadway scene.

As the women's movement gained momentum, many activists set about forming companies dedicated to making theatre by, about and for women. Martha Boesing, founder of the Minneapolis theatre At the Foot of the Mountain, remembers that she and other activists

> walked in the Civil Rights and the peace movements, 'turned on and dropped out', lived in communes, and created theater events that flew in the face of the linear, rational thought processes of our culture and led our audiences hollering and singing into the streets [...]. Gradually we began to notice that we were still baking the bread, raising the children, and bringing coffee to the organizers of the institutions both inside and outside of the mainstream. So we rebelled.
>
> (Boesing 1996: 1012)

One of the first feminist theatre groups, the short-lived New Feminist Theatre (NFT), was founded in New York by National Organization for Women (NOW) activists Anselma Dell'Olio, Jaqui Ceballos and Myrna Lamb. Lamb would become the group's main playwright; their first performance, at a Redstockings benefit at Washington Square Church in March 1969, featured three of her plays: *But What Have You Done for Me Lately?*, *In the Shadow of the Crematorium* and *Scyklon Z*. The NFT organized a successful NOW benefit in May of the same year and presented new works on Monday nights at the Village Gate until internal differences led to the group's demise (Rea 1972: 80–81).

The early 1970s saw the establishment, in New York and across the country, of other women's theatre collectives including It's All Right to Be Woman Theatre and the Westbeth Playwrights' Feminist Collective. In 1972, a group of playwrights including Maria Irene Fornés, Megan Terry, Rochelle Owens and Adrienne Kennedy founded the Women's Theatre Council with the aim of encouraging the increased presence of women in all areas of the theatre (Bemis 1987: 2). These companies had varying agendas and philosophies, but most promoted social change, not only with plays by and about women but also through a collective or collaborative approach that encouraged communication, egalitarianism and shared experience.

Unfortunately, what many women's theatre companies also had in common was tremendous pressure – both interior and exterior – which led to difficulties in making an immediate impact on the theatre landscape at large. The painstakingly egalitarian, collaborative approach to theatre preferred by companies like It's All Right to Be Woman Theatre proved maddeningly slow in practice, yet companies that relied on traditional hierarchies often faced criticism from within and without for not trying harder to counteract patriarchal models (Boesing 1996: 1021). Many women's theatre groups collapsed by the 1980s for these and a host of other reasons, including inadequate funding, burnout and lack of professional experience (Bemis 1987: 3–4). If internal problems were not damaging enough to women's theatre collectives and the individuals behind them, external pressures often took an additional toll.

The off-off-Broadway movement was often lauded by critics for its freshness and creativity in lieu of healthy budgets and workable performance spaces. Yet when it came to women's theatre, a perceived lack of professionalism was more often met with gruff impatience by the predominantly male critical corps, which was not necessarily supportive of the women's movement, let alone women's theatre. While much about off-off-Broadway remained artistically influential and commercially viable in New York City through the 1970s, theatre with a strong feminist bent did not prove especially popular with critics or mainstream audiences.

The conservative strictures and mainstream appeal of the musical theatre made it especially resistant to feminist influence. Thus it is notable that one of the first overtly feminist pieces to appear in a commercial house was the musical *Mod*

Donna by NFT co-founder Myrna Lamb, with music by Susan Hulsman Bingham.[6] Produced and directed by Joe Papp at the Public in 1970, the piece critiqued the ways that men and especially women are culturally conditioned to use sex as a weapon in their power struggles. Despite the strong sexual content of *Mod Donna*, Papp chose to buck the trend and keep his actors clothed. 'I feel it would be wrong, here', he stated, when asked why the musical contained no nudity. 'There is the nakedness of the idea, instead, a stripping away of things that are usually left unsaid' (Bender 1970: 79).

Narrated by an all-female Greek chorus and accompanied by an all-female instrumental ensemble, *Donna* focuses on four characters: Jeff, a wealthy company man; his bored, manipulative wife, Chris; his resentful but toady employee, Charlie; and Charlie's sexually pliant wife, Donna. Early in Act 1, Jeff and Chris invite Donna to join their marital bed with the aim of improving their sex life; in return, Jeff will see to it that Charlie advances at the office. The set-up initially makes everyone happy, but then Chris and Jeff grow bored with their sexual plaything and decide to rekindle their marriage in Europe, alone. They attempt to pay Donna off and send her back to Charlie, but she has become pregnant and refuses to leave the wealthier couple's opulent home. In the end, Jeff and Chris depart abruptly, and a jealous Charlie murders Donna.

True to their traditional role, the Greek chorus informs the audience of Donna's murder and offers the moral of the story: until class and gender inequalities are resolved, and people stop manipulating one another sexually, the Donnas of the world will continue to die violent, senseless deaths. The chorus then reprises 'Liberation Song', a tonally murky, rhythmically jagged number that appears in varied form several times throughout the show:

> They tell us we are bound by grave and gravity
> Yet we must bear ourselves against the stone
> The tablets of a prophet of depravity
> The rock is fathergod oppressor grown
> Let them tell the fields to be fruitful for the nation
> Let us not be compliant earth to wilful seed
> Let us cast another god from our true vision
> Our true need.
>
> (Lamb 1970: 40)

As *Mod Donna* ends, the chorus faces the audience with fists raised, shouting for liberation.

Lamb remembers that *Mod Donna* resonated with audience members, if only because, as far as feminist theatre went, 'it was the only game in town!' (Lamb

2007). Indeed, at least one review describes 'wild cheering' during performances (Brukenfeld 1970: 53). And the show received some positive reviews in the press. Barnes argued that while artistically inconsistent, *Donna* was, politically speaking, 'one of the most pertinent and stimulating offerings' the Public Theatre had produced to date (Barnes 1970: 48). Although slightly more ambivalent, Dick Brukenfeld for the *Village Voice* noted his appreciation for the musical's anger, courage and wit (Brukenfeld 1970: 53). Yet a majority of reviews for what the press corps quickly labelled 'the women's lib musical' were resolutely negative, and critics frequently moved beyond the piece to mock feminism in general.

Papp obviously anticipated controversy. In his programme notes, which read curiously like a circuitous apology, he explained that *Donna* was not about feminism:

> Though Myrna Lamb [...] is an activist in women's liberation and an ardent feminist, her work is much too ambiguous, too sophisticated, too comedic to satisfy the clear-cut political sloganeering required by a mass movement. However, the play digs into the very core of the matter out of which has sprung the struggle for women's liberation – frustration [...] the thwarting and distorting of natural aspirations. The heart of *Mod Donna* is the heart of the male-female relationship in our society: the use of sex as the ultimate weapon, the final solution in the bedroom [...]. Having more options, the man finds alternatives outside the boudoir, while the wife [...] wields the knife of castration [...]. Lamb has brewed a bitter, bitter medicine which we offer to you [...] on a sugar-coated spoon. We hope it will not be too hard to swallow.
>
> (Papp 1970)

Nevertheless, many critics found *Mod Donna* – not to mention the movement Papp insisted it had nothing to do with – most unpalatable indeed.

In his review of *Mod Donna* for the *Post*, Jerry Tallmer lamented the fact that Lamb had not addressed 'the woman question' as effectively as Strindberg, Ibsen and Coward had, but noted that at least the lead female characters were attractive:

> Sharon Laughlin as Chris has a beautifully modeled face and a Mona Lisa smile, which helps [...] and April Shawhan as Donna is just a trifle flat as an actress though not indeed – well, Sisters, I'm not going to say it.
>
> (Tallmer 1970: 23)

Kerr for the *New York Times* begins his review by deriding feminism:

> I am glad to learn from Joseph Papp's program notes for *Mod Donna* [...] that the evening is not to be construed as a pro-feminist entertainment. I am glad because if

it *were* a feminist entertainment, anything I might have to say against it would be taken as male-oriented, biased, vengeful, nearsighted, thick-headed and disloyal to that half of the population which has been making so much noise lately and to which I have hitherto been so intensely devoted. I'm off the hook, right?

(Kerr 1970: 1)

Like Tallmer, Kerr finds solace in the attractiveness of the female cast members: 'Sharon Laughlin is cool enough to have been carved from cold cream, with faint wisps of hair brushing her ivory cheeks'; April Shawhan is 'a lovely thing to look at in her pink silk and pink breasts', even though 'she does an increasing amount of snarling' as the play progresses (Kerr 1970: 1–3).

Such comments are par for the course when it comes to the critical reception of *Mod Donna*. Taken as a whole, the clips about the musical make abundantly clear the fact that New York's theatre critics were overwhelmingly male, and generally mocking of the women's movement to boot. Just as telling, however, is the content of the few articles written by women about the musical. For instance, fashion writer Marylin Bender's interview with Lamb, Bingham and Papp for the *New York Times* focuses less on *Donna* than on Lamb and Bingham's personal lives, physical appearances and husbands' backgrounds (Bender 1970: 79).

The treatment of *Donna* in the press prompted several terse responses from activists, including writer Vivian Gornick – who, in the *Village Voice*, lamented the 'patronizing and unilluminating criticism' heaped on the musical (Gornick 1970: 47) – and NOW Vice President Lucy Komisar, whose letter to the *Times* lambasted Kerr's review. 'Lamb's lyrics are vibrant and memorable – and to feminists, they are poetry that represents what we feel in our guts', Komisar concluded. '[W]e are fiercely proud of her and of the contribution *Mod Donna* has made to the literature of our movement and to the cause of our liberation' (Komisar 1970: 28).

The negative reviews, combined with a budget crunch at the Public, led to a mere six-week run for *Mod Donna*, and a dearth of overtly feminist musicals off- or on Broadway for a good decade. Feminism would be reflected more regularly in the American theatre by the late 1970s and early 1980s, but it remained at an arm's length from the theatrical mainstream through most of the 1970s, even as the women's movement was at its peak.

The women's movement and media representation

What confuses matters is that while feminist theatre failed to click with critics or mainstream audiences through much of the 1970s, the sexual revolution reverberated rather strongly during this time. Even further, since the women's movement was influenced in part by the sexual revolution, the two tended to become conflated in the media and in the minds of many Americans. This is perhaps unsurprising: the second wave of feminism was an enormously influential, far-reaching, extraordinarily complicated movement that encompassed not only the personal and the political, but also the economic, legal, cultural, linguistic, sexual and social (Echols 1994: 158–59). Because the movement prompted so many questions for which there were so few quick answers, and accepted so many challenges for which there were so few easy solutions, it strongly influenced 'the ways Americans understood gender in this period', but at the same time caused an enormous amount of cultural anxiety, in part because 'its positions were not coherent enough to offer a firm foundation to sympathizers and were various enough to provide a multiplicity of targets for opponents' (Bailey 2004: 109). One result of the perceived vagueness of the women's movement, then, was a tendency within mainstream culture to react with defensiveness, mockery or sensationalism (Carroll 1990: 113).

Sexuality as related to the concept of liberation was particularly complicated. During the 1970s, women sought liberation from oppression by attempting to reject aspects of American culture that reduced women to their sexual merits and, at the same time, by embracing sex on their own terms. Meanwhile the media wasted no time in sexualizing the movement:

> Sex sells [...] and titillating images of bra-less women and sexual freedom made for livelier stories than statistics about women's wages and the lack of affordable childcare. The mainstream media – and often for reasons no more Machiavellian than a desire to attract viewers or readers – often treated women's liberation and sexual freedom interchangeably. But opponents of women's liberation also purposely conflated women's liberation with the sexual revolution to brand the women's movement as radical, immoral, and antifamily. [The] conflation of the women's movement with the sexual revolution [...] reached beyond the ranks of avowed antifeminists. Many who were [...] sympathetic to the claims of the women's movement found the sexual revolution troubling, and the conflation of movements made it easier for them to draw a line between 'reasonable' demands for decent wages and (as they saw it) the sex-obliterating role reversals and illegitimate intrusions into the 'private' spheres of home, marriage, and the family demanded by 'radical' women's libbers.
>
> (Bailey 2004: 116–17)

The resultant slew of mixed messages about feminism and its relationship to sexuality fuelled the confusion that was – and continues to be – played out in the cultural landscape at large.

Because adult musicals were strongly influenced by off-off-Broadway theatre, many creators attempted to infuse their works with appropriate social or political messages. Yet as noted above, when it came to gender issues, the fringe itself was not especially liberated by the time adult musicals appeared. As a result, messages about gay and especially female liberation tended to get lost amid the jiggle of naked bodies that was a selling point for adult musicals.

Let My People Come

A case in point is *Let My People Come: A Sexual Musical*, which enjoyed a successful run that began off-Broadway at the Village Gate in January 1973, and ended after an ill-advised move to Broadway's Morosco Theatre in 1976. Written and composed by Earl Wilson, Jr., who developed the show with producer and director Phil Oesterman, *Let My People Come* was a response to *Oh! Calcutta!*, which both men saw as distressingly out of touch. '*Oh! Calcutta!* was a dirty show', Wilson remembers. 'It was old. It was my parents' generation. It [made] you feel dirty when you [left] it' (Wilson 2005). Wilson and Oesterman decided to try and represent contemporary sexuality more honestly, while being as 'outrageous as the law will allow, and the cast will go along with' (Wilson 2005). Once Wilson and Oesterman came up with the general idea for their revue, they held auditions in search of young, multiracial, non-union actors who, Wilson felt, would come across as more innocent than seasoned professionals. Of course, non-union actors would also likely be more willing to perform naked and simulate sex acts on stage in exchange for equity cards. Casting the show was thus quite easy.

Let My People Come began its run at the Village Gate in January 1973. In a shrewd move, Oesterman refused to allow critics to see the show unless they paid for tickets themselves, and never announced an official opening. Word spread fast; enough critics griped in the press about the nudie show they'd been shut out of that *Let My People Come* soon became a hot ticket in New York and beyond. During its run, the musical spawned national and international tours, an original cast album and spin-off productions in cities including Amsterdam, London, Paris and Toronto, where it ran for a decade (Gussow 1974: 52).

In keeping with the off-off-Broadway ancestry of adult musicals, the songs and sketches from *Let My People Come* were written largely in response to conversations between the original cast and the creative team during intense encounter sessions. Wilson recalls,

> We had the auditions and we said, 'We don't really have a show. We have a couple songs, we have an idea, and we're going to write it around you guys. It'll be based

on what you think. I don't want you to say anything you don't believe, because that will come across. It has to be honest, or nobody's gonna come to the show'. We had five months of rehearsal, five nights a week. We had encounter sessions, where we would all talk. Then I would go home and write a song for somebody, because I knew what they sounded like.

(Wilson 2005)

As a result of this inclusive process – which stems from experimental theatre and has since been used to develop such 'collective' shows as the musical *A Chorus Line* (1975) – the songs and sketches in *Let My People Come* are more inclusive and reflective of a broader swath of contemporary sexuality than most adult musicals staged in New York during the decade. Songs like 'Take Me Home With You', 'I Believe My Body', the spoof 'The Cunnilingus Champion of Company C', and the title song celebrated various aspects of the sexual revolution. The song 'Dirty Words', which consisted almost entirely of 'taboo' sexual terms and euphemisms, was a direct homage to Lenny Bruce and an inadvertent tribute to *Hair* and its own 'taboo' number, 'Sodomy'. The revue poked fun at the mainstream popularity of pornographic films with the song 'Linda, Georgina, Marilyn and Me', in which a female singer eager to appear in adult films opined, 'What have they got I haven't got more of? What they can take two of, I can take four of' (Wilson 1974).

Unlike *Oh! Calcutta!*, which Tynan demanded be heterosexual in content and appeal, Oesterman insisted that *Let My People Come* reflect both gay and straight perspectives. Wilson acknowledges that, as a straight man, he was daunted by the challenge of coming up with gay content. The cast and creative team, however, included several gay actors (albeit no lesbians), and a gay music director, all of whom contributed ideas (Wilson 2005). The song 'I'm Gay', for example, was inspired by conversations Wilson had with some of the gay cast members.

Performed by two male actors who were fully clothed and seated, centre-stage, on stools facing the audience, 'I'm Gay' was written in the style of a 'coming out' letter to parents:

Dear mom and pop, I'm really happy
And not ashamed at all of what I am.
Those who don't know or think it's funny
Don't pay much attention to them.
[…]
I'm hoping that you'll come to see
This is how God meant me to be.
This is my way, and I'm proud to come right out and say I'm gay.

(Wilson 1974)

As the two men repeated the line 'I'm Gay' at the end of the song, they were joined by the rest of the cast. The number, according to original cast member and assistant choreographer Tobie Columbus, was one of the strongest in the show, often bringing the house down and spectators to tears (Columbus 2006).

To their credit, the all-male creative team of *Let My People Come* also devised several numbers purporting to represent women's perspectives. Yet these numbers seem to lean more in favour of titillation than honest representation. Take, for example, 'And She Loved Me', a number depicting a lesbian love affair. Because there were no lesbians in the cast with whom to confer, Wilson turned to media representations of lesbians on which to base this song. 'There was a scene in – was it *Killing of Sister George*? It was some movie of the time that had a lesbian scene in it', he recalls. 'I thought, "I'm going to use that as my example in my head". So I didn't talk to any lesbians or go through any of that' (Wilson 2005). Yet, as Karen Hollinger points out, lesbian characters have traditionally been depicted through a heterosexual and highly critical lens as 'sinister villains, victims of mental illness, cultural freaks, or pornographic sexual turn-ons for a male audience' (Hollinger 1998: 10).

The last applies to 'And She Loved Me', the lyrics and original staging of which reflect lesbians primarily as seen through the male gaze. The fact that the women begin and end their lovemaking by weeping in one another's arms, for example, is likely indicative of Wilson's reliance on mainstream depictions of lesbians for inspiration:

> And she loved me, oh
> Took me in her arms
> I softly cried
> Then she held me, oh
> Ran her fingers through my hair
> 'Til my tears had dried
> [...]
> Then she woke me, oh,
> Gently like a child
> And I softly sighed
> And I loved her, oh
> Took her in my arms
> And then we cried
>
> (Wilson 1974)

Columbus recalls that the song was sung by two fully-clothed women who flanked the stage, while two other women danced naked centre-stage under soft lighting to give the impression of lovemaking. In Columbus' view, the number was not intended to be crude or titillating, but, instead, impressionistic and 'quite beautiful' (Columbus 2006). Nevertheless, it is telling that the sole lesbian number was performed in the nude and depicted women weeping after experiencing forbidden love, while 'I'm Gay' featured two fully-clothed men who, upon proclaiming their sexuality, were joined in cheery solidarity by the rest of the cast. In short, 'And She Loved Me' emphasized sex while 'I'm Gay' emphasized the struggle for acceptance and respect.

The tendency to conflate feminism with the sexual revolution is demonstrated in the number 'Give It to Me', which Wilson wrote with a particular cast member in mind. Even in his recollections of this actress, Wilson associates the women's movement with free sexuality. 'We had a girl in the show who [...] was very sexually liberated, sort of a women's libber', he remembers:

> She had a certain look about her – dungaree jacket, open shirt, 'I'll take home anybody' kind of attitude. So I came up with 'Give It To Me', and she was terrific with it because she really believed it. She could pull it off.
>
> (Wilson 2005).

In 'Give It To Me', a woman voices her desire for a man who is terrific in and out of bed:

> I want a man who loves to fuck and can keep it up for days
> Who's clever and smart and can make me come in a thousand different ways
> I want a man who knows how to love and loves all that sex can be
> And when he's driving me out of my mind I wanna know he's fucking me
> Give it to me, give it to me, give it to me, give it to me,
> Give it to me hard and strong
> Give it to me, give it to me, give it to me, give it to me,
> Give it to me all night long
> There's too many candy-assed lily-livered soft-bellied boys parading as men
> Find me a man who's got some balls – I'll be happier then.
>
> (Wilson 1974)

In keeping with the theme of *Let My People Come*, this song purports to offer a woman's perspective on desire, and can thus certainly be read as empowering. Nevertheless, as the only number directly reflective of second-wave feminism, 'Give It to Me' can also be read to imply that for all their complaining, what women really want is a good, old-fashioned roll in the hay.

Perhaps the most problematic number from a feminist perspective is the first one that Wilson wrote for *Let My People Come*. Composed before casting began,

'Come in My Mouth' was originally performed by Tobie Columbus, who sat alone onstage in a red dress, crooning into a microphone while bathed in light from a single pin-spot. Whereas much of the content of *Let My People Come* was meant to be satirical – comparatively serious declarations of sexual freedom like 'I'm Gay' notwithstanding – 'Come in My Mouth' was intended to be overtly erotic (Columbus 2006). The song, and the way it was performed, thus borrows a great deal from the aural techniques common to the pornographic films that had become fashionable by the early 1970s.

In 'Come in My Mouth', the singer describes in graphic detail the fellatio she professes to have been waiting all day to perform on her partner. Accompanied by a mechanical ostinato and the same ethereal, synthesized noodlings typical of just about every porn film soundtrack ever composed, the singer lavishly praises her man, all the while asserting his dominance over her:

> Put your feet up on the sofa
> Stretch out baby, close your eyes
> Feel my fingers walking over the part of you I idolize
> [...]
> All day long I've been planning on how I was going to love you tonight
> So I could show you how I absolutely adore you. So you know I am your woman
> [...]
> Run your fingers through my hair as you force my mouth to open wide
> Don't you just love it there as I drink you deep inside?
> I can feel all your strength. What would you like me to do? I'll take you inch by inch –
>   just let me worship you.
>
>   (Wilson 1974)

The song ends as the keyboard fades out and the singer erupts in orgasmic moans.

The primal reaction of the female singer is typical of much hard-core porn. Whereas male arousal in pornography is visually obvious – and the 'money shot' thus fetishized as proof of satisfaction – the female orgasm is far more complicated to render visually. Thus, sound is often used to prove a woman's sexual pleasure in the absence of visual representation (Corbett and Kapsalis 1996: 103). The orgasmic moans the singer elicits at the end of 'Come in My Mouth' can only imply a money shot, not only because the song was performed by a woman, but because the revue it appeared in relied on simulated and not actual sex. Both the pleasure the singer experiences and the climax she causes her man are transmitted to spectators via her cries.

Columbus remains ambivalent about this number, which she never enjoyed performing:

> the song was supposed to be every man's fantasy. I mean, what's a man's fantasy, gay or straight? But, you know, I was brought up a nice Jewish girl, and this wasn't something I did! This was dirty! Now, I couldn't *say* that, because this was the swinging seventies and you were supposed to be enlightened. But that was a male fantasy, not a woman's fantasy! Everything else I did in the show – including the nudity – was more comfortable for me.
>
> (Columbus 2006)

Columbus' ambivalence mirrors that of other women who have spoken to me about their experiences in *Let My People Come*, almost all of whom recall feeling pressure to be more sexually liberated than they were comfortable with. Actress Joanne Baron remembers,

> I had a lot of psychological trouble with being naked [onstage]. I found it frightening, confusing – I remember having pressure to loosen up, to be open to other people sexually. Not in any kind of overly aggressive way, but the tone was, 'hey, you have a great body, you're real sexy, don't be so scared of your sexuality'. But I felt like a good girl who had chanced upon this more free lifestyle. It wasn't a perfect psychological fit.
>
> (Baron 2005)

Other women remember feeling pressured to appear naked onstage, whether or not they were entirely willing to do so, and sometimes despite 'nudity-optional' company policies. For example, an actress who appeared under the sole name Peachena refused to sign a contract to appear in *Let My People Come* unless it stipulated that she would not have to appear nude during the run. Even though such a contract was granted, she remains convinced that her abrupt dismissal from the show after her contract was up a year later was based solely on her refusal to disrobe and has never been given any reason to believe otherwise (Peachena 2006). Columbus remembers that, like Peachena,

> if I could have stood my ground and said, look, I don't wanna be nude, I think I probably would have, but I could never voice that […] because doing that would have been unhip and I knew that I was there to be nude. And I think I would have lost my job.
>
> (Columbus 2006)

These experiences point to the fact that while many women during the 1970s were attempting to reject traditional sexual values in favour of more control over their own bodies, the sexual revolution's emphasis on detached sexuality often resulted in widespread pressure for women to either conform to male standards or appear prudish and unliberated (Carroll 1990: 25).

For all the messages of inclusion and the interest in depicting sexuality honestly and openly, distinctions between sexual freedom and exploitation were often lost behind the scenes as well. While everyone interviewed for this project remembers that relationships within the companies were largely respectful, the turmoil of the times and the barrage of social messages that adult musicals were ostensibly promoting often proved confusing in other ways. For example, many of the performers interviewed recall ignoring the 'no sex' policies imposed on them by producers, some of whom broke them themselves. Original *Oh! Calcutta!* cast member Barrett writes that some fellow cast members violated the production's 'No Fuck Law' – (christened 'the NFL' by the cast) – within hours of the first rehearsal (Barrett 1973: 17).

Barrett also remembers that the sexual freedom her show celebrated did not extend to all parties: despite the company's purported disgust at Tynan's homophobia, one particularly private male actor was so regularly taunted, alienated and labelled a 'fag' by his fellow cast members that he left the production. Meanwhile, despite the homophobia that hung in the air backstage, some female cast members – Barrett included – were subject to exercises during which the male director had them touch and fondle one another and then talk with him about how they felt; these 'lesbian rehearsals' were apparently deemed necessary so that the cast members would appear at ease with one another onstage (Barrett 1973: 23–24, 84–85). Clearly, lesbian overtones were acceptable in Tynan's review because they fuelled male fantasies in ways that gay men did not.

The distinctions between liberation and exploitation seem to have been blurred not only by companies of adult musicals, but by audiences as well. Visitors to *Let My People Come*, for example, included, on the one hand, Betty Friedan – who told the press that the show was so affirmative about sex that she'd seen it twice and planned to bring her daughter (Anon. 1974) – and, on the other hand, Larry Flynt and Hugh Hefner – both of whom devoted space to the show in their magazines and invited several female cast members to pose as centrefolds (Columbus 2006). One anecdote that points especially acutely to the blurring of women's liberation and exploitation is told by actor Barry Pearl:

> Every night, at the beginning of the show, the actors would walk out and schmooze with the audience before the show began. Clothed. Got into a relationship with the patrons, put them at ease, because at the end of the show, now we're all naked, and we go down into the audience again in a receiving line, and as the audience leaves, we shake hands standing there, perfectly, totally naked. [But a while into the run] the

women remained on the lip of the stage, with some male cast members just sitting there naked, protecting them, because they'd gotten groped too many times through the course of the run. So they decided to have the ladies stay on the stage. Only men basically were in that receiving line.

(Pearl 2005)

Despite the widespread ambivalence, everyone interviewed noted that overall, they found their experiences in adult musicals liberating. 'Once you take your clothes off in front of people you can certainly do just about anything. And in that way, it really served me as an actor', Pearl argues (Pearl 2005). Boni Bryant, original cast member of *Oh! Calcutta!*, agrees:

For me, it was enlightening, liberating. I was 24, and I had not really been that open about sex, or a man's body, or even my own body. So this was a real educational, growth experience. And it was really fun, and it was in a safe environment.

(Bryant 2005)

Columbus remembers that her work in *Let My People Come* solidified her beliefs in 'sexually being who you are, and not judging anybody else's sexuality', a message she remains proud to have been able to convey to audiences (Columbus 2006). And despite her concerns about appearing naked onstage, Baron argues that overall, *Let My People Come* was 'a fantastic lot of fun, and a great creative experience, and I met wonderful people, so I can't say I regret it' (Baron 2005).

This prevalence of doublespeak – in which many of the actors look back on their experiences in adult musicals as simultaneously exhilarating and confusing, embarrassing and liberating, freeing and exploitative – implies that not even the young performers advocating increased sexual freedom onstage nightly for eight shows a week were entirely comfortable with the changing times, or the social movements they were representing. The ambivalence expressed by the cast members serves as a reminder that just as culture at large can be confusing and contradictory, so are social movements, especially those that end up meaning so many different things to so many different people.

Todd Gitlin points out that during the late 1960s, there were 'many more weekend dope-smokers than hard-core "heads"; many more readers of the *Oracle* than writers for it; many more co-habiters than orgiasts; many more turners-on than droppers-out' (Gitlin 1987: 214). The same may be said of the sexual revolution as interpreted by the enthusiastic yet ambivalent companies of adult musicals. Ambivalence may be, in the end, the healthiest reaction to a production that paid cast members to cheerfully simulate a wide variety of sex acts – while singing! – before audiences comprised of as many Larry Flynts as Betty Friedans.

The actors' ambivalence easily extends to the audiences of adult musicals, and even to the question of why these shows existed at all at a time when there was so much other sexually steeped entertainment available. Why adult musicals, when one could go to the local cinema for an 8 p.m. showing of *Deep Throat*? Why bother with a musical meditation on sexuality when you could just as easily see a live sex show, with actual – not simulated – sex, on the next block?

In his 1969 *New York Times* article about the trendiness of stage nudity, Kerr wondered, 'Why are we, in our new [...] freedoms on the stage so dreadfully, laboriously humorless? Why are we so serious about sex and why do we dislike it so much?' (Kerr 1969: 26B). Perhaps adult musicals helped ease the collective gloom that Kerr describes and, like *Hair*, permitted audiences to revel in the simple idea that naked bodies can be pleasant to look at and that sex can be fun. Just as adult musicals allowed actors to experience the sexual revolution and its offshoots in a relatively safe environment, they also allowed audience members to live vicariously without having to think too deeply. These shows, after all, espoused sex that was fun, light-hearted and consequence-free, but there was ultimately nothing transgressive about them. Pretty, innocent-looking young actors simulated sexual activity; the message of even the most risqué songs and sketches was that our bodies and urges are not such a big deal, after all; and the whole package was almost always offered in a comforting, age-old format: the musical revue.

Adult musicals thus allowed performers and audience members alike to feel a little bit dirty, a little bit liberated, without having to brave the seediness of a peepshow, on the one hand, or having to confront the more serious ramifications of the sexual revolution and its offshoot movements, on the other. This may help explain why comparatively serious musicals with social and political messages – like *Mod Donna* and *The Faggot* – have largely faded from memory, while shows like *Oh! Calcutta!* – the most conservative of all – not only enjoyed such long runs, but eventually influenced such upbeat, conventional confections as *The Full Monty* and *Naked Boys Singing*. One of the most damning adjectives critics hurled at the many adult musicals they panned during the 1970s was 'innocent', but it is possible that, deep down, they were as relieved to apply that word as they were indignant.

The sexual revolution, gay liberation and second-wave feminism were all enormously influential, complicated movements that meant different things to as many different people. During the 1970s, Americans began a mighty struggle over issues of sexuality and gender in ways they had not before, and it is no wonder that the result was often feelings of liberation on the one hand and confusion – even fear – on the other. In the end, adult musicals succeeded not so much in challenging notions about sexuality and gender as they did in offering cheerful, conventional messages to audiences who might have felt, more than anything else, comforted by the gesture.

ACKNOWLEDGEMENTS

I am grateful to Stephen Amico, Susan Tenneriello and two anonymous peer reviewers for their comments on previous drafts of this essay. I am also grateful to the many people who agreed to be interviewed; special thanks go to Mod Donna composer Susan Hulsman Bingham for her music, memories and insight.

NOTES

1. See for example Reif (1983), Rich (1989), Atkinson (1990), Bordman (2001) and Ward (2005).
2. Coined around 1960 in the *Village Voice*, the term 'off-off-Broadway' initially denoted plays or workshops staged in small spaces anywhere in Manhattan, for which actors received little or no pay. The term, however, quickly took on more ideological associations, especially since many off-off-Broadway practitioners had no desire to cross into more commercial realms. For further discussion of the term and its ideological associations, see Bottoms (2006) and Crespy (2003).
3. For details on the development and impact of *Hair*, see Horn (1991) and Wollman (2006).
4. For far more extensive information on twentieth-century gay activism than this essay allows, see Marcus (1992), Duberman (1993), Kaiser (1997) and Loughery (1998).
5. One writer who did question the presence of Catherine the Great was Duberman (1973).
6. Very few women had attained recognition for writing musicals in New York City by 1970, with the exception of Gretchen Ford and Nancy Cryer, whose first effort, *Now Is the Time for All Good Men*, ran off-Broadway at the Lortel Theatre in 1967. *Mod Donna* seems to be the first musical by women to tackle human sexuality as primary subject matter, at least in New York.

REFERENCES

Anon. (1969), 'The theater: New musicals – A guide to Modcom', *Time*, 3 October.

Anon. (1971a), 'Homo Libs Razz off-B'way *Movie*, get the bounce', *Variety*, 13 January.

Anon. (1971b), 'Off-B'way *Stag Movie* Keeps Going: Still a Public for Porno Legit?', *Variety*, 3 March.

Anon. (1974), 'Show in "Village" Defended by Two: Mrs Friedan and Toffler back sexual musical', *New York Times*, 24 December.

Atkinson, B. (1990), *Broadway* [revised edition], New York: Limelight.

Bailey, B. (1994), 'Sexual revolution(s)', in D. Farber (ed.), *The Sixties: From Memory to History*, Chapel Hill: University of North Carolina Press, pp. 235–61.

Bailey, B. (2004), 'She "Can Bring Home the Bacon": Negotiating gender in seventies America', in B. Bailey and D. Farber (eds), *America in the Seventies*, Lawrence: University Press of Kansas, pp. 107–128.

Banham, M. (ed.), (1995), *The Cambridge Guide to Theatre*, Cambridge: Cambridge University Press.

Barnes, C. (1969), 'Theater: *Oh, Calcutta!* a most innocent dirty show', *New York Times*, 18 June.

Barnes, C. (1970), 'The stage: *Mod Donna*', *New York Times*, 4 May.

Barnes, C. (1971), 'Stage: 71 is off to a lamentable start', *New York Times*, 4 January.

Baron, J. (2005), personal communication, 14 September.

Barrett, R. (1973), *First Your Money, Then Your Clothes: My Life and* Oh! Calcutta!, New York: Signet.

Bemis, S. M. (1987), 'The difficulties facing feminist theater: The survival of at the foot of the mountain', *North Dakota Journal of Speech and Theatre*, 1:1, pp. 1–6.

Bender, M. (1970), 'Women's liberation taking to the stage', *New York Times*, 26 March.

Bigsby, C. W. E. (1985), *A Critical Introduction to Twentieth-Century American Drama. III: Beyond Broadway*, New York and London: Cambridge University Press.

Boesing, M. (1996), 'Rushing headlong into the fire at the foot of the mountain', *Signs*, 21:4, pp. 1011–1023.

Bordman, G. (2001), *American Musical Theatre: A Chronicle*, 3rd ed., New York: Oxford University Press.

Bottoms, S. J. (2004), *Playing Underground: A Critical History of the 1960s Off-Off-Broadway Movement*, Ann Arbor: University of Michigan Press.

Brukenfeld, D. (1970), 'Off-Off-: *Mod Donna*', *Village Voice*, 7 May.

Bryant, B. (2005), personal communication, 3 July.

Bunce, A. (1969), 'Stage: Erotic and otherwise', *Christian Science Monitor*, 20 June.

Canning, C. (1993), 'Constructing experience: Theorizing a feminist theatre history', *Theatre Journal*, 45:4, December, pp. 529–540.

Carmines, A. (1973), 'Drama mailbag: Politics is not art', *New York Times*, 9 July.

Carroll, P. (1990), *It Seemed Like Nothing Happened: America in the 1970s*, New Jersey: Rutgers University Press.

Columbus, T. (2006), personal communication, 14 September.

Corbett, J. and Kapsalis, T. (1996), 'Aural sex: The female orgasm in popular sound', *The Drama Review*, 40:3, pp. 102–111.

Crespy, D. A. (2003), *Off-Off-Broadway Explosion: How Provocative Playwrights of the 1960s Ignited a New American Theater*, New York: Back Stage Books.

Davis, J. (1969), 'Stag show opens to the general public', *The Daily News*, 18 June.

Drutman, I. (1966), ' ... Was Peter Brook its brain?', *New York Times*, 9 January.

Duberman, M. (1973), 'The gay life: Cartoon vs. reality?', *New York Times*, 22 July.

Duberman, M. (1993), *Stonewall*, New York: Dutton.

Dunbar, E. (1969), 'Levy of *Oh! Calcutta!*: A dropout makes it as a sex revolutionary', *Look*, 26 August.

Echols, A. (1994), 'Nothing distant about it: Women's liberation and sixties radicalism', in D. Farber (ed.), *The Sixties: From Memory to History*, Chapel Hill: University of North Carolina Press, pp. 149–174.

Enten, B. (2005), personal communication, 3 July.

Genauer, E. (1969), 'Art and the artist', *New York Post*, 21 June.

Gitlin, T. (1987), *The Sixties: Years of Hope, Days of Rage*, Toronto and New York: Bantam Books.

Gornick, V. (1970), 'Who is fairest of them all?', *Village Voice*, 28 May.

Guernsey, O. L., Jr. (ed.) (1969), *The Best Plays of 1968–69*, New York: Dodd, Mead, Inc.

Gussow, M. (1974), 'Stage: More success than just blurbs – *Let My People Come*, a sexual musical', *New York Times*, 7 May.

Gustavson, T. (1973), *'The Author Speaks'*, clipping from unnamed publication, Billy Rose Theatre Collection, New York Public Library at Lincoln Center.

Heidenry, J. (1997), *What Wild Ecstasy: The Rise and Fall of the Sexual Revolution*, New York: Simon and Schuster.

Hollinger, K. (1998), 'Theorizing mainstream female spectatorship: The case of the popular lesbian film', *Cinema Journal*, 37:2, pp. 3–17.

Horn, B. L. (1991), *The Age of Hair: Evolution and Impact of Broadway's First Rock Musical*, Westport, Connecticut: Greenwood Press.

Kaiser, C. (1997), *The Gay Metropolis, 1940–1996*, Boston: Houghton Mifflin.

Karpel, C. (1969), '*Oh! Calcutta!*: No Penetration in Eden', *Village Voice*, 15 May.

Kauffmann, S. (1979), 'New York: The city and the theatre', *Theatre Quarterly*, 8:32, pp. 34–40.

Kerr, W. (1969), 'What can they do for an encore?', *New York Times*, 2 February.

Kerr, W. (1970), 'Is it true – Women hate women?', *New York Times*, 10 May.

Komisar, L. (1970), 'Drama Mailbag: Women are the victims', *New York Times*, 31 May.

Lamb, M. (1970), *'Mod Donna'*, *The International Socialist Review*, 31:5, pp. 18–40.

Lamb, M. (2007), personal communication, 24 January.

Lewis, E. (1971), '*Stag Movie* is just an ambling vignette', *The Record*, 4 January.

Lingeman, R. R. (1971), 'I was an angel for *Stag Movie*', *New York Times*, 14 February.

Loughery, J. (1998), *The Other Side of Silence: Men's Lives and Gay Identities – A Twentieth-Century History*, New York: Henry Holt.

Marcus, E. (1992), *Making History: The Struggle for Gay and Lesbian Equal Rights, 1945–1990*, New York: HarperCollins.

Newburge, D. (2006a), personal communication, 13 June.

Newburge, D. (2006b), personal communication, 13 July.

O'Connor, J. J. (1969), 'Old message put to music', *Wall Street Journal*, 25 September.

Papp, J. (dir.) (1970), 'An Audience Guide', programme notes to *Mod Donna*, original off-Broadway production.

Patrick, R. (2005), personal communication, 8 February.

Peachena (2006), personal communication, 21 February.

Pearl, B. (2005), personal communication, 6 July.

Rea, C. (1972), 'Women's theater groups', *The Drama Review*, 16:2, pp. 79–89.

Reif, R. (1983), 'A 14th birthday for Broadway's long-running nude musical: *Oh! Calcutta!*' *Playbill*, June, pp. 14–20.

Rich, F. (1989), 'The asterisks of *Oh! Calcutta!*', *New York Times*, 8 August.

Tallmer, J. (1969), 'Tynan: A show for the thinking Voyeur', *New York Post*, 9 April.

Tallmer, J. (1970), 'And now … women's lib', *New York Post*, 4 May.

Tynan, K. (1969), 'Pornography? And is that bad?', *New York Times*, 15 June.

Valocchi, S. (2001), 'Individual identities, collective identities, and organizational structure: The relationship of the political left and gay liberation in the United States', *Sociological Perspectives*, 44:4, pp. 445–467.

Ward, J. (2002), 'Come In My Mouth: The Story of the Adult Musicals of the '70's', http://www.furious.com/perfect/adultmusicals.html. Accessed 22 August 2022.

Whitburn, J. (2000), *The Billboard Book of Top 40 Hits*, 7th ed., New York: Billboard Books.

Wilson, E., Jr (1974), Let My People Come: *Original Cast Recording*, CD, Libra: LR 1069.

Wilson, E., Jr (2005), personal communication, 22 June.

Wollman, E. L. (2006), *The Theater Will Rock: A History of the Rock Musical, from* Hair *to* Hedwig, Ann Arbor: University of Michigan Press.

8

A Substitute for Love: The Performance of Sex in *Spring Awakening*

Bryan M. Vandevender

In *Words and Music,* his 1972 seminal text on the American musical libretto, Lehman Engel cites romance as one of the six primary needs of a musical, claiming that the lyrical nature of the form requires romantic love as a *modus operandi.* As he contends, 'It should be clear that – to date – no musical without principal romantic involvement has worked. Romance is the fuel that ignited the music and lyrics' (Engel 2006: 113). Musical theatre scholars tend to agree that the musical is underpinned by romantic love, and that the romance in question is traditionally typified by a heterosexual couple that meet, resist each other, fall in love, pull apart and then reunite by the musical's end. Love and romance function as essential narrative devices that drive plot, create dramatic tension, and perhaps most importantly, give characters a reason to sing. In a more recent study, *The American Musical and the Performance of Personal Identity,* Raymond Knapp maintains Engel's view of love's centrality:

> The American Musical has been most consistently successful when its stories and themes resolve through the formation of conventional romantic relationships […] the dramatic crux will lie not in the larger trajectory (which is probably given) but in the ways in which the [romantic] relationships between and among the principals are delineated in musical and dramatic terms.
>
> (Knapp 2006: 264)

As Engel suggests and Knapp supports, romantic love is indispensable to the musical's structure. Moreover, their strong regard for romance tacitly suggests that no musical can function without it. As an axiom, this thinking is somewhat restrictive and discounts the many musicals that have successfully eschewed love in favor of more social or political themes, such as *Chicago* (1975), *Working* (1978), *Floyd Collins* (1996) or *Caroline, Or Change* (2004). It might be more accurate to regard romance as an effective *convention* of the musical theatre – one that naturalized and took root over the course of the twentieth century. A musical without love and romance is certainly possible. While Engel and Knapp do not necessarily claim that love must subsume the entire libretto, they do contend that it should feature prominently.

Sex, on the other hand, is both distinct from love and decidedly less requisite. In Engel's estimation, sex lacks love's capacity for building and sustaining narrative. As he states, 'When you've had your orgasm, you've had it. Maybe you sometimes start again. But this is repetition and not development […] sex as a substitute for love can go nowhere' (Engel 2006: 114). Sex then curtails what romance encourages – room to grow and a reason for song. This belief, however, has not kept sex from finding its way onto the musical stage, especially in the years surrounding and following *Words and Music*'s publication. Products of the sexual revolution – which appeared around the same time that Engel was writing – such as *Hair* (1968), *Company* (1970) and *Pippin* (1972) join together with later shows like *Jelly's Last Jam* (1992), *Hello, Again* (1993) and *Rent* (1996) to form a cohort of musicals that have used song or dance – the musical's primary modes of expression – to discuss or depict sex acts. While sex is a notable feature of all of these musicals, it is not a narrative though-line. To varying degrees, their librettos are still built upon romantic relationships or notions of love. Sex is often confined to a single scene or select production numbers. Moreover, sex in these musicals generally occurs between consenting adults.

Sexuality has also been a feature of several popular musicals about adolescents, however, these representations have been infrequent and significantly more veiled. Shows like *Bye, Bye Birdie* (1960), *Grease* (1972) and *Hairspray* (2002) have set the hormones of their wily teenagers to music. These urges manifest on stage in wild dance numbers and wobbly knees; that is, as metaphors or hyperbole, and not in descriptions or depictions of sex acts. The adolescent characters use a lexicon of broad generalities and double-entendres that gesture toward sex, but fail to cite it directly. If characters actually engage in intercourse, they do so off-stage, their behavior later confirmed by tangible consequences, such as pregnancy or sung admissions of guilt.

Steven Sater and Duncan Sheik's *Spring Awakening* (2006) is the first musical to offer direct representations of adolescent sexuality. Adapted from Frank Wedekind's infamous play *Spring's Awakening* (1906), the musical takes place in a nineteenth-century German village where talk of sex is verboten. The cast is predominately comprised of adolescent characters who inhabit two distinctly different worlds: the real world of words, strictly governed by parental writ, and an alternate world of music and dance. Unlike traditional book musicals in which songs emerge through the plot and serve to advance it, *Spring Awakening*'s songs mark a break in narrative and create a second space. Its production numbers give the adolescents an opportunity to escape the adult world and its rules in order to comment on events, express their discontent, assert themselves as subjects, and most importantly, articulate their erotic desires. *Spring Awakening*'s songs are not about love, but rather lust and longing. Here sex functions as a substitute for love, replacing romance as both a central theme and a *modus operandi*. This essay examines the ways in which *Spring Awakening* uses both song and dance to represent teenage sexuality. Duncan Sheik's rock score, Bill T. Jones's erotic choreography and Steven Sater's explicit lyrics work synchronously to provide the young characters with an aural and visual vocabulary that allows them to sing and dance their sexual desire, and in effect, *perform* sex.

In *The History of Sexuality: Volume One*, Michel Foucault describes the culture of sexual reticence that typified the Victorian era: 'On the subject of sex, silence became the rule [...] an affirmation of nonexistence, and, by implication, an admission that there was nothing to say about such things, nothing to see, and nothing to know' (Foucault 1990: 3–4). This directive is underpinned by a fear that allowing individuals to speak of sex will actually deploy sex and make it material. The silence that Foucault describes pervades *Spring Awakening*'s real world and is made apparent in the musical's opening scene. Frau Bergman refuses to explain to her daughter Wendla how a woman conceives a child. When Wendla claims that she no longer believes in the fable of the stork, the mother exclaims, 'I honestly don't know what I've done to deserve this kind of talk', suggesting that she finds the discussion inappropriate, and does not want to contribute to it (Sater 2007: 16). After much deliberation and hand wringing, Frau Bergman curtly claims that babies are the product of a loving marriage. With this swift explanation she brings this – and assumedly all future – conversations on the subject of sex to an abrupt end, leaving Wendla to lament in song that her mother has given her 'no way to handle things' (Sater 2007: 15). However, as Foucault notes, the imperative of silence ultimately fails. Sex as an immutable feature of human existence must be articulated in language. Speaking of sex is then speaking a paradox: it is at once human, inevitable and an act of 'deliberate transgression' (Foucault 1990: 6).

Under Foucault's rubric, singing of sex (even in the musical's alternate world) would also qualify as transgression. Therefore, the cast of *Spring Awakening* requires a musical genre that is both subversive and sexual in nature, one that can challenge societal norms and communicate eroticism. As Elizabeth L. Wollman suggests, rock music is equipped to accomplish both tasks effectively. By her charge, rock 'was associated from its inception in the 1950s with rebellion, sexual desire, physical and emotional empowerment, and the celebration of youth' (Wollman 2006: 69). Joan Anderman claims that genre's central tenets or values can be both traced and attributed to the origin of its name: 'the word rock, meaning to disturb or incite, was combined with the word roll, a centuries-old metaphor for sex' (Anderman 2007: 1).

In giving the characters a means of expressing their sexual desires, rock music allows the cast of *Spring Awakening* to follow the central conceit of the musical theatre and sing what cannot be said in words. Rock critic Deena Weinstein suggests that singing rock, a musical form already imbued by sex, redirects erotic energies as *performance* and provides the singer with a cathartic climax that is akin to sexual climax. As she notes, 'the cathartic function of [rock] music channels energies, including the anger and frustration caused by an oppressive and unjust society, into harmless release' (Weinstein 1994: 8). Sex and performance conflate and take residence in the world of song. In his review of *Spring Awakening* for the *New York Times*, Charles Isherwood describes what happens on stage when this transaction occurs:

> When the band cranks up, the floodgates in their souls holding back their emerging libidos and damaged egos fall away. They leave their specific identities in the world of 19th-century Germany behind and romp and rail like punks in a mosh pit.
> (Isherwood 2007: 6)

Romping and railing are particularly telling descriptions for *Spring Awakening*'s choreography. What cannot be said or even sung can and is expressed in dance. As a means of expression, dance, based in the body, is inherently erotic. Dance and sex share the same instrument. As Judith Lynne Hanna has asserted, dance 'can mediate between sexual stimulus and response. A dance performance embodies the dancer – a human sexual being' (Hanna 1998: 13). Mercedes Ellington claims that this correlation between dance and sex is natural and derives from the most elemental of human instincts: 'Dance is erotic, because it echoes back to our primary objective as human beings, which is to procreate. Dance is an echo of tribal memories and primitive ways of trying to fulfill that sexual directive' (cited in Gener 2003: 33). Moreover, dance is a mode of expression that exists outside of language and words. Through dance, the characters in *Spring Awakening* can express their sexual desires without ever marking them in speech. Gillian Hanson contends that naturalistic representation, based in relating concepts or narratives through words, is ill-suited for depicting the darker desires such as violence and eroticism. As she contends, 'The theatre [of sex] has been forced back into gesture [...] the word describes how we feel, the gesture expresses what we feel'

(Hanson 1970: 133). Hanson suggests that movement is a more powerful and therefore more compelling form of communication that can circumvent if not exceed language. In *Spring Awakening*, however, choreography works in concert with the libretto and score, enriching the musical's aural elements with potent visual pictures.

The songs in *Spring Awakening* function in one of three ways: to lament the teens' subordination by the adult world, to reflect on past acts of transgression, or to perform deliberate acts of transgression vis-à-vis the articulation of sexual desire. This final category of songs, which includes 'The Bitch of Living', 'Touch Me' and 'The Word of Your Body', affords the character the opportunity to *perform* sex. Their lyrics contain direct references to erotic desires, fantasies, or pleasure. The songs and their staging describe sexual longing and imagine sexual acts, and through the modes of musical theatre, longing and imagination are outwardly performed. To be clear, I am not arguing that these songs underscore or highlight actual sex acts. Melchior and Wendla's scene in the hayloft marks *Spring Awakening*'s only explicit act of copulation. What I do contend is that words and gestures come together in these songs to offer characters a means of expression and catharsis, a release that cannot occur in the non-singing, everyday world. The numbers, an amalgam of song and dance, effectively stand in the place of sex acts, allowing the adolescents to explore and experiment away from the world of adults.

'The Bitch of Living', sung by the entire male ensemble, articulates the boys' fantasies and dreams – dreams that are decidedly wet. The song is set in a schoolroom, an unlikely location for its frank subject matter. However, once talk of a sexual nature begins, the lights shift and an electric guitar begins a pulsating three-note riff. Student Moritz Stiefel, who has been both haunted and titillated by dreams of 'legs in sky blue stocking, climbing over the lecture podium', is the first to leave the classroom and escape into the world of song (Sater 2007: 23). Moments earlier, when classmate and friend Melchior Gabor asks Moritz to describe the nightmare, the young man is awkward and terrified and struggles to find the correct words. In song, however, he is confident and articulate. He begins by describing the angel who visits him at night and suggests ways to deal with his physical and emotional vexation. As he recounts:

> She said: 'Give me that hand, please, and the itch you can't control.
> Let me teach you how to handle all the sadness in your soul.
> Oh, we'll work that silver magic, then we'll aim it at the wall'.
> She said: 'Love might make you blind, kid – but I wouldn't mind at all'.
>
> (Sater 2007: 23–24)

This particular lyric is redolent with masturbation imagery. 'Silver magic' (presumably a reference to semen) and 'love might make you blind' (a caveat to boys who masturbate too much) are the most transparent references.

As Moritz starts to sing this lyric, his classmates (except for Melchior, who is engrossed in the task of translating Latin verses) begin tapping their feet and pulsing their shoulders in time to the music before joining Moritz in the chorus:

> It's the bitch of living
> With nothing but your hand.
> Just the bitch of living
> As someone you can't stand [...]

(Sater 2007: 24)

They continue the metaphor, insinuating (and foreshadowing, in the case of Hanschen) that their libidinal urges have driven them to masturbate behind closed doors. There is a palpable urgency that drives this chorus, consistent with what Weinstein identifies as a major tenet of rock music: 'Hard rock is redolent with themes of getting one's pleasure now [...] pleasure is not of the world of the adult; at best society metes out small dollops of it in return for what Freud terms "unpleasure" (*unlust*)' (Weinstein 1994: 16). The *unpleasure* to which she refers describes unreleased sexual tension that is the product of arousal and excitation (Freud 1962: 75–76). Masturbating or living 'with nothing but your hand' is then a way of releasing such tension.

The choreography for this moment complements the music's racing pulse and heated cadence. As the chorus begins, all of the boys (save Melchior) turn 90° in their chairs and begin to stomp fiercely. Even as the second verse begins and Georg describes his dream of his piano teacher's breasts, they continue to pound the ground. Once the second chorus begins, stomping evolves into jumping and leaping. The students bound across the stage, mounting chairs and kicking the air. This movement vocabulary closely resembles Judith Lynne Hanna's analysis of Shaker ritual and sexual sublimation. She asserts that dance in fact 'prevents sexual behavior: the cathartic energy or orgasm of dance dampens consummation' (Hanna 1998: 72). As the dictates of the real world forbid the students from expressing their erotic desires in words or onstage acts, the students retreat to the alternate world, where they can attempt to dampen (or perhaps more correctly fuel their longings. As the bridge culminates in a long, erotically charged moan that suggests climax, they effectively masturbate through movement and music.

Between its early placement within the libretto and its use of the male ensemble exclusively, 'The Bitch of Living' shows that *Spring Awakening* privileges representations of male sexuality. The libretto depicts the adolescent boys as hyper-sexualized and ruled by their hormones. A few of them take on the more active role of sexual aggressor.[1] Nearly every discussion of sex occurs between Melchior and Mortiz. Nearly every sexual fantasy that is revealed belongs to one of their male classmates. Conversely, the girls of the company do not speak of sex nearly as much. Their discussions centre on their respective family lives or current crushes. In the first song that they sing as a group, the reprise of 'Mama Who Bore Me', they align themselves with Wendla and claim sexual ignorance. In their second song, 'The Dark I Know Well', Martha and Ilse describe the sexual abuse they have endured at the hands of adult men. Those girls who do engage in sex are either forced into the act or consent under duress.[2] While the rest of the songs analyzed in this study offer a more balanced representation of gendered sexuality, this disparity is worth noting.

'Touch Me' is the first of only a handful of songs involving the entire adolescent company. Despite the fact that the song begins as a private conversation between Melchior and Moritz, it quickly becomes an ensemble number articulating a collective desire. They all yearn to be touched in some manner. Ernst is the first to sing the chorus:

Touch Me – just like that.
And that – O, yeah – now, that's heaven. Now, that I like.
God, that's so nice.
Now lower down, where the figs lie [...]

(Sater 2007: 35)

The ensemble will repeat these lyrics several times throughout the song, the final phrase alternating between 'where the figs lie', 'where the sins lie' and 'where the wind sighs' (Sater 2007: 36–37). These images allude to genitalia, transgression and post-coitus.

The phrase 'touch me – just like that' is conjugated in active voice in the form of a command. The speaker is giving both permission and direction. Constructed this way, the phrase can be reformed to read as '[I want you to] touch me – just like that'. In giving voice to a specific desire, 'Touch Me' can be categorized as an 'I Want/I Need' song. Borrowing the term from Engel, Stacy Wolf has explained that this type of song defines character and establishes subjectivity through the articulation of desires. It generally appears early in the musical, is sung by a single character and communicates cardinal information about the character. While its placement later within the libretto and the fact that it uses the entire ensemble make 'Touch Me' a questionable candidate for this classification, the song's steady pace, rising arc and clear musical apex recall the function of this particular kind of production number. As Wolf describes, 'the number builds gradually verse by verse to become an "I will/I can" song' (Wolf 2008: 11). Every member of the ensemble sings the chorus in unison and in the first person. Many voices become a single voice, suggesting that both the characters' lyrics and their desires are aligned – at least for the duration of the song.

The movement vocabulary employed in 'Touch Me' is a choreographed phrase that repeats throughout the entire musical. Individual characters perform the gestures in other songs: Wendla introduces the movement in 'Mama Who Bore Me', and Melchior repeats it in both 'The Mirror Blue Night' and 'Totally Fucked'. Here the entire ensemble executes it together. The players begin by placing their hands over their eyes and slowly sliding them down their necks and past their sternum. Then they gently trace their bust-line with their palms, twist their wrists to face their palms upward and then cross their arms and embrace their torso. Pulling their hands down to their waist, the dancers slowly slide them to the small of the back and then down the side of the legs. The movements that follow are a variation on this theme, forming a lexicon of gentle touches and caresses. The movement then abruptly stops, the ensemble turns to face the audience, and the song swells in both volume and intensity. The ensemble sings two more choruses, the second of which reaches the musical equivalent of a critical mass. Raymond Knapp describes musical climax in operatic terms and notes, 'In Wagner, these moments, especially as shaped through their wavelike preparations, simulate simultaneous orgasm' (Knapp 2006: 303). The build and release in 'Touch Me', particularly in the song's final moments, come to resemble this orgasmic shape. After reaching a clear musical apex, the song slowly deflates into dénouement.

'The Word of Your Body' marks a significant moment in the musical's narrative not only in that it is the first scene between Melchior and Wendla, but also in that is the only scene in which the central couple sings together alone. This effectively makes the song *Spring Awakening*'s only love duet. However, the presence of a love duet at this particular moment is somewhat conspicuous as love is not a salient feature of the song. Following the climactic conclusion of 'Touch Me', Wendla and Melchior encounter each other in the forest. After exchanging some pleasantries, they begin to discuss the nature of charity. Wendla is the only adolescent character in the musical to engage Melchior in debate. As he is cerebral, ideas and rhetoric are what excite him intellectually, and as suggested by the song, sexually.

Throughout 'The Word of Your Body', Melchior and Wendla negotiate proximity, both spatially and melodically. They come together, make brief contact, quickly separate and timidly return. In this way, 'The Word of Your Body' functions as musical foreplay. What follows is tentative, tantalizing and teasing. The song begins with the couple sitting next to each other, squarely facing the audience. They begin by expressing a singular, private thought. Wendla sings, 'Just too unreal, all this. Watching the words fall from my lips' (Sater 2007: 39). As we have learned in the musical's opening moments, Wendla is ignorant of anything to do with sex. However, her lyric suggests that she is aware that something significant is happening in this moment. Melchior counters with, 'Baiting some girl – with hypotheses!' (Sater 2007: 39). His thought suggests amazement that his intellectual life has aroused his sexual life. In using the word 'baiting', he also admits a desire to *have* Wendla. Having sung their first lines separately, Wendla and Melchior make brief melodic contact with the lyric, 'Haven't you heard the word of my body?' (Sater 2007: 39). They sing the same melody, but begin 'Haven't you heard' in different octaves. They start separated, but then meet on the same notes in the same register for 'word of your body'. The second verse follows a similar structure of tentative call and response. As Raymond Knapp notes, 'in a conventional love duet, there is generally a period of negotiation before the couple sings together in perfect alignment, without which it is no true duet' (Kanpp 2006: 305).

Erotically charged movement enters the song with the start of the second verse. As the libretto directs, 'Melchior reaches, tentatively, takes Wendla's hand. They begin a private pas de deux' (Sater 2007: 39). From their seated position, Melchior uses the back of his hand to gently caress Wendla's arm. Wendla responds by raising her arm and slowly wrapping it around his. She sings the lyric 'Grasping at pearls with my fingertips' and their fingers graze each other once and then return for a second moment of contact (Sater 2007: 39). They clench hands as Melchior sings, 'Holding her hand like some little tease' (Sater 2007: 40). The pair then rise to a standing position and come together in harmony for 'Haven't you heard the word of my wanting?' (Sater 2007: 40). They turn to face the audience again, holding hands and sing the song's refrain in unison. This is the longest span of song in which the pair sings the same notes, albeit in different octaves, at the same time. They continue to face front until Melchior sings, 'Playing with her in your fantasies' (Sater 2007: 40). At this moment, he pulls Wendla close to him, wraps his arms around her torso, and clasps his hands just under her bust-line. They linger here for a moment and sing the song's refrain once more before working their way back to their original seated positions. The staging for 'The Word of Your Body' may appear simple, but its movements teem with eroticism. As choreographer Martha Clarke asserts, 'the less that is done, in a way, the more erotic the image becomes [...] the more possibilities are available for the viewer to discern' (cited in Gener 2003: 34).

Spring Awakening's direct depictions of adolescent sexuality end abruptly with Wendla and Melchior's liaison at the close of the musical's first act – a sex act that is actually performed on stage. The second half of the libretto addresses the consequences that arise from their tryst: her pregnancy and death, his banishment and contemplation of suicide. As critic Charles McNulty notes, 'The second half

[…] rushes by in a tragic blur that is moving more as a tableau than as a narrative' (McNulty 2008: 2). With the possible exception of Wendla's 'Whispering' and Hanschen and Otto's reprise of 'The Word of Your Body' – songs representing female and queer sexuality that are far more abbreviated than the male-centred or ensemble numbers of the first act – there is no further discussion, sung or otherwise, of sexual longing or activity. *Spring Awakening's* rapid dénouement would seem to lend some credence to Lehman Engel's argument against sex as a musical's organizing principal. The first musical to exchange a narrative organized around love for one concerning sex appears to lose momentum after reaching its narrative climax. However, what keeps the musical from ending in the hayloft is the notion of agency. Underscoring the libretto as a whole, agency functions as a concurrent theme along with sexuality. A significant portion of the musical's plot revolves around the concept of knowledge. The adult characters in *Spring Awakening* fervently monitor and regulate knowledge, particularly sexual knowledge. Their restrictive rules attempt to discourage free thinking and restrict free will. As knowledge generally begets agency, the adolescents' exploration of sexuality is arguably an attempt to become a free agent. Their inability to think for themselves or act freely is precisely what drives them to the world of song. Sex, supported by the notion of agency, effectively sustains *Spring Awakening*.

Since its opening on Broadway in December of 2006, *Spring Awakening* won critical accolades, legions of fans and numerous awards, including the 2007 Tony Award for Best Musical. It spawned both touring and international companies and recouped its entire financial investment before closing in January of 2009. *Spring Awakening*, a musical fueled by sex, found success and – to borrow language from Engel – worked. This landmark piece of musical theatre not only demonstrates that sex as a *modus operandi* is indeed possible but also suggests that Engel's claims against sex are worth reconsidering. While much of the musical theatre created over the past century has been wrought from collectively accepted conventions or assumed requirements, *Spring Awakening* reminds us that convention, like tastes and sensibilities, changes over time. Sometimes a substitution is needed.

NOTES

1. For example, Hanschen masturbates while imagining the murder of *Othello's* Desdemona. Furthermore, Melchior beats Wendla with a switch during their first encounter in the forest.
2. In Wedekind's play, Melchior takes Wendla against her will. In the musical, Wendla relents to Melchior, but only after his insisting. Ilse infers that sex is a common occurrence within the colony to which she has been banished; however, the playful romps that she describes are marked by a possibility of violence. She tells Mortiz of being chased, prodded with a paintbrush or being awakened with a gun against her breast (Sater 2007: 67).

REFERENCES

Anderman, Joan (2007), 'Sexual discovery in song, and as electric as a concert', *Boston Globe*, 10 June, sec. N, p. 1.

Engel, Lehman (2006), *Words With Music: Creating the Broadway Music Libretto* (rev. H. Kissel), New York: Applause Cinema and Theatre.

Foucault, Michel (1990), *The History of Sexuality – Volume I: An Introduction* (trans. R. Hurley), New York: Vintage Books.

Freud, Sigmund (1962), *Three Essays on the Theory of Sexuality* (trans. J. Strachey), New York: Basic Books.

Gener, Randy (2003), 'Body heat', *American Theatre* 20, pp. 32–35, 77.

Hanna, Judith Lynne (1998), *Dance, Sex and Gender: Signs of Identity, Dominance, Defiance and Desire*, Chicago: University of Chicago Press.

Hanson, Gillian (1970), *Original Skin: Nudity and Sex in Cinema and Theatre*, London: Tom Stacey Ltd.

Isherwood, Charles (2007), 'On this rock, build a future for musicals', *New York Times*, 24 June, sec. AR, p. 5.

Knapp, Raymond (2006), *The American Musical and the Performance of Personal Identity*, Princeton: Princeton University Press.

McNulty, Charles (2008), 'Harmonic hormones: *Spring Awakening* not only smells like teen spirit, it sounds and looks like it too', *Los Angeles Times*, 1 November, sec. E, p. 1.

Sater, Steven (2007), Spring Awakening: *A New Musical*, New York: Theatre Communications Group.

Weinstein, Deena (1994), 'Rock: Youth and its music', in S. Epstein Jonathan (ed.), *Adolescents and Their Music: If It's Too Loud, You're Too Old*, New York: Garland Publishers, pp. 3–23.

Wolf, Stacy (2008), 'Defying gravity: Queer conventions in the musical *Wicked*', *Theatre Journal*, 60:1, pp. 1–21.

Wollman, Elizabeth (2006), *The Theater Will Rock: A History of the Rock Musical from* Hair *to* Hedwig, Ann Arbor: University of Michigan Press.

9

If You Were Gay, That'd Be Okay: Marketing LGBTQ+ Musicals from *La Cage* to *The Prom*

Ryan Donovan

Introduction

The Tony Awards, Broadway's biggest chance to promote itself to a mass audience, opened its televised portion in 2011 with host Neil Patrick Harris cheekily singing that Broadway 'is not just for gays anymore'. Broadway, it would seem, was in on the joke about how *out of the closet* it now supposedly was, even while baldly disavowing its longstanding association with *homosexuals* by featuring a song on primetime network television hoping to sell *heterosexuals* on the merits of Broadway. That it did so through openly gay actor Harris underlines how Broadway often makes LGBTQ+ people complicit in practices that marginalize and downplay their own queerness. And the fact that the lyrics only mention gays – omitting all other factions of the queer community – shows how Broadway had not yet focused on including or representing LBTQ+ identities. Despite the increasing inclusion of LGBTQ+ representation, Broadway marketing alternately reveals ambivalence and discomfort with queerness, which in turn admits what producers *think* audiences will tolerate or accept. Broadway never *was* 'just for gays', and even productions with queer content or appeal have always needed to appeal to a range of ticket buyers just to sustain a run. Given that most Broadway shows fail to even return their investment let alone make a profit, selling tickets to Broadway musicals remains a high stakes endeavour.

Marketing Broadway musicals has evolved according to the technologies available for distribution; during and since the 1970s, this typically meant using a mixture of print ads, billboards, bus ads and television commercials, while internet and social media marketing have become prominent modes of the twenty-first century. Notably, Facebook and Instagram were founded in 2004 and 2010, respectively, and have since become major locales for Broadway marketing. Creating a recognizable brand solidifies a marketing strategy used across various platforms. A musical's visual identity, in images like the key art (or logo) used in advertising, and its appearances on awards shows and talk shows, shape its brand in the consciousness of the ticket-buying public. In this essay, I chart various ways that musicals with LGBTQ+ content marketed themselves to the public as well as outline the sociopolitical context of each musical's era. While it may seem that Broadway has been an unequivocally safe space for LGBTQ+ people (especially for cisgender white gay men), the marketing and promotion of musicals (often *by* cisgender white gay men) with LGBTQ+ content has been decidedly equivocal. Broadway profits from the queer representations within these musicals by being coy about their actual content with ticket buyers.

Broadway is the centre of US *commercial* theatre, a fact central to discussing musicals and their politics of representation. As musical theatre scholar Elizabeth L. Wollman notes, 'A tendency to downplay the very commercial trappings the industry relies on to survive has surely been carefully cultivated over the years' (Wollman 2020). Musicals are commercial products as well as artistic statements, and they need to develop a competitive brand to succeed in the market. Just like the theatre it sells, branding is its own kind of cultural performance, one constructed with specific audiences in mind; theatre scholar David Savran explains, 'the study of branding facilitates an analysis of consumer culture's unconscious, of the desires the commodity both arouses and tries to satisfy, the fears and anxieties it both instigates and tries to allay' (Savran 2012: 77). Producers brand Broadway musicals in order to reach *specific* audiences, which matters because advertising 'serve[s] as a model of normativity by which we Americans must measure ourselves' (Schulman 1998: 103). How musicals are marketed matters as much as to whom they are being sold: mainstream audiences. According to the Broadway League's data on the 2018–19 season, 65 per cent of Broadway ticket buyers were domestic and international tourists, 68 per cent of spectators were female, the average age was 42, nearly 75 per cent of the audience was white and a vast majority had completed college (The Broadway League 2021). The intersection of these data points reveals the typical mainstream Broadway spectator: a white, 40-something, educated, female tourist. In terms of accepting queer content, these points matter; the Pew Research Center reports that age, gender and level of education are three primary factors driving the public's acceptance of homosexuality. Generalizing from this data, the typical Broadway ticket buyer can thus be presumed to be more accepting than not (Poushter and Kent 2020).

Musicals have increasingly incorporated LGBTQ+ characters and themes since the 1970s; this inclusion parallels changes in social attitudes towards and the legal recognition of LGBTQ+ people. For example, the percentage of US Americans opposed to same-sex marriage and those in support of it swapped between just 2004 and 2019, with 60 per cent opposed in 2004 falling to just 31 per cent in 2019 (Pew Research Center 2019). Despite the social and legal advances, selling musicals with queer content continues to reveal the limits of normativity. How musicals with notable LGBTQ+ content market themselves serves as a cultural barometer for the social position of LGBTQ+ people; how producers *closet* this content in advertising demonstrates that the price of *inclusion* on Broadway is often *evasion*.

Musicals come out in the 1970s and 1980s

By the late 1960s and early 1970s, Broadway musicals were featuring gay characters in sometimes coded and sometimes overt supporting roles. Before *A Chorus Line* (1975) and its more honest depiction of gays began its fifteen-year long Broadway run, gay characters existed to support female stars like Katherine Hepburn in *Coco* (1969), Lauren Bacall in *Applause* (1970) and Debbie Reynolds in her revival of *Irene* (1973) (Kirle 2005: 161–200). These advances followed decades of what Wollman refers to as 'coded references to gay culture and sexually ambiguous characters' (2013: 49). The 1970s inaugurated the musical's 'coming out' era, with the increased presence of LGBTQ+ characters as subjects deemed worthy of representation onstage, though not in any advertising since gay content was still a tough sell. This was markedly different from prior eras when, as feminist musical theatre scholar Stacy Wolf describes, queer spectators had 'to determine how lesbians appear[ed] where none officially exist[ed]' (Wolf 2003: 4). But within the newfound representations of the 1970s, white gay male characters outweighed the number of all others under the LGBTQ+ umbrella – and still do as of this writing, which reflects who has historically been permitted to write and direct musicals, as well as the long-standing assumption that gay men are the musical's most devoted consumers. Savran points to the limited notion of who historically counted as queer when he notes that, 'the very category 'queer' in the commercial theatre designates as a rule plays by and/or about gay men' (Savran 2003: 63).

After earlier homophile movements like the Daughters of Bilitis and the Mattachine Society in the 1950s and 1960s, the 1970s gay liberation movement coalesced following the Stonewall riots of 1969. Gay characters in mainstream stage productions went from being simply comic relief or the butt of jokes to more fully fleshed-out characters, as exemplified by *A Chorus Line*'s Paul, whose storyline culminates in a remarkable acknowledgement of his humanity – a first for a

Broadway musical. *A Chorus Line*'s frank depiction of gay men was duly remarkable given that its antecedents like *Coco* and *Applause* presented gay men as little more than camp. Regardless of this kind of significant textual shift, the iconic photograph of the chorus line used in the show's logo gives no indication that homosexuality is one of the show's themes. To be fair, it would have been unusual to sell this or any show based on supporting roles.

It was not until *La Cage aux Folles* in 1983 that a Broadway musical centred gay male characters as its leads. *La Cage* opened during a deeply conservative time in the US: the rise of the religious right had propelled Ronald Reagan to the presidency in 1980, and the stigmatization of AIDS and the ensuing demonization of gay men swiftly curtailed gay liberation's advances. On its unlikely road to the Tony Award for Best Musical and a four-year Broadway run, *La Cage* was faulted by many heterosexual theatre critics for not going far enough in its depiction of gay men. Despite being written and directed by gay men (Jerry Herman's score coupled with Harvey Fierstein's libretto and Arthur Laurents' direction), the musical was received by some straight critics as not gay enough. *New York Times* critic Frank Rich refers to Georges and Albin as 'homogenized homosexuals' and calls the show 'the schmaltziest, most old-fashioned major musical Broadway has seen since *Annie*'. He cautions audiences not to 'go expecting an earthquake', noting that 'in its eagerness to please all comers, this musical is sometimes as shamelessly calculating as a candidate for public office' (Rich 1983). Arguably, the musical had to do this. Its creators worked first and foremost to create entertainment and sidestep contemporary gay politics along the way, and Harvey Fierstein's libretto cannily appropriated the traditional family values promulgated by conservatives in the early 1980s and put them in drag (Hart 2003: 9–10). The writers decided to focus the musical on family values to ensure the content would be palatable to mainstream audiences. If it faced a bind in how to depict gays onstage, it confronted another one offstage when producers had to figure out how to get straight audiences to see the show.

Given that it was 1983, *La Cage* had to navigate a complex set of circumstances when it came to selling a musical about homosexuals to a largely homophobic society. There simply weren't enough gay ticket buyers to sustain a long and profitable run, so the musical couldn't just be marketed to gays. The show's original key art evokes that of an earlier Jerry Herman musical, 1966s Tony Award-winning *Mame*, as both feature illustrations of a woman clad in red along the entire right side of the frame. Whether or not this similarity was intentional, it ties *La Cage* to Herman's oeuvre while deftly avoiding the musical's plot. The art gives no indication that the show's plot revolves around a gay couple and their son. Later in the run, the production deliberately misled audiences about its primary content when a newer version of its advertising featured a female Cagelle in the foreground and the secondary heterosexual ingénue couple in the background. The show's central couple, Georges and Albin, were nowhere to be seen.

This strategy of obfuscation set the precedent taken up by subsequent musicals and highlighted the challenge of selling a musical to mainstream audiences whose blazing anthem was, paradoxically, 'I Am What I Am'. *La Cage*'s vague or even misleading imagery lured audiences in with the *illusion* of heterosexuality (Figure 9.1). When awards season came around, producers sent mixed messages again through two different televised performances of its most unapologetically gay number, 'I Am What I Am'. At the Grammy Awards, understudy Walter Charles

FIGURE 9.1: This heteronormatively-framed advertisement for *La Cage aux Folles* celebrating original star Gene Barry's return to the production appeared in the *New York Times* on 12 January 1986.

performed the song in full drag, while at the Tony Awards, Broadway's drag-clad Albin, George Hearn, sang the number in a tuxedo. Was it despite or because of this ambivalence that *La Cage* became a long running hit and won the Tony Award for Best Musical? The choice to skirt its gay content was at once political and financial, as Herman explains,

> If we had written a stronger, tougher political message into the material, the *New York Times* might have loved us more. But that would have given our show too narrow an appeal and it would never have found the huge universal audience that it did.
>
> (Herman and Stasio 1996: 228)

La Cage shied away from the courage of its onstage convictions repeatedly in its marketing, effectively confining its homosexuality to the theatre rather than being open with the world. Closeting the show worked: it ran for over four years.

Musicals and the gay 90s

It would be nine years before another Broadway musical with gay protagonists opened. When *Falsettos* opened in 1992, AIDS was on its way to becoming the number one leading cause of death for adult men in the US (Centers for Disease Control 1993), making it extremely topical. It was the first Broadway musical to directly address the plague, as one of the main characters dies of AIDS. It was also about divorced parents trying to raise their son and navigate parenting as a gay man and a single mother. *Falsettos* initially struggled to attract audiences; the *New York Times* described it as 'not exactly an easy sell to theatergoers looking for an evening of fun' (Collins 1992: C13). The show's original key art featured an illustration of three figures shaking their fists at a big red heart by openly gay pop and graffiti artist Keith Haring, who had died of AIDS in 1990. To those 'in the know' who recognized Haring's distinctive visual style, this might have signified the show's gay content. To those unfamiliar with Haring, its significance would have been ambiguous at best and completely lost at worst. Haring's illustration, while striking, did not help sell tickets nor did it really give much away about *Falsettos*. Producers Barry and Fran Weissler went through four ad campaigns after the opening as they 'struggle[d] constantly to sell the show to the mainstream Broadway audience it need[ed] to survive', which proved difficult with the Haring image, since, as Mr Weissler put it, 'many people felt the drawing was meant to attract a gay audience' (Collins 1992: C13). After switching ad agencies, the production settled on selling the family aspect of the show – family values had not lost their sway in US society – and the production went on to earn a profit and embark on a national tour. The hitch with removing hints of homosexuality from the advertising is that it worked, which is the point and the problem.

The following year, another Broadway musical with a gay male leading role, *Kiss of the Spider Woman*, opened and went on to win the Tony Award for Best Musical. Its key art featured a drawing of the show's star, Chita Rivera, with a spiderweb superimposed over her face, continuing Broadway's practice of obscuring gay content in advertising. One might argue that this closeted approach to marketing made sense since Broadway legend Rivera was the show's major draw. Thus, Rivera's figure filled the key art and producers selected her big numbers for television appearances and awards shows. But this continued trend in obscured queer content seems more anchored in cultural mores of the time than anything else. Given that the US was in the midst of heated public debates about the place of gays and lesbians in society and their inclusion in institutions like the US military, Broadway musical producers strategically closeted their marketing, even as they continued to produce musicals with openly gay characters (and lesbians in the case of *Falsettos*). Gay was not yet exactly commodifiable, even if it was becoming increasingly profitable for Broadway musical producers.

In 1996, *Rent* made queerness a selling point and the show became the hottest ticket on Broadway. This musical re-setting of *La Boheme* in the East Village of the 1990s notably featured queer characters beyond only gay men. *Rent*'s key art features a series of photographs of the original cast, and it might lead one to think it's about a group of twenty somethings who like to wear costumes (and this wouldn't be entirely wrong). The poster shows Idina Menzel's bisexual performance artist Maureen in a latex cat suit and Daphne Rubin-Vega's stripper-drug addict reclined with her legs apart wearing fishnet stockings, leather knee-high boots, and little else. The bottom center photo in the show's original window card features Wilson Jermaine Heredia in a mini-dress and heels as Angel, the show's HIV+ drag queen. *Rent*'s successful branding helped it run twelve years on Broadway. According to Savran, 'the true genius of *Rent* [was] its marketing', which 'allowed the producers to sell the show less as a play [...] than as a kind of lifestyle philosophy' (2003: 43, 45). On the 1996 Tony Awards, the youthful cast performed a medley of 'Seasons of Love' and 'La Vie Boheme', offering primetime television viewers a fuller glimpse at the kinds of queer representation they could find onstage at Broadway's Nederlander Theatre. *Rent* used Broadway's biggest stage to shout out in their performance of 'La Vie Boheme', 'To faggots, lezzies, dykes, cross-dressers, too', an act which took courage in 1996. The sociopolitical background of this ballsy performance was the congressional debate over the Defense of Marriage Act (DOMA), which would be signed into law later that year and limit federal recognition of marriage to opposite sex spouses; the federal government's discrimination enshrined the stigmatization of being LGBTQ+. But *Rent* had a healthy enough advance and enough buzz to spend some of its cultural capital, which only increased after winning the Pulitzer Prize for drama, and own its queerness in ways previous musicals had not. To be sure, *Rent*'s presence in this sociopolitical context was complex: despite President Clinton's anti-gay actions in office like signing DOMA and barring gays and lesbians from serving openly in the military, he invited the cast to sing in support of his re-election at the 1996 Democratic National Convention in Chicago.

We're here, are we queer? The new millennium

Broadway's marketing of gay content shifted again in the wake of the mainstream success of properties like NBC's hit sitcom *Will and Grace* (1998–2006) and films like *Brokeback Mountain* (2005). Two Broadway musicals in 2003 depicted gay men who reached the peak of fame in the 1980s: *The Boy from Oz* was about Australian singer–songwriter Peter Allen and *Taboo* featured British singer–songwriter Boy George both in its cast and its narrative. Neither musical completely shied away from gay content in its marketing, but their approaches diverged, demonstrating how queerness could successfully be sold and how it couldn't. Both musicals opened to mixed reviews (and neither was received as particularly good), yet *The Boy from Oz* was a hit while *Taboo* flopped.

X-Men film star Hugh Jackman's global celebrity and public heterosexuality mitigated the risk of playing the openly gay, flamboyant Allen in *The Boy from Oz*. Allen's over-the-top costumes and his failed marriage to Liza Minnelli had cemented his status as a gay icon, and Jackman's Tony-winning performance helped turn the biographical musical into a hot ticket. Various iterations of the show's art picture Jackman dancing in white pants and tropical-patterned shirt, which despite their connotative queerness were somewhat tamer than many of Allen's actual looks. *The Boy from Oz*'s playful art contrasts with that of *Taboo*, which opened less than a month later. More than any other musical up to that point, *Taboo* explicitly advertised gay sexuality in its artwork, with one poster even featuring star/writer Boy George as Leigh Bowery cruising a men's room, replete with urinals in the background.

Taboo eked out 100 performances before closing, while *Oz* ran three times as long and only closed when Jackman proved irreplaceable after his contract expired. *Taboo* was Broadway superfan, former talk show host, and newly out lesbian Rosie O'Donnell's first big project after coming out. It marked her debut as a Broadway producer and she financed the reported $10 million budget herself. The combination of O'Donnell and Boy George made *Taboo* about as openly queer as Broadway could get in 2003, and it also made the show a target. In a post-mortem assessment of what went wrong, *New York Post* theatre columnist Michael Riedel notes the 'ill-conceived marketing campaign' (2004). While the show surely had flaws contributing to its short run, perhaps the biggest taboo it tackled was the frank acknowledgement of queer sexuality in it marketing.

Taboo's failure and the failure of its marketing to attract audiences likely made Broadway marketers and producers reticent to fully embrace queerness in advertising throughout the rest of the decade. *The Color Purple* opened on Broadway in 2005, two years after *Taboo*, and it fell back into familiar patterns of evasion in its marketing. This evasion was particularly disappointing given the fact that the show's eleven o'clock number takes place as its protagonist, Celie, stands center stage and sings 'I'm Here' after her female lover, Shug Avery, leaves her for a younger man. *The Color Purple* is based on Alice Walker's Pulitzer Prize winning 1982 novel, but perhaps known best by some because of Steven Spielberg's 1985 film, one which had almost wholly obscured the lesbianism in the novel. The marketing of the Broadway production illustrates a paradox of lesbian representation: increased visibility onstage increases closeting in marketing. As Broadway's first musical with a Black lesbian protagonist, the show contained the potential to appeal to marginalized communities largely excluded from representation onstage in musicals. Talk show host Oprah Winfrey starred in the film and became attached to the Broadway production as the above-the-title producer and her promotional efforts on behalf of the show paid dividends. The production wildly succeeded in bringing Black audiences to Broadway. According to Sanders, 'about 50 per cent of the audience' was Black, compared with 3.8 per cent of all Broadway audiences in the 2004–05 season overall (Associated Press 2006).

Following old trends, however, the marketing for neither the original production nor the 2015 revival of *The Color Purple* gave any indication of the musical's central lesbian love story, with the original production's key art being an illustration of the show's two sisters playing patty-cake. Producer Scott Sanders explained that this image was focus-group tested and that the decision was made 'to distill it to the two sisters, Celie and Nettie. Their story had the strongest emotional and spiritual connection with audiences' (Hodges 2016: 116). Producers sold the musical using the tagline 'The Musical About Love', and although 'the love that dare not speak its name' was one of several kinds of love depicted in the show, it remained obscured in its marketing and publicity. When the original cast performed on *The View* for host Rosie O'Donnell's birthday, the show's original female stars La Chanze and Elizabeth Withers sang the Sapphic love duet 'What About Love?'. Performing for out lesbian O'Donnell's birthday, absent any narrative context indicating why these women are singing this song to each other, is another way *The Color Purple* hides its lesbianism in plain sight, leading viewers to wonder 'are they or aren't they' (jimmysappletv1 2011).

Selling out in the 2010s

Drag became a selling point in the 2010s, alongside the increasing popularity of VH1's competition program *RuPaul's Drag Race*. The 2010 revival of *La Cage* starring Kelsey Grammer and *Priscilla Queen of the Desert* (2011) show Broadway's approach to selling drag: lean in. *Priscilla* initially used an image drawn from its source film in its logo, one of a bus with an enormous high heel on top of it. This alternated with a picture of its stars draped in a feather boa and the name 'Bette Midler', its celebrity producer, prominently placed. It unabashedly relied on drag to sell itself and in the meantime owned its identity in a way that most musicals discussed here had not. The shifting cultural and legislative place of gays came through in choices in marketing. By the dawn of 2011, Congress had repealed Don't Ask, Don't Tell, marking a major victory against state-sanctioned discrimination and advancement toward greater mainstream acceptance. By then using high-profile celebrities to sell musicals with LGBTQ+ content had become commonplace, whether they were producers (Midler and Winfrey) or writers (Boy George and Cyndi Lauper) or heterosexual actors (Grammer). That so many of these (often straight) celebrities were already publicly associated to one degree or another with LGBTQ+ communities was yet another measure of increased social acceptance.

Starting in 2013, *Kinky Boots* would invert Broadway's usual relationship with marketing queer content. Its plot centres on a failing British shoe factory brought back to solvency by a Black drag queen named Lola, who popularizes the show's titular boots. *Kinky Boots* and its marketing are complicated by the fact that it relied upon drag tropes that read as gay even though its librettist Fierstein insisted, 'No one's gay in this!' (Signorile 2013). *Kinky Boots* commodified queerness to sell a musical in which it was simultaneously present and absent. Fierstein has never been one to back away from writing gay characters, so we must take him at his word regarding his intention. Yet *Kinky Boots* relies so much upon drag, an art form inextricably bound to gay and trans identities and performance traditions, that it capitalized on this association in its marketing and even promoted itself in conjunction with Gay Pride. The Broadway cast regularly performed at Pride festivals, and its social media profiles especially pushed this connection: a 2019 Instagram post features an image of the show's signature boot in the rainbow colours of the pride flag along with the message 'Everybody Say PRIDE!' (kinkybootsbway 2019).

On 26 June 2015, when the US Supreme Court decision in *Obergefell* v. *Hodges* granted same-sex couples the right to marry, Broadway helped celebrate. Onstage at *Kinky Boots*, star Billy Porter (who had been an out gay man in the industry since the 1990s) acknowledged the momentous occasion in a post-show speech given at the request of the show's producers. He connected the musical's message of self-acceptance to the newfound social and legal gains of gay equality in the age of Obama, saying 'you can change the world when you change your mind' (*Kinky Boots* on Broadway 2015). The production's official social media accounts shared this message with its followers. By this time, Broadway and the US had changed to the degree that queerness *without* queers could marketably exist in narratives, even while the musical was written by, directed by, and starred gay men. Was this progress or was it having it both ways? Like marriage equality, it represented both incorporation into the mainstream and an assertion that difference matters. *Kinky Boots*, with its not quite queer queerness, ultimately ran on Broadway for 2507 performances.

And then came *Fun Home*. In 2015, *Fun Home* broke new ground on Broadway, both in terms of form and content, but when it came to marketing, producers seemed to rely on older practices of obfuscation as they continued in the tradition of selling the show's family (read: 'universal') aspects rather than anything that would highlight the LGBTQ+ themes. *Fun Home* centres on the cartoonist Alison Bechdel's reckoning with her father's death as it presents her growing consciousness of her own lesbian identity alongside the realization that her father was a closeted gay man whose struggles with his own sexuality led the family to the brink of collapse. Gender studies scholar Maureen McDonnell argues that *Fun Home*'s marketers 'imagined that being forthright about the production's contents and its masculine lesbian protagonist would threaten the show's entertainment and economic potential' (McDonnell 2019). The producers decided to hide the show's content and its protagonist. The social status of LGBTQ+ people may have changed, but branding Broadway musicals still relied on the same old tactics of evasion.

Fun Home's producers note, 'The uptown hunch was *Fun Home*, however brilliant, could never work on Broadway'. They explain the predicament they found themselves in: 'Most Broadway show art represents what you'll experience at the show. Because *Fun Home* was unlike anything else on Broadway, this demand felt particularly oppressive […]. So you know? Don't explain' (Hodges 2016: 212). Along with design agency SpotCo, the producers settled on the idea of selling the show's acclaim through pull-quotes from reviews and listing the awards it had racked up Off-Broadway. Though the producers never articulate exactly *what* was so oppressive about representing *Fun Home*, they made it clear that the decision to avoid representing the show's queer content was deliberate – and apparently this decision worked, as *Fun Home* won the Tony Award for Best Musical, ran for over a year on tourist-sales-reliant Broadway, and went on a financially successful national tour, which recouped its investment in just seven months (Gans 2017). A prime example of Broadway's queerness hiding in plain sight, the strategy for *Fun Home*'s television commercial was to display itself as an award-winning musical about family (*Fun Home* on Broadway 2016). The ad's voiceover universalizes the very specific family experience portrayed in *Fun Home*: 'Welcome to a musical about a family that's nothing like yours. And exactly like yours'. The 30-second spot features Bechdel's cartoons interspersed throughout and Beth Malone as Alison drawing the scenes that then come to life on screen. It features the cast in moments from the show that emphasize the centrality of family, giving no indication that the show deals with sexuality and queer identity at all (Matilla 2016).

Yet like some of the other musicals addressed here, when the producers of *Fun Home* had to choose what number to perform on the Tony Awards telecast, they leaned into the show's queerness by choosing 'Ring of Keys' for the performance. This song dramatizes the moment when Young Alison spots an older butch lesbian and experiences a profound self-realization, making a stronger statement about visibility than had been seen in any of its marketing. Although the show's print ads and commercials had eschewed queerness, on Broadway's biggest night *Fun Home* used queer recognition (albeit edited for television) as its selling point. Perhaps unlike previous productions, *Fun Home*'s publicity team overtly changed its marketing tactics in response to larger cultural and political events affecting LGBTQ+ communities, namely the marriage equality decision and the 2016 Pulse mass shooting. McDonnell explains in her exploration of *Fun Home*'s branding that the production eventually took a contradictory 'two-pronged approach' that relied on universalizing the family story while also framing 'the production as politically engaged' and culturally significant, especially within gay and lesbian publications (McDonnell 2019).

What previously published accounts of *Fun Home*'s marketing glaringly omit is its social media presence, which was quite different than its traditional marketing because of social media's ability to selectively target specific demographics of potential ticket buyers as well as speak directly to the show's fans. Online, *Fun Home* was more open about its lesbian content, with the production's official YouTube page featuring excerpts of Malone's speech given on the night that marriage equality became the law (*Fun Home* on Broadway 2015). One of the first associations of queerness on *Fun Home*'s Instagram is a video of lesbian Broadway star Cherry Jones calling the show 'a landmark production' (funhomemusical 2015). *Fun Home* appeared most comfortable being out on Instagram, where multiple posts featured notable (to those in the know) lesbians like comic Lea DeLaria and activist Edie Windsor at the show's opening night. Once it was clear the Supreme Court was headed for a decision on marriage, *Fun Home*'s Instagram

FIGURE 9.2: Unlike its print campaign, *Fun Home*'s social media connected the show's message to queer-linked contemporary events, as seen in this Instagram post on the day the US Supreme Court made equal marriage the law. Image from *Fun Home*'s Instagram account, 26 June 2015, USA.

account posted a series of photos with the cast holding placards saying #lovemustwin. On the day that the marriage equality decision came down, the production shared an image with the words 'Equal justice under law' superimposed on the musical's key art (funhomemusical 2015) (Figure 9.2).

Six months after *Fun Home* won the Tony Awards for Best Musical, Score and Book, *The Color Purple* returned to Broadway in December 2015, arguably to a new world as far as LGBTQ+ rights were concerned. *The Color Purple*'s revival nonetheless sold itself by sidestepping the shows lesbian content and instead using an ad campaign featuring its three stars: Cynthia Erivo, Jennifer Hudson and Danielle Brooks. Could it have marketed and represented itself more fully in the age of Obama post-marriage equality? Perhaps, but like other musicals it reserved being out for digital spaces like Instagram rather than in its traditional marketing materials like newspaper ads and television commercials. *The Color Purple* revival contributed to what writer Sarah Schulman describes as the process by which 'lesbians, who have spent lifetimes translating subtext and innuendo in order to have the normative pleasure experience of seeing themselves represented' learn to see themselves in the void (1998: 117). Celie may have been 'here' onstage, but she wasn't fully present in the show's advertisements.[1] While drag musicals pushed queerness in their marketing, the two musicals with lesbian protagonists remained evasive about that fact except in digital spaces.

By the time 2018 saw *The Prom* opening on Broadway, the United States had undergone major shifts in public opinion toward LGBTQ+ people. A fuller range of gender and sexual identities was becoming more common on stage in musicals like *Head Over Heels* and on the small screen in shows like *Orange Is the New Black*. *The Prom* tells the story of a teenage girl who wants to bring her girlfriend to the prom, the homophobia that ensues, and the Broadway stars who swoop in to save the day and the dance. *The Prom* was typically more open about its content and its message in much of its marketing and television appearances than the other musicals with lesbian protagonists discussed above. In some cases, the musical's message was the selling point; one poster and ad for the production reads, 'BIG BROADWAY STARS. A SMALL TOWN. AND A LOVE THAT UNITES THEM ALL', above a picture of the young butch/femme lesbian couple dressed for the prom, holding hands raised in triumph (The Road Company website 2020). Even the show's merchandise was *out* – you could buy a t-shirt at the theatre reading, 'WE'RE ALL LESBIANS' (*The Prom* website 2020). Before the show opened, the Longacre Theatre festooned its façade with posters illustrating handmade protest signs blending queer activism and inside-Broadway jokes for passersby, including 'It's OK to love Guys and Dolls' and 'Annie Get Your Girl', among others (McBride 2018).

The Prom, however, used different approaches for different platforms, and this sometimes unfortunately closeted the musical. While on television appearances like the Macy's Thanksgiving Day Parade and the Tony Awards, the cast often performed the show's finale, 'It's Time to Dance', which features a kiss between the young girlfriends at their prom. This kiss was the first televised same-gender kiss in the history of the Macy's broadcast. Alongside this newfound openness, the production's online commercials took a different but all too familiar approach. One ad begins by calling the show 'the best-reviewed Broadway musical of the season', while another features superlative pull-quotes from newspaper critics (ispot.tv 2020). Given that *The Prom* opened in 2018, its marketing spread across too many digital and traditional channels to detail here, but in many ways *The Prom* and its marketing demonstrate both the culmination of and continuation of Broadway's relationship with marketing and closeting queer content. Sometimes it plays coy, sometimes it is outright evasive, and other times it sings out proudly. The major change that *The Prom* brought was that in much of its marketing, it *was* fully open with ticket buyers about what they were going to see, which makes its occasional obfuscation all the more surprising.

Yet even with the marked difference in public opinions towards LGBTQ+ issues, the newfound visibility in these Broadway musicals appears to place them in a double bind: risk alienating some ticket buyers by being up front about their content or hide it to sell more tickets. This bind means national tours of musicals like *Fun Home* and *The Prom* rely on Broadway itself as a brand to help sell tickets, i.e., 'Broadway's award-winning hit musical comes to Denver!' But the choice is no longer binary given the multiple marketing channels increasingly available to producers, who can run different campaigns based on which platform they are using as well as which demographics are targeted, i.e., a print ad in the *New York Times* sends a different, inherently constrained message than a musical's Facebook page can. Thus, marketing *Fun Home* in 2015 meant using tools that did not exist when *La Cage aux Folles* ran in the 1980s. Despite the paradoxes of their marketing, many of the musicals discussed here include revelatory representations in a form that Wolf has described as historically sending the message that 'heterosexuality is both natural and mandatory and that women should know their place' (2003: 9). The inherent tension between a musical's content, message, and its marketing is increased when they are in opposition with each other.

Conclusion

The deliberate disavowal of the queerness in the musicals discussed here is a strategic kind of closeting justified by fears that audiences are so conflictedly homophobic that they won't purposefully buy tickets to a queer musical but that they will enjoy it if they unwittingly do so. Marketing musicals is not trivial, because even as musicals themselves have evolved and become more inclusive of whose identities are deemed worthy subjects of representation, erasing this in marketing is a bait-and-switch not just on unaware or unsuspecting spectators but on the communities represented. It is less the case that LGBTQ+ people desire to see ourselves represented in advertising, than we demand to not be purposefully erased in it. Wolf explains, 'The dominance of heterosexuality in the musical is neither natural nor inevitable. On the contrary, it's a choice that conforms to most representations, a choice that producers likely don't even see as a choice – hence the power of dominant ideology' (Wolf 2003: 31). Due to homophobia and stigma, producers and marketers often feel they have no choice but to disavow queer content even as they depend on it. Ethnographer D. Soyini Madison exhorts us to remember, 'Representation has consequences: how people are represented is how they are treated' (Madison 2012: 4); the absence of queerness in marketing speaks volumes.

Broadway's ambivalence in its marketing is one way in which the queerest art form produced in the US exhibits the insidiousness of homophobia, as producers and marketers continuously adhere to perceived, but outdated, views of a society increasingly accepting of LGBTQ+ people. How ignorant do they think audiences are? The gap between social acceptance and Broadway marketing tells audiences and producers alike much about the commercial realities of Broadway. Broadway's Tony-winning R-rated *Sesame Street* sendup *Avenue Q* (2003) made denial part of its brand, with one of its posters reading 'I am NOT a closeted HOMOWHATEVER!' (broadwayposters.com n.d.). A puppet from *Avenue Q* could make this joke, but the joke is actually on the institution of Broadway itself. Why hide at all, if Broadway's closet is ultimately transparent. As gay cultural theorist D. A. Miller explains, 'the fact the secret is always known – and, in some obscure sense, known to be known – never interferes with the incessant activity of keeping it' (Miller 1998: 206). The paradox of queer visibility persists. Despite the strides made in representation, truth in advertising does not jibe with lying by omission. The fact that Broadway musicals with queer content are not always open in their branding and marketing admits uncomfortable truths about the status of LGBTQ+ stories and people, as well as how those truths have changed and how they perhaps have not.

Though the visibility of queer people has steadily increased since the 1970s, this alone has not been enough to destroy the closet. The practices of closeting musicals (of all cultural products!) in order to sell them to mainstream audiences indicates the amount of work that still needs to be done to liberate society – including Broadway producers – from homophobia, transphobia and misogyny. Closeting in marketing projects a sense of internalized oppression from an industry largely run by gay white men behind the scenes; this closeting sends the message that LGBTQ+ people are less worthy than straights. Broadway musicals may have come out onstage, but their marketing is still negotiating the closet.

ACKNOWLEDGEMENTS
The author originally shared an early version of this essay at Song, Stage and Screen XI in New York in 2016. The author thanks Sierra Gamble, Maia Gersten, Isaac Grivett, Samantha Levine and Emily McNally for their research assistance.

NOTE

1. The revival's marketing team by and large avoided sharing social media posts that addressed anything beyond marketing the musical itself, although it did post a picture of star Cynthia Erivo singing 'I'm Here' on June 26, 2016 with the caption, 'You're beautiful and you're here! Happy #Pride Day from #TheColorPurple family! #lovewins' (bwaycolorpurple 2016). Earlier that month, the production shared a production video on Instagram of Erivo and Heather Headley singing 'What About Love?' that made clear they were singing to and about each other.

REFERENCES

Associated Press (2006), '*Color Purple* drawing diverse crowds', *Today*, 6 June, https://www.today.com/popculture/color-purple-drawing-diverse-crowds-wbna13170487. Accessed 4 August 2020.

The Broadway League (2021), 'Research reports', https://www.broadwayleague.com/research/research-reports/. Accessed 28 June 2021.

broadwayposters.com (n.d.), '*Avenue Q* (Closeted)', https://broadwayposters.com/triton/posters/aveqcloseted.htm. Accessed 1 July 2020.

bwaycolorpurple (2016), Instagram post, 26 June, https://www.instagram.com/p/BHIhFhlgx/. Accessed 1 July 2020.

Centers for Disease Control (CDC) (1993), 'Update: Mortality attributable to HIV infection among persons aged 25–44 years – United States, 1991 and 1992', *Morbidity and Mortality Weekly Report*, 42:45, pp. 869–72, https://www.cdc.gov/mmwr/preview/mmwrhtml/00022174.htm#:~:text=During%20the%201980s%2C%20human%20immunodeficiency,men%20aged%2025%2D44%20years. Accessed 25 June 2020.

Collins, Glenn (1992), 'The many faces and facets of keeping *Falsettos* afloat', *New York Times*, 26 November, p. C13.

Fun Home on Broadway (2015), '*FUN HOME* – First performance after marriage equality ruling – June 26, 2015', YouTube, https://www.youtube.com/watch?v=mDyjv1uFvoE. Accessed 2 July 2020.

Fun Home on Broadway (2016), 'WELCOME to fun home on Broadway (commercial)', YouTube, https://www.youtube.com/watch?v=acqUs2AfPoc. Accessed 29 June 2020.

funhomemusical (2015), Instagram post, 26 February, https://www.instagram.com/p/zk4LzBlSRl/. Accessed 1 July 2020.

funhomemusical (2015), Instagram post, 26 June, https://www.instagram.com/p/4ZS66zFSR5/. Accessed 1 July 2020.

Gans, Andrew (2017), 'National tour of *Fun Home* recoups investment', *Playbill*, May 17, https://www.playbill.com/article/national-tour-of-fun-home-recoups-investment. Accessed 4 August 2020.

Hart, Norman (2003), 'The selling of *La Cage aux Folles*: How audiences were helped to read Broadway's first gay musical', *Theatre History Studies*, 23, pp. 5–24.

Herman, Jerry and Stasio, Marilyn (1996), *Showtune*, New York: Donald I. Fine Books.

Hodges, Drew (2016), *On Broadway: From* Rent *to* Revolution, New York: Rizzoli.

iSpot.tv, 'The Prom Musical TV commercial, The Best-Reviewed Broadway Musical of the Season', https://www.ispot.tv/ad/dUHr/the-prom-musical-the-best-reviewed-broadway-musical-of-the-season. Accessed 29 June 2020.

jimmysappletv1 (2011), 'What about love', YouTube, https://www.youtube.com/watch?v=yDl8BUreX1s. Accessed 26 June 2020.

kinkybootsbway (2019), Instagram post, 27 June, https://www.instagram.com/p/BzOFEyBH24C/. Accessed 26 June 2020.

Kinky Boots on Broadway (2015), '*KINKY BOOTS*: Marriage equality curtain call speech', YouTube, https://www.youtube.com/watch?v=cbBqq1JdHU. Accessed 26 June 2020.

Kirle, Bruce (2005), *Unfinished Show Business: Broadway Musicals as Works-in-Process*, Carbondale: Southern Illinois University Press.

Madison, D. Soyini (2012), *Critical Ethnography: Method, Ethics, and Performance*, Los Angeles: SAGE.

Matilla, Kalle Oskari (2016), 'Selling queerness: The curious case of *Fun Home*', *The Atlantic*, 25 April, https://www.theatlantic.com/entertainment/archive/2016/04/branding-queerness-the-curious-case-of-fun-home/479532/. Accessed 26 June 2020.

McBride, Walter (2018), '*The Prom*' – Theatre Marquee, Walter McBride Photography, n.d., https://www.waltermcbridephotography.com/gallery/The-Prom-Theatre-Marquee/G0000wmrPuuIRqfM. Accessed 13 April 2022.

McDonnell, Maureen (2019), 'Branding Bechdel's *Fun Home*: Activism and the advertising of a "Lesbian Suicide Musical"', *The Journal of American Drama and Theatre*, 31:2, https://jadtjournal.org/2019/01/28/branding-bechdels-fun-home-activism-and-the-advertising-of-a-lesbian-suicide-musical/. Accessed 26 June 2020.

Miller, D. A. (1988), *The Novel and the Police*, Berkeley: University of California Press.

Pew Research Center (2019), 'Attitudes on same-sex marriage', May 14, https://www.pewforum.org/fact-sheet/changing-attitudes-on-gay-marriage/. Accessed 29 June 2020.

Pushter, Jacob and Nicholas Kent, 'The global divide on homosexuality persists', *Pew Research Center*, 25 June, 2020, https://www.pewresearch.org/global/2020/06/25/global-divide-on-homosexuality-persists/. Accessed 24 August 2020.

The Prom (n.d.), 'Shop', http://theprommusicalshop.com/. Accessed 29 June 2020.

Rich, Frank (1983), '*La Cage aux Folles*, review', *New York Times*, 22 August 1983.

Riedel, Michael (2004), '*Taboo* postmortem; What & who went wrong', *New York Post*, 16 January, https://nypost.com/2004/01/16/taboo-postmortem-what-who-went-wrong/. Accessed 26 June 2020.

The Road Company (2020), '*The Prom*', https://theroadcompany.com/shows/prom.php. Accessed 29 June 2020.

Savran, David (2003), *A Queer Sort of Materialism: Recontextualizing American Theater*, Ann Arbor: University of Michigan Press.

Savran, David (2012), 'Branding the revolution: *Hair* redux', in L. D. Nielsen and P. Ybarra (eds), *Neoliberalism and Global Theatres*, London: Palgrave Macmillan, pp. 65–78.

Schulman, Sarah (1998), *Stage Struck: Theater, AIDS, and the Marketing of Gay American*, Durham: Duke University Press.

Signorile, Michaelangelo (2013), 'Harvey Fierstein on *Kinky Boots*, working with Cyndi Lauper and his show's big surprise', *Huffington Post*, 17 May (updated 2 February 2016), http://www.huffingtonpost.com/2013/05/17/harvey-fierstein-kinky-bootsn3292504.html. Accessed 26 June 2020.

Wolf, Stacy (2003), *A Problem Like Maria: Gender and Sexuality in the American Musical*, Ann Arbor: University of Michigan Press.

Wollman, Elizabeth L. (2013), *Hard Times: The Adult Musical in 1970s New York City*, New York: Oxford University Press.

Wollman, Elizabeth L. (2020), 'How to dismantle a [theatric] bomb: Broadway flops, Broadway money, and musical theater historiography', *Arts*, 9:2, 66, https://doi.org/10.3390/arts9020066. Accessed 24 June 2020.

PART 3

DIVAS DON'T CARE ABOUT NOBODY'S RULES

10

Embracing Excess: The Queer Feminist Power of Musical Theatre Diva Roles

Michelle Dvoskin

As act two of the 2002 Broadway hit *Hairspray* opens, most of the female characters are behind bars performing a song about their arrest and imprisonment entitled 'The Big Dollhouse'. At the end of the number, the chorus sings that 'The big dollhouse ain't big enough for me / for me / for me'; Edna Turnblad then steps forward, parts the bars centre stage, and belts out 'For me!'(O'Donnell et al. 2002: 83). Any audience member with even a passing familiarity with mid-century musical theatre will recognize the direct citation of one of the most famous moments in *Gypsy* (1959), when Rose, at the end of 'Rose's Turn', belts out 'This time for me / for me / for me / for me!'. Certainly, when thinking about 'living large and feeling big' in musical theatre, one of the first things that may spring to mind is the figure of a diva like Rose (or perhaps Edna). Scholars like Stacy Wolf (2002), John Clum (1999), D. A. Miller (1998) and others have noted that these larger-than-life female characters at the centre of many classic Broadway musicals can help encourage queer and/or feminist readings within the commercial, typically heteronormative genre of musical theatre that often textually reinforces gender norms. In this essay, I examine three musicals that focus on the world of popular entertainment – *Gypsy*, *Hairspray* and *Memphis* (2009) – in order to argue for an important distinction between *diva roles* and *diva characters*. By *diva roles*, I mean larger-than-life female characters who drive a musical's action and encourage a virtuosic, outsized performance style. *Diva characters*, on the other hand, are textually marked as divas in that they are performers, but they do not necessarily incorporate the productive, joyous excess of a diva role. Diva roles (whether or not they are also diva characters) are productive sites for queer feminist cultural critique, as their excess – their largeness – breaks the bounds of normative femininity and can allow audiences to glimpse it as a construction, rather than a 'natural' state. Diva characters who are *not* diva roles, on the other hand, can end up reinforcing troublesome normative ideas about gender and sexuality.

In arguing that diva roles function as queer feminist cultural critiques, it is important to clarify my terminology, as all three terms – queer, feminist and diva – have multiple, contested meanings. When I use the term queer, I am drawing on Michael Warner's work, with queer signifying 'resistance to the regimes of the normal', and finding its definition 'against the normal rather than the heterosexual' (1993: xxvi). While sexuality is important, it is not the only element: queer is about difference, about challenging normativity in a range of fields. By feminist, I mean interested in gender as a primary category of analysis, (1) a recognition that the binary gender system regulates and limits everyone; (2) an awareness that those identified as female are at a structural disadvantage; (3) a commitment to the idea that 1 and 2 are problems that should be addressed. Both feminism and queer theory, then, encompass similar issues. Feminism is more focused, however, and work that is queer – even queer work that significantly challenges heteronormativity – can be decidedly un-feminist. The two can also overlap in highly productive ways; when considered together they can help us see how systems of subordination (like heteronormativity and the gender binary) interact and support one another.

There is no precise definition for 'diva'; as Alexander Doty notes, 'There are many ways to be a diva – and many ways to understand divadom' (2008: 2–3). There are two main components to what makes a diva: one, a female performer, often a vocalist, with an excess of talent and ambition (and often attitude as well); the other, an outsized, starring performance by a performer marked as female. Within the context of a narrative performance, the first describes a diva character; the second, in the proper context, is a diva role.[1]

In general, diva roles are central female characters who sing loudly, take up space (both narratively and physically) and demand attention. Susan Leonardi and Rebecca Pope describe the diva as 'larger than life [...]. Chameleon, protean, vampiric, dramatic, regal, seductive, powerful, manipulative, ambitious, generous, life-enhancing, life-altering, extravagant' (1996: 10).

The multiplicity of this list of adjectives emphasizes the excess embedded in the notion of the diva, as well as the difficulty in defining her. They also point out that the very magnificence of the diva separates her from normativity in ways that are not necessarily socially acceptable, as 'to speak of the diva as gloriously extraordinary is a polite way of acknowledging that she is something of a freak' (1996: 45). While the concept derives from opera, the diva is also a key figure in musical theatre. Stacy Wolf notes that classic mid twentieth-century American musical theatre, while arguably 'appear[ing] to reflect the dominant values of the culture: conservative, sexist, and homophobic' was also 'the golden age of female stars and characters'. Some of those characters were diva roles (Wolf 2002: 9, 22). Musical theatre diva roles tend to share certain characteristics. Discussing the character of Elphaba in *Wicked* (2003), Wolf describes her as 'Broadway's traditional diva: she is the dark, alto outsider who sings the musical's well-known belting numbers [...]. She breaks the rules and is condemned for her strength and determination' and goes on to refer to 'the quintessential diva, the singer of big, belting songs of self-determination and self-celebration' (2007: 48, 51). A Broadway diva role, then, is about both content and form. It requires certain personality traits – 'strength and determination' coupled with resistance to normativity – as well as certain musical traits – a strong belt, most often in an alto register.

Typically, significant roles for women in classic book musicals can be classified as either ingénues or soubrettes. The diva offers a third path, blending the soubrette's lower, brassier voice with the ingénue's leading-lady status. Unlike both the soubrette and the ingénue, however, the diva typically does not depend on being part of a couple for her relevance. While she is often nominally part of a heterosexual romance, the diva's real story usually focuses on fulfilling her own needs and desires. In *Gypsy*, Momma Rose chooses her daughter's career (which is Rose's connection to show business) over marriage to Herbie; in *Hairspray*, Tracy Turnblad is head over heels for heartthrob Link, but her primary focus remains on achieving her goals: stardom, 'a graduate degree in musicology with a minor in ethnic studies' and racial integration (O'Donnell et al. 2002: 121).

A number of authors have emphasized the degree to which 'divahood is ever a gender disorder' (Leonardi and Pope 1996: 57). In a culture where normative femininity positions women as passive and located in the private sphere of the home, a woman who sings loudly and demands attention in the public space of performance challenges normative ideas of gender. As Wolf argues, 'The diva's excessive, performative display of self refutes the limits of femininity even as her voice and body are insistently female' (2007: 46). Divas require us to both see and hear women *as* women; divas are unmistakably female, even as these roles also exceed and in some cases refute certain core ideals of western femininity. Momma Rose may be that quintessentially feminine thing, a mother, but she is also intensely ambitious and the (loud, belting) singer of the bulk of the show's music.

This resonates with theorizing around women's ability to perform femininity deconstructively. Carole-Anne Tyler describes the product of much of this work as follows:

> In theory, the female mimic [of femininity] denaturalized ideology by calling attention to the conventions that encode her as a woman; she repeats femininity with

> a playful difference that is a critical difference, producing knowledge about it: that it is a role and not a nature.
>
> (2003: 38)

Tyler is concerned, however, that in practice this theory's insistence on a difference between masquerade (un-playful, uncritical repetition) and mimicry relies on a false notion of origins. She goes on to postulate that perhaps, to be legibly a mimic, a woman must 'impersonate a man impersonating a woman' (2003: 60). In other words, she must model herself not on a biological woman, but on a drag queen. Interestingly, this is often how critics and scholars describe diva roles in musical theatre. John Clum notes, for example, that 'the great roles of the Broadway divas are themselves, like drag queens' personae, distillations and exaggerations of certain feminine traits' (1999: 139–40). Perhaps this perceived connection between divas and drag helps explain the potential diva roles have to serve as critical mimicry, rather than masquerade.

The diva's disruption of gender roles also implies a challenge to the heterosexual order that the traditional gender system supports (and is supported by). As Leonardi and Pope suggest, there is something 'decidedly queer about divas today' (1996: 2). Certainly, the diva has long been a favoured figure among gay men. Her queerness goes beyond sexuality, however, encompassing her challenge to heteronormativity, her embrace of excess, and her overall deviance: as Doty notes, 'Divas [...] are about troubling and breaking out of their "proper" culturally assigned sex, gender, sexuality, class, national, ethnic, and racial spaces' (2007: 4). Divas, in other words, challenge all sorts of 'regimes of the normal' held sacred in contemporary US culture. So too can diva roles in musical theatre, as they (loudly) demand attention and investment regardless of how they 'should' behave based on their identity positions and their relationship to cultural norms.

A diva role in action: Gypsy

In literature or even in most forms of non-musical performance, it is difficult to imagine a diva role as distinct from a diva character. After all, on the page audiences can only discern divadom through character description and actions. Musical theatre, however, 'is insistently, exuberantly performative, always already aware of itself as performance, even in those musicals that observe fourth-wall realism in the spoken scenes' (Wolf 2011: 11). Even if the fourth wall is officially in place, in musical theatre, the presence of song challenges our suspension of disbelief. Raymond Knapp argues that the presence of musical numbers 'imposes, through its obvious and conventional artificiality, a kind of mask that both conceals and calls attention to the performer behind the persona' (2005: 12). In a musical, no matter how expertly presented, the performer can never truly disappear into their role. Wolf, drawing on opera and dance scholarship, asserts that in musical theatre, performance can exceed and even contradict text: 'What a character is like [...] matters [...] but her actions, what the actor does, matters, too' (2011: 7–8). As women in musicals sing and dance, the power of their voices and bodies, she argues, can potentially exceed the frame of the official narrative.

In the context of divadom, this allows for the presence of a diva role where there is, officially, not a diva character. A classic example of this is Momma Rose, the 'monster of fabulistic proportions' (Feingold 2003), and starring role in the classic musical *Gypsy* (1959). Arthur Laurents, Jule Styne and Stephen Sondheim's loose adaptation of the memoirs of stripper Gypsy Rose Lee focuses on Lee's mother, Rose, and Rose's determination to make her daughters stars. Since *Gypsy*'s initial production, with Broadway legend Ethel Merman in the role written for her, there have been four Broadway revivals, a film version and a television production, each a star vehicle for the actress playing Rose. Rose is not a performer by profession. Her songs, unlike some numbers in the show, are not diegetic. Yet Rose is unquestionably the central figure in the musical based on her daughter's life, and *Gypsy* is, in many ways, the quintessential diva musical. Ethan Mordden calls Rose the 'outstanding diva role' of the musical theatre (1998: 246), while Mark Steyn states that 'in a genre dominated by larger-than-life ladies [...] there is none like Rose' (2000: 133).

Since she is not a diva character, what makes her such a clear example of a diva role? First, Rose is not simply *Gypsy*'s central character; she is its structural core, the engine that drives it – a level of power that immediately sets her apart from normative femininity. From her arrival midway through the first scene, shouting her iconic line 'Sing out, Louise', Rose maintains control over *Gypsy*'s narrative. She decides to take her daughters' vaudeville act on the road; when she cannot persuade her father to give her the money she needs, she steals it from him. She finds the act a manager (and herself a boyfriend) when she persuades the candy-salesman Herbie, happily retired from show business, to take her and her girls on. She designs the vaudeville acts that the children perform. She sabotages her younger daughter June's big chance at success when a producer insists that she let June leave the act and study to become an actress, because it would mean relinquishing control and by extension her connection to show business. Even on the rare occasions when something happens *to* Rose (instead of Rose *making* something happen), she quickly regains her momentum. When June abandons her and the act to elope with her fellow performer Tulsa, Rose's shock almost immediately gives way to a declaration that her older, less obviously talented daughter Louise will become a star, reinforced by the ferocious 'Everything's Coming up

Roses'. This belted hymn of optimism and ambition in the face of despair ends act one and sends the plot careening in a new direction, as Rose puts her hand to the wheel and resumes control.

Rose is not precisely a likeable character – she is manipulative, overbearing, and as Feingold and others have commented, more than a bit of a 'monster' in her determination to make the world, and everyone in it, conform to her dreams. She is a creature of excess, a larger-than-life woman determined to achieve success through her daughters at any cost. It is precisely this outsized personality, however, that combines with the narrative structure of the show to allow her to lay claim to divadom. The ferocity of the character, and the virtuosic, expansive performance demanded of an actress playing her, allow the performance to 'exceed the frame' of the story. For example, at the end of *Gypsy* Rose is bereft; Herbie has left her, and more importantly, Louise – now the star performer Gypsy Rose Lee – has turned on her as well. Not only has her daughter rejected her, challenging Rose's understanding of herself as a mother, but Gypsy, Rose's connection to show business and the stage the diva demands, rejects her as well.

Rose channels this double betrayal into her musicalized nervous breakdown – and tour de force – 'Rose's Turn', a moment where the ostensibly realistic conventions of the show momentarily break down. In 'Rose's Turn', Rose engages directly with the audience and the orchestra, but although she is on a stage, there is no 'real' performance going on within the world of the show. In addition, Rose controls the space; as the band responds to her commands and lights enter and shift, the realism the show has employed temporarily fractures in service of the diva's grand moment. If marginalization destroys Rose, leading to her breakdown through song, the show counteracts that marginalization by making her utterly central and triumphant. As Wolf notes, 'Rose's failure is Merman's success', an observation that has held true for the other Broadway Roses as well (2002: 128). Rose recognizes that she cannot be a star in the ultimate star turn for the performer playing her. In the end, the primary pleasure offered by *Gypsy* is the character of Rose. In turn, the pleasure of Rose is the pleasure of the diva role; her excess, embodied by a gifted performer, makes her compelling. And that pleasure comes from enjoying, celebrating, and even rejoicing in a character who is both entirely female (she is the ultimate stage *mother*, after all) and utterly beyond the bounds of normative femininity.

Diva characters as diva roles: Hairspray

While *Gypsy* is arguably the breakout 'diva musical', its primary diva role is not also a diva character. A more current example of the genre, the 2002 musical

Hairspray adapted from the John Waters film of the same name, features several diva role-character hybrids. The musical depicts the adventures of Tracy, a white teenager in 1962 Baltimore, as she attempts to become a star on the local television dance show, *The Corny Collins Show*. *Hairspray* revolves around an array of diva roles: the protagonist, Tracy; her mother, Edna; her ally, African American DJ Motormouth Maybelle; and her antagonists, Velma Von Tussle and her daughter, diva (-in-training) Amber. Of these women at the core of the show, several, including Tracy, Maybelle and Amber, are diva characters as well as diva roles – that is, the characters are skilled, ambitious performers.

Hairspray's diva roles perform excess and queered femininity in a range of ways, as their various marginalized identity positions intersect with their gender. Both Tracy and Edna, for example, are overweight, described in the script as 'chubby' and 'hefty', respectively (O'Donnell et al. 2002: xv). The relationship of fatness and divadom is not a new one; opera divas are often heavier than traditional beauty standards would allow. Edna is also a drag role, originated onstage by the openly gay performer Harvey Fierstein. Making Edna a drag role adds a certain obvious degree of queerness to a musical that officially includes no gay characters. The African American diva who joins Tracy and Edna at *Hairspray*'s centre is Maybelle, DJ for 'Negro Day' on *The Corny Collins Show* and the mother of Tracy's friends Seaweed and Little Inez. 'Big, blonde, & beautiful' – and loud – Maybelle also speaks primarily in rhyme; the excess and theatricality of her presentation is central to her divadom.

Against these three divas who represent marginalized communities (beyond simply being women), *Hairspray* offers an antagonist who is also a diva. White, thin and cisgender, visually 'rich, bigoted, bossy' station manager and stage mother Velma Von Tussle is the diva who gets femininity 'right' (O'Donnell et al. 2002: xv). Her song '(The Legend of) Miss Baltimore Crabs' highlights her excessive performance of normative femininity as she recalls how she won a beauty pageant in her youth by 'hit[ting] the stage / Batons ablaze / While singing "Aida" / And preparing cheese soufflés'. At the same time, the song marks her as deviant since she also attributes her win to having 'screwed the judges'; women are not supposed to use their sexuality so overtly (O'Donnell et al. 2002: 28). Velma is a hyper-sexualized, hyper-ambitious version of hyper-femininity, and in this show, the evil diva. Although she is not a performer during the show, she remains tied to show business; we also know from her song that she was a performer when she was younger. Therefore, it seems reasonable to consider her, like Maybelle and Tracy, as a diva character as well as a diva role.

Hairspray focuses on these larger-than life female characters, and the show is campy, playful, and ultimately celebrates their excess. This tone is set from the opening number, 'Good Morning Baltimore'. In addition to establishing location, this song defines Tracy's character. As the first character we meet, singing a version of the 'I Want' song, she is the protagonist. The song sets up a number of key elements and conventions for the show. Visually, it highlights the importance of big hair and the excess it represents, as the first thing we see is Tracy in bed, covered by a sheet up to her neck, her enormous hair dressed with a blue bow. The song also introduces Tracy's weight as a plot point, not simply by showing it visually but by having her sing in the first verse about being 'hungry for something that I can't eat' (O'Donnell et al. 2002: 3). The lyrics, and her performance of them, also suggest her deviance from normative femininity in terms of class. As she interacts with Baltimore on her way to school, Marissa Jaret Winokur as the original Tracy on Broadway sings cheerfully, in her bubbly, bright voice with its excessive, elongated Baltimore vowels, that 'the rats on the street all dance round my feet', and acknowledges 'the flasher / who lives next door' and 'the drunk on his barroom stool' (O'Donnell et al. 2002: 4). Tracy's comfort and ease in this lower-class world marks her as outside of normative femininity. Musically, backing singers accompany Tracy, as would be typical for a pop diva. Non-diegetic numbers throughout the show include backing singers, which makes sense given that they all feature a diva (or, in one case, a diva-in-training, a performer in the process of coming into her power).

The musical as a whole is built around two narratives, both of which centre on the divas and particularly on Tracy. First is Tracy's determination to achieve success and fame. The second, arguably more important, narrative is the attempt to integrate *The Corny Collins Show*. Tracy is also the initial force propelling the story. Staging choices work to mark Tracy (although the character is clearly white) as a kind of interracial space in segregated Baltimore. The backing dancers in 'Good Morning Baltimore' are both Black and white; Tracy stands in the centre, with Black dancers on one side and white on the other. Throughout the show, Tracy connects with both white and Black characters and speaks in favour of integration at every opportunity. Tracy spearheads the initial integration effort with Maybelle. When the first attempt ends in failure Tracy considers giving up but Maybelle rallies her, along with the rest of their group.

Tracy does have a heterosexual romance, as she and *Corny Collins Show* heartthrob Link become a couple over the course of the show. Yet once again, largeness offers a queer feminist counterpoint to the officially normative narrative. Discussing the character of Glinda in *Wicked*, Wolf suggests that although the character performs stereotypical femininity, she 'is so over the top that she sustains a critique of those behaviors even as she plays them out' (2007: 46). Similarly, Tracy's over-the-top performance of heterosexuality offers a way of critiquing it and making it strange. For example, in her initial encounter with Link during her failed audition, Tracy's attraction to him is so intense that it literally stops time: when he bumps into her, Tracy freezes. After he apologizes, everyone except Penny becomes frozen as well. A chime sounds, and then voice shaking, still frozen, Tracy sings 'I can hear the bells' (O'Donnell et al. 2002: 23). She emerges from her frozen state to sing an extensive fantasy of her romance with Link, from its beginning to their romantic reminiscing in heaven. The other characters become props for her fantasy, participating in it during this moment out of time. The level of excess is incredible and seems (intentionally) more than a bit silly, making Tracy's heterosexual passion, in all its normativity, read as a bit silly as well.

In the end, despite her passionate desire to become Link's girlfriend, Tracy's focus on professional success remains paramount. When she sings with Link after becoming a hit on the television show, she tries to fit into proper femininity by emphasizing love at the expense of her career. However, she can't quite do it:

> Once I was a simple girl
> Then stardom came to me
> But I was still a nothing
> *Though a thousand fans may disagree*
> Fame was just a prison
> Signing autographs a bore
> I didn't have a clue
> Till you came banging on my door.
>
> (O'Donnell et al. 2002: 99, emphasis added)

She spends far more time singing about her fame than about her love – a typical diva response.[2]

Diminishing the diva: Memphis

Hairspray, in its willingness to let its diva characters become diva roles (and incorporate additional diva roles alongside them), focuses almost entirely on women, and asks us to attend to the complicated relationships between gender, race, class, size and sexuality – a project that seems to me both feminist and queer. Not all shows, however, permit their diva characters to be diva roles. Without the performance power found in the diva role, these characters are often unable to transcend their sometimes problematic narratives. As Doty points out, dominant cultures and narratives are thrilled by the diva's difference while frequently maligning or punishing her for not being a conforming good girl [...] however, the diva makes herself a force to be reckoned with, so that even in defeat there is something gloriously iconoclastic about the 'bitch'.

(2007: 2–3)

The problem is that the 'gloriously iconoclastic' quality he refers to is much more the province of a diva role than a diva character. Diva roles like Rose and Tracy can, to a certain extent, transcend any punishment the narrative cares to offer; a character like Felicia, the main female character in the 2009 musical *Memphis*, cannot. An ambitious, exceptionally talented African American singer, Felicia is nonetheless not the protagonist. *Memphis* centres on Huey, a white male DJ who plays Black music for white southern listeners in the 1950s. Felicia's primary role in the show is as his love interest. His choices, and his larger-than-life character, drive the action and in many cases control what happens to her.

Felicia's first number occurs in the prologue, which takes place in her brother's club where she is the star singer. She comes in and immediately claims the stage, saying, 'Now get outta my way and let me sing my song' – a promising beginning. The song, however, is about how her 'brother runs [her] life, [her] brother owns this bar [...] he won't let [her] be till he makes [her] a star' (DiPietro and Bryan 2011: 9). Felicia's initial 'diva moment' emphasizes how she isn't in control. Her song is also the vehicle to bring Huey onstage to sing the first big solo number of the show; he's attracted to her voice and 'wanted to see if you looked as pretty as you sound' (DiPietro and Bryan 2011: 13).

Throughout the musical, Huey pursues Felicia romantically, while also seeking to promote her career. She returns his affection, but is much more pragmatic about the danger facing an interracial couple in 1950s Memphis. Huey consistently makes choices for Felicia, both professionally and personally. For example, when he gets her on the radio for the first time, he has brought her musicians and backing singers to the studio so she can perform live, without her knowledge. While this is a loving and, in this moment, successful gesture, it highlights his control of her career.[3] Other choices he makes for her end far less successfully. At the end of act one, he kisses her in public, despite her warnings about the danger of such behaviour. This leads to a vicious attack that leaves her half-conscious and badly injured (we later learn the attack left her unable to have children). Rather than the 'act-1-finale-of-female-self-assertion', which Wolf notes is 'a conventional song type, repeated and reproduced in countless musicals', this act ends with the main female character brutalized and largely silenced (2011: 4).

While Felicia's body bears the brunt of racism, *Memphis* asks its audience to identify with the white male character, and the story centres on his battles with racism in the music world. While Felicia is able to stand up for herself in moments, in the end *Memphis* is not her story, and she cannot truly exceed its boundaries. Huey is the larger-than-life character, not her. *Memphis* is a musical that does not permit its diva character to become a diva role. It is also a musical about integrating rock-and-roll that is all about the well-meaning white guy. It wants to engage minoritarian experiences, but refuses to de-centre the majoritarian position in terms of gender or race.

This connection to race is one worth further exploration, as the same female (and therefore 'inappropriate') excess that is celebrated in a show like *Hairspray* and avoided in a show like *Memphis* resembles the affective excess often ascribed to racialized others in the United States. Performance scholar José Muñoz argues that ideas of appropriate affect are inherently racialized, as 'normativity is accessed in the majoritarian public sphere through the affective performance of ethnic and racial normativity'– that is, whiteness. He describes normative whiteness as 'minimalist to the point of emotional impoverishment. Whiteness claims affective normativity and neutrality, but [...] once we look at whiteness from a racialized perspective [...] it begins to appear to be flat and impoverished' (Muñoz 2000: 68, 70). A diva role is not 'minimalist'; her affect cannot be 'impoverished'. Divas are inherently excessive: too loud, too talented, too ambitious, too emotional, too visible. This excess allies them, affectively, with racial others marked as excessive in the national imaginary. It makes sense that a musical that is unable to fully embrace the deviant excess of the diva would also have difficulty engaging with racialized excess. *Hairspray* addresses race, racial oppression and appropriation in complicated, imperfect, but thoughtful ways that generally avoid the white-savior trope.[4] In *Memphis*, while much of the cast is African American, it is the white male protagonist who risks (and loses) everything in the struggle for integration and equality, while ignoring the advice and needs of the Black people who surround him.[5]

In the end, placing a diva role front-and-centre in a musical offers the greatest opportunity to encourage musical theatre audiences to productively push back against 'regimes of the normal' in terms of gender, as well as (hopefully) sexuality and race. As Doty argues, the diva's status as an excessive, unruly woman gives her 'plenty to say to women, queer men, blacks, Latinos, and other marginalized groups'. A diva, he suggests, 'will make certain that, as often as possible, it is tradition and convention that yield (or at least bend) to her' (2007: 2). Musicals that feature the exuberant largeness of diva roles, whether or not they are also diva characters, can help us imagine a different, queerer and more feminist kind of world – not just one where women are treated more equally, necessarily, but one where the idea of 'normal' versus 'different' holds less sway.

NOTES

1. The term 'diva' is also often used to refer to particular performers who share these qualities. For the purposes of this essay, however, I am interested in the construction of diva characters and roles within musicals. Performers are important in as much as their culturally understood 'divadom' intersects with these characters/roles, but what makes a female performer a diva is outside the scope of this work.
2. Leonardi and Pope note that particularly in texts by women, which they see as friendlier to the diva than texts in the 'masculinist tradition', divas 'are dedicated to their work, sometimes to the exclusion of sexual relationships' (1996: 18). While men wrote *Hairspray*, it nonetheless resonates with this description.
3. Following Felicia's performance, her brother Delray sends her home and he and Huey proceed to sing a song about which man knows what's best for her.
4. Unfortunately, this is less true of the 2007 film version, in which Tracy is the leader of the integration movement rather than the enthusiastic, highly motivated ally she is in the stage version.
5. In fact, late in the show, Huey accuses Felicia of being a sellout because she is willing to work within the system rather than make the kind of grand gestures he favours. She calls him out on the absurdity of his claim to be 'blacker than [her]', but he's the protagonist; even though she's right, audience sympathy has been set up to be with him (DiPietro and Bryan 2011: 131).

REFERENCES

Clum, J. (1999), *Something for the Boys: Musical Theater and Gay Culture*, New York: St. Martin's Press.

DiPietro, J. and Bryan, D. (2011), Memphis: *The Complete Book and Lyrics of the Broadway Musical*, Milwaukee: Applause.

Doty, A. (2007), 'Introduction: There's something about Mary', *Camera Obscura*, 22: 65, pp. 1–9.

Doty, A. (2008), 'Introduction: The good, the bad, and the fabulous; or, the diva issue strikes back', *Camera Obscura*, 23: 67, pp. 1–8.

Feingold, M. (2003), 'Revival of the fittest: Old's always better; the hard part is making it new', *The Village Voice*, 6 May, http://www.villagevoice.com/2003 05-06/theater/revival-of-the-fittest. Accessed 25 May 2015.

Knapp, R. (2005), *The American Musical and the Formation of National Identity*, Princeton: Princeton University Press.

Laurents, A., Styne, J. and Sondheim, S. ([1959] 1973), 'Gypsy', in S. Richards (ed.), *Ten Great Musicals of the American Theatre*, Radnor: Chilton Book Company, pp. 413–88.

Leonardi, S. and Pope, R. (1996), *The Diva's Mouth: Body, Voice, Prima Donna Politics*, New Brunswick: Rutgers University Press.

Miller, D. A. (1998), *Place for Us: Essay on the Broadway Musical*, Cambridge: Harvard University Press.

Mordden, E. (1998), *Coming up Roses: The Broadway Musical in the 1950s*, New York: Oxford University Press.

Muñoz, J. E. (2000), 'Feeling brown: Ethnicity and affect in Ricardo Bracho's *The Sweetest Hangover (and Other STDs)*', *Theatre Journal*, 52:1, pp. 67–79.

O'Donnell, M., Meehan, T., Shaiman, M. and Whitman, S. (2002), *Hairspray*, New York: Applause.

Steyn, M. (2000), *Broadway Babies Say Goodnight: Musicals Then & Now*, New York: Routledge.

Tyler, C. (2003), *Female Impersonation*, New York: Routledge.

Warner, M. (1993), 'Introduction', in M. Warner (ed.), *Fear of a Queer Planet: Queer Politics and Social Theory*, Minneapolis: University of Minnesota Press, pp. vii–xxxi.

Wolf, S. (2002), *A Problem Like Maria: Gender and Sexuality in the American Musical*, Ann Arbor: University of Michigan Press.

Wolf, S. (2007), 'Wicked divas, musical theater, and Internet girl fans', *Camera Obscura*, 22:65, pp. 39–71.

Wolf, S. (2011), *Changed for Good: A Feminist History of the Broadway Musical*, Oxford: Oxford University Press.

11

Stepping Out of Line: (Re)Claiming the Diva for the Dancers of Broadway

Dustyn Martincich

In *The Diva's Mouth: Body, Voice, and Prima Donna Politics*, cultural studies scholars Susan J. Leonardi and Rebecca A. Pope muse that 'every female star, singer, and artist [has] been dubbed diva' (1996: 1). The term 'diva' gets tossed around in performance communities and headlines, carrying a certain weight, reverence and notoriety for a feminine performer's reputation. We can trace the term's origin to opera, where the diva or prima donna possesses a distinct voice and dominant, unruly disposition. Alternatively, the diva of the classical ballet world, the prima ballerina, is plucked from the corps of dancers, often by a male choreographer, because she stands out for the exceptional talent or star quality that she exudes from the line. American musical theatre has created its own culture of divas, long celebrating female-led shows built for and around women who have a signature talent and a recognizable, marketable quality onstage and offstage. Michelle Dvoskin defines a musical theatre diva as 'a female performer, often a vocalist, with an excess of talent and ambition (and often attitude as well)' (2016: 94). Although vocalistas like Ethel Merman, Pearl Bailey, Patti LuPone, Audra MacDonald and Idina Menzel have often taken the title of diva, musical theatre performances rely on more than vocal virtuosity; given that dance is an integral part of musical theatre performance, dancers who have stepped out of the chorus line to create signature roles, highlighting the virtuosity of the body as well as the voice, have at times – although perhaps less often – also earned the title of diva. These dancers, however, have garnered far less scholarly attention.

Working from the terms and examples set in musical theatre, opera and dance, this chapter expands the definition of Broadway's diva to include the powerful performances of Broadway's dancing divas: Gwen Verdon, Chita Rivera and

Donna McKechnie. Drawing on the work of gender and queer studies performance scholars like Wayne Koestenbaum, John Clum, Stacy Wolf and Leonardi and Pope; musical theatre diva studies scholar Dvoskin; and dance studies scholar Susan Leigh Foster, this chapter reframes the musical theatre diva in a way that acknowledges the virtuosity of the body as tantamount to that of the voice. By highlighting the dancing diva, I make a case for her as collaborator, translator and independent artist, as opposed to acting as 'a loner par excellence' (Leonardi and Pope 1994: 265) or simply as muse for male directors, choreographers and composers. Finally, by featuring Verdon, Rivera and McKechnie, I point to the dancing diva's essential impact on the evolving artistry of musical theatre in the twentieth century by highlighting their contributions to the narrative power of dance and their roles in establishing unique expectations for the triple-threat performer.

Verdon, Rivera and McKechnie share common experiences and traits that echo those of recognized opera and musical theatre divas as well as prima ballerinas. All three come from intense training, with strong ballet technique and a wide range of experiences in other dance forms; all distinguished themselves from the chorus line of hopefuls and capitalized on their breaks; all had exceptional longevity in their careers, having what Koestenbaum calls 'a peculiarly poignant relation to the fiction of eternal youth' (1993: 116), ultimately outlasting most dancers of the chorus lines; all captured the attention of dominant choreographers, directors and creators because of their ability to convey story through movement and a signature performance quality; all served as translators of a choreographer's iconic style; and all inserted their voices into the creative process and helped develop new diva roles written expressly for them. These signature roles of the musical theatre canon, which Dvoskin terms as 'larger-than-life female characters who drive a musical's action and encourage a virtuosic, outsized performance style' (2016: 94–95), feature the diva's ability to 'perform both femininity and masculinity' (Leonardi and Pope 1996 : 21), which is highlighted through their costuming, staging and performance interpretation.

Despite sharing so many traits with other types of divas, these diva dancers have often been denied the diva title for several reasons. First, the diva's virtuosity is assumed to be the voice, featured in roles that, for musical theatre, Dvoskin describes as 'blending the soubrette's lower, brassier voice with the ingénue's leading lady status' (2016: 95). Though these dancing divas possess unique voices, their bodies are their primary virtuosic instruments. Musical theatre scholars and critics frequently overlook the value and expressive power of the body and view it as a secondary, sexualized entity to the voice. This tendency privileges the talents of singers over dancers. Second, the work of the choreographer often eclipses the virtuosity of the dancer's body. The personality of the ideal dancer is often conceived of as a subservient, agreeable, workable muse omitted from artistic input; she is a beautiful and highly trained machine who is not seen as an individual, but rather as part of a unit in service to the choreographer. Third, though highly sexualized anti-hero roles are typical for divas, diva dancers are often forced to share the spotlight with others, thereby foregoing the singularity often associated with the vocal diva. The diva dancer works with the vision and ego of the director-choreographer who, in the process of making dance a primary focus of the production, reunites the diva role with other characters, even the chorus, visually diminishing her power and in a sense making her compete for the spotlight.

Finally, the ephemerality of dance and the norms of theatrical archiving deny the diva dancer any record of her virtuosity akin to that of the vocal divas' cast recordings. With the exception of Verdon's Lola from the film version of *Damn Yankees* (1958), neither Verdon, nor Rivera nor McKechnie was filmed in any of the roles they created. Without this recording for mass distribution, the diva legacy must be imparted by passing down roles to other dancers (where the next dancer is always compared with the diva by audiences and fellow artists), creating an original show (Rivera's *A Dancer's Life* [2005]) or writing a memoir (McKechnie's *Time Steps*). Since so often the diva's productions are built around her specific signatures and strengths, the dancing diva's shows are not seen in revival as often, like Verdon's *Redhead* (1959) or *New Girl in Town* (1957) or Rivera's less dance-focused Kander and Ebb diva vehicle *The Rink* (1984), which co-starred Liza Minelli. Even if the shows are regularly revived, their standout dance numbers, like McKechnie's iconic 'Tick, Tock' from *Company* (1970), are often impossible to replicate and often either altered for the body of the new performer (who is then compared to the diva) or cut entirely. If their diva roles are not revived or featured, the dancing divas are forever trapped in history and not brought to new generations of performers or audiences.

This chapter seeks to expand existing perspectives on the diva, specifically with the idea that previous definitions did not consider the specificities of the dancing diva, thereby ignoring the range of skills, talents and personalities necessary to produce and perform a Broadway production. By turning toward dancer-singer-actors like Verdon, Rivera and McKechnie, we can arrive at a more inclusive notion of just who the musical theatre diva can be.

The diva body as virtuosity

Whereas opera and musical theatre have traditionally privileged the voice when crowning their divas, the 'virtuoso performances' of dancing divas instead demote vocal power as they offer 'the audience a glimpse of the extraordinary possibilities of the moving body' (Thomas 2003: 109). Like the voice, the body is a virtuosic instrument, capable of exceptional, signature talent, cultivated through training in styles, technique and repertory in a strict atmosphere known for harsh criticism, physical pain and an attitude of silent perseverance. Virtuosity, as Judith Hamera describes, is 'that critical container curiously hyperdisciplined, hyperlaboring thus hypervisible – yet somehow, ineffable, elusively more' (2000: 147). A dancer's body must be trained to withstand the rigorous show schedule, the athletic and unnatural nature of virtuosic choreography, constant, repetitive motion and crippling footwear. So often dancers are seen as beautiful machines, trained to repeat something given to them by choreographers. In dance studies, this is what Foster calls the 'hired body' where 'the body's character is reduced to principles of physics: can be enlarged here, elasticized there'. She goes further to ascribe a customizable quality, where the dancer body as 'a purely physical object, can be made over into whatever look one desires' (2003: 255). In other words, the dancer's body is often seen as something that can be shaped, something that is not owned by the dancer: 'the hard work, repetition, and structure of the daily class frequently results in "unthinking" dancers, trained to accept unquestioningly the professional requirements' (Adair 1992: 15). But the diva dancer steps out of that line, not only because of her abilities but because of her virtuosic 'it factor', a certain confidence and an ability to employ aspects of herself in a creative process.

A diva dancer's virtuosic body, like a diva's voice, is instantly recognizable. Through her career and training, 'the aim is nothing less than *creating the body*' as Foster describes. As the diva gains notoriety, 'the images used to describe the body and its action *become* the body' (2003: 239, original emphasis). A diva dancer's particular virtuosity is magnified when the body becomes the primary communicator. Audiences, reviewers and critics traditionally highlight the unique shape and form of the body when addressing these divas' significant performances, thereby proclaiming and further defining the body for which she becomes known. For Verdon, her tomboy body type, her comedic approach to the choreography, her girl-next-door-meets-pin-up look and (perhaps less importantly) her gravelly voice become expected in her roles. Rivera has become her long legs, the rasp in her voice and what Helen Thomas calls a 'flexible body' that 'might shift seamlessly' into all movement styles, from Jerome Robbins to Bob Fosse and then from Gower Champion to Jack Cole to Graciela Daniele (2003: 112). As Rivera told Glen Collins in an interview for the *New York Times*, 'My body is the sum total of all the choreographers who have trained me […] there is this instinctual memory of their styles' (Collins 1993). McKechnie's signature move (the lay out) highlights her long limbs, elegant neck and rubber band back. These diva dancers' bodies define the roles they have played throughout their careers because of these signature aspects in the same way that Merman or LuPone's voices set expectations for their diva turns.

The roles set out for these diva dancers feature their strengths and virtuosities, but with the choreography further sexualizing their bodies. Furthering the traditional notion that the diva is eroticized as she 'presents the uncomfortable and antipatriarchal spectacle of a woman taking her body seriously' (Koestenbaum 1993: 101), the diva dancer's virtuosic body invites the audiences to look at the diva as one who exercises immense control over a splendid instrument, often costumed in such a way that extends a particular fantasy. This kind of performer-audience connection is a virtuosity that is about 'a story of looking, of engaging corporeal and contextual difference' (Hamera 2000: 147).

The audience sees a live, refined body onstage and 'the power of the vicarious is activated by critical projections onto the screen of the exceptional laboring body of performer' (Hamera 2000: 147–48). The diva dancers' bodies in these roles, like other divas, succumb to the male gaze where, as film scholar Laura Mulvey argues, 'woman displayed as sexual object is the leit-motiff of erotic spectacle: from pin-ups to strip-tease, from Ziegfeld to Busby Berkeley, she holds the look, plays to and signifies male desire' (1999: 837). Both the dancing diva's translation of these roles and the stylized choreography play into this gaze, and at the same time, work with the choreography to subvert expectations: Verdon's campy striptease in *Damn Yankees*' (1955) 'Whatever Lola Wants', Rivera's half-hearted seduction gone awry in Gower Champion's 'Shriner Ballet' from *Bye, Bye, Birdie* (1960) or McKechnie's erotic and driving solo 'Tick Tock' in *Company*. In each example, the dancing diva extends beyond her virtuosic instrument (her body) in order to integrate acting, movement and music. This triple-threat ability disrupts the traditional sexualization of the body in choreography, giving the dancing diva a voice.

Surely Broadway audiences expected female dancers to inject sexual appeal into a musical comedy and drama at the height of the diva dancer's reign. Since live dance performance is, as Judith Hanna argues, 'immediate, emotionally charging the performer and audience in sporadic and continuous interchange', the diva dancer has the ability to impact the audience, embody and convey gender and sexual norms and promote the evolution of the musical theatre form in the 1950s, 1960s and 1970s using 'the power of dance to convey sexual imagery' (1988: 18–19). Another example of transforming what could be merely suggestive choreography into key narrative turns includes McKechnie's dream ballet solo 'Tick Tock'. The number is set to the internal monologues of Bobby and a woman (her character, Kathy) in the middle of intercourse. Through McKechnie's interpretation of Michael Bennett's choreography that features her signature long limbs and flexible back, she, dressed in a negligee, acts the subtext of the scene, connecting the intention with the music. As the piece evolves, her movements intensify, reaching out in a controlled frenzy of energy and ecstasy as the woman grows towards climax. Showcasing her command of musicality, dynamics, character interpretation and the *acting* of the dance, McKechnie's movements exquisitely translate a moment that transcends words in a way unlike any other body; as a diva, she employs her signature qualities in highly erotic, complex patterns to convey what cannot be said.

Verdon, whose diva body became synonymous with Fosse's choreography, is the queen of converting awkward and erotic movement into narrative expression for her anti-hero diva roles. In each role, Verdon capitalizes on her trademark of creating sexual dynamism with physical comedy as well as Hamera's performer-audience connective 'virtuosity' by playing into the male gaze while simultaneously subverting the expectations of what is considered sexy. Playing roles like Lola, a temptress turned good in *Damn Yankees*; Anna Christie, a prostitute in *Redhead*; Charity, a big-hearted taxi-dancer in *Sweet Charity* (1966) and Roxie, a murderer who gets everything she wants in *Chicago* (1975), Verdon's physical expression wins over audiences in spite of her less-than virtuous characters who, like all divas, exist in 'a culture where normative femininity positions women as passive and located in the private sphere of the home' but who 'demand attention in the public space of performance' (Dvoskin 2016: 95). The critics repeatedly capture Verdon's attributes in write-ups. In 1959, *Life* magazine *Redhead* reviewer Marc Prideux drew attention to her 'lovely double-action legs' and 'superior posterior', calling Verdon 'a special blend of pure sex and pure fun' (Prideux 1959). Fosse biographer Sam Wasson said that it took Verdon's knack for comedy in *Damn Yankees* 'to make sex safe for the American musical: it took a Cole dancer to read Fosse, and an actress to legitimize Lola's humanity' (2013: 111). Even her *New York Times* obituary noted Verdon's 'head-turning figure' and range of diva roles, from 'oozing seductive come-ons as the Devil's sexy troubleshooter' to 'brooding over a whiskey as a disillusioned prostitute' (Berkvist 2000). As a diva, Verdon took the material given by powerful male choreographers and converted it into *her* signature style. Verdon the dancing diva made Fosse's movements her own.

The body is elevated as a primary narrative communicator in the dancing diva's featured 'I Want' songs. For instance, 'The Music and the Mirror' from *A Chorus Line* (1975) is a marathon solo with a significant dance break that grows in intensity, allowing McKechnie to lose herself in a trance of emotion as she communicated Cassie's exhaustive passion for the stage. As Stacy Wolf describes, McKechnie 'has the stage all to herself, and the flats revolve to mirrors so that she is reflected many times', creating the illusion that she is not alone. Her interpretation of Bennett's choreography, which 'includes leaps and turns, back bends, and head rolls; that is, movements that are unique and individualized and that were, in fact, conceived to accentuate Donna McKechnie's strengths as a dancer' (2011: 123–24), provides her an opportunity to access her signature virtuosity while conveying Cassie's most urgent objectives. Like diva vocalistas in their solos, she showcases her most exceptional skills in this song. In a way, Bennett and McKechnie conventionalized the dance solo, making it a way to convey a character's emotional narrative in the same way a Merman or a LuPone would through monologue or song. This Bennett/McKechnie solo also illustrates that a female dance diva does not have to be comedic or sexy and that danced moments can be as narratively meaningful and truthful as *Gypsy*'s iconic diva 'I Want' number 'Everything's Coming Up Roses'.

An additional significant characteristic of the dance diva's virtuosic body is its ability to survive abuse, illness and injury. As Clum writes, 'divas are survivors, proud of their battle scars'(1999: 229). Diva dancers' bodies become symbols of survival and perseverance in the face of crises: like Verdon's vocal polyps, Rivera's car crash and McKechnie's debilitating arthritis. Rivera's comeback from a car accident to perform Aurora in Kander and Ebb's *Kiss of the Spider Woman* (1993) while in her 60s 'marked her as one who has resisted the ravages of age' (Weigman 2004: 406). Though she can be aligned with her vocal diva counterparts like Judy Garland who return to the stage after personal crisis, the dancing diva must work harder for audience accolades if her virtuosic body is hindered because the audience and collaborators demand the spectacle of the body, the spectacle of a superhuman. No matter the pain or personal sacrifice, the dancing diva exudes 'an aura of utter confidence that is the essence of a Broadway dancer's brassy spirit' (Rich 1993), even when facing adversity.

More than a muse: Diva as artist, collaborator and translator

The notion that the opera diva's attitude is as big as her talent might suggest that she is an impossible collaborator, developing roles with no concern for other artists in the process. The notion that a prima ballerina is simply a beautiful machine might suggest that she is simply a vessel or muse for someone else's creativity. Leonardi and Pope paint the picture of a 'lone and demanding and implacable and self-absorbed destructive screaming diva' (1994: 265–66) (perhaps perpetuated by male texts), but that kind of diva could not succeed in the dance world of musical theatre. Given that musical theatre is ultimately collaborative, and artistic genius is dependent on the bodies of others, the dancing diva of musical theatre must work in collaboration with other artists, acting as translator for the narrative power of movement. Because of her simultaneous need to collaborate and function as artistic translator, she then defies both the traditional perception that she cannot 'play well with others' (Leonardi and Pope 1994: 265) as well as the prima ballerina's image of a beautiful machine. The dancing diva instead ascribes to the role of 'diva' as historically written by women, using her 'voice' in the creative process 'as metaphor of and vehicle for female empowerment' (Leonardi and Pope 1994: 266), actively evolving roles alongside choreographers, composers and lyricists.

The diva dancer gained popularity at a time when dance became more complex and pivotal to the plot development of a musical. With the advent of director-choreographers, dancers had to act and sing. Rivera and Verdon worked towards diva status in the 1950s, when 'the musical play had made character the essence of performing, yet the concomitant explosion of narrative choreography made dancers more crucial, even in lead parts' (Mordden 1983 : 153). Rivera created the role of Anita under the dancing-acting direction of Jerome Robbins in *West Side Story* (1957), and Verdon claimed her diva status by upstaging French dancer Lilo in Michael Kidd's choreography in *Can-Can* (1953). After Verdon and Fosse worked together in *Damn Yankees*, she had enough diva power to bring him along with *her* on subsequent projects. Verdon vehicles like *New Girl in Town* and *Redhead* offered her the opportunity to create these new roles around *her* strengths, highlighting *her* ability to translate character through movement and that signature raspy voice. For instance, a highlight of *Redhead* featured Verdon dancing in a 30-minute, multi-section sequence where she 'appeared in every section, twirling, kicking, clowning, and once, flying' (Wasson 2013: 144). The show won her the Tony for Best Performance by a Leading Actress in a Musical and Fosse the award for Best Choreography. Though all three of these diva-dancers would contribute to the creation of iconic musical comedy roles, Verdon, as Robert Wahls notes in *The Sunday Times*, 'probably defines an era in American musical comedy history, a 25-year span during which audiences learn to accept musicals that totally integrate dance, drama, and music' (Wahls 1977).

The dancing diva gained status in the 1960s as the director-choreographer gained popularity and as the nature of a musical's leading female character evolved. As Wolf points out, 'by focusing on the female characters and the convention of choreography, these musicals offer a new perspective on the 1960s Single Girl' (2011: 60). For example, Verdon's character of Charity in Fosse's *Sweet Charity* (1966) is further developed and expressed by the dance numbers. Verdon applies Fosse's movement style to the character's physical expression, particularly in numbers like 'If My Friends Could See Me Now', which gives audiences a peek into Charity's joyful, yet quirky, hope not only for love, but for a better life. 'Verdon's style conjoined with his', Wolf points out, highlighting how Fosse and Verdon's collaborative work became a staple of the 1960s musical theatre landscape, 'shifting pointed feet to flexed, with turned-in toes, jutted-out hips, slouched shoulder, head cocked to the side, and a slack-jawed expression that David Van Leer calls the "desexualization of eroticism"' (2011: 62). Similarly, McKechnie's first diva-in-training Bennett feature on Broadway was as a lead in a trio of featured single-girl secretaries in the office-party Act I closer 'Turkey Lurkey Time' in *Promises, Promises* (1968). Like Verdon in *Can-Can*, McKechnie takes a diva turn in this piece, making her mark using Bennett's movement to add a vibrant physicality to an independent, flailing, single-girl secretary character. As dance continued to be a primary communicator for leads in musicals, diva dancers developed more roles that included Verdon's Roxie (*Chicago*), Rivera's Velma (*Chicago*) and Aurora (*Kiss of the Spider Woman*) and McKechnie's Kathy (*Company*) and Cassie (*A Chorus Line*). Each character is independent in some way. In each role, the diva's 'physicality, blocking, and gestures – their choreography, that is, whether set to music or to story – define their characters as much as song or speech' (Wolf 2011: 60). The dancing diva inserts her signature interpretation of the movement to give the character a powerful physical status as a woman of the era.

The diva dancer serves as a translator who interprets information from fellow artists and communicates it to the audience, while adding her specific signature. Like so many dancers, Verdon, Rivera and McKechnie were seen by many as 'female dancers who were "molded" into stars' by male choreographers or partners (Austin 1997 : 68). However, these divas had powerful voices in the creative process. Without the divas' very specific and unique bodies, talents and knack for translating style, the choreographers' styles could not have come to life. The movement creation relies on the diva's body to interpret and sculpt the ideas of the male choreographer into its embodied specificity. In this way, the dancing diva translates movement into her signature style, thereby inviting audiences to associate her with the role. Like her vocal counterparts, she shares the signature virtuosity that comes in translating another artist's work live for an audience. The 'tension between the dancer's personal presence and her performance presence makes her dance interesting to us' (Fraleigh 1987: 70). A diva lends her unique talents and signature to that character, never letting the audience forget that the diva dancer is present, because after all 'in a musical, no matter how expertly presented, the performer can never truly disappear into their role' (Dvoskin 2016: 96). This is notably the case for McKechnie's development of Cassie for *A Chorus Line*, as she had the rare opportunity to play a character largely based on her own life and experiences.

Unlike featured dancers or dancers in the chorus line, diva dancers like Verdon, Rivera and McKechnie collaborate closely with choreographers to help create the legendary dance styles that then define the choreographer. A choreographer needs the dancing diva because she can offer her signature style, not because she will imitate his. The diva dancer is not, as Foster describes, 'a mere vehicle for aestheticized expression'. Instead, the choreographer and diva dancer engage in what she terms as a 'playful probing of physical and semantic potential' where 'choreographers' and dancers' bodies create new images, relationships, concepts, and reflections' (1995: 15). The diva then participates in the creation and codification of a choreographer's signature style or process. As Graham McFee suggests 'authentic performances of a dancework [...] must also accommodate any *crucial* contribution from dancers' (2011: 75, original emphasis). Fosse actually acknowledged the contributions of Verdon and Rivera when they were developing *Chicago*. Though he described the divas as '"ideal instruments" [...]. He also acknowledged their creativity and intelligence, admitting that they often had choreography input into the numbers he was creating' (Austin 1997: 71). The diva, aware that others need her virtuosity in order to create, uses her status to have voice in the creative process.

If the dancing diva's body creates alongside the choreographer, then her body becomes a physical archive of a choreographic style. The dancing diva body holds the 'way' a style should be performed and how a role should be played. Her relationship with her choreographer can be tumultuous (for Verdon and McKechnie especially, as they married their choreographers), but it is symbiotic as each relies on one another to achieve legendary status. Verdon was accustomed to being the female translator of the male body for Jack Cole before she met Fosse. Judy Austin argues, 'Verdon was able to capture the precision of Cole's isolated choreography, yet we can argue against the idea that she was "created" by Cole' (1997: 68). When she discovered that her body and talents aligned with Fosse's style, she became as Austin says the 'ultimate Fosse dancer' (1997: 69), eventually translating his choreographic vision for other dancers and putting movement into understandable physical and verbal language they could interpret and execute. As Robert Berkvist points out in Verdon's obituary, Fosse 'found that working with Ms. Verdon was more of a collaboration than a tutorial' (Berkvist 2000). Verdon had the ability to execute Fosse's seductive feminine aspects of a hip or shoulder roll with the vaudevillian comedy of a foot twitch while simultaneously finding the more masculine athleticism and strength in every dynamic boxer's punch or burlesque hip bump. Her ease and fluidity made the movement evolve into more of a unisex style. Wasson writes, 'Verdon knew how Bob Fosse thought, which elevated her above assistant, above collaborator, into a sort of creative cohabitant, beyond anything she had ever done for Jack Cole'. She essentially codified Fosse's style, making her a 'living illustration of a burgeoning style that few, including Fosse, could put into words' (Wasson 2013: 130) and establishing a lasting 'technique' that is passed from dancer to dancer.

The diva dancer acts as muse and translator for composers and lyricists as well, developing pairings with fellow artists who align with her signature vocal and physical style. As Sally Banes notes, 'in dance, as in music and drama, a score or text provides the skeleton on which the musculature of the individual performer's interpretation is built' (1998: 9), and for Rivera, the work of Kander and Ebb inspired her to take new directions on her diva path. John Kander and Fred Ebb 'tailor-made works to showcase the talents of their favorite divas' (Leve 2009: 231), which included Liza Minnelli, Karen Ziemba and Rivera. After working with Rivera in *Chicago*, they wrote *The Rink* for her as a star vehicle, followed by *Kiss of the Spider Woman* nearly a decade later. She also worked with the duo on *The Mystery of Edwin Drood* (2012), as well as *The Visit* (2015), after Ebb passed away. Acknowledging her diva status while working on *Kiss of the Spider Woman*, Kander said in an interview with Marc Peyser of *Newsweek*, 'Without her, I don't think the show could work. Whenever you try to replace Chita, you always make a compromise [...]. It's not that there aren't any more left. I don't ever remember other Chitas' (Peyser 1993).

Rivera's work on *Kiss of the Spider Woman*, a show Clum refers to as 'the last diva musical of the twentieth century' (1999: 189), epitomizes the role of the dancing diva as an exaggerated figure. Her work with Kander and Ebb in developing Aurora, a fantasy character who provides escape for the homosexual political prisoner Molina, exemplifies the traditional diva's ability to inspire art and translate for artists in addition to the choreographer. With choreographers Vincent Paterson and Rob Marshall, Kander, Ebb and Rivera capitalized on her virtuosic, signature body and voice, presenting Aurora as dangerous, seductive and surrounded by a chorus of attractive, skin-baring men, 'a true diva in a gay-created musical about the role of divas in the life of an unliberated queen' (Clum 1999: 189). Rivera's Aurora is also a key example of what Koestenbaum points to as the diva's power to overturn 'the world's gendered ground by making femaleness seem at once powerful and artificial'. He further describes the diva costume, for him the 'gown', as it is essential in 'showing gender's dependence on costume' and that 'clothes give gender its social meanings' (1993: 104, 120). The biggest dance numbers for Rivera feature the most exaggerated forms of divadom, where costuming and movement denote status and thematic gender fluidity. In 'Gimme Love', for example, Rivera is a Carnival dancer or showgirl with headdress and feathers, striding through the space, whereas in 'Where You Are', she appears in an all-white tuxedo, complete with fedora and cane, 'a costume that heightens her androgynous qualities' (Weigman 2004: 407). The number features a classic jazz dance style, ideal for her body as she cuts across the stage with ease, turning sharply into the arms of the male partners, extending her legs as a spider would, sliding up and through the chorus' limbs. In 'Her Name is Aurora', which 'celebrates the diva as diva' (Leve 2009: 158), Rivera works a chair in a satin and feathered robe, her long legs on display, performing the subtlest of gestures that erupt into a full ménage-a-tango with her male ensemble. As Aurora, Rivera is 'a female star who is a reminder of the history of the last four decades of Broadway'

(Clum 1999: 189), translating the work of the composer, lyricist and librettist in each of these fantasy numbers.

Verdon, Rivera and McKechnie exemplify divadom in the signature roles they have created in collaboration with the choreographers, lyricists and composers with whom they have helped define. They represent the best of all Broadway worlds with their versatility as acting and singing dancers who have allowed for the conception of and helped in the creation of new kinds of musical roles for women.

The dancing diva's legacy

Providing further evidence of their power within the musical theatre world, Verdon, Rivera and McKechnie, like their vocal counterparts, impart a legacy in the roles they have created as well as their impact on the creative process for key choreographers, composers and lyricists. Their unique characteristics and collaborative ability in stylistic translation and physical character development have helped elevate the body to a virtuosic entity, a powerful tool just as effective at communicating narrative as the vocal diva's voice. In the process, they had a direct hand in the evolution of musical theatre dance and the role of dancers in modern musical theatre. By establishing expectations for both a dynamic body and voice, the dancing divas were leaders in establishing the artful triple-threat female performer in leading musical theatre roles by setting the bar for Broadway dancers to go beyond a 'heightened technical proficiency', 'ballet body' and the ability to 'be astonishingly virtuosic in a wide variety of dance styles' (McClean 2008: 219). Broadway dancers must sing and act, particularly if they hope to step out of the chorus line as the dancing divas did.

In leaving these legacies, Verdon, Rivera and McKechnie redefine what it means to be a Broadway diva and how audiences might view the body of a leading lady. Each diva dancer, with her ability to simultaneously lean into, transgress and subvert gender expectations, created female, dance-centred diva roles beyond the sexualized showgirl, using movement as a means to convey spectacle and narrative. Aligning with traditional diva traits, each diva established her signature style, capitalizing on her 'it factor', which inspired artistic collaborators and audiences to invest in iconic, dance-centred roles that would become part of the Broadway canon. This created opportunities for generations of dancers to follow the divas by emulating Charity, Roxie, Anita or Cassie, embracing complex, physical roles 'with the diva body as reference' (Adamy 2014: 274), knowing they will always be compared to these great divas who originated the roles.

With the trending ensemble-focused or dance-light musicals of the first couple decades of the twenty-first century, the days of the dancing diva may have come to a close. Though somewhat recent revivals have offered opportunities for exceptional dance-based performers like Ann Reinking and Bebe Neuwirth (*Chicago* [1996]), Sutton Foster (*Thoroughly Modern Millie* [2002] and *Anything Goes* [2011]), Stephanie Pope (*Pippin* [2013]) and Karen Ziemba (*Contact* [2000]), we look to Verdon, Rivera and McKechnie to give us a taste of the past, their bodies capturing a certain era and aesthetic. By elevating this trio of dancers to a diva title, we recognize the significance of dancers (and not just singers) in not only the creation of standout female performances but also the collaborative musical-making process. By celebrating the dancing diva and allowing the term 'diva' to be more inclusive in its exclusivity within musical theatre, we acknowledge powerful female artistic contributions, not just personalities, and accept the body as a valuable communicator of narrative and style.

The diva is an idea of a performer, and the performer performs the role of diva. She is 'not so much a person as a position, a condition, a situation'. Because of her virtuosity, she gains status, and because of her status, she becomes a symbol: 'the diva herself – constructed, fictional, conditional as she is – is larger (or louder) than life' (Leonardi and Pope 1996: 10). The diva dancer's virtuosic body is her primary instrument that she wields as powerfully as her vocal counterparts. Like the vocalistas, she offers this diva self to her audiences and collaborators, keeping her own signature on display every time she comes on stage. In the dance world, we use the term 'diva' with pride. The term calls out a dancer for performing with ferocity, for standing out because of what they bring to a performance beyond technique. It suggests something about attitude and the intentional pull of focus, of not dancing with the rest of the line. And the community supports this show of individuality. As true divas, Verdon, Rivera and McKechnie have carved out their legacies, sculpted history with their bodies and imparted their individual stamps on the next generation.

REFERENCES

Adair, C. (1992), *Women and Dance: Sylphs and Sirens*, New York: New York University Press.

Adamy, H. P. (2014), 'Always and already excessive: Theorize diva performativity in a TAMU studio soprano', *Studies in Musical Theatre*, 8:3, pp. 271–80.

Austin, J. (1997), 'Mentors of American Jazz dance', in S. E. Friedler and S. B. Glazer (eds), *Dancing Female: Lives and Issues of Women in Contemporary Dance*, Amsterdam: Harwood Academic Publishers, pp. 67–81.

Banes, S. (1998), *Dancing Women: Female Bodies on Stage*, London: Routledge.

Berkvist, R. (2000), 'Gwen Verdon, redhead who high-kicked her way to stardom, dies at 75', *New York Times*, 19 October, http://www.nytimes.com/2000/10/19/theater/gwen-verdon-redhead-who-high-kicked-her-way-to-stardom-dies-at-75.html. Accessed 15 May 2017.

Clum, J. M. (1999), *Something for the Boys: Musical Theatre and Gay Culture*, New York: Palgrave.

Collins, G. (1993), 'To the spider woman, Broadway is home', *New York Times*, 1 June, http://www.nytimes.com/1993/06/01/theater/to-the-spider woman-broadway-is-home.html. Accessed 28 September 2017.

Dvoskin, M. (2016), 'Embracing excess: The queer feminist power of musical theatre diva roles', *Studies in Musical Theatre*, 10:1, pp. 93–103.

Foster, S. L. (1995), 'Choreographing history', in S. L. Foster (ed.), *Choreographing History*, Bloomington: Indiana University Press, pp. 3–21.

Foster, S. L. (2003), 'Dancing bodies', in J. Desmond (ed.), *Meaning in Motion: New Cultural Studies of Dance*, Durham: Duke University Press, pp. 235–57.

Fraleigh, S. (1987), *Dance and the Lived Body: A Descriptive Aesthetics*, Pittsburgh: University of Pittsburgh Press.

Hamera, J. (2000), 'The romance of monsters: Theorizing the virtuoso body', *Theatre Topics*, 10:2, pp. 144–53.

Hanna, J. L. (1988), *Dance, Sex and Gender: Signs of Identity, Dominance, Defiance, and Desire*, Chicago: The University of Chicago Press.

Koestenbaum, W. (1993), *The Queen's Throat: Opera, Homosexuality, and the Mystery of Desire*, New York: Poseidon Press.

Leonardi, S. J. and Pope, R. A. (1994), 'Screaming divas: Collaboration as feminist practice', *Tulsa Studies in Women's Literature*, 13:2, pp. 259–70.

Leonardi, S. J. and Pope, R. A. (1996), *The Diva's Mouth: Body, Voice, Prima Donna Politics*, New Brunswick: Rutgers University Press.

Leve, J. (2009), *Kander and Ebb*, New Haven: Yale University Press.

McClean, A. L. (2008), *Dying Swans and Madmen: Ballet, the Body, and Narrative Cinema*, London: Rutgers University Press.

McFee, G. (2011), *The Philosophical Aesthetics of Dance: Identity, Performance and Understanding*, Basingstoke: Dance Books Ltd.

Mordden, E. (1983), *Broadway Babies: The People Who Made the American Musical*, New York: Oxford University Press.

Mulvey, L. (1999), 'Visual pleasure and narrative cinema', in L. Braudy and M. Cohen (eds), *Film Theory and Criticism: Introductory Readings*, New York: Oxford University Press, pp. 833–44.

Peyser, M. (1993), 'The dancing diva of Broadway', *Newsweek*, 23 May, http:// www.newsweek.com/dancing-diva-broadway-193474. Accessed 15 May 2017.

Prideux, T. (1959), 'Gwen knocks 'em in the aisles', *Life*, 23 February, pp. 81–84.

Rich, F. (1993), 'For the musical, a love affair beyond the liaison in a Latin jail', *New York Times*, 4 May, http://www.nytimes.com/1993/05/04/thea ter/review-theater-for-the-musical-a-love-affair-beyond-the-liaison-in-a latin-jail.html?pagewanted=all. Accessed 15 May 2017.

Thomas, H. (2003), *The Body, Dance and Cultural Theory*, New York: Palgrave Macmillan.

Wahls, R. (1977), 'The old razzle dazzle', *Sunday News*, 6 February, p. 4.

Wasson, S. (2013), *Fosse*, New York: Houghton Mifflin Harcourt.

Weigman, M. (2004), 'Re-visioning the spider woman archetype in *Kiss of the Spider Woman*', *Journal of Analytical Psychology*, 49:3, pp. 397–412.

Wolf, S. (2011), *Changed for the Good: A Feminist History of the Broadway Musical*, Oxford: Oxford University Press.

12

Diva Relations in *The Color Purple*, the 2015 Broadway Revival

Deborah Paredez

The diva, as a virtuosic and complicated woman, stands alone – invariably in the spotlight and in a full-front stance. She is known and sometimes revered and other times reviled for her stubborn singularity. She is singular in her unmatched virtuosity – *anything you can do, she can do better*. She is singular in her refusal or failure to be romantically attached or easily confined to coupledom – '*Mama's movin' on, Mama's all alone*' – which contributes considerably to her delicious queerness.[1] She is unruly and frequently does not play well with others and thus has a vexed relationship with notions of liberal feminist solidarity. She is inimitable, *sui generis*, the One and Only – or at least that is what so many of us, her devoted fans, have come to believe.[2]

The Broadway musical adaptation of *The Color Purple* (2005, 2015), based on Alice Walker's (1982) Pulitzer Prize-winning epistolary novel, features one such diva: Shug Avery, the juke-joint blues singer whose presence (and absence) catalyses changes for the show's main characters.[3] And yet, even as *The Color Purple* narratively and performatively delights in the exploits and conventions of the solo diva (and the diva solo), the musical encourages us to rethink the very notion of the diva as an inevitably singular force. *The Color Purple*'s 2015 revival, in particular, departs from Broadway musical conventions by showcasing not just one singular diva, but by depicting the performative prowess of three different divas – Celie, Sofia and Shug – in relation to one another. Divas cohabit the stage, and not in a predictably elbow-jabbing, diva-duelling spectacle of one-upmanship. Instead, the revival stages divaness as a liberatory mode of relations among women. Within this set of diva relations, each diva gains a deeper understanding of her own power and desires *in relation to other divas* (rather than in spite of them, as standard diva narratives go) and also acts as a force that generates, restores and reconfigures relations for the other divas within their respective communities. Divas here act as facilitators of female relationships that are otherwise foreclosed by racism and patriarchy. Divaness thus emerges as a radically reconfigured set of relations among women marked by the aspiration to occupy desire and the achievement of self-actualization rather than by the patriarchal constraints of (re)productivity or zero-sum-game competition. Throughout the musical revival, expressions of diva virtuosity serve to forge and solidify – rather than isolate the diva from – liberatory female bonds. The production's promotional materials and theatrical elements – including its conventional musical numbers, its unconventional trinity of diva performers and director John Doyle's signature character-focused approach to ensemble acting, Brechtian staging and minimalist design – amplify the centrality of diva relations at the heart of story's womanist aesthetics and upend traditional understandings of the Broadway diva by staging divaness as a mode of womanist relations.

The role of the diva as a relational rather than simply singular force, of course, has much to do with the centrality of Black feminism in Alice Walker's text and the role of the blues diva within Black feminism. Published in the year before her influential treatise, *In Search of Our Mother's Garden: Womanist Prose*, in which she coined and defined the term womanist as 'a black feminist or feminist of color [...] who loves other women sexually and/or nonsexually' (1983: xi), *The Color Purple* (1982) enacts Walker's womanist vision through the relationships forged among the female characters at the centre of the story. The novel's title itself signals the mutual influence between Walker's fictional and theoretical writing as expressed in her assertion that 'womanist is to feminist as purple is to lavender' (1983: xii). Walker's novel, told through Celie's letters to God and the letters exchanged between Celie and her absent sister, Nettie, chronicles several decades of Celie's life in rural Georgia during the first half of the twentieth century. Throughout the novel, Celie confides in both God and her sister about the abuses she endures at the hands of her stepfather and husband and about her gradual womanist awakening and radically reconfigured understanding of the divine activated by her contact with other Black women who challenge racist patriarchy in a range of ways: her sister, Nettie, who forgoes marriage and motherhood and escapes abuse to become a missionary in Africa; her step-daughter-in-law, Sofia, who boldly refuses the conventions of wifely subservience within her marriage; and the sexually capacious, world weary blues singer, Shug Avery, who becomes Celie's lover, mentor and catalyst for Celie and Nettie's eventual reunion.

Female blues performers, as Angela Davis observes, were instrumental in 'defining the blues as a site where women could articulate and communicate their protests against male dominance', and their performances thereby 'divulge unacknowledged traditions of feminist consciousness in working-class black communities' (1998: 128, xii). Throughout Walker's novel and Marsha Norman's libretto for the musical – which sticks closely to the source material's plot and characterization – the blues diva functions in relation to and as a catalyst of reconfigured relations among her community: even as she is the source of church lady gossip, she is primarily the agent of desire, sisterly and sexual love and mentorship to the other female protagonists. As such, *The Color Purple* narratively foregrounds a variety of ways that 'women's blues provided a cultural space for community building among working-class black women, as well as a space devoid of bourgeois notions of sexual purity and "true womanhood"' (Davis 1998: n.pag.). This articulation of blues feminism is especially pronounced in the 2015 Broadway revival directed by Doyle and featuring Cynthia Erivo, Jennifer Hudson (eventually succeeded by Heather Headley and Jennifer Holliday) and Danielle Brooks. The production's blues feminist aesthetic is central to both its delight in and departures from Broadway divadom.

The Broadway diva is a staple in musicals and, like the blues diva, is an instrumental figure in shaping popular understandings of gender, race and sexuality (Clum 1999; Dvoskin 2016; Flinn 2007; Miller 1998; Wolf 2002, 2011). Indeed, since Broadway's Golden Age, the diva has been a central component of the form (Wolf 2002). Traditionally, the Broadway diva is 'the dark, alto outsider who sings the musical's well-known belting numbers [and who] breaks the rules and is condemned for her strength and determination' (Wolf 2011: 48). Larger-than-life, she takes up space – sonically, lyrically and scenically – often exceeding the boundaries of propriety, gender norms and coupledom. As such, Broadway diva roles can provide 'productive sites for queer feminist cultural critique, as their excess – their largeness – breaks the bounds of normative femininity and can allow audiences to glimpse it as a construction, rather than a "natural" state' (Dvoskin 2016: 94). While the Broadway diva may combine elements of 'the soubrette's lower, brassier voice with the ingénue's leading lady status', she ultimately distinguishes herself from these other traditional female roles through her insistent singularity: 'the diva's real story usually focuses on fulfilling her own needs and desires' (Dvoskin 2016: 95).[4] In many ways, Celie, Shug and Sofia each embody the characteristics of a traditional Broadway diva: they sing loudly and often and with marked virtuosity; they ultimately refuse the bonds of conventional coupledom; they provide expansive models for enacting or questioning femininity. But, they depart from convention in two distinct and significant ways: they form a diva trinity of mutually supportive relations, and they are Black women who carry the show.

Despite the diva's popularity, it is unusual and, indeed, unprecedented for three divas to be showcased at once in a Broadway show. There are certainly famous Broadway musical female trios such as *Gypsy*'s Rose, June and Louise (1959) and famous female trio numbers such as *Fiddler on the Roof*'s

'Matchmaker' (1964) and *Sweet Charity*'s 'Something Better Than This' (1966), but more commonly the Broadway musical promotes and acts as a star vehicle for a singular diva: Ethel Merman as Mama Rose, Patti LuPone as Evita, Audra McDonald as Bess or Bette Midler as Dolly. A notable exception is *Wicked* (2003) which, as part of its feminist interventions in the genre, showcases two divas, Elphalba and Galinda, as its central couple (Wolf 2008, 2011). The new musical, *War Paint* (2017), featuring Patti LuPone and Christine Ebersole as dramatic foils, Helena Rubenstein and Elizabeth Arden, adopts this tradition established by *Wicked*.

As the aforementioned litany reveals, divaness on Broadway is often and conspicuously marked by whiteness. For all her disruption of gender and sexuality, the Broadway diva has not historically challenged the musical's racialized investments in community and utopic promise in which 'community really means *white* community, while people of color are often absent from the utopia that many musicals present' (Hoffman 2014: 6, original emphasis). The Broadway musical's promotion of whiteness in and through its frequent staging of unification and aspiration emerges not just thematically but formally, as well.

> With few exceptions [...] nonwhite characters, unless they are main characters in a show such as *Dreamgirls* or *Flower Drum Song*, are not given 'I want' songs. Musicals, then, are about freedom of expression, about longings, but only for a select group of people.
>
> (Hoffman 2014: 7)

While a few memorable Black diva roles exist – notably Effie from *Dreamgirls* (1981) or Motormouth Maybelle from *Hairspray* (2002) – these characters are not the show's main protagonists and, instead, can be seen as the exceptions that prove the rule of Broadway's pervasive whiteness. Dan Dinero classifies these roles within what he calls 'a big black lady stops the show' trope wherein 'excessive' Black female performances are staged as central to but ultimately segregated from Broadway musical theatre: 'big black lady songs marginalize black women, assigning them a limited role on the Broadway stage' (2012: 29). It is thus rare for a singular Black diva to command the spotlight and unheard-of for three of them to share it at once. The diva trinity of Celie, Shug and Sofia and the relations that are sustained and transformed among them thus constitute an important distinction within Broadway musical tradition: they are afforded – thematically, lyrically and formally – pleasurable and powerful aspects of the Broadway diva normally reserved for white female characters while simultaneously challenging the constraints of inevitable singularity that frequently define the most famous (white) female diva roles.

Diva promotion: A new take on the 'triple threat'

The Color Purple, particularly in its original 2005 production, follows in *Wicked*'s ruby red footsteps by foregrounding Celie and her sister, Nettie, as the central couple whose unification the musical is propelled to restore. The promotional poster for the original production highlights this bond by depicting two girls in straw hats facing one another as they play a clapping game, referencing an opening moment of the show when Celie and Nettie, as children, share the brief hand-clapping duet, 'Huckleberry Pie', as an expression of their sisterly bond (Figure 12.1). On the poster, the girls emerge out of an amber-hued field dotted with lavender and are set against a cumulous-cloud-filled sky that fills most of the backdrop. The softened watercolour edges and warm colour tones of the poster's design combined with the straw hats and bucolic setting suggest that the world of this musical is rural, female-centric, historical and centred on a bond between two girls above all else (although not above Oprah Winfrey's name which is featured at the top of the poster – 'Oprah Winfrey Presents' – thereby showcasing not simply a diva couple but a singular diva producer, as well).

In contrast, the promotional posters for the 2015 Broadway revival feature the headlined names and close-up faces of the three actresses who portray Celie, Shug and Sofia: Erivo, Hudson and Brooks, respectively. At the completion of Hudson's run as Shug, her photo and name were replaced by Headley's, thereby consistently emphasizing that this production centres on *three* Black women. Unlike the 2005 poster, the women here are not costumed nor made up in ways that locate them at a temporal or geographical distance (Figures 12.2 and 12.3). In this way, the revival posters do not distinguish between the show's diva characters and the diva performers who play them, a merging that is not uncommon among Broadway diva roles (Wolf 2002). While Erivo's and Hudson's/Headley's names appear above and in larger font than Brooks' name and while Erivo's face is positioned in the foreground in a more full-front pose, all the women face the camera with similar closed-lipped, self-possessed expressions. All of their faces are in close proximity to one another and share the same horizontal plane, conveying a sense of close relation and equal footing among them. This featuring of three rather than two performers/characters also disrupts the focus on a central couple common in musicals and thereby highlights how this production of *The Color Purple* departs from – and perhaps even queers – these coupling principals/principles within Broadway musicals rather than, as the original production poster suggested, positioning itself within this legacy.

The press surrounding the 2015 revival – including televised interviews, reviews and feature articles depicting the star status of the leading actresses – established

FIGURE 12.1: *The Color Purple* original Broadway musical poster (2005). Artist Unknown. TMG – The Marketing Group.

all three performers and the characters they play as virtuosic divas who support and facilitate one another's achievement of greatness both on- and offstage. The actresses' appearance, along with director Doyle, on the 27 February 2016 episode of the public television talk show, *Theater Talk*, hosted by Susan Haskins and Michael Riedel, foregrounds their status as divas and promotes the revival's emphasis on the relationships among their characters. Host Michael Riedel exclaims that, among the revival's many virtues, 'I love the chemistry among these three [women]' and proceeds to anoint them affectionately as 'three very

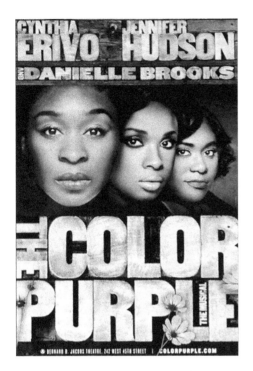 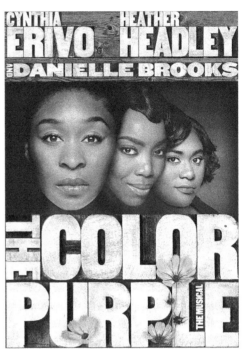

FIGURES 12.2 and 12.3: *The Color Purple* Broadway musical revival posters (2015, 2016). Photographer Unknown. Type A Marketing.

strong personalities, three divas, if you will' – to which all three actresses interrupt at once, 'Good divas! Divas in the good sense!' (*Theatre Talk* 2016). The women's collective qualification of Riedel's classification emphasizes how the diva 'chemistry' among their 'strong personalities' counters the commonly held (mis)understanding of the diva as a demanding and thus often isolated figure. At another point in the interview, Doyle situates and notes the distinctiveness of the female characters in *The Color Purple* within the history of Broadway musicals:

> If we look back in time at the strong women, you know, the Mermans and the LuPones and Bernadette Peters – and all of those women who are all strong – I worked with some of them – I know they're all strong, wonderful forces of nature – we've not until now had the opportunity to see black women take on that mantle. [...] That's not to say Audra [McDonald] hasn't played strong women, don't get me wrong, but [...] this piece, in particular, is about women, fundamentally about women. And a lot of the musical theatre writers have chosen *a* woman to write about but not *women* to write about.
>
> (*Theatre Talk* 2016, emphasis added)

Doyle's observation highlights the racial and relational – that is, the womanist – interventions that *The Color Purple* makes in the historical formation of Broadway divas. The show, and certainly this production, does not simply offer an additive model of inclusion for a Black diva but, perhaps more significantly, offers new possibilities of diva collectivity or relationality that re-imagines traditional Broadway musical constructions of its solitary, predominately white divas.

News features about the lead actresses emphasized the relationship between their emergent or established stardom and their subsequent, rightful place as divas. Each of the actresses who played Celie, Shug and Sofia was the subject of at least one feature news or magazine story: Erivo and Hudson in (among others) *New York Times*; Brooks in *The Washington Post*; Headley in the *New York Post* and Holliday in *People* magazine (Paulson 2015; Marks 2016; Riedel 2016; Soloski 2015; Quinn 2016). These feature stories, along with the reviews and online fan videos, bolstered the diva status of all of these performers and encouraged the elision between the diva performers with their respective diva roles. The press coverage of Erivo stressed her ascendency as an overnight Broadway star and the pleasures that witnessing her diva emergence afforded audiences: 'the greatest joy of all, at least for longtime believers in theater mythology, is the ascendancy of Ms. Erivo' (Brantley 2015). Brooks's relational diva status was reinforced by popular accounts of her concurrent role as 'Taystee' in the gyno-centric world of the Netflix women's prison drama, *Orange Is the New Black*. Hudson's and Holliday's diva performances as Shug were ghosted and bolstered by their shared associations with award-winning performances as Effie and her show-stopping diva solo, 'And I'm Telling You', in *Dreamgirls*; Holliday won the Tony for her role on Broadway in 1982, and Hudson garnered an Oscar for the role in the 2007 motion picture.[5] Given the paucity of Black diva roles on Broadway and in Hollywood and given the legendary star-making status of Effie's musical number, Hudson's and Holiday's affiliation with *Dreamgirls* authenticated their respective statuses as established divas. Press accounts of Headley channelled her star text into a narrative of the diva's triumphant comeback noting that her performance as Shug marked her long-anticipated return to Broadway after her Tony Award-winning performance in *Aida* (2000). This emphasis on the leading actresses' star texts served to establish and justify their collective status as divas, thereby underscoring the relationship between stardom and divaness and revealing the ways that 'the diva is both an on- and offstage phenomenon; she is both the character and the self' (Wolf 2011: 54).

Reviews of the production reinforced the horizon of expectations established by the promotional and press materials that showcased the revival's emphasis on diva relations. The revival received universal acclaim from critics across the country, and the source of many reviewers' delight was the diva triumvirate at its centre. Chris Jones titled his *Chicago Tribune* review, '*The Color Purple* lifted by trio of strong women' and observed, 'Clearly, Doyle's *Color Purple* has been conceived (and marketed) as the story of three strong women' (2015: 6). Jones offered praise for both the divas' skills and the relationships they established not only with one another but with the audience as well: 'They are staring at three powerful characters, played by powerful actresses who sing like the angels and who are staring back at them' (6). *New York Times* critic, Ben Brantley, delighted in the ways 'Mr. Doyle's version [...] puts Celie and her sisters in suffering and triumph front and center' (2015) and Charles McNulty of the *Los Angeles Times* noted favourably how 'The women are the backbone of *TCP*, and the actresses here find common cause' (2015: E12). Even while reviewers expressed unqualified astonishment over Erivo's transcendent Broadway debut performance, many, like Marilyn Stasio in her review for *Variety*, emphasized the performative power of all three actresses:

> The ladies wear the pants in John Doyle's ravishing revival of *TCP*. Jennifer Hudson is radiant as love machine Shug Avery. Danielle Brooks shakes the house as the earthy Sofia. And Cynthia Erivo [...] brings the audience roaring to its feet as Celie. [...] All three performers are making their Broadway debuts, which makes it all the more thrilling.
>
> (2015: 118)

The reviews' widespread focus on this 'trio of strong women' who simultaneously shared positions as virtuosic divas and Broadway neophytes underscored the production's promotional emphasis on *The Color Purple* as a show populated and propelled by the collective power of three dynamic divas and the mutually supportive relationships among them.

Relational structure, relational staging

The revival re-contextualizes Broadway musical divas within a relational frame through its plot structure, unconventional approach to production elements like direction and scenography and conventional musical numbers like the diva solo. Throughout both the original production and the revival, the plot maintains its central focus on Celie's individual journey towards self-actualization while simultaneously emphasizing her character development in relation to and as a result of her connections with other women. Structurally, the musical signals this relational world immediately and lyrically when Celie sings the opening line, 'Hey, Sista, Whatcha Gon Do', which works at both the literal and idiomatic level. The launching of the show in this interrogative mode invites the audience to assume a more active role in their spectator-ship and highlights the show's focus on a mode of interaction and entreaty that will convey and shape Celie's character and story. On the literal level, Celie directs the question to her sister, Nettie, as part of their clapping game to which Nettie responds in rhythm, 'Goin' Down by the River/ Gonna Play with You' (Russell et al. 2016).[6] The call-and-response play between the sisters establishes their intimate bond and foregrounds our understanding of Celie's character in relation to other female characters. The line also simultaneously conveys its idiomatic connotation as a rhetorical question addressed to all 'sistas', expressing a sense of resignation, as in, 'Sista, what is there to do/what can be done?' for a girl trapped by the patriarchal confines of a 'Papa [who] don't like no/Screamin' "round here"'. The revival underscores the question's more expansive address through the staging of Celie up-centre and facing the audience when she delivers the line before crossing downstage to kneel facing her sister for the rest of the hand-clapping game. The song's structure also works to position the sisters' exchange within a larger community: Celie and Nettie's brief duet is actually a prelude for the longer gospel number, 'Mysterious Ways', performed by the company's ensemble. The seamless transition between the girls' call and response chant and the Church Ladies' call and response exclamation, 'It's Sunday morning [...] So make a joyful noise!' introduces the centrality of Celie's relationship with God while also distinguishing this relationship from Celie's more fraught positioning within institutional powers like the church and its chorus of Church Ladies who move from Sunday praise for the Lord's 'mysterious ways' to catty gossip about Celie's fate. The musical thus encourages the audience from the outset to regard Celie and her relationship with her actual sister dialectically – that is, in relation to and shaped by larger structural, social and 'sista-ly', or diva, forces.

Doyle's spare scenic design and ensemble-driven direction facilitates a dialectical and diva relational consideration of Celie's story and character. Doyle, a Scottish director whom reviewers regularly praise for his signature 'minimalism' (Brantley 2015; Catton 2015; Rooney 2015), has achieved notoriety in the United States for his pared-down approach to musicals, most notably his Tony Award-winning Broadway revivals of Stephen Sondheim's *Sweeney Todd* (2005) and *Company* (2006). As Doyle has frequently asserted in interviews, his restrained direction and design foreground story and relationships among characters within his productions (Healy 2013). For *The Color Purple*, Doyle trimmed nearly 30 minutes off the production's running time, creating a sense of vitality and quick tempo by making cuts to plodding exposition in Norman's book, truncating transitions and eliminating the 'Overture'. The music and lyrics of the musical's score, written by Brenda Russell, Allee Willis and Stephen Bray, remain intact but are livened up with new orchestrations by Joseph Joubert and Catherine Jayes. Doyle's bare and flexible set consists of platforms made from rough-hewn wooden planks that cover the stage floor and extend across the length and width of the back wall. Along the back wall's slatted platforms, which are pocked with holes, hang more than a dozen straight-backed wooden chairs that the ensemble take down and use as props and furniture throughout the course of the show. The chairs play an integral role in the show's sparse prop economy, in which the few items that appear onstage become freighted with multiple and mutable meanings: chairs are transformed from indoor seating to hoes in the field, from guns among insurgents in Africa to the bars of a Georgia jail cell; a swaddled sheet signifies Celie's newborn baby and its brisk unfurling represents the moment Celie's abusive stepfather gives the child away against Celie's wishes. The warm, faded palette of Doyle's wood-covered set works with the earth tones and sepia-wash of Ann Hould-Ward's costume design and Jane Cox's lighting design to evoke abstractly rather than mimetically the show's rural and historical setting.[7]

This scenography conveys Doyle's aesthetic of abstraction and subtraction in favour of realist mimesis or high-tech spectacle more common on the Broadway musical stage. For example, the set certainly suggests the battered clapboard siding and austere feel of the humble wood-framed house that encloses Celie's world: as one reviewer noted, 'We can practically feel the splinters in those rough boards and the hard seats of those stiff-backed chairs' (Stasio 2015). Yet, even as the set establishes this dreary domestic world, it simultaneously conveys a sense of spaciousness and possibility: the stage uncluttered with excessive props or furniture and undivided by walls or partitions, the high fly space filled by the wood-slatted back wall which, while menacing in its length and width, is also made porous by its many holes. Simply, there is an abundance of unbounded physical space onstage. All of this empty space ultimately allows for the possibility of three divas in all of their diva glory to occupy the stage at once without elbowing each other out. Throughout the production, divas share the stage without having to sacrifice either their boundless performative prowess or their ties to other women. Scenic expansiveness thus encourages an expansive re-staging and re-thinking of relationships among women, and among divas, in particular, otherwise bound or foreclosed by patriarchal and racist confines or by the lavish scenography that often fills the conventional Broadway musical stage.

This relational staging is not unusual for Doyle, whose ensemble-focused directing style, along with the sparse visual economy of his set designs, engages the audience in a contract of interpretive participation and negotiation that is arguably more active than that demanded from most other Broadway musicals. Doyle's ensemble ethos resonates with the gospel aesthetic of the show wherein diva performers and performances are understood not as exceptional to or isolated from the community but as an intrinsic component or signal of the strength of the collective. In *The Color Purple*, Doyle stages the company within dialectical, pedagogical and presentational configurations that serve to reconfigure conventional Broadway relationships between the audience and the performers and among the divas who propel the action. Here, as in his previous productions, the entire company remains onstage for much of the show, acting alternately as implicated bystanders and compassionate witnesses to Celie's journey towards self-assertion. In one scene, a female ensemble member abruptly shakes out the sheet representing Celie's newborn to convey the moment in which Celie is forced to give up the child, while in another scene, the women of the company quilt or fold laundry (using the same aforementioned sheet) as they bear witness to Celie and Nettie's expressions of aspiration in their duet, 'Our Prayer'. Throughout the production, Doyle positions the actors – especially the women – as spectators: Church Ladies observe Celie and Nettie, Celie watches Sofia and everyone keeps their eyes on Shug. Doyle's privileging of staged spectatorship encourages a dialectical view of Celie's plight; she is always seen in relation to others and, in fact, is never alone onstage except for when she sings her liberatory 11 o'clock number, 'I'm Here'.

Doyle's Brechtian actor/spectator ethos works – like all Brechtian staging – not just dialectically but pedagogically, offering audiences a model for active engagement as is evident when the company enters and remains onstage midway through the intimate musical numbers between Celie and Shug: 'Too Beautiful for Words', 'What About Love' and 'The Color Purple'. The ensemble's presence during these moments in which they stand upstage and look on without judgment serves to affirm the romantic and sexual intimacy between Celie and Shug. This staged act of witnessing shows the audience how to view, accept and celebrate these moments of queer diva relations as integral to Celie's transformation. Moreover, these scenes of staged spectatorship semiotically incorporate Celie and Shug's private, non-normative bond into the larger public world of the play, thereby transforming, or more precisely, queering, the community in which Celie is embedded. The presentational acting style in these scenes and throughout the production also serves explicitly to encourage its audience to assume a more participatory, communal role. While Broadway musicals often rely on presentational modes of delivery, especially for the principal's solo numbers, the performers in this revival frequently exchange dialogue or deliver their songs to the audience rather than to one another. This non-mimetic staging favoured by Doyle is especially effective at reconfiguring audience/actor relations in the intimate scenes between Shug and Celie. In their duet, 'What About Love?' that closes the first act, the women explore the contours of and questions about their new-found love for one another. Keeping with the interrogative mode established by Celie at the musical's outset, the women launch their exchange of vulnerable questioning – 'What about trust? What about tenderness?' – while each facing the audience, thereby inviting spectators to share in this moment of intimacy. In this interactive rather than hermetic staging, the enactment of diva intimacy serves to forge an actor/audience intimacy that reconfigures the more conventional relationship of adoring distance between the singular Broadway diva and her fans. The audience/actor relationship is also transformed in the opening and closing ensemble numbers, 'Mysterious Ways' and 'The Color Purple (Reprise)'. The performers in these songs do not just sing out *towards* the audience but sing out *with* them, 'as if', Doyle remarks, 'everyone is in the same church at the same time' (Gerard 2016). Thus, within the context of *The Color Purple*, Doyle's signature ensemble-emphasis and non-mimetic performance style achieve 'the force and fluidity of a Gospel service [in which] the cast melds with the audience into a congregation' (McNulty 2015). In this way, Doyle's aesthetic resonates with and provides space for the amplification of Black spiritual and feminist traditions – from gospel call-and-response to a womanist ethos of sisterhood – in which diva virtuosity is showcased as an expression of and catalyst for collectivity rather than isolated singularity. Through this communal resonance and reconfiguration, the revival powerfully positions – indeed, interpolates – its audiences as not simply interpretively active spectators but as womanist witnesses who share in the show's understanding of diva relations as a model of and catalyst for liberatory female bonds.

Diva solos, not solo divas

Divas in *The Color Purple* activate self-awareness and forge emancipating female bonds by singing, loudly and often, to and for one another – even in songs that are not ostensibly directed to other women. Sofia sings her diva solo, 'Hell No!', to Celie and later, in the group number, 'Uh Oh', punctuates her defiant responses to Harpo with a conspiratorial affirmation directed at Celie: 'A woman need to have some fun. Ain't that right, Miss Celie?' In her diva solos, Shug instructs the women at the juke joint how to 'Push da Button' of their sexual desires and helps Celie see herself as 'Too Beautiful for Words'. Celie pronounces her diva skills as a seamstress in 'Miss Celie's Pants', launching the number as a letter addressed to Nettie and proceeding to sing to and with the women in the company, including Shug and Sofia, who show off Celie's bold and colourful designs. In response to Celie singing that her styles 'Make you/Feel like a queen', the chorus of women repeat, 'Who dat say/Who dat?', as Sofia stands on a chair and proclaims, 'Sofia's back/And I'm here to stay'. 'Miss Celie's Pants' not only showcases Celie's burgeoning self-assertion and status as a diva-in-the-making but foregrounds how her diva virtuosity reactivates Sofia's diva defiance. This marks the first time that Sofia sings after her spirit was crushed and her voice silenced when she was arrested for speaking back to a white woman, severely beaten in jail and forced upon release to work as the white woman's maid.

The women-centred world that the revival stages is, in some ways, not unlike the homosocial lyrical, musical and choreographic worlds often emphasized in other Broadway musicals – from *West Side Story* (1959) to *Wicked*. But what distinguishes *The Color Purple*, as 'Miss Celie's Pants' reveals, is that divas not only forge sustaining bonds with one another that remain intact at the end – already a remarkable feat for a Broadway show – but that expressions of diva virtuosity serve to animate and restore liberatory relations and a sense of selfhood, even divahood, previously wrecked by the forces of racist patriarchy. Narratively, these acts of restoration occur when, for example, Shug restores the bond between Celie and Nettie or when Celie's curse on Mister reanimates Sofia's broken spirit. At the close of the first act, Shug, upon discovering that Mister has been hiding Nettie's letters from Africa, steals them back and delivers them to Celie, who, having received no response from Nettie over the years, became convinced she was dead. Doyle's direction foregrounds the restorative power of this diva relation in his staging of Shug and Celie's duet, 'What About Love', that occurs just before the narrative revelation of Nettie's letters. During the second half of their duet, as Celie and Shug are slowly surrounded by the ensemble, Nettie emerges from upstage carrying her letters and crosses downstage between the two women as they profess their love to one another. This staging underscores how the expression of diva relations and specifically the sexual desire awakened by the diva facilitates the restoration of other female relations rather than foreclosing or compromising them. Near the top of the second act, when Celie decides to leave Mister and curses him as 'nothin' but some dead horse's shit', she provokes from Sofia – recently broken into silence by the forces of racist patriarchy – a series of long, low, life-activating peals of laughter. Upon hearing Sofia's long-absent laughter, Mister remarks, 'Look who's come back from the grave?' to which Sofia defiantly and loudly responds, 'Dead horse's shit! Oh, yeah, Sofia home now!' In this scene, Celie's assertion of her own discursive power (her delivery of a curse against Mister) and her own new-found vocal power (her movement from speech into fulsome song on the line, 'I may be poor/I may be Black/I may be ugly/But I'm here!') – serves to restore Sofia's voice (and vocal power), as well.

Nowhere is the activating and restorative power of the diva more palpable than in the diva solos, 'Hell No!' (Sofia), 'Push da Button' (Shug) and 'I'm Here' (Celie). *The Color Purple* narratively and lyrically foregrounds diva relations and scenographically provides space for divas to share the stage without denying its audience the pleasure of delighting in the rafter-raising diva solo. In fact, the revival's approach to diva solos challenges the standard function of this conventional musical number. Many of the most renowned musical diva solos – 'Rose's Turn' from *Gypsy*, 'Cabaret' from *Cabaret* (1966) and 'No Good Deed' from *Wicked*, to name a few – serve to showcase the diva's singular vocal power while simultaneously enacting her often tragically singular, or solitary, fate. Diva solos derive their emotional force precisely from this tension between the power of the performer's voice and the character's impotent attempts to forge lasting bonds. The seemingly inevitable foreclosure of relations for the diva is thus tied to, and sometimes regarded as the result of, the (often belting) enunciation of her overpowering diva voice within and through her show-stopping solo. But the diva solos in *The Color Purple*, while adhering to the lung-busting, crowd-rousing, star-vehicle pleasures of the conventional form, actually function to activate a set of relations rather than a sense of isolation for the diva and for the women who surround her.

The Color Purple narratively and performatively establishes Sofia and Shug (and their non-conformist approaches to marriage, motherhood and musical numbers) as recognizable Broadway divas whose 'excess breaks bounds of normative femininity [...] [and] who sing loudly, take up space (both narratively and physically) and demand attention' (Dvoskin 2016: 94). Both Sofia's 'Hell No' and Shug's 'Push da Button' function relationally in part because they function pedagogically: Sofia teaches Celie how to stand up for herself and stand together with other women while Shug teaches the townswomen how to access and fulfil their sexual desires. Sofia sings 'Hell No!' – a rhythmand-blues and gospel-inflected song built for a vocal powerhouse – upon learning that Celie told Sofia's husband Harpo to beat her. The song conveys Sofia's long-practiced 'fight' against family violence as a child, her subsequent refusal to 'fight in my own house', her decision to leave Harpo as a result of his attempted abuse and her insistence that Celie 'better learn how to fight while you're still alive'. Sofia's solo reprimands Celie for her collusion with patriarchy and, as such, could easily have served to foreclose the possibility of a continued relationship between the women. Instead, the song's primary purpose is to forge a bond between the two women in spite of the misogynist structures that Celie has internalized and that seek to divide and isolate them. Sofia's solo announces her departure from the household, but not without urging Celie to 'Let me take you away'. Doyle's staging of the solo positions Celie seated downstage centre facing away from the audience and up towards Sofia who stands centre stage. The female ensemble observes their exchange before accompanying Sofia as backup singers. In this way, Celie and the female ensemble act as surrogates for the audience, reinforcing the pedagogical force and relational bonds generated by the lyrical content of Sofia's solo.

Despite being encircled by men at the juke joint, Shug begins her bluesy solo, 'Push da Button', by addressing the women: 'Now there's somethin' 'bout good lovin'/That all you ladies should know'. While the song proceeds, lyrically, to direct its lesson on sexual fulfilment to both sexes, it functions choreographically to reconfigure the relationship between Shug and the townswomen from one based on suspicion and presumed threat to one based on shared delight in bodily pleasure. This is especially evident in the performance by Headley, for whom Doyle adjusted his choreography (Riedel 2016). Doyle's choreography and Headley's deft execution of it emphasize Shug's bodily ease and direct interaction with the other women onstage. Thus, a song that could easily have reinforced the women's view of Shug as a sexual threat (who tempts their men with her lascivious lyrics and attitude) is transformed into a song in which Shug wins over the women by teaching them her skills at acquiring sexual fulfilment. Prior to this number, the female chorus members regularly express their contempt for Shug's 'low moral character' ('All We Got to Say') and respond to her arrival in town with the admonishments, 'Lock up all yo mens/And young boys, too' or 'She ain't got no friends/'cept the ones she screw' ('Shug Avery Comin' to Town'). It is no surprise, then, that when Shug starts singing about how 'to light your man on fire', the women respond as scandalized listeners seated with their arms crossed, eyes cast down, wagging a finger of reproach and making a sign of the cross. But by the song's first chorus, the women join Shug downstage centre and attempt to follow her self-possessed, hip-shaking, knee-bending choreography. For the remainder of the song, the women mimic Shug's moves as they gain an increasing comfort and delight in the pleasures of their bodies. Even while suggestively interacting with men throughout the song, Headley encourages the women's participation, at one point interjecting her unscripted instruction to the ladies, 'You need to slow that down a little bit. Now you can speed it up!' In this way, Headley's performance underscores Shug's relational diva status as 'a role that's a star turn and yet also an integral part of an ensemble' (Rooney 2015). Within Shug's diva solo, the incorporation of Shug's choreography represents the incorporation of a lesson about inhabiting, affirming and fulfilling female desire. The women's shared dance moves serve to convey their unifying bond with Shug and with each other as sexual *subjects*, in contrast to their previous division (and unshared choreographical vocabulary with Shug) as sexual *objects* within patriarchy's gaze. The reconfigured relations between the women and Shug in her diva solo implicate patriarchy's derisive (and divisive) conception of the diva as a means of preventing women from inhabiting and sharing knowledge about sexual desire and foregrounds the ways that the diva's sexual capaciousness is central to her pedagogical function and her womanist power.

At first glance, Celie's diva solo, 'I'm Here', and Erivo's show-stopping delivery of it closely resemble the classic 11 o'clock female belting number 'composed and designed as an emotional tour-de-force' in which 'the leading female principal sings her most expressive song' (Wolf 2011: 167). Like Rose in *Gypsy* or Caroline in *Caroline, or Change* (2003), Celie sings her 11 o'clock number following what seems like the irreparable severing of her relational ties: she has left her husband, Shug has left her for one last fling and Nettie's whereabouts remain unknown. But, unlike 'Rose's Turn', the paragon of 11 o'clock numbers, Celie's song is not motivated by nor performed as a compensatory act in response to foreclosed relationships or a sense of isolation. Rather, as Celie's ultimate expression of self-love and assertion of her voice, 'I'm Here' is a product of the culmination of diva relations she has forged throughout the show and, furthermore, serves to re-incorporate Celie into a community that has been radically reconfigured by the divas who move through it. Lyrically, the song expresses Celie's new-found self-love and the faith she maintains in the love she feels from her absent sister and children ('They may not be here/But they still mine') and in her ability to keep loving despite loss ('Showin' my heart/To the folks that I'm close to'). The song is an enunciation of her selfhood achieved through the loving enumeration of her relationships, her body (her hands, heart and eyes) and her desire ('I'm gonna flirt with somebody'); but, above all, the song insists that her self-definition arises from her virtuosic ability to 'sing out [...] Sing ooouuuut'. Celie does not just become liberated, she becomes a diva; or, she becomes liberated precisely by becoming a diva.

Structurally, 'I'm Here' moves across different musical modes: it begins with Celie's tentative voice supported by light accompaniment; the second section shifts to a bluesy drive in which it gains vocal and musical momentum; the song culminates in an uptempo pop-rock ballad before circling back in its final lines to light accompaniment that showcases Celie's/Erivo's powerful belt. The effect of these shifts is that the song, as Stacy Wolf observes, 'almost feels like three different numbers, as if Celie is experimenting with a range of musical linguistic self-expressions' (2011: 187). The changing styles thus chart Celie's process of diva-becoming; through the course of the song we hear her, as Wolf notes, come into her voice before our very ears (2011: 188). This effect is profoundly and movingly reinforced in the revival by the collapsing of Celie's transformation with Erivo's transformation from a relatively unknown actress making her Broadway debut to a Tony Award-winning diva. A large part of what makes Erivo's astonishing delivery of 'I'm Here', which stopped the show with standing ovations nightly, so exhilarating is witnessing the simultaneous and co-constitutive emergence of Erivo and/as Celie as divas. 'The greatest joy of all', *New York Times* critic Brantley observed, 'at least for longtime believers in theater mythology, is the ascendancy of Ms. Erivo' (2015). This marks another way in which 'I'm Here' distinguishes itself from other classic 11 o'clock female belting numbers (or even previous versions of this same song) that frequently serve as vehicles for established divas to showcase why they are rightly crowned or for an ageing diva to assert her comeback. Instead, the revival's version of 'I'm Here' shows us how the right song makes the diva just as much as the right diva makes the song.

The 11 o'clock number is not the last time we see or hear from a diva in *The Color Purple*. Immediately after the song ends in the revival, Celie struts upstage and grabs the sheet which, over the course of the show, has become laden with associations with Celie's relational ties to her lost children (Celie's swaddling of it and its subsequent heart-wrenching unfurling) and to a female-centric domestic world (women witnessing her transformation as they fold laundry). Following 'I'm Here', Celie takes a long moment to carry the sheet downstage – as the audience settles back into their seats after their extended ovation – before shaking it out onto the stage for a picnic at which she will re-define her relationship with Mister, reunite with Nettie, Celie and Sofia and at which the entire company will gather for the final ensemble number, 'The Color Purple (Reprise)'. In her conversation with Mister while sitting together atop the sheet, Celie acknowledges the redemptive changes he has undergone, refuses his marriage proposal and establishes instead a bond with him based on their shared love of a diva: Shug Avery. Celie and Mister's exchange reveals how within a world shaped by diva relations, everyone is afforded the possibility of redemption and reincorporation into a community based on womanist rather than (hetero)sexist terms. The timing of this final transformation of the sheet into the very platform on which Celie reintegrates into her community in radical new ways underscores the relational power of diva virtuosity: Celie delivers her song and her song delivers her over into reconfigured and restored relationships.

In their closing moment of reconciliation, Celie asks Mister, 'What do you love best about Shug?' to which Mister responds, 'Her style'. Throughout *The Color Purple* revival, divahood is characterized not only by the ability to stop the show or elicit rapturous delight and desire through one's distinctive vocal power. Divahood here is also a style of living in and fighting back against and triumphing over the world. Divahood is a mode of womanist relations and an activating force for self-liberation. Divahood provides a clearing, a space marked by liberatory female bonds, a divahood, in which we can view divas as women of colour have long viewed and loved them; that is, as the vessels of virtuosity crafted from and inaugurating a sense of communion rather than isolation. Divahood here is a clearing on which the diva's centrality to womanist thought and practice can be more fully animated and appreciated. Divahood is the unfolded sheet on which we make room for and revisit and unfurl our understanding of Black feminism and on which we implicate and revise our racialized conceptions of the diva's power and its relationship to her seemingly inevitable solitariness. In the revival of *The Color Purple*, divahood is the cleared stage on which we reconstruct the Great White Way that we have come to think about divas.

NOTES

1. Italicized lyrics are from diva standards, 'Anything You Can Do, I Can Do Better' (*Annie Get Your Gun*) by Irving Berlin and 'Rose's Turn' (*Gypsy*) by Jule Styne and Stephen Sondheim.
2. For more on the virtuosity, singularity and queerness of diva figures, see Clum (1999), Doty (2007, 2008), Koestenbaum (1993), Leonardi and Pope (1996), Miller (1998) and Wolf (2002, 2007, 2011).
3. Although not the lead, Shug, unlike Celie, fits easily within standard definitions of the diva as a singular, well-known performer (both in the role and in the casting) who disrupts gender norms. In the musical and in the novel on which it is based, Shug is immediately recognizable as a diva, whereas Celie slowly emerges as one by the end.
4. Dvoskin distinguishes between what she calls 'diva roles' and 'diva characters' on the Broadway stage wherein diva roles are larger-than-life female characters who drive a musical's action and encourage a virtuosic, outsized performance style', while diva characters are 'textually marked as divas in that they are performers, but they do not necessarily incorporate the productive, joyous excess of a diva role' (2016: 94). Following her distinction, I would categorize Celie, Sofia and Shug as diva roles, with Shug also classified as a diva character who, unlike other diva characters that Dvoskin discusses, does manage to simultaneously incorporate the 'joyous excess of the diva role'.
5. Carlson (2003) provides insights about how performers' roles are ghosted or haunted by the previous roles they have played.
6. All subsequent quotations from the revival's song lyrics are taken from Russell et al. (2016). All Lyrics Used By Permission of Natasha's Holding Music (BMI). All Rights for Natasha's Holding Music Administered by Painted Desert Music Corp (BMI).
7. I draw my observations about the revival's production elements from my attendance at three performances: 5 May 2016 featuring Jennifer Hudson; 19 August 2016 featuring Heather Headley and 4 January 2017 featuring Jennifer Holliday.

REFERENCES

Brantley, B. (2015), 'Blazing spirits, distilled', *New York Times*, 11 December, p. C1.

Carlson, M. (2003), *The Haunted Stage: The Theatre as Memory Machine*, Ann Arbor: University of Michigan Press.

Catton, P. (2015), 'Minimalism brings down barriers in *The Color Purple*', *Wall Street Journal*, 8 December, p. A17.

Clum, J. (1999), *Something for the Boys: Musical Theater and Gay Culture*, New York: St. Martin's Press.

Davis, A. (1998), *Blues Legacies and Black Feminism: Gertrude 'Ma' Rainey, Bessie Smith, and Billie Holiday*, New York: Vintage Books.

Dinero, D. (2012), 'A big black lady stops the show: Black women, performances of excess and the power of saying no', *Studies in Musical Theatre*, 6:1, pp. 29–41.

Doty, A. (2007), 'Introduction: There's something about Mary', *Camera Obscura*, 22:65, pp. 1–9.

Doty, A. (2008), 'Introduction: The good, the bad, and the fabulous; or, the diva issue strikes back', *Camera Obscura*, 23:67, pp. 1–8.

Doyle, J. (dir.) (2015–17), *The Color Purple*, written by M. Norman, performed at the Bernard B. Jacobs Theatre, New York: 10 November–8 January.

Dvoskin, M. (2016), 'Embracing excess: The queer feminist power of musical theatre diva roles', *Studies in Musical Theatre*, 10:1, pp. 93–103.

Flinn, C. (2007), *Brass Diva: The Life and Legends of Ethel Merman*, Berkeley: University of California Press.

Gerard, J. (2016), 'Disruptive *Color Purple* director John Doyle swings the scythe brilliantly on Broadway (and off)', *Deadline Hollywood*, 7 April, http://deadline.com/2016/04/john-doyle-color-purple-tony-awards watch-1201733579/. Accessed 25 February 2017.

Haskins, S. and Riedel, M. (2016), interview with Cynthia Erivo, Jennifer Hudson, Danielle Brooks and John Doyle, *Theater Talk*, 27 February, CUNY TV, New York: PBS.

Healy, P. (2013), 'Stripping a Southern musical to its core', *New York Times*, 18 August, p. AR4.

Hoffman, W. (2014), *The Great White Way: Race and the Broadway Musical*, New Brunswick: Rutgers University Press.

Jones, C. (2015), '*The Color Purple* lifted by trio of strong women', *Chicago Tribune*, 11 December, p. 6.

Koestenbaum, W. (1993), *The Queen's Throat: Opera, Homosexuality, and the Mystery of Desire*, New York: Da Capo Press.

Leonardi, S. and Pope, R. (1996), *The Diva's Mouth: Body, Voice, Prima Donna Politics*, New Brunswick: Rutgers University Press.

Marks, P. (2016), 'From *Orange* to *Purple*: The multi-hued performance ride of Danielle Brooks', *The Washington Post – Blogs*, 29 April, https://www.washingtonpost.com/news/arts-and-entertainment/wp/2016/04/29/from-orange-to-purple-the-multi-hued-performance-ride-of-daniellebrooks/?utmterm=.d80df959c867. Accessed 19 January 2017.

McNulty, C. (2015), '*Color Purple* has a divine spirit', *Los Angeles Times*, 11 December, p. E12.

Miller, D. A. (1998), *Place for Us: Essay on the Broadway Musical in the 1950s*, New York: Oxford University Press.

Paulson, M. (2015), 'The actress Cynthia Erivo rises with *The Color Purple*', *New York Times*, 22 December, p. C1.

Quinn, D. (2016), 'How Broadway icon Jennifer Holliday overcame depression, body issues and temporary blindness to stage a comeback in *The Color Purple*', *People Magazine*, 26 October, http://people.com/theater/ how-broadway-icon-jennifer-holliday-overcame-depression-body-issues and-temporary-blindness-to-stage-a-comeback-in-the-color-purple/. Accessed 20 February 2017.

Riedel, M. (2016), 'Purple reign: Jennifer Hudson who? Heather Headley's the new draw', *New York Post*, 13 May, p. 32.

Rooney, D. (2015), '*The Color Purple*: Theater review', *Hollywood Reporter*, 10 December, http://www.hollywoodreporter.com/review/jennifer-hudson color-purple-theater-847846. Accessed 28 January 2017.

Russell, B., Willis, A. and Bray, S. (2016), *The Color Purple*, *The Color Purple Musical* (New Broadway Cast Recording), sleeve notes, New York: Broadway Records.

Soloski, A. (2015), 'Jennifer Hudson, safety net is not included', *New York Times*, 6 December, p. AR1.

Stasio, M. (2015), '*The Color Purple* review', *Variety*, 15 December, p. 118.

Walker, A. (1982), *The Color Purple*, New York: Harcourt Brace Jovanovich.

Walker, A. (1983), *In Search of Our Mother's Gardens: Womanist Prose*, New York: Harcourt Brace Jovanovich.

Wolf, S. (2002), *A Problem Like Maria: Gender and Sexuality in the American Musical*, Ann Arbor: University of Michigan Press.

Wolf, S. (2007), 'Wicked divas, musical theater, and Internet girl fans', *Camera Obscura*, 22:65, pp. 39–71.

Wolf, S. (2008), 'Defying gravity: Queer conventions in the musical *Wicked*', *Theatre Journal*, 60:1, pp. 1–21.

Wolf, S. (2011), *Changed for Good: A Feminist History of the Broadway Musical*, Oxford: Oxford University Press.

13

How Can the Small Screen Contain Her? Television, Genre and the Twenty-First-Century Broadway Diva Onslaught

Kelly Kessler

The Broadway diva has been a part of American television from the get-go. Ethel Merman and Mary Martin's omnipresence in the early days of television helped to establish the New York-based medium's sense of style and place. At times, however, the theatrical grandiosity of musical divas like Carol Channing, Judy Garland and Patti LuPone has pushed up against the form and displayed a contentious relationship with stylistic specificities of this box-bound medium. I argue, however, that the twenty-first-century television industry has shifted in various ways, allowing for a more nuanced symbiotic relationship between the Broadway diva and American television programming. Old and new Broadway divas alike have become staples of network, cable and streaming programming in the 2000s, with such iconic figures as Liza Minnelli, Elaine Stritch, Bernadette Peters, Audra McDonald, Megan Hilty and Sutton Foster appearing on TVs and mobile devices across America. Importantly, and much more so than in previous eras, the musical diva of millennial television has been able to *embrace* her true divadom within small screen performances. Whereas the grandeur and power of divas like Channing and Garland may have once clashed with the more diminutive expectations of television aesthetics and stories, she now finds her grandness economically, spatially and narratively in demand. After briefly exploring the notion of divadom and providing a (too) short history of the diva-television relationship, I posit why the 2000s is the era of Broadway's televisual diva. Examining shifts in television marketing, generic norms, shooting practices and viewing habits, I argue that a confluence of events has made twenty-first-century television a natural home for Broadway's grande dames.

But who are these divas? When I began considering the recent deluge of divas to the small screen, I first had to wrap my head around the very meaning of the term. Broadway actresses were and certainly had been making the sojourn from the footlights to the small screen for decades: Carol Lawrence, Channing, Gwen Verdon, Carol Haney and the list goes on. Were they all divas? Just who is the diva? Is she simply a Broadway legend? She whose name on the marquee can sell out a Broadway house? Certain names appear and reappear through anecdotal evidence and popular press articles addressing contemporary divas, names like Foster, Hilty, Idina Menzel, Kristin Chenoweth, Lupone and Peters (Musto 2014; Feldman and Cote 2012; Wontorek 2015). Although initial research on this archetypal role often centred on the operatic diva, scholars have approached this iconic female figure from various performance platforms – opera, popular music, film and soap opera – and intellectual vantage points such as gay male spectatorship, camp, consumerism and queer female fandom (Koestenbaum 1993; Leonardi and Pope 1996; O'Neill 2007; Salvato 2007; Wolf 2007; Wlodarz 2008). In many of these contexts, her gist (if she can be associated with something so common as a gist) comes through in her excess.

Across scholarship, excess, power and transgression define the diva. Edward O'Neill, in his discussion of the intersection of divas, camp and commodity, describes diva roles as providing space for women 'whose talents exceed the limited boundaries of romantic interests' and instead 'provide the opportunity for extraordinarily talented women to give awesome, admirable and even frightening performances' (2007: 23–24). Stacy Wolf describes 'the quintessential musical diva, [as] the singer of big, belting songs of self-determination and self-celebration' (2007: 51), while Michelle Dvoskin argues that musicals' diva roles 'are productive sites for queer feminist cultural critique, as their excess – their largeness – breaks the bounds of normative femininity' (2016: 94). Further, Wolf argues, 'The diva is both an on- and offstage phenomenon' (2007: 54). In short, she is a force with which to be reckoned whether playing a character or simply performing her own celebrity. She exudes attitude. Onstage and off, the character (and actress) is larger-than-life and needs to be if she is going to fill a Broadway theatre, up to the cheap seats, with the raw emotion of a gut-wrenching performance.

Enter the challenge of transplanting the diva onto the small screen. Currently, the main attempt to theorize the television diva has focused on the narratively over-the-top and visually opulent feminized genre of the soap opera. In his discussion of the soapy diva, Nick Salvato piles onto the diva's excessiveness with loaded words and phrases like 'difficult', 'roar', 'hissy fit', 'hyperbolic' and 'bigger-than-life'

(2007: 106–12). Although scholars differ in their approach and precise definition of the diva, her power both while in character and offstage remains constant. As a figure larger-than-life and pushing at the boundaries of acceptable gendered behaviour, the diva would seem to have been too big for traditional American television. As illustrated through its slang moniker, the television lacked the grandiosity of the diva; it was simply the 'small screen'. This apparent tension begs the question: how did American television of the twenty-first century find the space to so fervently embrace the Broadway diva's excess? How did the – largely nonmusical – small screen expand to house her big performances? Through an examination of shifts in American television marketing, production and style, I will explore just that.

American television welcomes the Broadway diva with open arms

To be clear, the diva in various forms has been hanging around American television for decades, at times as a featured star and at others just dropping by for a short visit. In the early 1950s, the struggling television industry used its proximity to the Great White Way to help establish its legitimacy and provide American viewers with something unique: access to Broadway's performances and performers (Kessler 2013). With NBC, ABC and CBS helmed in New York City and programmers partial towards variety shows, anthology dramas and specials, the new medium embraced the likes of Merman, Martin and Stritch, allowing them to appear in their natural habitat of the musical play or as themselves. Merman reprised the title role of Panama Hattie on *The Best of Broadway* (1954); Martin made television history as *Peter Pan* (NBC 1955, 1956, 1960) and the two divas turned in a nearly thirteen-minute duelling duet on the *Ford 50th Anniversary Show*, airing in 1953 and simulcast on both CBS and NBC. Their *tour de force* included portions of nearly 30 songs, including many of their signature numbers: 'There's No Business Like Show Business' (*Annie Get Your Gun*), 'I Got Rhythm' (*Girl Crazy*), 'Cock-Eyed Optimist' (*South Pacific*) and 'My Heart Belongs to Daddy' (*Leave It to Me*). As they took centre stage in front of posters from their most popular Broadway shows, they belted to the people in the back row – or in Albuquerque – and ultimately came together for a diva battle with a friendly scuffle as they jokingly attempted to out-belt each other with battling versions of 'Indian Love Song' and 'Tea for Two'. Add in appearances on shows like *Texaco Star Theatre* (Merman in 1949), *The Colgate Comedy Hour* (Merman in 1953 and 1954), Edward R. Murrow's *Person to Person* (Merman in 1955; Martin in 1954) and *Toast of the Town* (Merman eight times between 1955 and 1968; Martin in 1958), and the divas were singing up and down the dial.

Despite dwindling opportunities for live theatrical performances on television, the diva still cropped up in sixties and seventies TV with varying levels of success. Carol Burnett and Julie Andrews scored with their successful concert specials, *Julie and Carol at Carnegie Hall* (1962) and *Julie and Carol at Lincoln Center* (1971), and Burnett found lasting success with her variety show. Barbra Streisand blended her Broadway and pop successes through a series of televised specials for CBS, whose Columbia Records then benefitted financially from the associated record sales. Minnelli wowed audiences in the Emmy-winning, Bob Fosse directed, Kander and Ebb vehicle *Liza with a Z* (1972), while Channing only found a modicum of success trying to bring the stage to the small screen in a number of televised specials. In 1966, the *New York Times* described *An Evening with Carol Channing* as having, 'the look of a stylish production', but a sense of wit that 'was right out of *Green Acres*' (Anon. 1966: 55). The reviewer also challenged the fit of her 'sophisticated talents' for the 'unsophisticated dimensions of television'.

Forays into fictional series were historically lacklustre for Broadway's musical divas. Stars like Debbie Reynolds, Channing and Dorothy Loudon, whose film and Broadway successes – *The Unsinkable Molly Brown* (1964), *Hello Dolly!* (1964) and *Annie* (1977), respectively – relied on their over-the-top performances of unflappable dames, left a string of sitcom failures in their wake. Channing's 1966 pilot failed to ever air, while Reynolds's two-year contract for *The Debbie Reynolds Show* (1969, NBC) was truncated after she, in grand diva fashion, quit after a drawn-out game of chicken over a dispute regarding cigarette advertising (Browning 1972: SCL 1; Anon. 1969: 58). Following her Tony win for *Annie*'s Miss Hannigan, Loudon premiered the short-lived situation comedy *Dorothy* (1979). Capitalizing on Hannigan juxtaposition, she played a lovable ex-showgirl teaching music and drama at a stuffy Connecticut girls' school. The series only lasted four episodes but includes classic Loudon shtick as she belts and dances throughout. She portrays the role as if playing for the back row of a Broadway house, rather than a small studio audience. Channing, Merman and Ann Miller were able to go big and fleetingly strut their stuff on a super-sized, two-part musical episode of Aaron Spelling's nautical comedy *The Love Boat* entitled 'The Love Boat Follies' (1982). All in all, however, divas found little *recurring* success into the eighties.

Not until the mid to late eighties did Angela Lansbury and LuPone break the diva through into series television. Lansbury's *Murder She Wrote* (1984–96) ran for 264 episodes and garnered the actress twelve consecutive Emmy nominations (Figure 13.1). In contrast to many of the previous theatre-to-television diva transfers, however, Lansbury left her excess on the stage and reveled in the intimacy provided by television. Her bicycle-riding sleuth played *against* her diva image. When interviewed by the *New York Times*, the *Mame*, *Gypsy* and *Sweeney Todd* Tony Award winner said, 'What appealed to me about Jessica Fletcher is that

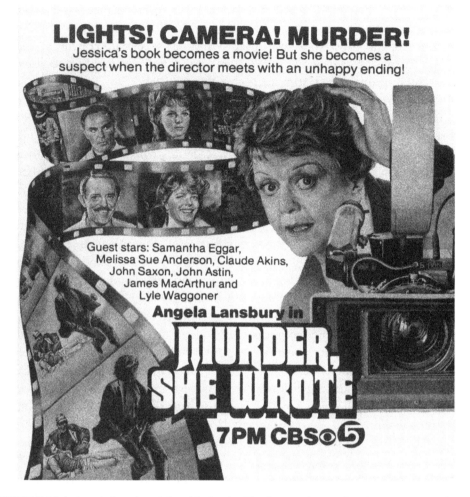

FIGURE 13.1: Angela Lansbury's lovable Jessica Fletcher made *Murder She Wrote* an audience favorite, thrusting the Broadway diva's iconic Mama Rose, Mame and Mrs Lovett into the rearview mirror (*TV Guide* advertisement, 27 October–2 November 1984).

I could do what I do best and have little chance to play – a sincere, down-to-earth woman. Mostly, I've played very spectacular bitches' (Harmetz 1985: H25). To the contrary, the infamously combative LuPone found herself butting heads with the more restrictive style of the family melodrama. Just two years after taking on Merman's role of Reno Sweeney in *Anything Goes*, she stepped into the character of suburban mom Libby Thatcher on the Down's Syndrome family drama *Life Goes On* (1989–93). Whereas the elder diva reveled in her chance to go small, LuPone was reportedly in need of being handled. In meetings, the director was continuously told to tame LuPone and make sure she was 'grounded and not too big' (Lange 2014). After three episodes worth of similar criticism, director Michael Lange confronted producer Michael Braverman and asked 'why in the hell did you cast her' if they wanted someone small (Lange 2014)? In a 1993 interview, LuPone herself articulated what she saw as the stifling (and counter-diva) nature of playing small. 'My character is just filled with lethargy and so subservient. I don't even know how I played it for (so long)' (Isenberg 1993).

From the fifties through the nineties, musical divas were surely present across television forms. Brushing up against emergent and shifting television norms, these theatrical women of stature struggled to find sustainable success in a medium so contrary to the theatrical stage. Shifts in the industry, however, would come to innovate the medium to the diva's benefit.

The diva returns with a vengeance

Despite the repeated appearances of the diva on the small screen through the latter part of the twentieth century, I argue the twenty-first century provided a brand-new environment just right for these women who defied both narrative and visual bounds of traditional, theatrical femininity. Whereas the likes of LuPone, Loudon and Channing stumbled over TV's generic and aesthetic norms, shifts within the industry opened up a space welcoming to the diva. The 2000s have brought a flood of Broadway's big belters across genres ranging from live television musicals to situation comedies to hard-core prison dramas. Whereas location and in vogue generic styles helped welcome the divas of the fifties, a string of major events occurred in the latter part of the twentieth and first decades of the twenty-first centuries that provided a more comfortable fit for these women who once appeared too big for the medium.[1] No longer stumbling over the constraints of live or filmed television, the televisual Broadway diva has not only been thriving but also providing some of the defining moments and characters of television's millennial turn. Over the last decade and a half, the likes of Stritch, Minnelli, LuPone, Rita Moreno, Betty Buckley, Chenoweth and Peters – just to hit the high notes – have had recurring or major roles on contemporary TV fare and managed to neither drive the shows into the ground nor dwarf the rest of the cast.

It's all about location

The relocation of television production hubs back to New York in the late 1990s and early 2000s offers one possible (and somewhat simple) explanation for the recent diva onslaught. The majority of production had shifted to Los Angeles in the early 1960s when television moved away from live performance and toward filmed programming. During this transition, a move toward Hollywood and the motion picture industry was a logical one. After that move, only a handful of shows had carried out primary shooting in New York. Here and there a show like *East Side/West Side* (1963–64), *The Patty Duke Show* (1963–66), *The Cosby Show* (1984–92) or *Kate and Allie* (1984–89) had taken up residence in New York, but for the most part, television production remained a west coast phenomenon for the last four decades of the twentieth century. Even when iconic New York sitcoms like *Seinfeld* (1989–98), *Mad About You* (1992–99), *Friends* (1994–2004) and *Will and Grace* (1998–2006) dominated Nielsen ratings and NBC's 'Must See TV' lineup in the 1990s and early 2000s, they were shot in Los Angeles, Studio City or Culver City, with potential infrequent jaunts to New York for location shooting. After a 40-year hiatus, television began its return to the Big Apple, making cameos and small recurring roles easier for those musical broads who call New York and the New York stage their homes.

By the early 2000s, the tide had clearly begun to turn, and not simply because everyone in New York was appearing in *Law and Order* (1990–2010). By 2008, New York City and state were touting a 35 per cent tax credit incentive for New York-based television and film production, a move that pushed shows like *Ugly Betty* (2006–10) which were narratively based in the city but shot in Los Angeles back to the Big Apple (Kinon 2008). By 2011, *The Huffington Post* noted that a 'record' 23 shows were filming in New York, and *The Wall Street Journal* reported that the 2011–12 season would bring eight new shows to join existing programmes like *30 Rock* (2006–13) and *The Good Wife* (2009–16), notably a show *set* in Chicago but *shot* in New York (Anon. 2011; Orden 2011). As of the writing of this chapter in 2017, the New York City Mayor's office listed 32 'Primetime TV/Online Episodic Shows and Miniseries' shooting in the city (NYC.gov).

Of course, divas have done their share of Los Angeles-based television work, but the increased volume of New York shows allowed for an easy-in for New Yorkers, especially if they wanted to pop in and out through cameo or non-ensemble appearances. In the early years of the New York production resurgence and cable's original programming boom, the graphic HBO prison drama *Oz* (1997–2003), shot in Bayonne, New Jersey and New York City, landed a hat trick of divas, casting Moreno as series regular/prison councillor Sister Peter Marie and both Buckley and LuPone as recurring characters with multiple-episode arcs. LuPone went on to make cameos and recurring appearances on high-profile, New York-based shows like *Girls* (2012–17), *30 Rock* and *Glee* (2009–15, when shot on location in New York). Many of these appearances either directly coincided with Broadway work or snuck into the margins, with her work on *30 Rock* occurring in 2009, 2010 and 2012, potentially overlapping with her Broadway stints in *Gypsy* (2008–09), *Women on the Verge of a Nervous Breakdown* (2010–11), *An Evening with Patti LuPone and Mandy Patinkin* (2011–12) and/or *The Anarchist* (2012). Stritch balanced Broadway- and New York-based small screen work as well, with nine appearances on *30 Rock* between 2007 and 2012, all surrounding her stint as Lansbury's replacement in *A Little Night Music* between July 2010 and January 2011. Her *Night Music* co-star Peters was also juggling television appearances, with a 2009 recurring role in the relocated *Ugly Betty*. She would go on to star in two more locally shot shows, *Smash* (2012–13) and *Mozart in the Jungle* (2014–18). A string of big female voices and personas went on to juggle television and theatre in this new amenable system, including Megan Hilty (*Smash* and Broadway's *Noises Off*), Laura Benanti (*Law and Order: SVU* and Broadway's *Women on the Verge of a Nervous Breakdown*) and more recently Danielle Brooks (Netflix's *Orange is the New Black* and the Broadway revival of *The Color Purple*). Although location certainly is not everything, it surely opens up a space for these women to flow in and out of shows without relocation or upheaval to their routines.

Technology, money and audience share

Another impetus for the diva onslaught has been the network struggle to find audiences in the new century and their at least temporary reliance on musical event programming. The 1970s has been hailed as the height of the three-network system in American television, one in which ABC, CBS and NBC controlled the game and viewers' eyeballs. By the 1980s, this had started to turn and by the 1990s the networks – now including newcomers Fox, the WB and UPN – started to face major challenges from the increasing penetration of cable television and the resultant competition for advertiser dollars (Becker 2006: 82–92). The associated decline in network viewership has been a thorn in the side of programmers for nearly three decades. By the turn of the millennium, the audience share enjoyed by the broadcast networks had dropped to 58 per cent and an associated rise in multi-platform viewing occurred, with 85 per cent of households subscribing to cable or satellite by 2003 (Lotz 2007: 13). Following the rising threat of cable came an increasing ease by which viewers could 'time shift' or watch shows at a time other than the one designated by the network. By 2005, digital video recorders (DVRs) were present in 8 per cent of American homes, rising to 44 per cent by 2011 and 50 per cent by 2016 (Spangler 2011; Anon. 2016).[2] These cable and technology-related challenges to broadcasters have been compounded by the rise of 'on-demand' streaming services like Hulu, Netflix, Amazon and iTunes, services also integrated into 50 per cent of American households by 2016 (Anon. 2016). Amid these shifts in viewing practices and platforms, broadcasters scramble to capture viewers for *synchronous* viewing, meaning the viewing of programming in its *scheduled* time slot. Practices like time shifting via DVR and streaming present major hurdles regarding capturing and maintaining advertising dollars directly associated with Nielsen ratings. Although Nielsen has begun reporting ratings based on both live viewing and some delayed DVR viewing, the audience's ability to time shift and stream, along with their yen for original programming on outlets like Netflix, Hulu and cable, have created major hardships for the broadcast networks.

Enter the live musical. Today's seemingly endless choices regarding *the what* and *the when* of television viewing seem ideal from a viewer's perspective, but it has sent programmers scrambling for alternative production models. In the post-network, multi-platform viewing era, live events like sports and reality show finales, where their 'now-ness' is paramount, have been the most reliable for bringing viewers back to synchronous television viewing in droves. During the 2012–13 season, for example, in the coveted 18–49 demographic, *NBC's Sunday Night Football* took the top Nielsen spot, with reality shows *The Voice* (#3 and #5) and *American Idol* (#6 and #7) taking up four of the next six spots (Patten 2013). With a need to lure advertisers with strong Nielsen numbers into this hostile ratings environment, both NBC and Fox took a page from the 1950s television playbook and ushered in a resurgence of live televised musicals or musical events: *The Sound of Music Live!* (NBC, 2013), *Peter Pan Live!* (NBC, 2014), *The Wiz Live!* (NBC, 2015), *Grease: Live!* (Fox, 2016), *The Passion* (Fox, 2016) and *Hairspray Live!* (NBC, 2016).[3] Although these televised spectaculars have had hit and miss ratings and ushered in a new trend in *synchronous* musical hate-watching,[4] the networks appear sold on the concept. Despite a pan by critics and a Twitter storm of derision directed at *The Sound of Music Live!*, the show scored a huge advertising partnership with Walmart, a 10.5 Nielsen rating, nearly 18.5 million viewers and 450,000 unique tweets (Hetrick 2013; Rice 2014).[5] This compares favourably to the top Nielsen rated series of that season, *NBC's Sunday Night Football*, which received an average 12.5 rating with approximately 21.3 million viewers (Anon. 2014). Viewers may be snarky, but they are there and the money appears to be good.

In an attempt to wrest lucrative, young, hip viewers from their time-shifting devices and redirect them back to live television broadcasts, most of the live musicals have gone after television stars (Amber Riley of *Glee* in *The Wiz*, Stephen Moyer of *True Blood* in *The Sound of Music*), film stars (Christopher Walken as *Peter Pan*'s Captain Hook) and popular music (rather than musical) figures (Mary J. Blige as *The Wiz*'s Evilene, Ariana Grande as *Hairspray*'s Penny) to fill their casts, at times resulting in less than stellar reviews. Reviewers described Carrie Underwood (Maria in *The Sound of Music*) and Allison Williams (Peter in *Peter*

Pan), respectively, as having 'blank stares and placid smiles' and being 'the worst thing the iconic cross-dressing orphan with the Oedipus complex could be: just fine' (Bernardin 2013; Fallon 2014). The larger casts, however, have included their share of Broadway performers. Although the women appearing in these new musicals were not taking on title roles like Martin and Merman before them, these shows provided the opportunity for Americans to see some of Broadway's best in their (somewhat) natural habitat.

Sure, none of the aforementioned live musicals include a LuPone or a Peters, but they have opened up a space for various Broadway divas and Broadway-television crossovers to strut their divalicious stuff: Chenoweth in *Hairspray*, Stephanie Mills in *The Wiz*, Benanti and McDonald in *The Sound of Music* and Kelli O'Hara in *Peter Pan*. Notably, these Broadway transplants are at times the ones receiving rave reviews from television critics, as they are often the only ones who seem to know how to act and sing live. *Rolling Stone* decried 'The Broadway Veterans Ruled' when describing the otherwise rather disastrous *The Sound of Music Live!* and noted that 'Audra McDonald, as the Mother Abbess, totally earned her right to drop the mic with her rendition of "Climb Every Mountain"' (Leeds 2013). Having broken through with Tony-winning roles in 1994's revival of *Carousel* and as a diva-in-training in 1996's *Master Class*, McDonald had conquered stage and small screen, taking home additional Tony Awards for *Ragtime* (1998) and *Raisin in the Sun* (2004) prior to starring in the television medical melodrama *Private Practice* (2007–13). Taking a slightly different route, rags-to-riches *American Idol* (2002–present) reject/*Dreamgirls* (2006) Academy Award winner/Broadway star as diegetic diva Shug in *The Color Purple*, Jennifer Hudson garnered raves as Motormouth Maybelle in *Hairspray Live! Variety* and *The Hollywood Reporter* described her as having offered a 'knockout performance' and '[tearing] the roof off' in her televised performance of 'I Know Where I've Been' (Saraiya 2016; Rooney 2016). These women, schooled on the stage and screen musical, have embodied or created diva roles in vehicles where at least one of the assigned divas, in these cases Underwood as Maria and newcomer Maddie Baillio as Tracy, perhaps failed to rise to the occasion. McDonald's and Hudson's respective diva turns come through in narrative moments where the Mother Abbess and Motormouth project what John Clum identifies as 'hallmarks' of the diva, their 'feminine assertiveness and [propensity for] survival' (1999: 137). Although both divas were sequestered into relatively small supporting roles, their power and presence were clear. As McDonald forcefully sends Underwood's Maria back into the world and Hudson's Motormouth powerfully leads the ensemble into a potentially dangerous civil rights march, the *real* divas dwarf the lead actresses and remind those at home watching just which actresses bring the experience, power and Broadway chops to the broadcast.

The longevity of this televised musical trend remains to be seen; however, NBC has already announced its upcoming productions of *Jesus Christ Superstar* and *Bye Bye Birdie* (starring pop-diva Jennifer Lopez) and Fox has announced that they will be presenting live productions of *A Christmas Story* and *Rent*.[6] Most recently, ABC has announced that it will enter into the live musical fray, contributing a star-studded, live/animated hybrid musical event around *The Little Mermaid* (Stanhope 2017). As long as the musical keeps coming to the small screen, one can assume that the Broadway diva will continue to find her way front and centre, even if only for a single breakout number. These vehicles also, perhaps, prove to be ideal for Broadway's leading ladies, commonly taking minimal time away from their potential theatrical schedules and providing immediate performance platforms accessing millions of viewers.[7] It only makes sense that the diva would find her way into these shows. In the 1950s, after all, such shows were aptly called 'spectaculars'.

Shifts in story, style and excess

Although shifts in economics, technology and location surely helped make television more convenient for and unexpectedly needy of performers from Broadway, perhaps the most important and dynamic changes occurring within the industry, as it relates to the musical diva onslaught, relate to major shifts that have occurred over the last twenty years in terms of American television's *narrative* and *visual* form. Significant narrative and visual evolutions have occurred on both ends of the generic spectrum, through a continued rise in dramatic and near-epic seriality and the popularity of highly stylized, self-referential and satirical comedy and dramedy. Such shifts have helped push the medium in directions more embracing of these divas' at times overpowering performance styles and convention-busting connotations.

By the late 1990s and early 2000s, as production hubs were shifting and networks were scrambling for viewers, programming was also more heavily embracing what Jason Mittell describes as contemporary television's tendency towards 'narrative complexity' (2006: 29–31).[8] Included in this style of storytelling is an increase in irony/satire (*Arrested Development* [2003–06, 2013, 2018], *30 Rock*), more detailed narratives with rich story worlds (*Lost* [2004–10], *Heroes* [2006–10], *Buffy the Vampire Slayer* [1997–2003]), a heightened level of seriality (*Oz* [1997–2003], *The Sopranos* [1999–2007], *The Wire* [2002–08]) and/or an increased focus on the 'pyrotechnics' of storytelling (like *Heroes'* confounding shifts in time and space), at times resulting in special one-off episodes (e.g. *Buffy*'s musical and silent episodes) that formally deviate from the rest of the series. Mittell associates such shifts with TV's heightened cultural cachet, an influx of film writers to television and viewers' increased ability to re-watch episodes – through DVR, DVD or streaming services – to capture the nuances of deep seriality and irony (2006: 29–31). These narrative and visual shifts occurring in both drama and comedy push at the seams of established generic norms as they drive the shows in question to exceed their traditional forms. This embrace of visual, narrative and satirical excess marks an important moment for the musical diva and her ability to more comfortably take front and centre on the small screen. Finally, the dramatic and emotional levels of television were big enough for her diva turn, and comedies were so self-aware that the diva's over-the-top performances of herself or fictional characters would fit nicely into the form.

Whereas divas' performances once seemed either too big – like Merman – or in need of being toned down – as Lansbury had chosen to do – because of the rise in complex narratives and an accompanying increased acceptability of televised sex and violence, today's serial melodramas often rise to the level of the diva's – operatic or theatrical – emotional extremes. Historically, the television melodrama would have seemed to have been a solid fit for the Broadway diva and her penchant for embodying strong, assertive women with a tendency towards the dramatic or traumatic. David Thorburn likens the genre's emotional excess and at times over-the-top dramatic scenarios to the operatic tradition (2007: 442–43). He argues that those who 'complain about the genre's improbability' refuse to acknowledge melodrama's *operatic* rather than conventionally dramatic form, stating further that 'no one goes to Italian opera expecting a realistic plot' (2007: 442). The same can certainly be said for television melodrama's aptly named daytime cousin, the soap *opera*. Thorburn further notes the similarity between television melodrama's convention of building to highly emotional moments, only to then cut to commercial, and the practice in opera – and relatedly musical theatre and certainly diva vehicles – of following emotional displays of song with narrative-halting applause (2007: 442–43).

Today these dramatic conventions – feuds, affairs and murder with a climactic commercial break – remain, but the dramatic and serial scenarios have inflated exponentially, providing televisual contexts more suitable for the diva than LuPone's ill-fitting *Life Goes On*. Over the last twenty years, in addition to providing more deeply serialized night-time drama, television has seen a stark increase in the acceptability of sex and violence on both cable and network television. Moreno (2000) describes her HBO prison drama *Oz* as 'graphically violent, graphically sexual, all of the big, big nonos [...]. It is really biblical. It is epic. It's like Bruegel's painting of hell'. Today's female-driven serial dramas (*Grey's Anatomy* [2005–present], *Scandal* [2012–present], *How to Get Away with Murder* [2014–present]) are often those that take narrative and performative excess to new heights, allowing the actresses to embody what Koestenbaum identifies as the diva's 'art of anger' and her 'will to power' through the depiction of characters akin to those Clum describes as divas: 'survivors, proud of their battle scars' (Koestenbaum 1993: 90, 113; Clum 1999: 229). These vehicles provide fitting narrative and emotive opportunities for Broadway's musical divas. McDonald's *Private Practice* trafficked in the fertility hopes of patients and the bed hopping, out-of-womb baby stealing and drug addiction surrounding the main medical ensemble. Moreno's *Oz* was a weekly tragedy of Greek proportions, filled with stabbings, rapes, poisoning, turf wars and overdoses. Like many of the diva roles of the stage – *Evita*'s Eva Peron, *Gypsy*'s Mama Rose or *Cabaret*'s Sally Bowles – the emotional and ideological stakes for these television characters are high and allow the actresses the ability to emerge as 'seductive, powerful, manipulative, [and/or] ambitious', just as Leonardi and Pope frame the diva (1996: 10). The increased level of seriality, as well, allows those levels of drama to continue week to week, rather than finding comfortable resolution at the end of each episode. It is not that any diva cannot play these roles, but finally the musical diva could find a dramatic television role that did not constrain her excessive performance of emotion and power.

In addition to these shifts in narrative conventions, shifting stylistic norms also work to the diva's advantage, with many millennial dramas forgoing the once rather neutered visuals dubbed by scholars as 'zero degree style'.[9] Canonical television scholarship addressing melodrama has highlighted how the medium's diminutive frame was befitting of a visual, emotional articulation of the genre. Thorburn points to the genre's prevalence of close-ups and argues that 'in the kind of psychologically nuanced performance elicited by good melodrama, the smaller television screen would seem even more appropriate' (2007: 446–47). Similarly, Horace Newcomb argues that the smallness of television encouraged a focus on 'faces, reactions, explorations of emotions' (1974: 245–46). Contemporary melodrama often both adheres to these spatial norms and infuses them with more highly stylized visuals: short shot lengths, Steadicams, quick movements and swirling cameras. This combination of traditional and more highly stylized visuals aids in providing the musical diva a tele*visual* – not just narrative – space in which she can flourish. Whereas she often finds herself separated from her traditional mode of conveying her emotional strength – song – the stylized, yet intimate, visuals associated with contemporary melodrama reassign the locus of her excessive performance. Instead of her command emerging through sheer vocal power, the diva – typically separated from the audience by the gulf between the proscenium and the house – projects her power through the focus on her emotionally wrought face as presented through stylized cinematography and editing. It is as if the raw emotion of an 11 o'clock diva number comes through in the close-up and potentially frantic camerawork that helps underscore her powerful emotions.

Television's newer melodramas have also invited narrative flourishes that at times allow the musical theatre diva to perform at her most diva-ish. Within this world of complex narratives, generic flourishes and 'very special episodes', a single episode that disrupts the stylistic norms of the series does not overall upset the series' equilibrium. Mittell exemplifies both 'narrative pyrotechnics' and 'narrative spectacle' via his discussion of *Buffy the Vampire Slayer*'s one-off musical episode ('Once More with Feeling') (2006: 35–36). Both Moreno and Sara Ramirez have been able to take advantage of this kind of post-network flourish. In *Oz*'s musical episode 'Variety', Moreno sings a full-front, to the audience, quasi-in-and-out of character soulful rendition of Janis Ian's 'Days Like These'. Ramirez is able to go full diva in *Grey's Anatomy*'s musical episode. The actress snatched a Tony for both *playing* diva and *feigning* diva as *Spamalot*'s intertextual, musical-trope-mocking Lady of the Lake. After seeing her performance, ABC executives offered Ramirez a spot on any show she wanted to join, landing the relative television newbie on one of the network's hottest night-time melodramas (Anon. 2006). In 2011, she starred as the central focus of 'The Song Beneath the Song', a one-off musical episode in which her character experiences catastrophic injuries in a car accident. Callie (Ramirez) appears as a musicalized out-of-body version of herself, ultimately performing her breakout diva number – that notably wakes up the comatose Callie – 'The Story' (Figure 13.2). In this number, diva tropes of the stage blend with norms of the melodrama and the more highly stylized aesthetics of post-network televisuality. Callie, almost unhinged, belts out the episode's version of a tormented 'Rose's Turn' or 'Memory' as the camera swirls around her going in and out of close-up. Her vocal power, maintained and adjusted for the closeness of television, complements her bodily power as she storms from one set to another, at times with arms outstretched in a near 'Don't Cry for Me Argentina' vein. The next week, she steps back from the footlights and returns to the show's established serialized, non-musical drama, but for that moment the diva is unleashed.[10]

Despite this new comfortable locale of excess, the ladies have certainly not been sequestered to melodramas. Television comedy's turn toward the satirical, big and self-referential has also provided a space for Broadway divas' big personalities to flourish. Alongside his discussion of deep seriality and narrative pyrotechnics, Mittell highlights emergent trends in television comedy that have proved welcoming to the diva (2006: 34). He argues that contemporary comedies like *Arrested Development* and *Curb Your Enthusiasm* (2010–present) engage a high level of self-referentiality, while rejecting the notion of stasis commonly associated with the episodic sitcom.[11] Similarly, Ethan Thompson points to the popularization of 'comedy verité', which he argues combines 'the "don'ts" of observational documentary' with 'its claim to capturing reality' to a desired comedic end (2007: 67). Shows like *Arrested Development* and *30 Rock* that embrace this notion of capturing 'reality' with an associated wink and nod have been hotbeds of activity

FIGURE 13.2: The millennial trend of producing one-off musical episodes of fictional television shows created a perfect opportunity for crossover actresses like *Spamalot* Tony-winner Sara Ramirez to show off her diva chops. Here she blows out 'The Story' to the comatose version of her character in *Grey's Anatomy*'s (2011, Episode 'Song Beneath the Song').

for the larger-than-life personalities of Stritch, LuPone and Minnelli. Although almost wholly bereft of opportunities for the women to flaunt their musical power, their transgressiveness, assertiveness and over-the-top performance styles fit nicely into these rather off-the-wall satires.

Stritch's Colleen Donaghy – mother of Alec Baldwin's NBC exec, Jack Donaghy – stormed into nine episodes of *30 Rock* shouting lines like 'Tell him his mother's here, and she loves him, but not in a queer way', 'My father did not kill dozens of Germans so his daughter could die in a van!' and 'This is supposed to be a hospital, not a Japanese internment camp I volunteered at during the war!' Although largely denied the opportunity to share her 'whisky soaked alto' singing voice (Faires 2014), she still stood as a looming power that could disrupt the show at any moment, with each appearance converting her guest spot into a diva role, that described by Dvoskin as 'central female characters who sing loudly, take up space (both narratively and physically) and demand attention' (2016: 94). Stritch may not have been singing, but she was certainly loud and, as she flung her body and copious accusations, she surely took up physical and psychic space. Further, as the racist, sexist, homophobic and less-than-maternal diva Colleen, she 'breaks the bounds of normative femininity' and is able to metaphorically take the stage, belt out a series of one-liners and head off into the dressing room (Dvoskin 2016: 94).

Similarly, Minnelli appeared in the faux soap opera *Arrested Development* as the archrival to the show's matriarch. She plays Lucille Austero: widow, rival, extreme vertigo sufferer and quintessential diva, unwilling to adhere to the bounds of gendered decorum as she begins dating her rival's son. Cinematography, editing and narrator voice-over repeatedly highlight the inanity of the characters and the resultant scenarios. The prospective inability of audience members to separate the offstage Minnelli diva persona from an over-the-top on-screen Lucille only adds to the potential narrative pleasure of such hyper-aware instances of comedy verité. In these comedies – unlike the tamer variety of earlier decades – it simply does not matter if the diva and her out-of-character persona burst through the fourth wall. In a similar vein, twenty-first-century generic norms do not restrain LuPone as they had on *Life Goes On*. Like Stritch, she goes full diva, converting guest spots to fleeting diva roles as an over-bearing mother on *30 Rock*, a homophobic cat-fancying mother on *Ugly Betty* (2006–10) and an irate LuPone herself on HBO's millennial dramedy *Girls*.[12] In the era of post-network self-awareness and complex narratives, a willing suspension of disbelief is no longer a required skill or affect.

I would be remiss to not mention Chenoweth's contributions to post-network stylized dramedy. In both the romantic-detective-fantasy *Pushing Daisies* (2007–09) and the Christian-critique melo-dramedy *GCB* (2012, based on the novel *Good Christian Bitches*), the diva shows off her pipes. In the former, Olive, a lovesick waitress yearning for her pie-making boss – who (literally) has the power to wake the dead – busts into a rendition of *Grease*'s 'Hopelessly Devoted' as she cleans and dances around a seemingly unaware floor polisher and then later – joined by *Little Shop of Horrors*' Ellen Greene – sings a duet of They Might Be Giants' 'Birdhouse in Your Soul'. In *GCB*, her petty Carlene Cockburn graces the congregation with an overdramatic and bitchy version of 'Jesus Take the Wheel' (directed at a rival whose husband had just tragically died in a car accident). Truly, the type of hyperstylization, self-awareness and over-the-top narratives and characters who have come to define much of twenty-first-century television have provided an easy-in for the Broadway diva. The very characteristics identified by diva scholars as setting her apart – and those often preventing her from peacefully coexisting (if that is something she does) within earlier television content – had come to define cutting-edge television. The Broadway diva had found her televisual niche.

Divas down the road

Who knows what the near future will bring? Who even knows what will become of the form we have known as 'television' for the last 70 years, as technology, funding and delivery systems change? But in this moment, TV loves the diva. In the first two decades of the twenty-first century, she has proven to be a welcome addition to small screen fare. Production has shifted to the backyard of Shubert Alley. Programmers have sought to draw in viewers through generic innovation (*Pushing Daisies*, *Smash*) and special programming (*The Sound of Music Live!*). Perhaps most importantly, contemporary programming has aggressively pushed the visual and narrative extremes of comedy and drama (*30 Rock*, *Pushing Daises* and *Oz*) such that the emotional and performative excesses of the Broadway diva can stretch to their full grandeur. As the performance platforms of the stage and big and small screens have become increasingly porous, allowing celebrities to float from one locale to the next, it only makes sense that the diva would find her small screen throne. Now, I am just waiting with bated breath in hopes that Wontorek's (2015) *Broadway.com* article 'Lockdown! Eight Broadway divas we'd kill to see behind bars on *Orange is the New Black*' will come to fruition. If Buckley, LuPone and Moreno could survive the ironically named Emerald City wing of Oswald State Penitentiary in *Oz*, then surely Menzel, Hilty and Orfeh can survive *Orange is the New Black*'s Litchfield Penitentiary. After all, according to Salvato's and O'Neill's constructions of the diva, she is a 'difficult' woman who can elicit a 'frightening' performance (Salvato 2007: 106; O'Neill 2007: 24). Netflix, do everyone a favour and prepare Litchfield for the diva onslaught.

NOTES

1. The runs of television show noted in the text of the chapter reflect the article's original time of publication in *Studies of Musical Theatre* (2018). By the time of this anthology's publication (2022), shows such as *Mozart in the Jungle* (2014–18) and *Scandal* (2012–18) had ended their runs. For consistency, however, original dates have been left in the text.
2. Although network programmers saw VCR-based time shifting in the 1980s as somewhat problematic, the sheer volume of time shifting allowed by the DVR at a time when the networks were already under siege by cable and then later streaming content upped the ante on this front.
3. Fox also aired *The Rocky Horror Picture Show: Let's Do the Time Warp Again* in 2016, but this was a wholly filmed (meaning not live) special.
4. The flood of negative and catty Twitter traffic related to *The Sound of Music Live!* and *Peter Pan Live!* culturally linked these new live television musicals to the process of hate-watching or watching something for the sheer pleasure of hating it. For more on the link between social media, hate-watching and the live TV musical, see Kessler (2020).
5. Viewership increased to 21.8 million with 'Live-plus-7', which counts DVR views in the seven days following the scheduled telecast (O'Connell 2013).
6. By the publication of this book, the live television musical had waned, with a disastrous *Rent: Live* in 2019, cancellations of planned future projects, and a weird, if numerically successful, hybrid *The Little Mermaid Live!* finally hitting the ABC airwaves in late 2019.

7. Notably, McDonald appeared in *The Sound of Music Live!* just shy of four months prior to premiering at Circle in the Square as Billie Holliday in *Lady Day at Emerson's Bar & Grill*. Hudson performed her last show of *The Color Purple* on 8 May 2016 and appeared in *Hairspray Live!* on 7 December 2016.
8. Although Mittell anchors the stark rise of complex narratives in the late nineties and early 2000s, the seeds for these generic transformations were sewn earlier. Caldwell (1995: 631) pinpoints the rise of what he terms 'televisuality' or 'excessive style' to the late 1980s and early 1990s and highlights an increased reliance on visual excess, cinematic visual stylings, intertextuality and 'very special episodes'. It was also during the 1980s when serial narratives – those akin to soap operas that continue their plotlines from episode to episode – escaped the daytime ghetto and took their place in the night-time lineup (e.g. *Dallas*, *Dynasty* and *Falcon Crest*). Nonetheless, the late 1990s and 2000s took these changes to new heights.
9. Caldwell (1995: 56) positions 'zero degree style' – one more simply communicative than flashy – as reflective of TV's theatrical roots, when 'the technical apparatus was just in place only to allow the televised stage play to unfold'.
10. For more on the one-off musical episode of otherwise non-musical television series, see Kessler (2015).
11. In this context, episodic refers to comedies like *The Golden Girls* or *Everybody Loves Raymond*, in which very little plot development occurs from one episode to the next. Rather, each episode serves as its own closed-off storyline.
12. Stacy Wolf argues that 'The diva's excessive, performative display of self refutes the limits of femininity even as her voice and body are insistently female' (2007: 46). Stritch, Minnelli and LuPone each embrace this in their roles as monstrous and overbearing mothers or widows preying on someone else's son.

REFERENCES

Anon. (1966), 'TV: Sunflower in shade', *New York Times*, 19 February, p. 55.

Anon. (1969), 'Cigarette advertiser drops *The Debbie Reynolds Show*', *New York Times*, 20 September, p. 58.

Anon. (2006), 'The Anatomy of *Grey's*', *Oprah*, 17 November, http://www.oprah.com/oprahshow/The-Anatomy-of-Greys. Accessed 15 February 2017.

Anon. (2007), 'US DVR penetration 17.2%; timeshifting lifts *House*, *Lost*, *The Office*', *Marketing Charts*, 1 May, http://www.marketingcharts.com/television/us-dvr-penetration-172-timeshifing-lifts-house-lost-the-office-306/. Accessed 5 March 2017.

Anon. (2011), '23 TV shows filming in New York, a record high, boosting economy: Bloomberg', *Huffington Post*, 23 August, http://www.huffingtonpost.com/2011/08/23/23-tv-shows-filming-in-nen934090.html. Accessed 15 February 2017.

Anon. (2014), 'NBC's *Sunday Night Football* concludes regular season as primetime television's #1 show', *TV By the Numbers*, 30 December, http://tvbythenumbers.zap2it.com/

network-press-releases/nbcs-sundaynight-football-concludes-regular-season-as-primetime-televisions1-show/344772/. Accessed 5 March 2017.

Anon. (2016), 'Milestone marker: SVOD and DVR penetration are now on par with one another', *Nielsen*, 27 June, http://www.nielsen.com/us/en/insights/news/2016/milestone-marker-svod-and-dvr-penetration-on-parwith-one-another.html. Accessed 15 February 2017.

Becker, R. (2006), *Gay TV and Straight America*, New Brunswick: Rutgers University Press.

Bernardin, M. (2013), '*The Sound of Music Live!*: TV review', *The Hollywood Reporter*, 5 December, http://www.hollywoodreporter.com/review/soundmusic-live-tv-review-663346. Accessed 15 February 2017.

Browning, N. L. (1972), 'Debbie Reynolds takes on Eva, Mae, Pearl, and *The Kid*', *Chicago Tribune*, 19 March, p. SCL 1.

Caldwell, J. T. (1995), *Televisuality: Style, Crisis, and Authority in American Television*, New Brunswick: Rutgers University Press.

Clum, J. (1999), *Something for the Boys: Musical Theatre and Gay Culture*, New York: St. Martin's Press.

Dvoskin, M. (2016), 'Embracing excess: The queer feminist power of musical theatre diva roles', *Studies in Musical Theatre*, 10:1, pp. 93–103.

Faires, R. (2014), 'Elaine Stritch (1925–2014): Brassy Broadway legend truly at liberty now', *The Austin Chronicle*, 17 July, https://www.austinchronicle.com/daily/arts/2014-07-17/elaine-stritch-1925-2014/. Accessed 11 September 2017.

Fallon, K. (2014), '*Peter Pan Live!* review: No amount of clapping brings it to life', *The Daily Beast*, 4 December, http://www.thedailybeast.com/articles/2014/12/05/peter-pan-live-review-no-amount-of-clapping-brings-it-tolife.html. Accessed 15 February 2017.

Feldman, A. and Cote, D. (2012), 'The 25 best divas of all times', *Time Out*, 23 January, https://www.timeout.com/newyork/theater/broadways-25-all-timegreatest-divas-broadway. Accessed 1 March 2017.

Gould, J. (1968), 'TV: *Carol Channing and 101 Men*', *New York Times*, 1 March, p. 75.

Harmetz, A. (1985), 'Angela Lansbury's unlikely sleuth has staying power: *Murder, She Wrote*', *New York Times*, 27 October, p. H25.

Hetrick, A. (2013), 'Updated: *The Sound of Music Live!* is ratings smash for NBC', *Playbill*, 6 December, http://www.playbill.com/article/updated-thesound-of-music-live-is-ratings-smash-for-nbc-com-212511. Accessed 15 February 2017.

Internet Broadway Database (2017), http://ibdb.com. Accessed 11 February 2017.

Isenberg, B. (1993), 'Q&A with Patti LuPone: "Basically, I'm an actress for hire"', *Los Angeles Times*, 9 January, http://articles.latimes.com/1993-01-09/entertainment/ca-9361q-a-with-patti-lupone. Accessed 15 February 2017.

Kessler, K. (2013), 'Broadway in the box: Television's infancy and the cultural cachet of the Great White Way', *Journal of Popular Music Studies*, 25:3, pp. 349–70.

Kessler, K. (2015), 'Primetime goes Hammerstein: The musicalization of fictional Primetime television in the post-network era', *Journal of e-Media Studies*, 4:1, http://journals.

dartmouth.edu/cgi-bin/WebObjects/Journals.woa/1/xmlpage/4/article/452. Accessed 12 March 2018.

Kessler, K. (2019), 'Trash talk and virtual protests: The musical genre's personal and political edge in the age of the internet', in E. L. Wollman and J. Sternfeld (eds), *Routledge Companion to the Post 1970s American Stage Musical*, New York: Routledge.

Kessler, K. (2020), *Broadway in the Box: Television's Lasting Love Affair with the Musical*, New York: Oxford University Press.

Kinon, C. (2008), '*Ugly Betty* production moving to NYC', *Daily News*, 12 May, http://www.nydailynews.com/entertainment/tv-movies/ugly-bettyproduction-moving-nyc-article-1.332338. Accessed 15 February 2017.

Koestenbaum, W. (1993), *The Queen's Throat: Opera, Homosexuality, and the Mystery of Desire*, New York: Poseidon Press.

Lange, M. (2014), interview with Kelly Kessler, Los Angeles, CA, 13 November.

Leeds, S. (2013), 'The best and worst moments of the new *Sound of Music*: A few of our favorite and not so favorite things', *Rolling Stone*, 6 December, http://www.rollingstone.com/movies/news/the-best-and-worst-moments-ofthe-new-sound-of-music-20131206. Accessed 15 February 2017.

Leonardi, S. J. and Pope, R. A. (1996), *The Diva's Mouth: Body, Voice, and Prima Donna Politics*, New Brunswick: Rutgers University Press.

Lotz, A. D. (2007), *The Television Will Be Revolutionized*, New York: New York University Press.

Mittell, J. (2006), 'Narrative complexity in contemporary American television', *Velvet Light Trap*, 58, Fall, pp. 29–40.

Moreno, R. (2000), interview with Marla Miller, Archive of American Television, 22 June, http://www.emmytvlegends.org/interviews/people/rita-moreno. Accessed 15 February 2017.

Musto, M. (2014), 'Michael Musto's definitive rankings of the top 10 Broadway divas onstage today', *Paper Mag*, 17 September, http://www.papermag.com/michael-mustos-definitive-ranking-of-the-top-10-broadway-divasonstage-1427411097.html. Accessed 5 March 2017.

Newcomb, H. (1974), *TV: The Most Popular Art*, Garden City: Anchor Books.

NYC.gov (2017), 'Filming now in New York city', NYC.gov website, http://www1.nyc.gov/site/mome/production-in-nyc/filming-now-in-nyc.page. Accessed 28 September 2017.

O'Connell, M. (2013), 'TV ratings: NBC's *Sound of Music Live* nears 22 million viewers with DVR', *The Hollywood Reporter*, 23 December, http://www.hollywoodreporter.com/live-feed/tv-ratings-nbcs-sound-music-667543. Accessed 1 March 2017.

Oliver, W. (1955), '"$5.80 ticket" for *Peter Pan*: TV of Broadway play set tomorrow', *Chicago Daily Tribune*, 6 March, p. NW12B.

O'Neill, E. R. (2007), 'The m-m-mama of us all: Divas and the cultural logic of late ca(m)pitalism', *Camera Obscura*, 65:22, pp. 11–37.

Orden, E. (2011), 'TV shows channel city', *Wall Street Journal*, 25 May, https://www.wsj.com/articles/SB10001424052702304066504576343673162864838. Accessed 15 February 2017.

Patten, D. (2013), 'Full 2012–2013 TV season series rankings', *Deadline*, 23 May, http://deadline.com/2013/05/tv-season-series-rankings-2013-fulllist-506970/. Accessed 5 March 2017.

Rice, L. (2014), '*Peter Pan Live!* was no *The Sound of Music Live!*', *People*, 5 December, http://people.com/tv/peter-pan-live-was-no-the-sound-ofmusic-live/. Accessed 15 February 2017.

Rooney, D. (2016), '*Hairspray Live!*: TV review', *The Hollywood Reporter*, 7 December, http://www.hollywoodreporter.com/review/hairspraylive-953980. Accessed 15 February 2017.

Salvato, N. (2007), 'On the bubble: The soap opera diva's ambivalent orbit', *Camera Obscura*, 65:22, pp. 102–23.

Saraiya, S. (2016), 'TV review: *Hairspray*', *Variety*, 7 December, http://variety.com/2016/tv/reviews/tv-review-hairspray-live-jennifer-hudson-arianagrande-1201936567/. Accessed 15 February 2017.

Spangler, T. (2011), 'DVR penetration: VOD monthly usage hit new heights in US', *Broadcasting & Cable*, 13 October, http://www.broadcastingcable.com/news/technology/dvr-penetration-vod-monthly-usage-hit-newhighs-us/48739. Accessed 15 February 2017.

Stanhope, K. (2017), 'ABC slates *Little Mermaid* and *Rolling Stone* live musicals', *The Hollywood Reporter*, 16 May, http://www.hollywoodreporter.com/live-feed/abc-little-mermaid-rolling-stone-live-musicals-1004221. Accessed 11 September 2017.

Thompson, E. (2007), 'Comedy verité? The observational documentary meets the televisual sitcom', *The Velvet Light Trap*, 60:1, pp. 63–72.

Thorburn, D. (2007), 'Television melodrama', in H. Newcomb (ed.), *Television: The Critical View*, 6th ed., New York and Oxford: Oxford University Press, pp. 595–608.

Vries, H. De (1992), 'For actors, TV can upstage Broadway', *New York Times*, 19 January, p. H31.

Whitburn, J. (1996), *Top Pop Albums: 1955–1996*, Menomonee Falls: Record Research, Inc.

Wlodarz, J. (2008), 'Love letter to Jane', *Camera Obscura*, 67:23.1, pp. 160–64.

Wolf, S. (2007), 'Wicked divas, musical theater, and Internet girl fans', *Camera Obscura*, 65:22, pp. 39–71.

Wontorek, P. (2015), 'Lockdown! Eight Broadway divas we'd kill to see behind bars on *Orange is the New Black*', *Broadway*, 15 June, http://www.broadway.com/buzz/181207/lockdown-eight-broadway-divas-wed-kill-to-seebehind-bars-on-orange-is-the-new-black/. Accessed 5 March 2017.

PART 4

ONSTAGE, OFFSTAGE AND ONLINE: GENDER AND SEXUALITY IN PERSONAL AND PROFESSIONAL MUSICAL PRACTICE

14

The Queerness of *Copla*: Musical Hope for the Spanish LGBTQ

Alejandro Postigo

Not much information exists on the 'Spanish musical', at least musicals akin to those performed on Broadway and the West End and having originated in Spain and in Spanish language, and maybe (only maybe) having been translated and performed outside Spanish-speaking borders. Narrow this search down to Spanish musicals developed in the twentieth century and brought to the non-Spanish world, and the results are close to zero. This lack can partially be explained by the disruption of an autochthonous Spanish musical theatre during the Francoist dictatorship (1939–75) and that form being progressively replaced by the importation of American musicals during the period following Spain's transition to democracy (post-1975). This historical disruption of Spanish musical theatre paralleled the growth of the American 'book musical' or those musicals which were more reliant on the integration of song and plot. Up to that point, Spanish musical theatre had been limited to the remains of the hybridized form *zarzuela*,[1] which integrated popular and operatic music as well as song and spoken word, and a series of variety revues largely comprised of *copla*, a folkloric, storytelling and theatrical songform which arguably became a key component for the development of Spanish musical theatre throughout the twentieth century.

Although Spain's primary musical form deviates stylistically from the American book musicals, revues and cabarets, *copla*, like various forms of American musical theatre performance, possesses historical links to both queer audiences and artists. Many LGBT poets, musicians and lyricists like Federico García Lorca or Rafael de León authored the form; LGBT popular singers like Miguel de Molina served as its primary performers; and LGBT audiences embraced the form, first covertly during the dictatorship, later openly after the transition to democracy, and still to this day.

This chapter explores LGBT connections and queer undertones of the *copla* artform. The LGBT struggle of the Spanish people follows the development of *copla*, moving from a dark period of censorship and repression during the Francoist dictatorship into a period of liberation and empowerment in the era of Spanish democracy. *Copla* accompanied the LGBT collective throughout the twentieth century, with many of the songs that were cherished in secret during the fascist regime becoming queer anthems in democracy. LGBT artists wrote and performed *copla* songs, first secretively and then publicly, and the songs' messages resonated with the LGBT community in times of persecution, torture and isolation. My aim as an artist–scholar has been to take *copla* into the twenty-first century world and beyond Spanish borders. My artistic research and creative work present, for the first time, *copla* songs performed in English in the context of a musical theatre narrative, creating points of access to the artform for English-speakers around the world. This chapter presents *copla*'s historical framework to highlight its emergence as a queer musical form in the shadow of the Franco regime, and then concludes with a brief exploration of my original performance piece, *The Copla Musical*, and its cross-cultural articulation of Spain's musical history and the space it created and continues to create for queer identity.

The role of copla *as the musical theatre of Spain's twentieth century*

Copla songs existed as popular components of Spanish variety shows during the Second Republic (1931–36), the Spanish Civil War (1936–39) and the subsequent fascist dictatorship (1939–75). While an array of musical revue formats including burlesque, minstrelsy, vaudeville, extravaganzas and musical comedies were in vogue in American musical theatre at the beginning of the twentieth century, the revue shows of Spain leaned heavily on the *copla* songform. In both Spanish and US forms of revue, musical numbers were often only loosely connected through a thematic argument if at all. A Spanish revue, for example, would commonly present back-to-back a flamenco dance number, a bullfighting parody sketch, and a deeply heartfelt *copla* song. In Broadway revues such as The Garrick Gaieties and The Ziegfeld Follies, cohesive plots often took a back seat to the spectacle of song and dance. Within this same period, the Tin Pan Alley songs of George and Ira Gershwin, Cole Porter and Irving Berlin fed the growing industry of early Broadway by popularizing a formula with dialogue and action interspersed with loosely related songs and dance numbers, as exhibited in shows such as Cole Porter's *Anything Goes* (1934). *Copla* songs rarely integrated into any sort of narrative larger than the songs' own and thus remained outside of any larger theatrical development. The non-integration or self-contained nature of *copla* songs within these theatrical revues perhaps contributed to Spanish musical theatre failing to develop in a manner similar to the more integrated Broadway form. Unlike with *copla*, the narrative integration of Porter's and Berlin's music within Broadway's musical comedies facilitated a step towards a uniquely American integrated musical form that eventually developed into the 'book musicals' seen around the world.

Although formal and performative similarities exist between American revues of the early twentieth century and Spanish *copla* shows, the *copla* songs of Spanish revues find their musical foundations in non-theatrical, folkloric forms such as *pasodoble* and *flamenco*. The popularity of *copla* relied on the telling of a self-contained story that could be dramatized and staged with a beginning, a climax and an ending all within one number. This ran in contrast to other musical theatre songs that presented a character or situation that transcended that single song's narrative. In the late 1920s and early 1930s, *copla* became a dominant genre within Spain's intellectual, political and artistic spheres, performed in cafes and cabarets with audiences that blended different social classes. During the years of the Second Republic (1931–36), a period of political liberalism and ideological progressivism wedged between fascist dictatorships, a divided population of diverse social classes and opposing ideologies popularized and embraced *copla* songs. Considered one of the most socially advanced periods of Spanish history, the Second Republic saw the emergence of LGBT figures and sensibilities on Spanish stages. Such advances were then abruptly interrupted by the Spanish Civil War (1936–39) and the start of the fascist dictatorship (1939), a time which saw the eradication of LGBT visibility and new legislation that singled-out and persecuted the LGBT community.

From the start of the war, fascist propaganda appropriated and manipulated *copla* songs. During the Francoist regime, *copla* songs, their themes and performers, suddenly projected strong conservative images in tune with National-Catholic ideals of the regime. But even within this time of ideological conflict, the songs kept their diverse popularity, drawing audiences from opposing political factions: victorious fascist rebels identifying with their new *overt* nationalistic contents and defeated Republican liberals finding a certain level of release in the lyrics' *encrypted* messages – ones that went unnoticed by the regime's strict censorship body. In this period of extreme political and social repression, one especially oppressive for LGBT collectives, these songs became, in both content and performance, a means to experience a certain degree of freedom. Performers were able to pass on implicit messages of diversity within a particularly authoritarian Spanish society, an act especially salient for an oppressed Spanish homosexual community. Since the transition to democracy, *copla* songs have been progressively and openly adopted by LGBT performers and audiences, creating an artistic space for an increasingly visible Spanish 'queer' collective.

A Spanish contextualization of 'queer' from Franco to Spanish democracy

To this day, the term 'queer' lacks a recognized translation to Spanish, and its use in Spain has proven confusing. While in Britain and the United States queer theory occupies a notable space within many University programs, in Spain a stigma remains against queer studies, a discipline considered a mere intellectual novelty that challenges sexual taboos (Mérida 2006: 71). Popularly, the concept of 'queer' is still relatively new in Spanish culture and is commonly confused with 'gay, drag-queen, transvestite and transsexual', although none of these reflect its functional definition (Mérida 2006: 70). The queer *Spanish* political movement generally rejects sexual classifications and instead focuses energies on promoting social change against heteronormativity. Since the start of Spanish democracy (1975), the country's LGBT collective has been more concerned with the recognition of LGBT rights than a transgression of sexual norms and definitions. The queer movement in Spain has run intellectually behind its Anglo counterparts with regard to more identity-based queer theorization. After almost 40 years of fascist oppression, the priority of the Spanish LGBT collective has been to acquire visibility and acceptance, before joining the international discourse of varied queer identities. Even within homophile discourse and gay activism, concepts like 'camp' have often been rejected and subsequently accused of being frivolous and escapist. During the first years of the transition to democracy, transvestites and 'queens' were excluded from progressive homosexual collectives – and to a certain degree they still are – as they were seen as confirming gay stereotypes and taking the focus away from political struggle.[2]

The ultra-Catholic social model imposed by Franco's dictatorship from 1939 to 1975 sought to control and repress any deviance from conservative heteronormative canons. This had particularly tough consequences for all women and gay men. Gay men were legally targeted by the *Ley de Vagos y Maleantes*, literally translated as 'law of lazy and mischievous people'. The law had been active since the Second Republic, targeting groups such as nomads and pimps, but Franco's regime modified it in 1954 to include homosexuals. The revised 1970s Spanish penal code, the *Ley de Peligrosidad y Rehabilitación Social* or 'law of danger and social rehabilitation', addressed acts of homosexuality and instituted a spectrum of punishments for those caught engaging in such acts (Pérez 2009: 65). Between August 1970 and the end of 1978, 4000–5000 homosexuals fell victim to this law, with thousands of gay people condemned without apparent motive, at least none beyond the exercise of the repressor's power (Mérida 2015). Gay prisoners were at times divided by their sexual practices: 'top' and overly-masculine homosexuals were sent to a prison in Huelva and 'bottom' and effeminate homosexuals to another in Badajoz, with the two being administered different 'cures' (Ruiz Mantilla 2013: 52). In prison, these men would be 're-educated' into heterosexuality while enduring extreme therapies, including electric shock treatments.[3] The medical community at large, which ascribed to the notion that homosexuality could be cured, only compounded the oppression exhibited towards the homosexual community via Spain's political and legal systems (Arnalte 2003).

In the late 1960s, such repressive legislation coexisted alongside a marginally increased tolerance for new venues that embraced LGBT networks and showcased LGBT performers. In big cities such as Barcelona, new small nightclubs and cabarets offered shows with female impersonators, transvestites and transsexuals. Autobiographical testimonies from artists such as Pierrot (2006) and Dolly Van Doll (Matos 2007) describe in detail some of these experiences (in Mérida, 2015). Although in 1970, the legal system still classified homosexual acts as criminal, men were not so concerned with hiding all mannerisms which might be deemed suspect. From 1975 onward, homosexual references and innuendo became more prominent within the music industry, through both song lyrics and the flamboyant appearances or drag performances of the singers. It was also at this time, following three decades of cultural autarchy, that Spain began to open up to foreign artforms, and homosexual representation took on more of an international dimension, with international anthems such as Gloria Gaynor's 1978 disco hit 'I Will Survive' making their way into the Spanish LGBT scene.

According to Javier Ugarte, although European countries had sweepingly instituted repressive legislation singling-out homosexuals, Spain stood apart from the rest of the continent in terms of what drove its homophobia. While European laws targeting homosexuals tended to focus on psychological deficiencies, in Spain morality and the influence of the Catholic church drove such laws (Ruiz Mantilla 2013: 52). The dictatorial regime penalized men who were single more heavily than those who were married, giving the latter group less punitive sentences so they could return to their wives. Gayness remained stigmatized during the early years of democracy, as the Law of Social Danger remained intact. Not until 1999 did the Spanish government approve the Law of Data Protection, purging and deleting all of the information the government had collected regarding arrests of homosexuals during the Franco years and those to follow (Ruiz Mantilla 2013: 57).

After the death of Franco in 1975, Spain started a process of transition to democracy, during which time political activism began to publicly address LGBT rights. Barcelona saw the birth of Spain's first homosexual movement and the organization of the nation's first Gay Pride parade. Public personalities like cartoonist Nazario and painter Ocaña participated in and attended such events in drag, but there was a long path ahead in the establishment of gay acceptance. Even the LGBT community was divided, with gay activists reluctant to allow drag queens and performers to become central to political demonstrations (Mira 2013: 60). During those years, artists were concerned with political change and made efforts to normalize a 'moderate' LGBT presence in a Spanish society still experiencing the echoes of the dictatorship. This period saw 'a short-lived obsession with political change, morality, and sexual issues': because of the 1977 abolition of existing censorship laws, LGBT visibility and representation strongly increased in both film and TV (Mira 2013). Within the cultural manifestations of the transition to democracy, an incipient obsession for *morbo* emerged: a popular word of the period denoting prurient curiosity for what was forbidden (Mira 2013: 58). Here, some cultural anchors helped the transition by merging old and new. *Copla* songs, now able to overtly offer all the implicit messages constrained during the dictatorship, provided one such anchor.

The role of copla *as marker of gender identity*

Prior to the popularization of cinema and a widespread adoption of radio in Spanish homes, rural areas of post-war Spain relied on communitarian celebrations of song and dance as their primary forms of affordable entertainment. Through such celebrations and a process of oral transmission, *copla* expanded during the 1940s, bringing along with it resultant role models for women that were in tune with the official canons of the dictatorship. This presentation of *copla* singers/stars as virtuous women aligned with the regime's larger strategy to create a 'national' conscience. Various stereotypes were subsequently disseminated via *copla*, images and symbols that coalesced around what it meant to 'be Spanish'. Many songs share a common denominator: stories featuring key roles for women displaying behaviour and facing situations the regime considered to be transgressions against the official morality of Franco's Spain and therefore worthy of punishment. These transgressions include 'deviances' such as prostitution, adultery, maternity outside marriages, pre-marital cohabitation, concubinage, independency and spinsterhood. *Copla* songs warned about the dangers of straying from the regime-sanctioned path.

In contrast to the songs themselves, female singers of *copla* embodied 'Spanish virtues', and stories of their private lives spread throughout the media, framing them as ideals of Hispanic femininity and making them role models for what Spanish women should aspire to be (Zurián 2005). In Francoist Spain, stardom served a political agenda of alienation, demonizing or admonishing any women who could not live up to the stars' depictions of ideal Spanish femininity and morality. As Eva Woods suggests, the regime's use of entertainment stars in the shaping of female Spanishness drew on a precedent established in the star system of Spanish folklore. Stars of Spanish spectacle were called *folklóricas*, a label originally denoting performers of Spanish folklore but later restricted to women doing Andalusian-flavoured spectacle.[4] Within the *folklórica* star system of the 1930s and 1940s, only women thought to have national-Catholic virtues were allowed to go on stage: only they could risk singing about passions not easily tolerated by the conservative regime.

The female protagonists of *copla* inhabit a sensorial world of emotions, characterized by being over-affectionate, whimsical, exaggeratedly emotive and compliant. From a medical point of view, women in *copla* have often been framed as hysterical and sexually mature but intellectually infantile. In the early to mid 1930s, during the Second Republic, *copla* became popularized as a vehicle for the transgressive and sinning woman,[5] but this halted by the end of the decade with the onset of the dictatorship, when songs were quickly censored and adapted to fit the conservative ideological bill of the regime (Prieto 2016: 317). The Spanish Civil War of 1936–39 had resulted in the exile of established artists who had failed to embody the ideals of Franco's Spain, and subsequently a new generation of *folklóricas* emerged. According to Woods, these new *folklóricas* were: 'women of strong Catholic values, virgin until marriage, but passionate and feminine'. She goes on to argue that 'although the *folklórica* icon was not a model of revolutionary resistance but rather one of negotiated class interests, the potential for imagined and vicarious solidarity for Spanish spectators was certainly possible' (2004: 40–41).

If the regime saw *copla* as a contemporary cultural product open to political use and manipulation, others read them emotionally and ahistorically, placing them instead in what Acosta Díez et al. describe as 'the timeless space of feeling' (1994). During this time, such double meanings of *copla* seemed to slip by the powers-that-be. Satisfied with the strong conservative images the female singers presented, those in power and their censors ignored the polyvalent possibilities of the narratives and lyrics themselves. Even when censors intervened and made changes to lyrics, *copla* songs still seemed to reflect the emotional experiences of those the regime had condemned to silence because of their sexuality and gender identity: homosexuals, transgender people, etc.[6] Because these communities possessed very few artistic models through which they could embrace these forbidden emotions, *copla* became a shared vehicle for such identification. *Copla* lyricists like Rafael de León hid strong male homosexual innuendo within verses narrated by female voices, attracting huge gay crowds which identified with the narratives, despite their performance by a female vocalist. Examples of this type of homosexual innuendo appear in songs such as 'ced*Romance de la otra*' ('Romance of the Other One'), in which the lyrics '*yo soy la otra que a nada tiene derecho*' translate to 'I am the "other one" that has no rights'. Such phrasing could as easily refer to the homosexual experience as to the female experience and slip past censors (Pérez 2009: 63–64).

In early to mid-twentieth-century Spain, male homosexuals would largely have to settle for finding themselves within the performances of women. Despite other European countries popularizing male theatrical performance and even female impersonation, early twentieth-century Spain shied away from men appearing on the variety stage. As Spanish women slowly achieved some level of social liberation, the most progressive embracing more traditionally masculine acts such as smoking, driving and wearing trousers, men needed to maintain their gender-compliant macho image. This meant neither publicly expressing feelings nor performing in variety shows. Variety spectacles including cross-dressing and all other 'immoral manifestations of art' all but ceased to exist at the 1939 outset of Franco's dictatorship (Pérez 2006: 61). A tight adherence to cultural norms meant that Spanish *copla* during the dictatorship was almost exclusively performed by women or homosexuals rejected by the regime. It was notably at this time that out-homosexual Miguel de Molina became one of the first male *copla* performers to gain considerable fame, concreting associations between *copla* and homosexuality.[7]

De Molina stood as a gendered outlier, performing feminized *copla*. The form's songs themselves typically centred on culturally feminized experiences, predominantly displaying emotions in relation to love affairs, the kind men were not expected to publicly express during Franco's male-dominated macho culture. The few male singers who performed *copla* and wanted to preserve an image of virility adapted their repertoire to songs devoid of such feminized emotion. Performances like Pepe Blanco's '*Cocidito Madrileño*' ('Madrilenian Stew') or Juanito Valderrama's '*El emigrante*' ('The Emigrant') and '*Mi Salamanca*' ('My Salamanca') side-lined relationships for Spanish food and locales. Such masculinized songs also served the regime's goal to use popular entertainment to expound the grandiosity of Spanish geography and gastronomy. Male artists such as de Molina, Rafael Conde, and Tomás de Antequera resisted this change of focus and instead sang the repertoire popularized by female performers such as Concha Piquer or Juanita Reina, consequently advocating a more mannered (gay) art. All three of these male *copla* performers acquired a relative level of success in their native Spain and then subsequently in their respective places of exile.

Over the decades, the popular stars of *copla* seemed to wind a path through the LGBT communities of Spain. Although a handful of male singers were performing feminized versions of the form in the 1950s, in what many consider the golden age of Francoist *copla*, the form was largely defined by popular female singers such as

Lola Flores, stars who projected an aspirational femininity for Spanish women: strong but pure, sexy but chaste, and unequivocally 'Spanish' in their mannerisms and expressions. In addition to her more expected appeal to female audiences in need of Francoist indoctrination, the duality of Flores' persona made her an ideal point of identification and admiration for many closeted homosexuals as well. The 1960s brought with them shifts in *copla*'s evocation of Spanish femininity, a move from the regime-approved sensual duality of Flores to the sexually experienced cosmopolitanism of Sara Montiel, the latter of whom would become a gay icon and favourite subject of star impersonators of the 1970s (Pérez 2009: 65; Castro de Paz 2005: 112).[8] By the late 1960s and early 1970s, new flamboyant but straight singers like Raphael began attracting young homosexual audiences to the waning form. In the absence of queer national idols, gay men clung to Raphael's songs like '*Digan lo que digan*' ('Whatever They Say') and '*Qué sabe nadie*' ('What Do They Know?'). By the 1970s, Franco's death seemed imminent and a sense of sexual liberation led to more explicitly sexually empowered messages within lyrics, and a new visible strain of cross-dressing celebrity impersonators and transvestites started to perform *copla* songs for wider audiences in subversive venues (Pérez 2009: 64).

Copla *in democracy: The emergence of trans presence and camp re-appropriation*

After Franco's death and the abolition of government-sanctioned censorship, Spain witnessed an erotic boom that gave way to the rise of a Spanish variety of trans spectacle (Mérida 2015). Post 1975, in the early years of Spanish democracy, 'trans' mainly refers to 'transvestite' or 'cross-dressing'. Transgender as an identity was not prevalent or as visible at the time. Police raids became more irregular and trans presence became less stigmatized and more visible; simultaneously, audiences were drawn by their curiosity for what had been long forbidden. In this period of the late 1970s and early 1980s, trans theatre flourished and became central to a cultural movement known as La Movida, one with its epicentre in Madrid and popularizing artists such as film director Pedro Almodóvar and singer Alaska. This post-Franco trans moment recuperated and updated early 1930s pre-Civil war shows in which 'star impersonators' had cross-dressed to imitate *copla* singers. The cross-dressing scene practically disappeared during the dictatorship, but in democracy it acquired more visibility and political presence than ever before. During these early democratic years of the 1970s and 1980s, trans visibility increased both on and off stage, and these performances of *copla* songs became statements of identity and politics as much as artistic expression.

This new trans Spanish tradition provided an outlet for emotions that could not have been expressed in the previous political era due to the regime's political silencing. In the transition to democracy this re-appropriation of *copla* became very popular, with an increasing number of artists performing the songs in drag. Spanish painter Ocaña, primarily known for his role in promoting sexual liberation during the transition to democracy, promenaded in full drag 'along the Ramblas followed by crowds of onlookers, sing[ing] the Quintero, León, and Quiroga *copla* "*Yo soy esa*" ("I am That Woman")' (Mira 2013: 60). *Copla* began to more overtly represent a queer demographic which had once embraced the form privately and was now free to do so publicly, leading to the establishment of a new explicit political dimension for both the genre and community.

In democracy, *copla* became associated with characteristics of gay camp. Spanish queer scholar Alberto Mira associates camp with a homosexual positioning of contents proceeding from popular arts and whose sense emerges from a recycling of these forms (2004: 145). Given the popularity of *copla* throughout the dictatorship and its long relationship with LGBT audiences, it seems only natural that the covert contents of *copla* songs would become overt in democracy. But *copla* in the 1970s felt outdated, stylistically old and full of stereotypes. It needed a makeover. Mira argues that camp addresses homosexuality without making it explicit: 'It's cultivated by homosexuals with effort, style, gesture. It's a response to the stereotype rather than a reproduction of it. It is a gay gaze that activates parody, recognizes kitsch, and questions gender roles' (2004: 147). He argues that identification with marginality is the only faithful interpretation of the *copla* texts. As during the Franco era, nothing associated with sexual perversion would have been tolerated, the frivolous language of a camp-infused *copla* and its forerunner *cuplé* would have damaged the Francoist sensibilities focused on the worthy and noble nature of the dictatorship and its notably homophobic ideals. This explains, in part, why light and frivolous *cuplé* songs were slowly replaced during the Franquismo with *copla* songs, ones which were deeper, more dramatic, and involved a lesser risk of camp interpretations.

Into the twenty-first century, *copla* has been more openly embraced by transgender and queer artists such as Falete. He performs sentimental *copla* while dressed in feminine outfits but without hiding his male gender, thereby flaunting a sense of androgyny. As Mira suggests, the performance of camp is the processing of potentially oppressive heterosexist cultural myths to transform them into a discourse of pleasure and affirmation of marginality (2004: 349). Rather than helping LGBT audiences escape from the harsh realities of homosexual erasure, post-democracy *copla* now helps reaffirm their existence in all its richness and diversity. Therefore, many gay, transgender and queer artists look to *copla* in the twenty-first century as a vehicle to express their feelings. This very affirmation of marginality inspired me, a twenty-first century Spanish gay immigrant living in the United Kingdom, to channel my artistic position. This affirmation of identity comes through my project *The Copla Musical,* a performance piece through which I seek to export the new and empowered queer *copla* into the Anglo-speaking world through a process of intercultural adaptation.

The future of copla: *Creating* The Copla Musical *for international audiences*

Despite *copla*'s continued popularity in Spain and its relationship to other popular song styles and musical theatre forms in the United Kingdom and the United States, the form has not been explored with any degree of detail. Although *copla* has succeeded as popular music across different social groups in Spain and its theatricality has been evidenced and repurposed in many cabarets and TV shows, attention to its origins as a form of Spanish musical theatre has failed to take hold, culturally diminished by an increasing affinity towards megamusical imports.[9] Even after the post-Franco return to democracy, no homegrown Spanish musical theatre akin to that of the United States and United Kingdom took shape, leaving *copla* as Spain's dominant indigenous musical theatre form. Well into Spain's twenty-first century, the strong musico-theatrical anchor of *copla* remains; with the exception of a few jukebox musicals and local initiatives which rarely find an afterlife beyond their short runs, very little composition and production of new Spanish musical theatre has emerged. Instead, globalized Anglo-American musicals translated into Spanish language currently fill most Spanish theatres and create the majority of Spain's theatrical revenue.

My research and related performance practice look back to *copla* in an attempt to re-imagine an artistic avenue for an intercultural intervention with a new type of Spanish musical, one putting *copla* in dialogue with other international manifestations of musical theatre.[10] *The Copla Musical* (2014) explores how *copla* songs of the past might now be adapted for and integrated into a contemporary musical theatre show conceived and presented outside of Spain in such a way that they negotiate *copla*'s cultural identity within an alternate linguistic and cultural context. My current artistic practice thus aims to combine this Spanish folkloric songform with principles inherent to musical theatre artworks found in the United Kingdom and United States. Such principles include the integration of songs and narrative, acting through song and storytelling, and dramaturgical principles from the book musical and jukebox musical. In that sense, my artistic practice-as-research holds a double objective. On the one hand, I aim to reduce the historical gap that separates Spanish and Anglo-American musical theatre, one that dates back to the Spanish Francoist dictatorship. Whereas Anglo-American musicals have continuously developed in form *and* reached Spanish theatres – throughout the dictatorship and beyond – *copla* practically disappeared from theatre stages during the dictatorship. Although the form has continued to enjoy popularity and acquired a whole new significance in democracy, it has been almost wholly detached from its theatrical origins until recent years. On the other hand, I strive to make *copla*'s once implicit LGBT contents now explicit, not only in terms of camp re-appropriation but also by making what was once only queer lyrical subtext the overt text of the songs, allowing them to achieve their full expressive, ideological and even revolutionary potential, now in an international context.

I first developed this project as a book musical version of *The Copla Musical* between 2011 and 2013. The show explored the Spain of the Civil War era via the American exile of transsexual Spanish artist La Gitana. Following a musical theatre two-act conventional format, the self-contained *copla* narratives were expanded to become part of a whole new narrative. In adapting the language and musical structure of songs, I did make some musical compromises, like the blending of some flamenco rhythms, Spanish imagery and musical ornamentation with Anglo idiosyncrasies defined either by the English language itself or by the tone of Anglo musical theatre works (Postigo 2016).

In 2014, I converted the musical into a solo show, attending to a new dramaturgy that paralleled the story of La Gitana with that of a contemporary migrant narrator and set in twenty-first century London. The narrator figure allows for a historical contextualization of La Gitana while providing a contemporary perspective and commentary on gender and queer narratives. The show became a one-hour piece in which one actor plays both the narrator and La Gitana. Within the show, all songs contribute to tell the story of La Gitana. Whereas in the ensemble piece they did this from a present narrative perspective, in the solo we look at this narrative in retrospect. The songs themselves carry the weight of representing and unravelling La Gitana's character, as the narrator keeps investigating her life. The musical and narrative development of La Gitana leads to an organic presentation and historical contextualization of the development of *copla*. The solo piece trims the band down to a piano and violin which provide accompaniment and underscoring and help to create different atmospheres through musical motives of *copla* songs.

The marketing description of the show reads as follows:

> In contemporary London, a Spanish immigrant sets out on a journey of self-acceptance, inspired by the remarkable story of drag artist La Gitana who escaped from Franco's dictatorship to perform her passion-filled Spanish folk music in America. Through the passion and subversion of Spanish *copla*, La Gitana will eventually transform his life and understand what it takes to come to terms with who you are born to be.

Explored in retrospect through the use of *copla* songs, the idea of identity becomes central to the solo piece.

This reimagining of *The Copla Musical* as a solo show emerged through a lens of queer theory, one that was able to aid in the exploration and excavation of gendered and sexual identities and expressions that informed the evolution of *copla* from its origins on through to today. In *The Copla Musical 'Solo'*, a narrator looks to the character of La Gitana and her songs as inspiration to unlock his own sexuality and gender identity. Through their shared passion for *copla*, the narrator identifies with La Gitana's longing for the homeland, her love affairs and her desire for freedom. The songs, sung by both La Gitana and the narrator, unify their emotional yearning and create a queer narrative journey between the two temporally separated characters. La Gitana draws inspiration from the Spanish divas of dictatorship era folkloric films, *folklóricas*, who exhibited *gypsy* features such as black curly hair (often tied up in a bun with a perfect curl adorning the forehead), dark skin, self-confidence, temper and nerve, but also charm and '*duende*' (Hurtado 2003: 29) (Figure 14.1).[11] Such features evoke an image of the *gypsy race*[12] associated with Andalusia, but also those that came to symbolize Spain within the international imagination. In both forms of *The Copla Musical*, La Gitana subverts such an entrenched gendered and ethnic visage through her trans-identity. Influenced by La Gitana, the narrator too experiences a personal transformation and embarks on a journey which ultimately leads to him going to the office dressed as a woman. The characters of the narrator and La Gitana eventually merge into one through the performance of *copla* songs. The narrator starts the piece by exploring who La Gitana was and how/where/when/why she performed *copla* and the significance of these songs. Eventually, he is able to channel the character into his own experiences and comprehend the quest for identity and homeland that La Gitana experienced a century prior. The *coplas* he and La Gitana sing as the show advances become more heartfelt and reflective of the migrant experience, as well as of their queer identities.

My original aim in the creation of this project was to rejuvenate *copla* outside of Spain and to defend its dramatic value abroad. Anglophone musical theatre has historically drawn on and adopted a variety of indigenous art forms such as jazz, blues and Irish jig ... so why not *copla*? An association with the internationally recognized Anglophone musical form could arguably help facilitate the integration of Spanish *copla* into a more broadly visible musical theatre landscape and generate new interest in the genre outside of Spain. For audiences completely new to *copla*, *The Copla Musical* provides an easily accessible, culturally Spanish flavoured, and historically and politically charged presentation of the form for the first time in English, following the narrative rules that musical theatre shows have featured all over the world. This intercultural approach paves a future for

FIGURE 14.1: *The Copla Musical*'s protagonist La Gitana drawing inspiration from the Spanish *folklórica*'s gypsy features (*The Copla Musical*. Photograph courtesy of Alejandro Postigo).

copla, as well as provides an opportunity to expand the possibilities of musicals beyond the mainly Anglo-generated content that currently exists across the globe.

The intercultural creation of this modern *copla* musical engages with the principles underpinning the creation of musicals in a globalized twenty-first century. Through my creation of *The Copla Musical*, I retraced the process of crafting a hybrid form of musical theatre. Musical theatre conventions such as the form's monomyth structure, the unification of dialogue and musical storytelling, and a jukebox-style integration of songs drive the epic story of La Gitana. In my composition of the show, I considered the traditional narrative functions of musical numbers within Anglophone musical theatre: openings, I am/want songs, character songs and comedy numbers, eleven o'clock numbers, climatic finales. I then streamlined these characteristics into a more intimate piece with the solo show. Authors are often encouraged to first know the rules and then bend them as needed. With *Copla*, a significant amount of bending was necessary to find a balance of cultural compromises. As well, I had to consider the financial implications of being able to produce an intimate show that could travel across the world.

Perhaps most importantly, and mirroring the popular genre's development in the United States, I embraced a collaborative process that appropriated forms and functions from other local and foreign cultures. The birth of musical theatre in the United States was a result of collaborative processes wherein several artists came together to assemble stories, music and lyrics to eventually form what we know as musicals today. Similarly, an international team of artists assembled to rejuvenate *copla* outside of its original Spanish language and cultural context. Throughout a five-year process of development, collaborators included artists from various nationalities, although mainly British and Spanish. I worked with British lyricists with whom I negotiated an accurate translation and adaptation of songs into ones that could be read correctly in the English language. Such a collaboration allowed us to convey the narrative information necessary for the story, while keeping the songs true to their originals. In addition, British musical directors, Spanish actors with prior experience singing *copla*, and a selection of international creatives with their own musical theatre backgrounds and cultural referents became part of the collaborative process, embracing *copla* through my eyes and those of the Spanish members of the team and ultimately becoming culture bearers of this songform.

Through several stages of development and cultural negotiation, *The Copla Musical* was born. At the start of the twentieth century in the United States, many artists involved in the first steps of integrated musical theatre brought their cultural referents into play: Irish jig, African-American and Jewish musical elements, etc. Similarly, in the diaspora of a global twenty-first century, where artists find themselves in foreign countries and yet seek to preserve their own cultural influences, such a cultural-infusion must continue to expand musical theatre beyond its Anglocentrism. The identity quest of *The Copla Musical* has been two-fold: to bring this beautiful poetic musical theatre work to non-Spanish audiences through the experience of the migrant artist, and in doing so, rescue its subversive potential as a queer form of expression, one which was particularly significant in a historical time of oppression. Simultaneous to its larger generic venture, this artistic project generates questions that challenge, renew and complement historical knowledge of Spanish LGBT collectives.

My performance experience, one that includes cross-gendering in my own embodiment of the *copla* heroine, offers another lens for queer analysis. The same actor plays both the male narrator, who cross-dresses, and La Gitana, a trans character. The queer embodiment existent within *The Copla Musical* echoes past experiences of the marginal communities who originally identified with *copla*. Being displaced from my country, although for my own professional pursuits and not by the same homophobic regime that exiled and oppressed the Spanish LGBT community for much of the twentieth century, sparked a new-born interest in exploring my Spanish cultural identity through the study of *copla*. To this day, *copla* songs help me reconnect with my Spanish identity while living abroad. As a gay immigrant, I embrace *copla*'s evocative power and practice a personal approach to these songs that drives me to reflect upon and share my experience of *copla* with those of other cultures, much liked the exiled queer *copla* singers of an earlier era. *The Copla Musical* has been staged several times in the UK and European countries such as Bulgaria, the Czech Republic and even Spain, where Spanish audiences have been able to experience this newly re-imagined English *copla*. The show has also travelled to Latin America, where *copla* singers living in exile had popularized the form for older generations. For each audience demographic, I have changed individual referents within the show or offered further contextualization. In Latin America, the show required a re-adaptation to Spanish; whereas, when performed in Spain, I played with a combination of English and Spanish lyrics to confront *copla* connoisseurs with the new English *copla*.

In each new country and cultural context, I have had to consider and somehow adapt based on the audience's prior experience (or lack thereof) with *copla* and/or various forms of musical theatre. Q&As, workshops, and interviews commonly accompany the performance to provide background on and context for *copla* and my research, so that the audience's experience can be as rich as possible. The audience often has many questions about *copla*; they want to know more as they experience this oppressive period of Spanish history through an artform of such beauty. Often such exchanges prove to be extraordinarily illuminating, especially when audience members are able to establish cultural parallels of their own, for instance regarding their own linking of culturally specific art forms to the LGBT experience. One of the biggest assets of *The Copla Musical* has been its ability to spread the form to new audiences, one of my main objectives at the core of the project. In conjunction, through my research, and most viscerally through the performances of *The Copla Musical,* I am able to present snippets of Spanish queer history to help audiences understand the potential formal and ideological role *copla* could play in the current musical theatre space.

Despite its contextualization within regimes that oppressed and attempted to erase the Spanish LGBTQ community, *copla* has been strongly associated with LGBT sensibilities since its birth in the early twentieth century. Gay writers and performers have been key in its development, but one cannot overlook the role LGBT audiences have played in embracing the genre throughout its difficult history. *Copla* provided hope in times of oppression and empowerment in times of liberation. It is no wonder scholar Stephanie Sieburth speaks of *copla* as 'survival songs' (2014). *Copla* was at the forefront of musical theatre in early twentieth century Spain, paralleling the musical theatre forms emerging in the United Kingdom and the United States, forms also often spearheaded by minority communities. In a global twenty-first century, it simply makes sense to rescue this historically, socially and poetically charged songform and present it internationally through a new intercultural lens. That has been and remains my aim with *The Copla Musical*: a lens that embraces *copla's* queer history, recuperates *copla* to potentially revive the Spanish musical, and provides an opportunity for global audiences to encounter bits of Spanish cultural history and identity within these brief moments of a song.

NOTES

1. *Zarzuela* emerged as a popular response to the monarchic impositions of foreign genres. The form, evolving from its mid seventeenth century Baroque period to its mid twentieth century Romantic period, combines operatic and popular song and dance with spoken word. For more information about the origins of musical theatre in Spain, see Fernández Cid (1975).
2. For more information about the evolution of queer theory and gender studies in Spain, the reader can check Alberto Mira's *De Sodoma a Chueca. Una historia cultural de la homosexualidad en España en el siglo XX* (2014) and Rafael M. Mérida Jiménez's publications: *Sexualidades transgresoras. Una antología de estudios 'queer'* (2002), *Manifiestos gays, lesbianos y queer* (2009), as well as *Minorías sexuales en España* (2013) and *Las Masculinidades en la Transición* (2015).
3. The felony known as *escándalo público* (public scandal) legitimized the persecution of LGBT collectives and led to the imprisonment of many with the invasive therapies mentioned above. This treatment was exposed by activist Armand de Fluvià (2003) and subsequently examined by Arnalte (2003), Mira (2004) and Olmeda (2004), among others.
4. Eva Woods frames the term *folklórica* as originally referring to 'female, male, and sometimes transvestite artists whose repertory included traditional regional songs or dances with hints of regional flourishes, regardless of the artist's own regional identity'. She goes on to argue that 'the reduction of the term to mean only women who performed Andalusian folklore produced a negative connotation, partly because the term indiscriminately referred to any artist that dedicated themselves to any kind of remotely Andalusian spectacle'. She contends that the term 'deserves problematizing given its instrumental links to shaping of female Spanishness' (Woods 2004: 57).
5. Narratives also presented women who reacted to their unhappy destinies and humiliations by killing others. Prieto defines these heroines as *las justicieras* (the righteous ones) (2016: 311).

6. The regime tried to forbid or alter the lyrics of popular songs like *Tatuaje* (Tattoo) or *Ojos verdes* (Green Eyes), but those attempts were rarely successful, as people knew and remained true to the original versions. In *Ojos verdes*, for instance there was an attempted substitution of '*mancebía*' (brothel) for '*casa mía*' (my house).
7. A flamboyant singer who popularized many *copla* songs, De Molina displayed a strong political affiliation to the Second Republic and was forced into exile in Argentina following harassment and persecution by the fascist regime at the start of the dictatorship.
8. Presumed gypsy, Flores distanced herself from flamenco canons to conform to the ideals of Spanish 'racial' femininity. She was succeeded by Montiel in 1960s, bringing a new sexualized canon of beauty that became exportable to the Hollywood industry, where she participated in a few film projects.
9. Marta Mateo (2008) and Mia Patterson (2010) explain in detail the growing demand of Anglo-American megamusicals in Spain throughout the twentieth and twenty-first centuries.
10. For more details on the artistic form, content, and process related to *The Copla Musical*, refer to my prior publications listed in the bibliography (Postigo Gómez 2014 & 2015).
11. *Duende* is a Spanish term, often associated with flamenco that refers to the power to attract through personal magnetism and charm.
12. Although recent discourse has addressed problematic connotations of this term, the gypsy race and culture were heavily featured in *copla* narratives. The protagonists of many *copla* songs present themselves as gypsy, and many *copla* singers identified as gypsy within Spanish society. *The Copla Musical* renders a small tribute to this culture by naming its protagonist La Gitana, which translates as 'The Gypsy'.

REFERENCES

Acosta Díaz, Josefa, Manuel, Gómez Lara and Jorge, Jiménez Barrientos (1994), *Poemas y canciones de Rafael de León*, Seville: Ediciones Alfar.

Arnalte, Arturo (2003), *Redada de violetas. La represión de los homosexuales durante el franquismo*, Madrid: La Esfera de los Libros.

Castro de Paz, José Luis and Josetxo, Cerdán (2005), *Suevia Films-Cesáreo González. Treinta años de cine español*, A Coruña: Xunta de Galicia.

Fernández-Cid, Antonio (1975), *Cien años de teatro musical en España (1875–1975)*, Madrid: Real Musical, D.L.

Hurtado Balbuena, Sonia (2003), *Aspectos léxico-semánticos de la* copla *española: Los poemas y canciones de Rafael de León*, Ph.D. thesis, Universidad de Málaga.

Mateo, Marta (2008), 'Anglo-American musicals in Spanish theatres', *The Translator*, Special Issue: '*Translation and Music*', 14:2, pp. 319–42.

Matos, Pilar (2007), *De niño a mujer. Biografía de Dolly van Doll*, Cordoba: Arco Press.

Mérida Jiménez, Rafael Manuel (2002), *Sexualidades transgresoras. Una antología de estudios 'queer'*, Barcelona: Icaria, 'Mujeres y culturas'.

Mérida Jiménez, Rafael M. (2006), 'Estudios queer y sexualidades transgresoras', *Dossier de: Asociación Educación y Bibliotecas Tilde*, 18:152, pp. 69–71.

Mérida Jiménez, Rafael M. (2015), 'De Rodríguez Méndez a Olea/Azcona: flores de otoño en fuga', in R. M. Mérida and J. L. Peralta (eds), *Las masculinidades en la Transición*, Barcelona-Madrid: Egales, pp. 123–36.

Mira, Alberto (2004), *De Sodoma a Chueca. Una historia cultural de la homosexualidad en España en el siglo XX*, Barcelona: Egales.

Mira, Alberto (2013), '*Ocaña*. An intermittent portrait (Ventura Pons, 1977): The Mediterranean movida and the passing away of Francoist Barcelona', in M. M. Delgado and R. Fiddian (eds.), *Spanish Cinema 1973-2010. Auteurism, Politics, Landscape and Memory*, Manchester: Manchester University Press, pp. 193–210.

Olmeda, Fernando (2004), *El látigo y la pluma. Homosexuales en la España de Franco*, Madrid: Oberon.

Patterson, Mia (2010), *75 años de historia del musical en España (1930–2005)*, Madrid: Ediciones y Publicaciones Autor, SRL; Tramart.

Pérez, David (2009), 'La homosexualidad en la canción española', *Ogigia. Revista electrónica de estudios hispánicos*, 6, pp. 55–71.

Pierrot (2006), *Memorias trans. Transexuales – Travestis – Transformistas*, Barcelona: Morales i Torres.

Postigo Gómez, Alejandro (2014), 'Rediscovering Spanish musical theatre: Exploring an intercultural adaptation of *copla*', in F. J. Schopf (ed.), *Music on Stage Volume I*, Cambridge Scholars Publishing, pp. 184–97.

Postigo Gómez, Alejandro (2015), '*The Copla Musical*: Exchanges between English and Spanish musical theatre', *Acotaciones*, 34, pp. 53–81.

Postigo Gomez, Alejandro (2016), 'New insights into the notion of interculturalism and hybridity in musical theatre', in F. J. Schopf (ed.), *Music on Stage Volume II*, Cambridge: Cambridge Scholars Publishing, pp. 96–110.

Prieto Borrego, Lucía (2016), 'La *copla*: un instrumento para el proyecto de moralización de la sociedad española durante el primer franquismo', Arenal: *Revista de historia de mujeres*, 23:2, pp. 287–320.

Ruiz Mantilla, Jesús (2013), 'Humillados por diferentes', *El País Semanal*, 12 May.

Sieburth, Stephanie (2014), *Survival Songs: Conchita Piquer's coplas and Franco's regime of terror*, Toronto: University of Toronto Press.

Woods, Eva (2004), 'From rags to riches: The ideology of stardom in folkloric musical comedy films of the late 1930s and 1940s', in A. Lázaro-Reboll and A. Willis (eds), *Spanish Popular Cinema*, Manchester: Manchester University Press, pp. 40–59.

Zurián Hernández, Francisco (2005), 'Mirada y pasión: Reflexiones en torno a la obra Almodovariana', in F. Zurián Hernández and C. Vázquez Varela (eds), *Almodóvar, El Cine Como Pasión*, 1st ed., Cuenca: Ediciones de la Universidad de Castilla-La Mancha, pp. 21–44.

15

Queering Brechtian Feminism: Breaking Down Gender Binaries in Musical Theatre Pedagogical Performance Practices

Sherrill Gow

This essay draws on my practice directing postgraduate musical theatre students in a production of *Pippin* (1972) at Mountview, London, United Kingdom.[1] Working from the premise that musical theatre is open, unfinished (Kirle 2005) and thus malleable to feminist interpretations, and that the disjunctive qualities of song and dance (McMillin 2006; Taylor 2012) offer disruptive possibilities, I argue that musical theatre presents productive unrealized territory for feminist practice in conservatoire training.[2] While vocational training provides the intensive contact hours needed to hone a high level of practical skill, it lags behind university programmes in engaging critical concepts and developing students' political sensibilities. My practice as a director/teacher seeks to activate the intersection between critical thinking and practically focused training in order to realize the feminist potential of musical theatre in pedagogical contexts. My experience with *Pippin* and other student productions has demonstrated that rehearsal processes provide natural opportunities to highlight these intersections, and I suggest that creatives in training contexts have a pedagogic responsibility to do so.

Our Pippin was a creative and skilled performer, with an exemplary sense of artistic discipline; he was also a trans man, and his casting set in motion a process of queering our feminist rehearsal and production process. Casting was only one element of an inclusive practice: in this case, I developed a hybrid approach that honoured students' identities and took a critical view of the material being presented. We brought queer concepts such as heteronormativity and chrononormativity into play with a feminist performance practice.[3] Heteronormativity can be broadly understood as a homogenous bias towards traditional gender roles and relationships that reinforces masculine and feminine binaries. Berlant and Warner observe how heteronormativity shapes wider societal structures and privileges heterosexuality:

> By heteronormativity we mean the institutions, structures of understanding and practical orientations that make heterosexuality seem not only coherent – that is, organized as a sexuality – but also privileged. Its coherence is always provisional, and its privilege can take several (sometimes contradictory) forms: unmarked, as the basic idiom of the personal and the social; or marked as a natural state; or projected as an ideal or moral accomplishment.
>
> (1998: 548)

In *Time Binds: Queer Temporalities, Queer Histories*, Elizabeth Freeman describes chrononormativity as 'the use of time to organize individual human bodies toward maximum productivity' (2010: 3) and 'the interlocking temporal schemes necessary for genealogies of descent and for the mundane workings of domestic life' (2010: xxii). I put these terms in dialogue with feminist performance scholarship, which recognized the potential of a Brechtian approach starting in the late 1980s and 1990s. As David Barnett notes in *Brecht in Practice: Theatre, Theory and Performance*, '[f]eminist theatre theorists and practitioners [...] have looked to Brecht for ways of confronting and combating sexism in performance by revealing patriarchal structures and dramatizing the dialectic of oppression and liberation' (2015: 208). This avenue of feminist performance scholarship proposes staging gender as a performance, 'rather than with practices that encouraged actors to live a gendered role with the forceful commitment of a Stanislavskian or "Method" actor' (Solga 2016: 38). Elin Diamond firmly established Brechtian feminism with her seminal essay 'Brechtian theory/Feminist theory' (1988) and later, *Unmaking Mimesis* (1997). Diamond advocates an approach extracted from Brecht's theory of gestus, 'the moment in performance when a play's implied social attitudes become visible to the spectator' (1996: xiv). She explains:

> Brecht theorizes that if the performer remains outside the character's feelings, the audience may also and thus freely analyze and form opinions about the play's 'fable'. *Verfremdungseffeckt* also challenges the mimetic property of acting that semioticians call iconicity, or the conventional resemblance between the performer's body and the object, or character to which it refers. This is why gender critique in the theater can be so powerful.
>
> (Diamond 1996: 45)

Diamond defines gender critique as 'the words, gestures, appearances, ideas and behaviour that dominant culture understands as indices of feminine or masculine identity' (1996: 45). She explains, '[a] feminist practice that seeks as the effect, not the precondition, of regulatory practices, usually uses some version of the Brechtian A-effect' (1996: 46).[4] I suggest that this mode of feminist performance practice is renewed, refined and developed further by bringing queer concepts into conversation with Brechtian feminism; this approach can then be usefully activated in musical theatre processes. As Stacy Wolf explains in *The Oxford Handbook of the American Musical*, musical theatre is a rich arena for ongoing gender critique:

> Even as the terms, definitions, and performances of masculinity and femininity in culture shift and morph into bi, trans, queer and so on, the musical remains reliant on bodies and voices, movements and sounds, characters; and performers alone and in relation. These categories of identity and presence will always constitute a rich and important area of analysis for the musical.
>
> (Knapp et al. 2011: 222)

We are in a moment where the rights of women and marginalized identities, including trans people, are both regularly debated and placed at risk. Conservatoire training should not be separate from political conversations; on the contrary, it can function as a productive forum in which to explore dynamics of gender, sexuality, race and class.[5]

It is important to acknowledge the plurality and differences between feminism*s*; I position myself in opposition to trans-exclusionary radical feminism. Writer and scholar Sara Ahmed, whose work intersects feminist, queer and race studies, critiques trans-exclusionary radical feminists who claim 'that transphobia is being misused as a way of silencing or censoring critical feminist speech' (2016: 22).[6] She posits that, through the insistence that trans people 'provide evidence of their existence' they endure a 'hammering', a 'constant chipping away' (Ahmed 2016: 22). Ahmed further asserts that 'transphobia within feminism needs to be understood in relation to cis privilege: not having to come into contact with this hammering' (2016: 22) but offers a 'model of hope resting on "an affinity of hammers"; that is, affinity can be acquired through the work of chipping away at the system' (2016: 22). I am inspired by this compelling metaphor and ask how musical theatre pedagogy might contribute to the work of 'chipping away' at a system that perpetuates exclusion and dualistic, gendered perspectives. As a vocational training system, the conservatoire is positioned to uphold dominant modes of performance that can ignore or perpetuate sexist, racist, homophobic and transphobic practices in the theatre and entertainment industries; equally, it is positioned to foster change. Ahmed's image of hammering also resonates with the direct, subversive approach we took in rehearsing *Pippin* with the goal of breaking down gender binaries and exposing stereotypes.

Bruce Kirle argues that musicals are open, fluid texts, and that new productions of musicals 'will inevitably adapt to new cultural moments and to new audiences [...] the musical is innately open, subject to a plurality of readings' (2005: xix). *Pippin* exhibits this interpretive flexibility, as Stephanie Lim's (2017) account of two Los Angeles-based productions of the musical demonstrates. Lim considers one production at East West Players, promoting Asian American performers, the other at Deaf West Theatre, featuring deaf and hearing performers onstage together.[7] Beyond showing ways in which *Pippin* can be conceptually reimagined, Lim's article shows how musicals can provide an artistic arena for marginalized identities, and as I argue, the subversion of stereotypes.

The flexibility and potential for re-conceptualization and gender-malleable casting made *Pippin* an agreeable option to programme as a public production for Mountview's postgraduate (Mountview Academy of Theatre Arts 2017) season.[8] The Leading Player was portrayed by Ben Vereen in the original 1972 Broadway production, and later by Patina Miller in the 2013 Broadway revival; both are significant examples of people of colour taking centre stage, since the part is arguably larger than Pippin's. Nothing indicates that the role is gendered, but even this ostensibly neutral role fails to exempt a female performer from objectification. Reviews of Ben Vereen's Leading Player highlight his authority and skill, while reviews of Patina Miller's interpretation of the same role regularly refer to her appearance and perceived sexiness: 'Miller, with her lithe body and megawatt smile, makes the Player both temptress and confidante, guiding Pippin with her siren's voice and sharp, sinuous dancing through a string of seductive but finally unfulfilling life choices' (USA TODAY 2018). Thus, a 'gender neutral' approach does not necessarily solve the problematic issues associated with gender politics, beyond simply redressing the balance of roles.[9]

My task was to find a conceptual frame that avoided reinforcing sexist representations and allowed the group's individual identities to be present. Alongside a range of nationalities and the trans lead, the company included a performer with a physical disability.[10] I chose glam rock as a conceptual frame for its anarchic spirit and use of fluid, non-traditional gender roles. As a style of rock that developed in Britain in the early 1970s, it resonates with *Pippin* stylistically (perhaps unsurprisingly, as Schwartz wrote the musical in 1972). This frame shifted the piece away from an American sensibility towards a more British-European feel, with a rock concert setting that suited the musical's 'real time' form (Miller 1996: 189). A glam rock construct would also encourage young performers to make conscious choices outside of the stereotypically feminine and masculine behaviours regularly enacted in musical theatre. Taylor identifies David Bowie/Ziggy

Stardust as an iconic glam rock artist and recognizes that the genre is affiliated with ideas of 'subversion and resistance' (2012: 29). In the preface to *Trans**, Jack Halberstam writes of Bowie:

> [Bowie] represented the possibility of stretching beyond social norms and hackneyed cultural forms of expression and generic expectation [...]. David Bowie was able to sustain, with considerable vigor, a meaningful and lasting relation to musical experimentation, and he was able to articulate those experiments through bodily gestures and a series of ambiguously gendered personae.
>
> (2018: xi)

We established the glam rock frame with set design featuring a band onstage and large speaker stacks framing the proscenium arch, as well as with costumes inspired by Ziggy Stardust and Elton John. Glam rock was also our starting point for practical approaches to rehearsing, which included exploring bodily gesture and signification.

Queer/feminist Fabel

I developed the approach of applying a queer/feminist lens to Brecht's Fabel as a practical rehearsal tool rather than a theoretical paradigm. Not to be confused with the same word in English, a play's Fabel is *'an interpreted version of events*, not simply the events themselves' (2015: 86, original emphasis).[11] To activate Brecht's Fabel, we did not concern ourselves with events as changes that affected the characters from a psychological perspective, but rather identified 'what happens' in a scene on a basic level, noting these events in black on one side of a flip chart. We then put on 'green glasses', as we called it, so named for the routine of writing the micro-Fabel, our queer/feminist interpretation of events in green, on the other side, of the chart. Barnett emphasizes that '[t]he *Fabel* is concerned with interpreting *fictional* events through the lens of *real* social contradictions' (2015: 89, original emphasis). In our rehearsal process, we interpreted fictional events through a queer/feminist lens to reveal real social constructs including hegemonic masculinity and patriarchy.[12] For example, real-world events such as President Trump's 'grab 'em by the pussy' resonated in our micro-Fabel 'locker room banter'. The binarized female appears in other microFabel: evil stepmother, old/wise grandmother and young widow. Throughout this process, the company recognized the ubiquitousness of heteronormativity. Heteronorms, as Ahmed suggests, are 'rules of conduct that direct girls towards boys and that render heterosexuality the right or best or happiest destination' (2016: 23). The pervasive pressure to find heteronormative love and happiness (as reinforced by romantic comedies and like narratives) became increasingly visible as our practice progressed, both in the textual analysis establishing the micro-Fabel as well as through the process of staging.

The performer playing Pippin noted the pressure of time passing, as demonstrated in the song 'On the Right Track', and we designated this section 'chrononormativity'. Freeman defines this term:

> Chrononormativity is a mode of implantation, a technique by which institutional forces come to seem like somatic facts. Schedules, calendars, time zones, and even wristwatches inculcate what sociologist Evitar Zurubavel calls 'hidden rhythms', forms of temporal experience that seem natural to those whom they privilege.
>
> (2010: 3)

Chrononormativity became a through-line for our narrative, emphasizing the absurdity of trying to find 'complete fulfilment' as defined by Pippin (success, happiness and love by a certain age). The interpretation moves away from an individual's narrative or psychology towards highlighting social contradiction; in this case, how societal expectations of time become a precedent for 'failure'. In Brechtian theatre, contradiction is used to highlight difference and address issues that might be passed over in everyday life, with Brecht asking spectators to 'confront contradiction' (Barnett 2015: 80–81). Applying a feminist/queer lens to the Fabel allowed us to articulate the paradoxical social constructs that subsume our everyday life, which in turn galvanized the company to embody and show these contradictions onstage. Our Fabel challenged the archetypal male hero journey (a narrative that *Pippin* easily fits), with students observing that storytelling traditionally privileges patriarchal systems. This queer/feminist Fabel became the 'thematic blueprint' (Barnett 2015: 86) for the staging and realization of the piece.

The body as social signifier

From very early on, my aim was to create a play world where women would take up space and not revert to playing 'sexy', a behaviour often coached and reinforced in performer training. In 'Play fair: Feminist tools for teaching improv', Amy Seham notes that male characters tend to assume higher status in terms of using the space; in her teaching, she encourages low-status players to 'TAKE UP SPACE' (2007: 147) and warns '[u]se the stereotype, but don't let the stereotype use you' (2007: 142). With *Pippin*, we aimed to expose and subvert the stereotype. The sexy housewife and powerful patriarch become grotesque, while chorus

TABLE 15.1: Examples of our events and micro-Fabel.

Events	Fabel
Leading player enters	Female takes charge
King introduced	Establish patriarchal society
Fastrada signals her part in plot	Trope of evil, sexy woman
King establishes family lineage	White male privilege
Charles greets Pippin formally and awkwardly	Received idea that men do not know how to communicate
Charles entrusts the future to Pippin	Performing/re-establishing patriarchy
Fastrada compares Lewis/Pippin	Judging masculinity
Fastrada tells Charles that she is overdrawn	Trope that women are financially dependent on men/incapable of handling money
Charles makes sex joke	Locker room banter
Baron makes request to King, which is denied	Establishing class structure
Charles explains protocol of war then prays	Religion as tool of hegemony
Pippin has sex with multiple people at the same time	Breaking heteronormative expectations of the hero

Events	Fabel
Pippin expresses concerns about time	Chrononormativity
Leading player introduces the young widow Catherine	Introduces heteronormative love as last resort for happiness
Catherine asks Pippin to help her on the estate	Nagging wife trope
Catherine reveals it is Pippin's anniversary of being on the estate	Relationship-specific chrononormativity
Catherine repeats her speech about her husband's death, forgetting her lines	Woman trapped in male-centric narrative
Catherine asks for more lights, sings against Leading Player's orders	Actress gives the character a voice

girls are dynamic women dominating the space. Recognizing oppressive patterns of behaviours that binarize the masculine and feminine was a starting point for rejecting, or in some cases embracing, those bodily gestures; this was most apparent in the arrangements.

Once the Fabel has been established, Barnett explains, the next step is to create an arrangement, 'the visual representation of the *Fabel* onstage' or 'a tableau that makes the social relations on stage readable for an audience' (2015: 90). Two examples of tableaux in our production used extremes of masculine and feminine to expose stereotypes. In the micro-Fabel we named 'Locker Room Banter', the performers took on stereotypically masculine postures, with wide legs, arms behind head, elbows spread wide. In contrast, when Fastrada sings 'Spread a Little Sunshine', manipulating Lewis, Charles and Pippin into serving her own interests, the players created a tableau reminiscent of *Desperate Housewives*: hands on hips, legs crossed, lips pouted, chests out. Barnett notes how a Brechtian approach makes invisible gendered behaviour visible:

> By observing the differences between the male and female body, and between masculine and feminine behaviour, the actress can draw attention to those aspects that a man may simply take for granted and ignore in performance. The distance between actors and their roles allows them to identify difference (in class, in age, in opinion, etc.) and to explore it, not to submerge it by 'completely transforming' into the role.
> (2015: 113)

Through the practice of activating the Fabel, I saw that recognizing gendered behaviour helped to address the problem of young women unconsciously enacting sexualized or other damaging stereotypes. It is worth noting, however, that Barnett assumes coherence of sex and gender, maintaining gender binaries. He is progressive in exposing gendered behaviour, but this essentialist, binarizing perspective remains problematic from a materialist feminist and/or queer point of view. My approach addresses this shortcoming by engaging Diamond's feminist theoretical framing of Brecht and introducing queer concepts into Barnett's practical applications. This intersection offers additional layers, nuance and political possibility.

Our 'heteronormative love montage' was another piece of staging that subverted societal expectations of romantic love. As Pippin and Catherine sing 'Love Song' (itself sending up the notion of true love with the lyric, 'Love Song, la la la la la, la la la la la la'), two male–female pairs enacted a variety of stereotypical love scenes in slow motion. Barnett notes that, '[t]o Brecht, montage was a powerful way of organizing material to activate spectators because *they* have to make the connections, not the actors' (2015: 51, original emphasis).

Our 'heteronormative montage' shows how happily-ever-after social constructs can be exposed and mocked; this gestic feminist criticism, as Solga explains, is 'a practice where feminist performers do not simply reflect the male gaze but refract it' (2016: 34). Our montage refracted heteronormative societal expectations by exposing and subverting them. We also engaged the feminist technique of returning the gaze throughout our production. Performers activated the consciousness of 'seeing and being seen' from the opening lyric 'Join us' through to the concluding scene where they moved into the auditorium and made direct contact with the audience, enacting Diamond's concept of 'looking-at-being looked-at-ness' (1997: 52) and Jill Soloway's 'I see you seeing me' (YouTube 2018).

Brecht expected actors to make 'offers' and solve problems rather than waiting to be briefed by the director (Barnett 2015: 117). Our '[h]eteronormative love montage' was devised primarily by the company, as was 'With You', a musical number whereby Pippin engages in sexual experimentation. Since it is in effect an orgy, this was a number that neither I nor the choreographer wanted to dictate. The students led a conversation about how much physical contact each performer felt comfortable with, then used the Frantic Assembly Exercise 'Round/By/Through' (Graham and Hoggett 2009: 131) to construct physical duets, trios and quartets.[13] Unlike Fosse's version, which painted the orgy as dark and perverse, we wanted to express sexual exploration without judgement. To avoid reinforcing normative views of sexuality, it was important that this scene avoid a heteronormative, male-centric tone (i.e. multiple women pleasuring one man) and include same-sex groupings, in turn challenging the presumption that Pippin is heterosexual and dominant heteronormative narratives in musical theatre repertoire.

Separating the actor from the role

One of the main feminist critiques of a Stanislavskian approach applied to realist material is that it conflates the actor and character, oppressing them in service of a narrow, dominant ideology. Barnett shares how a Brechtian approach 'cleaves' the actor from character:

> Brecht proposes that actors should both play their roles *and* display their personalities. That is, the audience should never believe that the actor on stage *is* the character, but rather that there is an actor *playing* a character by showing the difference between actor and role.
>
> (2015: 111, original emphasis)

Several Brechtian tools in our process facilitated this 'cleaving', including asking the performers to use their own accents or regional dialect (Barnett 2015: 130). With a cast comprised of many nationalities, it relieved the burden of enforcing a homogenous British or American dialect, and Players used Irish and South African accents to playfully define figures. The act of performing a song can also show the join between actor and character; as Raymond Knapp suggests, adding music to drama 'does not simply heighten emotions; rather, it also imposes through its obvious and conventional artificiality, a kind of mask that both conceals and calls attention to the performer behind the persona' (2005: 12). The student playing Berthe (in our production, inspired by Elton John) played the keyboard for her number 'No Time at All'. This showed her skill as a performer and highlighted the 'performer behind the persona'. We also relied on costume to show the difference between actor and role, with performers removing signifying items of clothing or props in the final scene.

The performer playing Fastrada, for example, removed her long, blonde wig to reveal a slicked back, androgynous hairstyle. We further separated actor from character by reading stage directions aloud. I engaged this technique in setting up the love scene by having the Leading Player direct Pippin and Catherine to kiss. The student playing Pippin, having just performed an extremely energetic number, was usually dripping with sweat at this point. The actors could acknowledge their physical state whilst having to perform a love scene, reinforcing the performative nature of the piece – the performance of performing a story is part of the diegetic nature of *Pippin*. Not all musicals are seamlessly integrated, and as a form, its disjunctive qualities highlight the join or distinction between actor and character. The disruptive qualities of song and dance can often offer these natural fissures for political intervention.

According to Barnett, showing the difference between actor and figure is not the only channel to demonstrate that an actor is playing a role (2015: 112). Bringing personal biography to the stage can also 'show a join' and inform how a role is played:

> Brecht praised Ernst Busch, an actor whom he cast in several central roles with the Berliner Ensemble, because he brought his working-class biography on stage, along with his role. […] He believed that Busch could not only 'show the join' between himself and his role, but that his experiences could also inform the way he played a role.
>
> (2015: 112)

This resonated with the student playing Pippin:

> Because I'm a queer, trans actor, I feel like whatever I do is political, whatever I'm cast as – a gay trans guy is playing this role – even though it doesn't necessarily show onstage and it's not something that directly affects my work or that people can see necessarily. In this example – this actor who brought his working class biography on stage along with his role – I feel like my background is with me. Especially in this one when I'm able to drop into being [me]. In the end, it brings a personal and political aspect to the role.
>
> (Mountview 2017)

This student's gender identity was neither foregrounded nor hidden in our production. I was led by his choices in interpreting the material and how much of his identity he wanted to bring to the performance. His contribution to the process was significant, both in leading the company and in bringing a queer perspective to our work. Musical theatre is a form regularly dismissed as mainstream and innocuous entertainment, but our endeavours to activate a queer/feminist approach demonstrate its potential for creating space to explore identity and gender politics and challenge dominant ideologies. This production is just one example, and I am hopeful that this work contributes to Ahmed's 'chipping away'. As she writes,

> An affinity of hammers does not assume we will automatically be attuned to others who are stopped by what allows us to pass through, even when we ourselves have the experience of being stopped. We have to acquire that affinity. It is what we work toward.
>
> (Ahmed 2016: 23)

I cannot offer a comprehensive queer/feminist practice for musical theatre training and production processes. I acknowledge that these approaches do not always line up neatly. I do suggest that feminist and queer approaches can work together to usefully critique patriarchy and heteronormativity in musical theatre training and performance. I argue that using musical theatre as a platform for political exploration increases students' critical and artistic facility and that when approached with intention, musical theatre presents productive potential for resisting or subverting the same narrow or negative stereotypes it frequently perpetuates. By introducing critical thinking to musical theatre pedagogy and production processes, we can activate political potential in training contexts; moreover, because of its role in shaping future artists, conservatoire training can play a pivotal role in driving changes across the wider industry.

NOTES

1. With music and lyrics by Stephen Schwartz and a book by Roger Hirson, *Pippin* follows Prince Pippin on a journey to find fulfilment, accompanied by a troupe of *Commedia dell'Arte* players. Bob Fosse directed the first Broadway production. *Pippin* won five Tony awards in 1972, including best director and best choreographer (Miller 1996: 191).
2. By 'conservatoire', I mean a training that is vocationally driven and discipline-focused on acting, singing, dancing, vocal or instrumental performance. Both conservatoires and universities award degrees, but a university programme places more emphasis on such subjects as analysis, criticism and history. While my practice research focuses on UK conservatoire training, earning a Bachelor of Fine Arts in musical theatre at The Boston Conservatory has also given me insight into American contexts.
3. I describe feminism broadly as thinking about 'gendered experience from a human rights perspective' (Solga 2016: 1); queer 'acquires its meaning from its oppositional relation to the norm, the legitimate, the dominant' (Halperin in Wolf 2010: 18).

4. *Verfremdung* is sometimes translated as 'alienation' (Barnett 2015: 7). Barnett explains, '[t]he term has been rendered in English over the years as "alienation", "estrangement" and "defamiliarization", among other things. A better translation, however, is "making the familiar strange"' (2015: 76).
5. In contrast to the abundant literature on approaches to acting and performance, there is limited critique on the politics of performer training. See, for example, *The Politics of American Actor Training* (Margolis and Renaud 2010), whose editors claim it is the first of its kind. I suggest there is further scope for critiquing, documenting and taking formal account of conservatoire practices that give specific consideration to the broader hegemonic forces influencing training.
6. Ahmed's article 'An affinity of hammers' builds on Susan Stryker and Talia M. Bettcher's assertion that 'feminist transphobia is not universal nor is living a translife, or a life that contests the gender binary, antithetical to feminist politics' (2016: 7–8).
7. Lim describes how *Pippin*, originally set in the Middle Ages, was reconceived with 'very modern, relevant re-appropriations' and finds similarities in the two communities' experiences, suggesting that Deaf and Asian American people face similar 'issues of social injustice and inequality' and 'are often recognized as not measuring up fully to normative identities' (2017: 26). She describes how each production used the theme of belonging in *Pippin* to give prominence to the narratives of Deaf and Asian American people 'in a way that reshapes, subverts and disrupts national notions of Deaf and Asian identities' (Lim 2017: 35).
8. The company was comprised of three male-identifying and nine female-identifying students.
9. *The Stage* recently reported that a new system, Neropa, is being launched in the United Kingdom to encourage gender parity in theatre and television casting. Invented by German actor/researcher Belinde Ruth Stieve, Neropa is designed to reduce the imbalance of male to female roles for performers by determining which roles in scripts are gender neutral (Masso 2018).
10. The students' nationalities included American, British, Irish, Dutch, Gibraltarian, Finnish, Norwegian, Swedish, South African and New Zealand.
11. The term 'events' is used in various practices. In *Acting in Musical Theatre*, Deer and Dal Vera suggest that '[o]ne of the simplest ways to find story events is with French scenes […]. A French scene begins with the entrance or exit of a character' (2008: 103). In her Stanislavski-based *The Director's Craft* (2009), Katie Mitchell also states that entrances and exits are events, and that events are changes affecting the behaviour of a character, with actors choosing a new intention for their character for each bit between events. This is the version of events that my students were familiar with, having been taught primarily in a Stanislavskian tradition.
12. We used Anne Cranny Francis's definition of patriarchy and posted it on the rehearsal room wall: 'a social system in which structural difference in privilege, power and authority are invested in masculinity and/or social positions of [white, heterosexual, cisgender] men' (2003: 15).

13. Graham and Hoggett explain the exercise in *The Frantic Assembly Book of Devising Theatre*: '[t]he partners stand opposite one another and choose A and B status. A is then given the task of changing the physical and spatial configuration between the two using any one of the instructions "Round", "By" or "Through"' (2009: 131–32).

REFERENCES

Ahmed, S. (2016), 'An affinity of hammers', *TSQ: Transgender Studies Quarterly*, 3:1&2, pp. 22–34.

Armstrong, A. and Juhl, K. (2007), *Radical Acts*, San Francisco: Aunt Lute Books.

Barnett, D. (2015), *Brecht in Practice*, London: Bloomsbury Methuen Drama.

Berlant, L. and Warner, M. (1998), 'Sex in public', *Critical Inquiry*, 24:2, pp. 547–66.

Cranny-Francis, A. (2003), *Gender Studies*, Basingstoke: Palgrave Macmillan.

Deer, J. and Dal Vera, R. (2008), *Acting in Musical Theatre: A Comprehensive Course*, London and New York: Routledge.

Diamond, E. (1988),'Brechtian theory/feminist theory: Toward a gestic feminist criticism', *TDR*, 32:1, p. 82.

Diamond, E. (1997), *Unmaking Mimesis*, London: Routledge.

Freeman, E. (2010), *Time Binds: Queer Temporalities, Queer Histories*, Durham: Duke University Press.

Graham, S. and Hoggett, S. (2009), *The Frantic Assembly Book of Devising Theatre*, London: Routledge.

Halberstam, J. (2018), *Trans*: A Quick and Quirky Account of Gender Variability*, Oakland: University of California Press.

Kirle, B. (2005), *Unfinished Show Business: Broadway Musicals as Works-in-Process*, Carbondale: Southern Illinois University Press.

Knapp, R. (2005), *The American Musical and the Performance of Personal Identity*, Princeton: Princeton University Press.

Knapp, R., Morris, M. and Wolf, S. (2011), *The Oxford Handbook of the American Musical*, Oxford: Oxford University Press.

Lim, S. (2017), 'At the intersection of Deaf and Asian American performativity in Los Angeles: Deaf West Theatre's and East West Players' adaptations of *Pippin*', *Studies in Musical Theatre*, 11:1, pp. 23–37.

Margolis, E. and Renaud, L. (2010), *The Politics of American Actor Training*, New York: Routledge.

Masso, G. (2018), 'Casting tool to create gender parity in theatre launches in UK', *The Stage*, https://www.thestage.co.uk/news/2018/casting-toolcreate-gender-parity-theatre-launches-uk. Accessed 13 September 2018.

McMillin, S. (2006), *The Musical as Drama*, Princeton: Princeton University Press.

Miller, S. (1996), *From Assassins to West Side Story*, Portsmouth: Heinemann.

Mitchell, K. (2009), *The Director's Craft*, Abingdon: Routledge.

Mountview (2017), '"Student feedback" following public production of *Pippin*', *Mountview*, London, July.

Solga, K. (2016), *Theatre & Feminism*, London and New York: Palgrave MacMillan.

Stryker, S. and Bettcher, T. (2016), 'Introduction', *TSQ: Transgender Studies Quarterly*, 3:1&2, pp. 5–14.

Taylor, M. (2012), *Musical Theatre, Realism and Entertainment*, 1st ed., Farnham: Ashgate.

USA TODAY (2018), '*Pippin*: Season's best musical, jazz hands down', https://www.usatoday.com/story/life/2013/04/25/broadway-review-pippin/2106973. Accessed 28 January 2018.

Wolf, S. (2010), *Changed for Good: A Feminist History of the Broadway Musical*, New York: Oxford University Press.

YouTube (2018), 'Jill Soloway on The Female Gaze | MASTER CLASS | TIFF 2016', YouTube, https://www.youtube.com/watch?v=pnBvppooD9I. Accessed 28 January 2018.

16

For Progress or Profit: The Possibilities and Limitations of Playing with Gender in Twenty-First-Century Musical Theatre

Stephanie Lim

Eight years before the Broadway revival of *Pippin* saw the light of day, participants in a BroadwayWorld forum argued over the hypothetical notion of a female Leading Player (Anon. 2005). Several users suggested such casting would be generally okay, as long as the actress were sinister enough, but they also believed certain scenes and songs like 'Glory' would not work dramaturgically. Others argued that a female Leading Player would only complicate the character's relationship to Pippin, that such a mental tug of war could only truthfully or authentically occur between two men. A female presence would simply be distracting, as audiences would surely be bound to read sexual tension between the two leads. In the end, gender-blind casting calls led to Patina Miller being cast as the Leading Player in Diane Paulus's 2013 revival of the show. The production went on to win the Tony Award for Best Revival of a Musical, and Miller herself won for her performance, making her and Broadway's original Leading Player, Ben Vereen, the first pair of performers to win Tonys for the same role in *different* categories – Leading Actress and Leading Actor respectively. Significantly, all subsequent casting of the revival's Leading Player, including understudies and national tour casts, has kept women in the role, indicating that the contemporary Leading Player is in fact not gender-blind but specifically female.

In the years since, musical theatre creative teams have implemented more and more instances of gender-swapped or gender-flipped casting: in 2018, Oregon Shakespeare Festival (OSF) produced *Oklahoma!* with a female Curly, male Ado Annie/Ado Andy, and a trans woman as Aunt Eller; the 2018 West End revival – now

2020 Broadway revival – of *Company* rewrote several characters' genders in order to feature a female Bobbie; in 2016, Tony-winner Lena Hall tackled the role of Hedwig during the show's national tour; and the 2017 revival of *Once on this Island*'s original cast featured gender nonconforming actor Alex Newell in the role of Asaka (the Mother of the Earth) and a female Papa Ge (the demon of Death). Such a rise in what many scholars are calling 'gender play' (Garcia 2018) does not count the many years of benefit concerts featuring performers singing in gender-flipped roles, like the 2016 male-led Miscast performance of *RENT*'s 'Take Me or Leave Me' and the 2015 Broadway Backwards all-male version of *Chicago*'s 'Cell Block Tango'. These fundraising concerts, hosted by MCC Theater and Broadway Cares/Equity Fights AIDS, respectively, specifically take advantage of audiences' curiosities and desires to, as MCC promotes it, 'see Broadway's hottest stars perform songs from roles in which they would NEVER be cast' (Anon. n.d.).[1] The growing interest in this type of queered casting reveals the industry's simultaneous impulse towards *progressivism* and *profit*.

By comparing new and 'traditional' casting choices and drawing on reviews of performances, this chapter highlights the increased focus on and engagement with gender-conscious and gender-disrupting performance in musical theatre. I first explore the implications of gender-centric casting practices through lenses of drag and cosplay. Then, I chart the varying dramaturgical shifts and consequences that have occurred within major professional productions of musicals, from 'safe' and commercially-driven decisions, to ambivalent and problematic effects, and finally to more significant reworkings of musical narratives and ideologies. Regardless of the initial intentions behind the industry's practices, and although such casting has become incredibly popular over the last decade, I argue that simply changing a pre-existing character's gender and/or allowing space for non-traditional casting in already well-known narratives cannot be the end goals of musical theatre.

In their discussions of theatrical gender play, scholars and critics commonly use the terms 'gender-flipped' and 'gender-swapped' interchangeably to identify any non-traditional casting decisions. I instead turn to the world of cosplay (the abbreviated term for 'costume play') for two more nuanced ways to understand these casting choices: 'crossplaying' and 'gender-bending'. Crossplay occurs when a participant takes on the target character's gender, one *different* than their own, as in Stacie Bono's performance as Pirelli in Barrow Street's *Sweeny Todd* (2017). Gender-bent casting occurs when the actor or participant changes the target character's gender to better fit their *own* identity, such as Patina Miller's stint as *Pippin*'s Leading Player. Whereas in crossplay, performers take on the pre-written gender of an existing character, gender-bending allows characters to be revisited with a new gendered approach, matching the gender identity of the performer and consciously shifting the narratives on stage in the process. But not all gender-centric casting practices are equal.

Uses of drag and crossplay can be constraining to the possibilities of gender play. Many instances of drag in musical theatre have been restricted to larger-than-life, comedic roles, as in the cases of *Hairspray*'s Edna Turnblad, *Chicago*'s Mary Sunshine, *Matilda*'s Miss Trunchbull and *A Gentlemen's Guide to Love and Murder*'s Lady D'Ysquith. These roles were also originally written as drag for the stage, rather than gender-flipped in revivals or through replacements. In addition, the use of drag in a show like *La Cage Aux Folles* (1983) 'was constructed upon a fantasy of gender' (Donovan 2019: 130), due to the homophobia surrounding the cultural moment in which the show was produced (Donovan 2019: 142). As such, drag roles are not representations of real female bodies, but rather of stereotypes about female bodies. Broadway's *Tootsie* (2019) goes as far as reserving both the 'leading lady' (Dorothy Michaels) and 'leading man' (Michael Dorsey) roles for a single male performer. In cases like *Tootsie* and *La Cage*, male performers *perform femaleness*, erasing the possibility of actual female-identifying bodies on stage. Such performances subsequently position drag and crossplay as a limited or even problematic casting practice, one perpetuating and exploiting stereotypes of brash, eccentric and unattractive women.

Regardless of potential limitations, discourses of drag and cosplay offer productive parallels to understanding the dramatic and dramaturgical work occurring within musical theatre because many who take part in drag and cosplay intentionally disrupt and expose the malleability of gender through their performances and embodiments. Exploring the subversive nature of cosplay, Joel Gn notes, 'Like drag […] cosplay offers opportunities of resistance to the dominant discourses of gender that reproduce the binary between masculinity and femininity' (Ramirez 2017: 12). Musical theatre's more recent gender-swapped casting practices attempt to move beyond pure gimmick and comedy, instead offering performers and audiences blank slates for otherwise known characters and accentuating the subversive nature found at the heart of drag and cosplay. Writing about the cosplay scene in Australia, Craig Norris and Jason Bainbridge echo Judith Butler's notion that 'gender is performative', arguing that if gender is 'something we unconsciously do, inscribed by societal norms and repetition – then cosplay is a performance, through costume and the assumption of another identity, that reveals the performativity of gender' (Norris and Bainbridge 2009). In creating opportunities for crossplay and gender-bending, musical theatre productions take part in exposing such performativity and provide room to question the original narratives and tropes.

Overall, responses to musical theatre's recent forays into gender play have been positive, with critics and reviewers celebrating such moves as feminist and a step in the right direction. British theatre critic Lyn Gardner asks, 'If the last

2000 years of theatre has mostly put men centre stage, isn't it fascinating to see what happens to those plays and musicals, often also written by men, when the leads' genders are swapped?' (Gardner 2018). NPR station KQED senior editor Rachael Myrow claims, too, that musical theatre can be freed from tired, old attitudes through such casting efforts (Myrow 2019). And University of Michigan student reporter Eli Rallo praises the growing practice, asserting that 'The future of the world is female. The future of art is female. The future of theatre is female' (Rallo 2017). Surely *some* representation is better than no representation at all, and at the very least, gender-swapped shows like *Oklahoma!* and *Pippin* can work to reclaim and reengage female voices within existing narratives where they may not have previously existed. Even though *The Telegraph*'s theatre critic Dominic Cavendish sounds the alarm about how gender equality 'risks the death of the great male actor' (Cavendish 2017), a review of the 2018–19 Broadway season by ProductionPro revealed that women made up only 32 per cent of that season's 365 titled characters (with 61 per cent being men), demonstrating no shortage of male roles or title characters, even with Broadway engaging in increased gender play (Anon. n.d.). In fact, the 2018–19 season showed a 5 per cent decrease in female principal characters from just one year prior (Anon. n.d.).

Many fans, critics and scholars also see gender play as mirroring American popular culture at large and its progressive impetus towards diversity and inclusion. Coming on the heels of movements such as #MeToo and #TimesUp, the industry's fascination with gender-swapped casting supports the global effort to make female voices and narratives heard. Such (re)casting also envisions a new or different world wherein marginalized identities can emerge as equal to otherwise dominant identities found within musical theatre, i.e. white, heterosexual and cis male. The cultural success of Tony Award-winning revivals like *Pippin* and *Once on This Island* and the national attention paid to big and small screen productions of *Cats* and *The Rocky Horror Picture Show* demonstrate a massively piqued interest among critics and audiences to see *something different*.

Often, however, such acts of innovation seem more profit-driven than politically motivated. To be sure, commercial theatre and film are by nature and necessity profit-driven, but in many of these revivals and reconceptualizations, the gender play may only *perform* progressivism. As with Hollywood films and television shows, Broadway has fallen into a 're-incarnation trap', continually reviving and reimagining popular work from earlier eras. For *New York Times* critic Amanda Hess, this recurrence of *playing with* gender, race and sexuality in Hollywood films 'satisfies a couple of-the-moment entertainment industry imperatives: It allows Hollywood to reanimate lucrative old properties [...] while recasting them with diverse casts and woke politics' (Hess 2018). By re-imagining characters' genders in well-known stories, Broadway producers exercise within a large financial safety net, since audiences will likely watch such a familiar show regardless of the cast.

Moreover, 'celebrity casting' (or 'stunt casting') provides both an added incentive for theatregoers and economic security for producers. The earliest reports of gender-swapped revival productions or replacement casts emerge in the 1990s. Billy Porter first revived the character of Teen Angel in the 1994 revival of *Grease*, but notable female performers such as Jennifer Holliday, Darlene Love and Mary Bond Davis subsequently stepped into the role. In 1995, Whoopi Goldberg took over for Nathan Lane as Pseudolus in the revival of *A Funny Thing Happened on the Way to the Forum*. In 1999, Ally Sheedy took over the title from Michael Cerveris in the original off-Broadway run of *Hedwig and the Angry Inch*, and, in 2000 Rosie O'Donnell replaced David Shiner as Cat in the Hat in Broadway's *Seussical*. In each of these instances, known celebrities stepped-in as replacements, making the choices seem largely profit-driven. As well, all four shows were mid-run at the time of their casting changes, so the creative teams' casting decisions directly helped continue the shows' successes. The popularity and availability of the 'stage door' as a meeting place after shows – one where fans are given a chance to meet performers with whom they may not otherwise have been able to engage – motivates the team's decision to utilize celebrity casting. For example, between 2018 and 2019, Vicky Vox (a popular drag queen), Amber Riley (*Glee*) and MJ Rodriguez (*POSE*) all appeared in productions of *Little Shop of Horrors*. Such stunt casting across registers of gender performance and gender identity allowed producers to exercise within a large financial safety net: theatre audiences will likely turn out in droves for the chance to see and potentially meet celebrity performers, whether truly interested in the show itself or not.

Casting celebrities, particularly high-profile trans and drag performers, as gender-bent non-human characters allows productions to benefit financially and feign a sense of progressiveness, while avoiding actual engagement with the ideological realities of having such performers embody human and gendered characters. Both Regent's Park and Pasadena Playhouse productions of *Little Shop of Horrors* feature female celebrities in the role of Audrey II, a character usually voiced by a male actor. For Regent's Park, drag performer Vicky Vox became an anthropomorphic embodiment of the man-eating plant, performing the finale number, 'Mean Green Mother from Outer Space', in plant-inspired drag. In cases such as these, the gendered stakes are low. Gender play within the 'character' of Audrey II negligibly impacts the interpersonal conflicts within the story itself. Critics praised Vox's performance for bringing a *sassiness* to a traditionally animatronic character and – in the words of *attitude* magazine's Simon Button – giving 'the oft-revived musical a stiletto-heeled kick up the tush' (Button 2018). Pasadena Playhouse's production also feminized Audrey II but in vocals only, with *Glee*'s

Amber Riley not physically appearing on stage except during the curtain call. The production used puppetry to generate the rapidly growing plant on stage; the puppet itself, however, remained devoid of any gendered costuming.

Both the Regent's Park and Pasadena Playhouse productions emphasize the alienness of Audrey II: for Pasadena Playhouse, puppet designer Sean Cawelti explains, 'I wanted to make something that seems alien and extra terrestrial but also that gives an emotional reaction' (Lee 2019). For Regent's Park, Vox's appearance in plant-drag for 'Mean Green Mother from Outer Space', a song originally written for the 1986 film, similarly emphasizes Audrey II's true alien identity and further distances the character from any human roots: Audrey II is either plant or alien, neither of which requires specific gendering on stage. While reviewers praised Pasadena Playhouse's casting as generating a 'fresh, inclusive iteration' (Ramos 2019) and Regent's Park's version for supporting the director's 'subversive, queer approach' (Saville 2018), Audrey II's re-stylizing as female, drag, and alien adds nothing to the show narratively or dramaturgically, while adding an in-vogue selling point.

The star-studded 2019 movie adaptation of Andrew Lloyd Webber's *CATS* similarly takes advantage of its non-human characters and the popularity of its title. The film features musically inclined celebrities like James Corden, Jason Derulo, Taylor Swift, Jennifer Hudson and Idris Elba, as well as Judi Dench in the traditionally-male role of Old Deuteronomy. Although Hollywood has relied on celebrity casting for musical adaptations like *Hairspray* (2007), *Les Miserables* (2012) and *Into the Woods* (2014), Dench is the first to appear in a role differently gendered than the way it had traditionally and originally been played on stage. Dench's own take on her performance calls attention to the intermediate space she inhabits as Old Deuteronomy. In one interview, she describes her performance as 'trans Deuteronomy' (Dommu 2019), while in another she explains that her performance follows in 'the same spirit, the same old cat' but with a '[d]ifferent gender' (Alexander 2019). For Webber and director Tom Hooper, Dench's casting emerged as a full-circle moment. Dench had been set to play Grizabella in the original 1981 West End production, but she ended up withdrawing due to a torn Achilles tendon. Nearly 40 years later, they reimagined the film's Old Deuteronomy 'as a woman' to make a space for Dench (Anon. 2019). In a movie already driven by celebrity casting, Dench's inclusion engages gender play at the levels of both profit and nostalgia. On the surface, gender-bent casting in both *Little Shop of Horrors* and *CATS* seems progressive, as women almost never play these roles. However, the casting choices leave the shows' dramaturgies untouched in any substantive way.

Even in the spirit of progressivism, gender-flipped casting can be questionable if not damaging, as seen in *The Rocky Horror Picture Show: Let's Do the Time*

Warp Again. In the 2016 made-for-television film by FOX, trans actress Laverne Cox (*Orange is the New Black*) appears in the role of Dr Frank-N-Furter, a character *The Washington Post*'s Travis M. Andrews describes as 'a mad scientist who is actually a cross-dressing alien from the planet Transsexual, which resides in the Transylvania galaxy' (Andrews 2016). The production, like many of its 'live' musical siblings, includes numerous celebrities from screen and stage, such as Adam Lambert, Victoria Justice, Reeve Carney, Ben Vereen and the original 1975 film's Frank-N-Furter, Tim Curry. Cox's clear profit-driven advantages bring with them layers of radicalism, as arguably the first high-profile trans actress to take on a role almost always played by men in professional productions. Despite such apparent groundbreaking achievements on the part of Cox, many of the movie's reviewers and fans voiced discomfort with her casting. *FlavorWire*'s Mari Brighe notes the potential harm of the casting choice:

> In an era where trans people (and trans women in particular) are still consistently struggling to shed the social view that we are little more than men in dresses, the once sexually subversive *Rocky Horror Picture Show* becomes simply a tool for the re-entrenchment of oppressive and harmful tropes about transgender people.
> (Brighe 2015)

Such criticism rings particularly ironic, given the fact that *Rocky Horror Picture Show* has been a subversive beacon of camp and fluid sexuality. Performer Sarah de Ugarte offers an alternative perspective to that of Brighe, maintaining that the show in general provides a space for 'people [to be] accepted as they are: fabulous, regardless of gender or sexuality or race or body type' (Schwab 2015). For her, Cox's casting generates a similar telos to the original show. As with Audrey II, however, Frank-N-Furter's true nature allows creatives a way to circumvent gender-based criticisms: Frank-N-Furter is an alien, not a human. Despite the show's mixed reviews, its initial airing drew 89 per cent more viewers for FOX than the same timeslot one week prior (Schwindt 2016). Financially, it turns out, producers did not take much of a risk in casting Cox; nostalgia fuels the profitability of *Rocky Horror Picture Show*.

As with Cox, Lena Hall's performance as Hedwig in *Hedwig and the Angry Inch* has also been met with ambivalence, even though the casting choice appears unique and seemingly progressive. Similar to *Rocky Horror Picture Show*, *Hedwig and the Angry Inch* explores, challenges and questions gender and sexuality at every turn. *Hedwig and the Angry Inch* thus seems like a perfect text through which to employ gender play: the titular character is genderqueer, and the plot highlights the character's journey through their shifting gender identity. During the show's 2016 national tour run, where she reprised her Tony-winning performance as Yitzhak, Hall made history stepping into the role of Hedwig for a limited number of performances in Los Angeles and San Francisco. In an interview, Hall explains the empowerment she felt playing Hedwig: 'even though I am a woman, I can do it just like the boys do' (Gioia 2016). She went on to frame this within the very nature of Hedwig the character, asking 'What does gender even mean? Does it identify anyone as a person?' (Gioia 2016). While Hall's performance was generally praised, and her versions of the songs turned into an EP with Ghostlight Records, fans commented on the limitations and complications of casting a female Hedwig. Since Hall crossplays as Hedwig, taking on the character's complicated gender identity and story, the show's political intentions and narrative arc become muddied. In the show, Hedwig is trapped in the transition between man and woman, so Sheedy and Hall's performances as Hedwig create further confusion: they are women playing a man who is trapped in the transition (back?) to womanhood. In this case, crossplay becomes a limitation and liability: if the *character*'s gender is fixed, audiences seem to expect and demand a traditional take on the role, leaving little room for the *actor* to recreate and challenge the role with their own (gender) identities.

Gender-flipped casting, as seen in *Pippin*, *Once on this Island* and *Into the Woods*, arguably creates more potential and power for characters and narratives. The 2013 revival production of *Pippin* set itself apart from the original, integrating a hyper-circus aesthetic. This marked distinction from the 1972 Broadway premiere made the Leading Player's casting change one among many in the re-imagined *Pippin*. In the original production, Ben Vereen's performance, and the production as a whole, created an air of mysticism; the show's opening number, 'Magic to Do', featured Vereen dressed in all black, with disembodied hands mysteriously floating behind him, inviting and enticing the audience to 'join' them. The entire number took place in front of a black curtain, with the show-within-a-show's troupe members emerging throughout, dressed almost entirely in white. With the exception of individual circus-like acts that appear on stage, such as levitators and a knife-swallower, the troupe moves in sync choreographically. The revival's opening number pays homage to the original, with Patina Miller's silhouetted figure eventually emerging from behind a dark curtain. Yet, the production brings new life and colour to the show: as characters emerge in bright-coloured outfits, the curtain drops to reveal the stage as being the inside of a circus ring, with all of the characters performing different acts. Miller's all-black outfit, while similar to Vereen's original, creates an alluring yet sinister Leading Player with its sleeveless bodice cut at the shoulders.

Ben Brantley's review of the Broadway production concurs that the revival 'push[es] the musical from seduction into sensory assault', and he perceives Miller's smile as 'more confrontational than invitational', contending 'we never glimpse the likable, fallible human beneath the polish' as audiences had with Vereen's performance (Brantley 2013). *Pippin*'s creator Stephen Schwartz claims that the Leading Player need not be male to fulfill the show's story arc: 'The motivation of the Leading Player [...] is to lead the character of Pippin to his destruction, and that seems essentially genderless to me' (Anon. n.d.). Schwartz also told director Diane Paulus that the Leading Player and Pippin are first and foremost opposites, as 'The Leading Player is meant to represent The Other – the other thing that Pippin has never experienced' (Haun 2013). Despite fans' initial unwillingness to see past the character's potential gender, Miller's performance reminds knowing audiences of the truer nature of the Leading Player as someone/something that exists *beyond* standard humanness. S/he symbolizes something much larger in Pippin's life: the voice inside our heads that tells us we need to do something spectacular in order to be important – a role that is neither man nor woman.

The gods of *Once on this Island* also exist beyond the bounds of gender. For Asaka, the Mother of the Earth, Newell performs in a liminal space between crossplay and his own real-life gender non-conforming identity (Pham 2017). Although Alex Newell uses he/him/his pronouns, his performance of Asaka is as a *mother*, in the traditional feminine sense of the term, a choice further generated by the character's costume and vocals, altogether defining the gender expression of the character as 'female'. The Asaka costume presents the character as female and includes a headdress made of grass and a red cropped jersey on top of a long yellow, flowery dress. Newell's understudies were both female performers, adhering to the original production, and understudy Loren Lott's behind-the-scenes video of her first performance as Asaka shows her costume as exactly the same as Newell's (Lott 2018).

The same was not true for the show's gender-bent casting of Papa Ge, played by actresses Merle Dandridge and temporary replacement Tamyra Gray, both of whom had male understudies. Costumes conformed to the performer's own gender. For female Papa Ges, the costume included a black bra, torn black skirt, dark leather faux-suspender and a headpiece with two small horns; for male Papa Ges, longer black shorts replaced the skirt, and a singular, phallic long horn replaced the pair worn by the women. These performances of Asaka and Papa Ge evoke a type of gender-fluidity, which falls in line with director Michael Arden's own insistence that the gods are not bound by gender. In interviews, Arden – who has made a directorial name for himself with non-traditional casting in musical theatre – asked: 'so many gay men do take on a motherly role, taking care of others, so why shouldn't we depict that in an honest way?' (Voss 2017). He also defended the production's casting choices, as he had with Deaf West's *Spring Awakening* and a diverse Los Angeles production of *Merrily We Roll Along*, by emphasizing inclusivity on the stage for the sake of the audiences' own inclusion:

> In casting the Gods that inhabit our island, it became imperative for me to break expectations and stretch beyond the bounds in which Gods are traditionally represented. It felt important that young people watching our production see themselves reflected back from the stage at them. The Gods are simply that: Gods. They are not bound by gender, race, sexuality or being human at all.
>
> (Kacala 2017)

If, in Arden's view, a god is not bound by gender, then his production emphasizes the social roles of the gods (over water, earth, love, and death) and removes any stereotypical connotations typically associated with traditional gender binaries of male/female roles.

In Barrington Stage Company's 2019 production of *Into the Woods*, gender-flipped casting created new possibilities for a well-known character. In the role of the Witch, most famously played in the original Broadway production by Bernadette Peters and in the 2014 movie adaptation by Meryl Streep, Barrington Stage cast African American actor Mykal Kilgore, re-inventing the character in both gendered and racialized terms.[2] In Dan Dwyer's review of the show, he describes the Witch's transformation in the second act as Kilgore 'morph[ing] into a gorgeous Amazonian queen, bedecked in a billowing, glimmering, white satin, gold-festooned gown. Kilgore's Witch has both sass AND soul' (Dwyer 2019). Reviewer Steve Barnes similarly looks beyond the gender play of the Witch, contending 'That she happens to be played by a man, Mykal Kilgore, is both essential and incidental to the success of the performance, and it's irrelevant to the grandly realized vision of director Joe Calarco' (Barnes 2019). Playing the Witch allows Kilgore to reinvent and reclaim the character, as he told a local newspaper, 'It's my responsibility to shake the audience as fast as I can from comparison. You're in for a brand new ride, don't think you know the direction we're going, you have no idea' (Smullen 2019). Since Peters and Streep had established well-known and memorable versions of the Witch, Calarco's casting of Kilgore creates an instant and productive distancing from the originals. Kilgore had space to engender his own version of the Witch without constant comparison to the Peters and Streep versions.

Arguably, two of the most recent and significant uses of gender-centric recasting occurred in OSF's *Oklahoma!* and Marianne Elliott's *Company*. In *Oklahoma!*, Black Jewish actress Tatiana Wechsler performs a gender-bent Curly, and Jonathan Luke Stevens performs a gender-bent Ado Annie, now Ado Andy (Figure 16.1). As a result, the two romantic relationships at the crux of the story become LGBTQ pairings. As well, trans actress Bobbi Charlton plays Aunt Eller. In an interview, Bill Rauch describes this particular production of the Rogers and Hammerstein classic as being simultaneously nostalgic and revolutionary, bringing new

FIGURE 16.1: Heralding the ideological impact of its gender-bent casting and narrative reworking, the Oregon Shakespeare Festival posted the heartfelt sentiments of one of its *Oklahoma!* cast members on its Twitter feed, 17 July 2020, US.

meanings into this classic context (Anon. 2018). Traditionally, the song 'People Will Say We're In Love' embodies a fear between a man and woman about their romance being public, but Rauch explains the characters' 'fear that people will say [they're] in love takes on a completely different resonance and a completely different depth when it's sung by two women' (Anon. 2018). He goes on to say that 'when they [finally] sing, "Let people say we're in love"', the theatrical audience 'just cries and cheers, because it's an affirmation in a completely different way' (Anon. 2018).

In consciously re-casting specific characters, the OSF creative team thus inscribes LGBTQ voices and relationships into a historical context, the 1906 frontier (Collins-Hughes 2018), which otherwise privilege heterosexual stories. That Rauch's creative re-imagining of *Oklahoma!* includes genderqueer and gay/lesbian coupling also reclaims characters such as Curly McLain, Ado Andy/Annie, and Aunt Eller for gender-non-conforming and LGBTQ+ communities, as well as for communities of colour. At the same time, such innovative casting proves how much work remains to be done in the world off-stage. DeAnn Welker points to the real-world and politically affective possibilities generated by OSF's gender-swapped revival, expounding that:

> Despite the legalization of gay marriage, Black Lives Matter, and #MeToo, we are very much still living in a hetero white man's world – especially in the past couple of years. This *Oklahoma!* allows us to imagine a different world, a new, wide-open prairie frontier. In this world, a female Curly can win the heart of Laurey, a male Will Parker can tame the wild Ado Andy, and the happily married couples are all mixed-race.
> (Welker 2018)

OSF's *Oklahoma!* produces two powerful narrative shifts: first, the show disrupts the male dominance of Rodgers and Hammerstein's original love triangle by having a man *and* a woman fight for Laurey's affection. Rauch notes that in their version, 'Jud's frustration that Laurey won't choose him is also part of frustration that she would choose to be with a woman and not with him as a man' (Anon. 2018). The second shift occurs dramaturgically, as OSF creates a unique, female-heavy storyline; rather than highlight the traditional white male hero, this production showcases a heroine of colour when Curly rescues Laurey from her plight with Jud. OSF surely takes advantage of a popular musical to ensure profitability, but their version also presents progressive performances, etching complex gendered and racial connotations into the show's already-complicated love triangles.

The 2018 UK gender-bent revival of *Company* also generates powerful and progressive narrative shifts. In traditional productions, a male Bobby celebrates his 35th birthday surrounded by his coupled/married friends and various on-again, off-again girlfriends. *Company* typically revolves around Bobby's own hesitance to marry and inability to commit to long-term relationships and marriage. Marianne Elliott's reimagining of *Company* integrates a female 'Bobbie', which raises the stakes for the character because of 'her ever-ticking biological clock' (Billington 2018). This gender-swap works to expose existing double standards regarding gender, sex, and sexuality. One reviewer describes the song 'Barcelona' as presenting 'our sexually rapacious heroine with a sweet, smiling flight attendant, Andy, as dim as he is hunky' (Wolf 2018). With this overtly sexualized Andy, the production calls attention to the real-life, hyper-sexualized, predominantly female occupation, whose required dress code still reportedly includes makeup, lipstick, high heels, and no visible body hair (Oppenheim 2019). Popular culture typically erases women's sexual desire and agency, seldom presenting female characters who sleep around or simply have sex for their own pleasure. However, this revival brings Bobbie's sexual desire and sexual promiscuity to the fore, highlighting her inability to decide between her three male lovers.

In the 'Introduction' for the *Company* revival libretto, David Benedict notes how Elliott's choice to swap genders responds to and reflects on current social attitudes surrounding men, who 'no longer feel urgency around being thirty-five', and women, for whom 'the stakes are [still] dramatically higher' (Benedict 2019: 7). Still, Elliot's gender-bent Bobbie rings less progressive than it could have been: the show swaps the genders of all of Bobbie's exes and sticks only to heterosexual relationships, when any one of her three male lovers could have been cast as female. Additionally, the penultimate scene between Bobbie and her friend Joanne clings to heteronormativity. In the original version of the production, Joanne proposes an affair with Bobby. In the revival, she instead offers Bobbie her own husband, Larry. For *American Theatre*'s Emily Garside, Joanne's character becomes 'a terrifying mirror to Bobbie' (Garside 2018), an example of what road might lie ahead of her if she were to get married. However, Joanne's offering of Larry proves a dissatisfying choice for anyone who might have wanted Joanne to propose a lesbian affair of her own, or alternatively, for the revival to have reimagined Joanne as a male character who proposes an affair to Bobbie. Nonetheless, *Company*'s gender-bent take gives whole new meaning to Bobby/ie's narrative, an apt reminder that women also deal with the societal and cultural pressures associated with marriage, perhaps even more so than men.

Over the last ten years, musical theatre's increased attention towards gender-flipped casting echoes many cosplayers' own reasons for engaging in such practices: gender-bending in particular provides a blank slate for cosplayers, as well as creative teams, to re-envision well-known characters and break away from their traditional desires, motivations, and – of course – genders. It also compels creative teams to be mindful of *all* the ways that characters act and interact within their respective worlds. Arguably, drag and crossplay seem more restrictive than gender-bent casting. Drag is commonly relegated to comedic or outlandish characters, as in cases of roles always-already drag-performed like Edna Turnblad, Miss Trunchbull and Lady D'Ysquith. In crossplay, too, performers must act within the parameters of a character's given gender, reinforcing and/or complicating the performance, as with Sheedy and Hall as Hedwig. Because crossplay and drag retain the originally written gender (roles), their use in musical theatre – and theatre in general – inhibits any further discussion about the characters, their relationships, and their worlds. To the contrary, when productions engage in gender-bending – Curly, Ado Andy, Bobbie and her lovers – they provide new perspectives on well-known narratives, giving audiences and performers increased chances to see themselves on stage in unique ways.

Scholars must be careful of idealizing gender play, as it also has the potential to merely reinforce gender norms and re-inscribe traditional notions of masculinity and femininity. Theatre critics note that gender-bending commonly occurs with characters already coded as *feminine* or those who exhibit so-called female qualities (Stoll 2019), thereby perpetuating dominant stereotypes about gender. This has occurred, for example, with characters written to embody traditional feminine qualities of gentleness, seduction and/or submissiveness (Hedwig, Papa Ge, Leading Player, St. Jimmy) and those who project a blurred sexuality (Hedwig, Bobby, Frank-N-Furter). Crossplay may also perpetuate or exaggerate stereotypical ideals of femininity or masculinity. Scholar Alison Shaw maintains that 'cross-gender impersonation is often highly stereotypical, usually serving to reinforce, for the audience, local ideas of femininity or masculinity as much as they challenge them' (Shaw 2005: 16). Eli Rallo points to the Catch 22 of gender-swapped casting, arguing that recasting some narratives with female leads, or revising the portrayal of some female characters, ignores the actual problem occurring within the theatre community: the absence of narratives *written for* strong women in the first place (Rallo 2017). Strong female characters can be written in new stories, not just recreated in old ones. In her article on Hollywood's obsession with gender play, *New York Times*' Amanda Hess lists recent gender-flipped movies like *Ocean's 8* (2018), the female-led *Ghostbusters* (2016) and the announced and then abandoned controversial all-female – yet male directed and penned – *Lord of the Flies*. Hess argues,

> These reboots require women to relive men's stories instead of fashioning their own. And they're subtly expected to fix these old films, to neutralize their sexism and infuse them with feminism, to rebuild them into good movies with good politics, too. They have to do everything the men did, except backwards and with ideals.
>
> (Hess 2018)

Hess's point makes me wonder: until film, television and Broadway can do better, are we unfairly asking female Curlys and Bobbies to bear a greater responsibility than they should?

For the time being, at least, gender play practices offer a temporary solution to the larger problem of male-domination that currently plagues Broadway musicals. And, when used on stage, gender-bending practices can strengthen a show's dramaturgical intent, particularly fruitful in giving audiences new ways to view the world – and to momentarily see love, marriage, life, and death through new perspectives. Such gender play provides a way for creative teams to carve out new territory with guaranteed money-makers, but Broadway must make a more concerted effort to carve out room for original shows that feature leading characters who are not simply white, cis, heterosexual men. Instead of focusing on how to recast, rewrite and reimagine existing characters, the musical theatre world must turn its focus to casting, writing and imagining diverse worlds the first time around.

NOTES

1. MCC Theater's *Miscast* began in 2020. A similar event, *Broadway Backwards*, started in 2006 by the Broadway Cares organization (Anon. [n.d.]).
2. Patina Miller performed the role of the Witch in Hollywood Bowl's 2019 production; the production also included other diverse casting, such as Hailey Kilgore as Rapunzel, Shanice Williams as Little Red and Tamyra Gray as Granny/Cinderella's Mother, as well as featuring Edelyn Okano, Stella Kim and Grace Yoo as Cinderella's family.

REFERENCES

Alexander, Bryan (2019), 'Judi Dench turns *Cats* catastrophe into triumph playing Old Deuteronomy in movie version', *USA Today*, 15 April, https://www.usatoday.com/story/life/movies/2019/04/15/judi-dench-cats-movie-dropped-out-of-west-end/3434462002/. Accessed 1 September 2020.

Andrews, Travis M. (2016), 'The new *Rocky Horror* stars trans actress Laverne Cox: Why some in the LGBT community are not pleased', *The Washington Post*, 17 May, https://www.washingtonpost.com/news/morning-mix/wp/2016/05/17/trailer-released-for-new-rocky-horror-starring-trans-actress-laverne-cox-though-not-all-in-the-lgbt-community-are-pleased/. Accessed 1 September 2020.

Anon. (n.d.), 'Broadway Backwards', Broadway Cares/Equity Fights AIDS, https://broadway-cares.org/category/post-event/broadway-backwards/. Accessed 26 July 2020.

Anon. (2005), '*Pippin* – Female leading player?' *BroadwayWorld*, April, https://www.broadwayworld.com/board/readmessage.php?thread=844883. Accessed 5 August 2019.

Anon. (2018), '*Oklahoma!* adaptation featuring same-sex couples hits the stage', *NPR Illinois*, 10 September, https://www.nprillinois.org/post/oklahoma-adaptation-featuring-same-sex-couples-hits-stage#stream/0. Accessed 5 August 2019.

Anon. (2019), 'Taylor swift on side-stepping into acting, owning what you make & loving the "Weirdness" of *Cats*', *Vogue*, 1 December, https://www.vogue.co.uk/news/article/taylor-swift-andrew-lloyd-webber-on-cats-musical. Accessed 1 September 2020.

Anon. (n.d.a), '*Miscast*', MCC Theater, https://mcctheater.org/miscast/. Accessed 5 August 2019.

Anon. (n.d.b), 'Stephen Schwartz answers questions about the show', *Stephen Schwartz*, https://www.stephenschwartz.com/wp-content/uploads/2017/04/Pippin.pdf. Accessed 5 August 2019.

Anon. (n.d.c), 'Broadway By the Numbers 2018', https://production.pro/broadway-by-the-numbers-2018. Accessed 1 September 2020.

Anon. (n.d.d), 'Broadway By the Numbers 2019', https://production.pro/broadway-by-the-numbers. Accessed 1 September 2020.

Barnes, Steve (2019), 'Review: *Into the Woods* @ Barrington Stage, 6/22/19', *Times Union*, 23 June, https://www.timesunion.com/entertainment/article/Review-Into-the-Woods-Barrington-Stage-14032128.php. Accessed 1 September 2020.

Benedict, David (2019), Company: *A Musical Comedy*, London: Nick Hern Book, pp. 5–10.

Billington, Michael (2018), '*Company* review – Sex-switch Sondheim proves a heavenly fling', *The Guardian*, 17 October, https://www.theguardian.com/stage/2018/oct/17/company-review-sex-switch-sondheim-gielgud-theatre-london. Accessed 5 August 2019.

Brighe, Mari (2015), 'Why casting Laverne Cox in the *Rocky Horror Picture Show* reboot isn't a slam dunk idea', *FlavorWire*, 23 October, https://www.flavorwire.com/544321/why-casting-laverne-cox-in-the-rocky-horror-picture-show-reboot-isnt-a-slam-dunk-idea. Accessed 1 September 2020.

Button, Simon (2018), 'Drag legend Vicky Vox steals the show in *Little Shop Of Horrors* at Regent's Park Open Air Theatre – Review', *Attitude*, 14 August, https://attitude.co.uk/article/drag-legend-vicky-vox-steals-the-show-in-little-shop-of-horrors-at-regents-park-open-air-theatre-review/18811/. Accessed 5 August 2019.

Brantley, Ben (2013), 'The Old Razzle-Dazzle, Fit for a Prince', 25 April, https://www.nytimes.com/2013/04/26/theater/reviews/pippin-directed-by-diane-paulus-at-the-music-box-theater.html. Accessed 5 August 2019.

Cavendish, Dominic (2017), 'The thought police's rush for gender equality on stage risks the death of the great male actor', *The Telegraph*, 23 February, https://www.telegraph.co.uk/theatre/what-to-see/thought-polices-rush-gender-equality-stage-risks-death-great/. Accessed 5 August 2019.

Collins-Hughes, Laura (2018), 'In this *Oklahoma!*, she loves her and he loves him', *New York Times*, 15 August, https://www.nytimes.com/2018/08/15/theater/oklahoma-same-sex-oregon-shakespeare-festival.html. Accessed 5 August 2019.

Dommu, Rose (2019), 'Judi Dench says her *Cats* character is trans', *Out*, 20 December, https://www.out.com/film/2019/12/20/judi-dench-says-her-cats-character-trans. Accessed 1 September 2020.

Donovan, Ryan (2019), 'Broadway bodies: Casting, stigma, and difference in Broadway musicals since *A Chorus Line* (1975)', *CUNY Academic Works*, https://academicworks.cuny.edu/gc_etds/3084/. Accessed 24 October 2022.

Dwyer, Dan (2019), 'Review: *Into the Woods* at Barrington Stage is totally entrancing', *The Berkshire Edge*, 25 June, https://theberkshireedge.com/review-into-the-woods-at-barrington-stage-is-totally-entrancing/. Accessed 1 September 2020.

Garcia, Lucas (2018), 'Gender on Shakespeare's stage: A brief history', *Writers Theater*, 21 November, https://www.writerstheatre.org/blog/gender-shakespeares-stage-history/. Accessed 5 August 2019.

Gardner, Lyn (2018), 'Gender-swapped revivals like company keep theatre alive, relevant and exciting', *The Stage*, 29 October, https://www.thestage.co.uk/opinion/2018/lyn-gardner-gender-swapped-revivals-like-company-keep-theatre-alive-relevant-and-exciting/. Accessed 5 August 2019.

Garside, Emily (2018), 'Everything's different, nothing's changed: *Company* with a female Bobbie', *American Theatre*, 22 October, https://www.americantheatre.org/2018/10/22/

everythings-different-nothings-changed-company-with-a-female-bobbie/. Accessed 5 August 2019.

Gioia, Michael (2016), 'Lena Hall recounts her first night as Hedwig', *Playbill*, 10 October, http://www.playbill.com/article/lena-hall-recounts-her-first-night-as-hedwig. Accessed 5 August 2019.

Haun, Harry (2013), 'The daring leading player on the flying trapeze: Diane Paulus takes *Pippin* to the Circus', *Observer*, 23 April, https://observer.com/2013/04/the-daring-leading-player-on-the-flying-trapeze-diane-paulus-takes-pippin-to-the-circus/. Accessed 5 August 2019.

Hess, Amanda (2018), 'The trouble with Hollywood's gender flips', *New York Times*, 12 June, https://www.nytimes.com/2018/06/12/movies/oceans-8-gender-swap.html. Accessed 5 August 2019.

Kacala, Alexander (2017), 'Alex Newell gets cast as a female lead in *Once on This Island* Broadway revival', *Hornet*, 8 August, https://hornet.com/stories/alex-newell-broadway-asaka-island/. Accessed 5 August 2019.

Lee, Ashley (2019), '*Little Shop of Horrors* in Pasadena: Secrets of a radically reconceived Audrey II', *Los Angeles Times*, https://www.latimes.com/entertainment-arts/story/2019-10-17/pasadena-playhouse-little-shop-horrors-audrey-plant-design. Accessed 18 October 2020.

Lott, Loren (2018). 'NEW Asaka understudy Debut (Loren Lott) behind the scenes in *Once on This Island* on Broadway', YouTube, 29 April, https://www.youtube.com/watch?v=dhzgwHo3qY8. Accessed 1 September 2020.

Myrow, Rachael (2019), '"Gender Bent Broadway" frees musical theater from tired, old attitudes', *KQED*, 1 June, https://www.kqed.org/arts/13858627/gender-bent-broadway-frees-musical-theater-from-tired-old-attitudes. Accessed 5 August 2019.

Norris, Craig and Bainbridge, Jason (2009), 'Selling Otaku? Mapping the relationship between industry and fandom in the Australian Cosplay Scene', *Intersections: Gender and Sexuality in Asia and the Pacific*, no. 20, April, http://intersections.anu.edu.au/issue20/norris_bainbridge.htm. Accessed 24 October 2022.

Oppenheim, Maya (2019), '"Shameful and dangerous": Airlines condemned for forcing female staff to wear lipstick, high heels and no body hair', *Independent*, 26 July, https://www.independent.co.uk/news/uk/home-news/airport-workers-sexism-heels-makeup-gmb-union-report-a9022011.html. Accessed 5 August 2019.

Pham, Jason (2017), 'Alex Newell won't fit into your mold, but he might squeeze into your shoes', *StyleCaster*, 30 June, https://stylecaster.com/alex-newell-glee-sexuality-body-image/. Accessed 1 September 2020.

Rallo, Eli (2017), 'Where women play the role in gender bent theatre', *The Michigan Daily*, 4 April, https://www.michigandaily.com/section/arts/how-women-play-role-gender-bent-theatre. Accessed 5 August 2019.

Ramos, Dino-Ray (2019), '*Little Shop of Horrors* review: Campy Classic Devours Pasadena playhouse with soul, heart and inclusivity', *Deadline*, 1 October, https://deadline.com/2019/10/little-shop-of-horrors-review-pasdena-playhouse-mj-rodriguez-george-salazar-amber-riley-1202748229/. Accessed 18 October 2020.

Ramirez, Manuel Andres (2017), 'From the panels to the Margins: Identity, marginalization, and subversion in cosplay', Tampa: *University of South Florida Scholar Commons*, 8 March.

Saville, Alice (2018), 'Why drag queen Vicky Vox is starring in the summer's big musical *Little Shop of Horrors*', *Independent*, 13 August, https://www.independent.co.uk/arts-entertainment/theatre-dance/features/little-shop-horrors-drag-queen-vicky-vox-regents-park-theatre-trans-transgender-a8483436.html. Accessed 18 October 2020.

Schwab, Katharine (2015), 'After 40 years, *Rocky Horror* has become mainstream', *The Atlantic*, 26 September 2015, https://www.theatlantic.com/entertainment/archive/2015/09/after-40-years-rocky-horror-has-become-mainstream/407491/. Accessed 1 September 2020.

Schwindt, Oriana (2016), 'TV ratings: *Rocky Horror* Doesn't Wow, *Thursday Night Football* wins', *Variety*, 21 October, https://variety.com/2016/tv/ratings/tv-ratings-rocky-horror-picture-show-1201896680/. Accessed 18 October 2020.

Shaw, Alison (2005), 'An introduction', in A. Shaw and S. Ardener (eds), *Changing Sex and Bending Gender*, New York: Berghahn Books, pp. 1–19.

Stoll, Emily Ann (2019), '"When in Other Habits": Gender-flipping and cross-gender casting in Shakespearean performance', *University of Buffalo Institutional Repository*, 1 February, https://ubir.buffalo.edu/xmlui/bitstream/handle/10477/79382/Stoll_buffalo_0656M_16204.pdf?sequence=3. Accessed 1 September 2020.

Smullen, Sharon (2019), 'Director and cast chart a different course with Sondheim's *Into the Woods* at Barrington Stage Company', *Berkshire Eagle*, 20 June, https://www.berkshireeagle.com/stories/director-and-cast-chart-a-different-course-with-sondheims-into-the-woods-at-barrington-stage,577254. Accessed 1 September 2020.

Voss, Brandon (2017), 'Why gods transcend gender in Broadway's *Once On This Island*', *NewNowNext*, 28 November, http://www.newnownext.com/broadway-once-on-this-island-michael-arden-alex-newell/11/2017/. Accessed 5 August 2019.

Welker, Deann (2018), 'Ashland: *Oklahoma!* for today', *Oregon ArtsWatch*, 6 May, https://www.orartswatch.org/ashland-oklahoma-for-today/. Accessed 5 August 2019.

Wolf, Matt (2018), 'A gender swap makes Sondheim's *Company* soar', *New York Times*, 25 October, https://www.nytimes.com/2018/10/25/theater/sondheim-company-london.html. Accessed 5 August 2019.

17

The Right to See and Not be Seen: South Korean Musicals and Young Feminist Activism

Jiyoon Jung

On the night of 8 February 2018, an anonymous post on the 'play/musical' gallery in https://www.dcinside.com alleged an unnamed stage actor's habitual sexual assault on female staff members.[1] The 'play/musical' gallery, which among the audiences and practitioners is generally called '*yŏnmyugael*' for short, is South Korea's biggest online fan forum for contemporary musical theatre and play performances.[2] On the forum, fans upload their own analyses, reviews, useful information and passing thoughts related to performances. Given the usual contents of the site (*yŏnmyugael*), the accusatory post seemed quite uncommon and was quickly deleted.[3] While the original post only appeared momentarily late at night, fans reacted strongly to the allegation. Hundreds of forum users wrote over 800 comments on the scandal within a few hours. Although only the actor's initials were mentioned in the initial post, forum participants, who share a lot of knowledge and information about current South Korean musical theatre, quickly realized it was Myeonghaeng Yi (a beloved performer among South Korean audiences) and unveiled his identity online by the next morning. Fans declared a boycott of his performances and demanded that the actor be expelled from theatres.[4] Three days later, Yi was under police investigation and dropped out of all his performances.[5] These events played out against a backdrop of the American #MeToo movement, founded in 2016 and brought online in 2017, when American celebrities, feminists and social media users began using the hashtag #MeToo to address their own stories of sexual harassment.[6] Two weeks prior, moreover, female South Korean prosecutor Ji-hyeon Seo had appeared on television news to share her own stories of suffering at work, which sparked nationwide attention to the prevalence of sexual harassment in South Korea.

Throughout 2018, feminism, the loanword of which is pronounced *p'eminijŭm* in Korean, truly stood in the spotlight in South Korea as a buzzword that invited the whole society to consider women's perspectives that had long been neglected. Interestingly, the female fan community of musical theatre showed the most immediate and active response to the Koreanized #MeToo movement and other feminist activities during that period. Since the aforementioned case of Myeonghaeng Yi in early February 2018, a number of female victims, mostly associated with musical theatre or theatre in general, have continued revealing dozens of sexual harassment cases through the online spaces used by musical fans, such as *yŏnmyugael* or Twitter. Online fan community members expressed their deep empathy with the female victims' experiences as women. Their powerful collective action has had a substantial effect on South Korean musical society as it reconsiders male-centred conventions. For example, many male actors, musical directors, producers and university educators who committed sexual misconduct resigned from their positions as the result of the #MeToo movement. At the height of this activity in February 2018, audiences went beyond online spaces into the streets to raise women's voices against gender inequality and threats of sexual violence. In February, details of the first street protest, titled #WithYou, was publicized on the *yŏnmyugael* bulletin board.[7] Over 300 protesters, all wearing masks, gathered on the street in Taehangno – the theatrical hub in Seoul.[8] These monumental protests led by musical theatre audience members provided momentum for South Korea's social debates around feminism. Their demands to change male-centred narratives and staging conventions in the theatre world resonated beyond theatrical circles. Taehangno, originally known primarily for being the theatre district, became instead a symbol of and locus for feminist activity where South Korean young women could assert their rights and state their opinions.

But why musicals? How did this genre become a wellspring for feminism among South Korean young people? This essay explores the unique correlation between musicals and feminist activism in South Korea by examining how South Korean musicals empower today's young South Korean women. In South Korea, musical theatre is regarded as 'women's culture', with a high percentage of female audience members and a preponderance of female fan subcultures. Women represent approximately 80 per cent of the audience of South Korean musical performances (Kim 2018: 37). Several South Korean-originated production practices such as star-based productions, the 'multicast' system of casting two or more performers in a role and the 'revolving-door audience' that sees a show multiple times, all depend on female fans' consumption of the genre.[9] These practices further confirm how important and influential female musical fandom is in the South Korean musical theatre industry (Kim 2018b: 430–34). The fans, primarily adult women, are targeted not only by musical companies as consumers but also potentially by misogynists as an archetypal flock of young women in the society. Female musical fans' belligerent reactions during the 2018 scandals reflect the women's anger, as well as the shifting awareness of gender and feminism in South Korean society.

Based on fieldwork in 2017 and 2018 in Seoul and archival research on South Korean musicals, this essay gives attention to the ways in which female fans project themselves in three common spaces: in dark theatre auditoriums, in online fan forums and in feminist protests. First I explore how shifting gender stratification and musical theatre fandoms in South Korea have produced feminist identities among young women. Then I examine how female musical fans nurture and enact their own version of feminism in each of the three spaces. While these women amplify their voices in online fan forums and at the Taehangno protest, their individual identities are hidden in those spaces. To account for this seeming contradiction, I propose 'half-visibility' as a mode of resisting misogynistic power structures. Being half-visible is the way that individual feminists choose to engage in feminist discussion without taking risk. The discourse of 'voyeurism', which American feminist film theorist Laura Mulvey brought to theatre and film studies (Mulvey 1975), provides a useful tool for understanding how young South Korean women navigate patriarchal capitalist society. I ultimately argue that today's South Korean musicals empower young South Korean women by providing safe spaces to engage with feminism.

Female musical fans and feminism

This female musical fandom emerged with the generation of women who were born around 1980. South Korea's dynamic social shifts of the 1980s–1990s – such as the establishment of democracy, rapid economic and technological development, national globalization policies and the 1997 Asian financial crisis (Lee 2015: 2–3) – created the space for today's young South Korean women who do not identify with the mores of their parents. Most of these women's mothers were born in the ashes of the Korean War, grew up under a dictatorship and led national growth, married and bore children in their twenties and sacrificed themselves to support their families. The new generation of South Korean women, however, do not necessarily see them as role models. They generally reject the roles of devoted mother, wife and daughter-in-law as part of the patrilineal structure based on the country's neo-Confucianism. Recent portrayals of this new female subjectivity, such as the 2017 film *Pigŭmmyŏnŭri* (B-rated daughter-in-law), the 2018 TV show *Isangan naraŭi myŏnŭri* (daughter-in-law in wonderland) and the 2016 novel *Kim Ji Young born in 1982*, demonstrate how women in their thirties clearly sense distance between conventional gender stratification in South Korean society and their preferred role in that society. Job insecurity in South Korea, which has worsened since the Asian financial crisis, also led to an increased number of young women who choose not to marry or date but would rather pursue pleasures in their work and leisure activities. South Korean economist Hasung Jang refers to this generation of South Koreans in their thirties as '*3p'o sedae*' (the generation giving up three things): they abandon dating, marriage and having kids as costly and potentially life-long commitments, because they feel hopeless about achieving financial stability (Jang 2015: 380). At the same time, the individualized, urbanized, liberal, educated and materially comfortable but economically unsettled post-1980s generation of women seek a new social order, lifestyle and cultural products. They are young but unmarried, earn their own money and are willing to spend it on entertainment, thus creating new economic possibilities.

Musical theatre has been a venue for this new generation of South Korean women to express themselves since the mid 2000s – a time when the post-1980s generation became adults and the South Korean musical theatre industry simultaneously started to shape its current forms of production, performance practices and culture. The commercial success of western touring musicals in the early 2000s encouraged public interest in musicals. Subsequently, many domestic musical companies were established in South Korea, which began to stage original South Korean productions in relatively small-scale theatres in Seoul's Taehangno (College Street) district. Many performance spaces and headquarters of cultural organizations subsequently settled around the district's Marronnier Park, which in turn attracted many young people and artists to the area. By the mid 2000s, these developments had helped to usher in a kind of golden age for the South Korean musical theatre industry.

Beyond just attending musicals, this generation of South Korean women also contributes to the feminist nature of current musical theatre fandom by bringing a new social awareness. The demographics of female musical theatre fans, such as age, education level and income level, coincide with those of young South Korean feminist activists. According to the statistics reporting audience demography of recent South Korean musicals, female fans are mostly in their thirties, unmarried, college-educated, residents of Seoul or its suburbs and middle-class workers (approximate annual income of 24–34 million won or $22–34 thousand).[10] On internet forums, fans frequently self-identify as financially independent single women with jobs who spend most of their time on their careers and hobbies, in this case attending musicals. While the female fan community exists outside the traditional domains of hegemonic power, its members must inevitably stand against dominant powers in the patriarchal capitalist society, and these young women are smart enough to be aware of social ideologies or to claim their own voice and pleasures. Through their performance reviews on blogs and Internet fan sites, the women often analyse and criticize what elements of performance or musical theatre conventions would be problematic or should be changed from a woman's point of view. For example, fans strongly object to scenes depicting passive or victimized female characters in musical theatre performances.[11]

In addition, several queer or queer-coded performances gained female musical fandom throughout the middle-late 2000s.[12] Musical performances adopted queer expressions of male characters or romance among male characters in order to show unconventional displays of masculinity and to objectify men on stage. Literary scholar Hyewon Kim, in her study of South Korean musical theatre, writes that she has witnessed women dominating the audiences for performances of *Hedwig and the Angry Inch* since its 2005 premiere. The title transgender character in *Hedwig* is played by a male performer, and this production of *Hedwig* introduced the revolving-audience system as well as a quadruple cast system (meaning four actors are cast for the lead role), thus offering an array of star-studded choices from which women audiences could choose (Kim 2018b: 425, 432). The musical *Thrill Me* (premiered in 2007), which solidified the revolving-door audience (Kim 2018b: 432), also features a homosexual romance between the two male characters. Both the revolving-door phenomenon and multicast system reflect women's fandom and their large influence on ticket sales in performance. Relying upon male performers' power to drive ticket sales in these contexts encouraged South Korean musical production companies to keep coming up with new performance and promotion strategies. In addition to the multicast system and prevailing male displays in South Korean musical productions, competitive marketing promotions attract female spectators to musical performances.[13] Performing male queerness, from this angle, reinforced patronage by a valued population that could spur further growth.

The South Korean musical theatre industry's attention to women's tastes and preferences also contributes to the public's gendered view of 'women's culture'. Even though not every female spectator attends shows to watch male actors, these fans are often mocked for their perceived sexual desperation. During my research, I observed fans often described as 'fat, ugly, poor women desiring a romance with a man'. In several posts on online fan forums and in informal conversations with practitioners, female fans are depicted as hopeless women who follow fantasy and get vicarious satisfaction from watching kind and nice-looking male actors in theatres, the kind such women could not acquire as boyfriends or husbands in real life.[14] In this scenario, the 'ugly' women are supposed to come to theatres to compensate for their failed status as women. One South Korean musical director explained:

> It's really unwarranted and groundless, but obviously there is such a discourse regarding the female fans. People's hypothesis is that highly successful and beautiful adult

women must not cling to theater performances because they would have to spend their time and money on their boyfriends or on achieving goals and career success in reality.

(Jung 2018a)

Musical theatre scholar Stacy Wolf insists that depreciation of women's cultural consumption is not new, writing that 'historicizing the devaluation of girls' tastes shows how categories of cultural worth are highly gendered, thereby contesting the media's negative, demeaning characterizations of girls as easily fooled, as unreliable, as possessing bad and fickle taste' (Wolf 2011: 222). In South Korean theatre, too, women's fandom is easily degraded.

The properties that are intrinsic to South Korean musicals have also been connected with women's positions in society, and used to legitimize female culture as cut-rate. Although musical theatre is currently one of the most promising mainstream cultural industries in South Korea, its status is still indebted to Broadway musicals. Hyunjung Lee's article '"Broadway" as the Superior "Other": Situating South Korean Theater in the Era of Globalization' (Lee 2012) points out the ingrained hierarchical relation between western musicals and original productions in South Korea. While South Korean musicals now have their unique history, styles, practices and subcultures, the longstanding cultural hegemony of the West continues to haunt South Korean productions and remind Koreans of their 'secondariness' to Broadway shows. Also, many performers and creators of South Korean musicals prefer working for other media productions such as films or TV dramas rather than theatre performances because these media reach a wider audience and provide more success and fame. Moreover, the relatively short history of musicals in South Korea undermines their status as an authentic artistic form. As the nature of musical theatre incorporates diverse artistic genres, musical theatre is often regarded as less authentic, less professional and less sophisticated compared to the genres of drama, music and dance that musical theatre embraces.[15] Anthropologist Mary Douglas considers how institutions selectively use and expand analogies to strengthen the existing hegemonic order. Douglas writes,

> individuals, as they pick and choose among the analogies from nature those they will give credence to, are also picking and choosing at the same time their allies and opponents and the pattern of their future relations [...] when an analogy matches a structure of authority or precedence, the social pattern reinforces the logical patterns and gives it prominence.
>
> (Douglas 1986: 63, 65)

The subjects of women, South Korean musicals and theatre culture are confined oppositionally to their counterparts: men, Broadway musicals and mass media culture, respectively. As Douglas suggests, the socially and culturally connected analogies between the South Korean musical theatre and South Korean women reaffirm them as less powerful, less authentic, less professional and deficient.

Spectatorship in theatres

Scholars have noted how patriarchal capitalist societies have constrained women and their public activities in the cultural mainstream. Ethnomusicologist Ellen Koskoff mentions that Korean women's involvement as music specialists has historically been severely limited and relegated to the home or to the periphery (Koskoff 2014: 44–55). Koskoff finds that women's public musical performances cross-culturally, especially in patriarchal societies, have suffered from gender stratification in accordance with society's gendered economic structure.[16] In modern South Korea, there is an earlier genre of women's musical theatre culture called *yŏsŏng kukkŭk*, a traditional style of musical theatre performed by all-female ensembles that emerged in 1948, but had trouble gaining ground in South Korea after its short heyday in the 1950s (when men were absent because of the war). This example, among others, illustrates how South Korean patriarchal traditions have tacitly forbidden women to be on a stage in public or to have their subcultures by themselves. British sociologist Angela McRobbie warns that in contemporary consumer culture, the seemingly autonomous images and pleasures of women might obstruct development of feminist politics by making young female consumers presume feminist politics are outmoded, thus leading them to settle for the status quo (McRobbie 2009). According to McRobbie, women's participation in mainstream cultures (along with their participation in civil society, education and employment with a notional form of equality) is conferred on today's young women as an exchange for reinvented feminist politics (McRobbie 2009: 1–3).

Given that women mainly participate in the South Korean musical scene as consumers rather than performers or producers, Koskoff's and McRobbie's arguments concerning women's passivity in patriarchal capitalist cultures seem valid. Although recent feminist movements urge more diversified women's roles in musical performances and in the field of musical theatre, such feminist attempts are in an inchoate stage, and men continue to feature on South Korean musical stages as performers, as characters and in male-centred narratives. Only women's 'fandom' is emphasized. However, if the female fandom of South Korean musicals is mere passive consumption of cultural products of dominant ideologies, then how to explain the 2018 feminist politics playing out among musical theatre fans?

In my fieldwork research on South Korean musical theatres, I noticed women's unique spectatorship and their presence as 'voyeurs': exerting an instinctive pleasure from watching an objectified other, in an active controlling sense.[17] Theatre studies scholar Eleni Papalexiou writes, 'the etymology of the word "theatre" leads us to the term "view", meaning look, contemplation, while *theatron* signifies the place where someone both watches and is being watched' (Papalexiou 2015: 50). This reference to the origins of the theatre is not coincidental. Her point here is that the theatre is the place for watching and being watched, which inherently connotes voyeurism. Theatrical audiences are plunged into darkness and actors into light when a performance begins: a special division that facilitates if not institutionalizes audiences' voyeurism (Rodothenous 2015: 9). Feminist film theorist Laura Mulvey argues in her study of classical Hollywood films that women's sexuality is commercialized for 'the male gaze' in many modern artistic forms.[18] Performance studies scholar Spyros Papaioannou agrees:

> Most accounts of theatrical voyeurism place the discussion within a feminist terrain, arguing for the de-traditionalization of conventional watching and the de-objectification of the image of women that used to be perceived as a passive 'spectacle', available exclusively for male gazing.
>
> (Papaioannou 2014: 170)

Yet these gender roles appear to shift in South Korean musical theatre. Given the conventional objectification of women in the discourse of theatrical voyeurism, women's voyeurism in South Korean musical theatre is subversive. As I already clarified, in many South Korean musical performances, audiences comprise mostly women and performers mostly men. In musical theatre, female voyeurs indulge themselves with the outright appropriation of male performers. The opera glasses and cameras that many fans enjoy using grant them a unilateral 'female gaze'.

Furthermore, 'voyeur' is the only role that women can take as members of the audience; watching without any movement and sound during the performance is common among South Korean musical fans. The term *sich'egwan'gŭk*, which literally means 'corpse spectatorship', was newly coined around 2013 to indicate the audience member who watches a performance as if they were a dead body. Among South Korean musical fans, *sich'egwan'gŭk* is commonly regarded as proper manners while attending musical performances. As soon as an audience member finds their seat, they turn off their mobile phone and set down every belonging so as to avoid interfering with their viewing pleasure. Once the performance begins, the fans do not allow even the faintest noise or motion typically made by audiences, such as the rustling sound of a padded-coat or occasional posture changes. I was frequently surprised to notice that all audience members steadfastly sat upright with their backs to the back of the chair and did not make any noise during the two- or three-hour performance. Even the faint sounds of breathing were unperceivable. The intentness and deathly silent atmosphere are overwhelming. A second neologism, *kwank'ŭ,* which translates to 'critically disruptive behaviour', also demonstrates how musical fans want to completely focus on the stage performance. *Kwank'ŭ* refers to an audience member's experience of others' disruptive behaviour during the performance. The fans complain of their experience of *kwank'ŭ* to a theatre usher or on Internet fan sites. Becoming as unobtrusive as possible thus maximizes the women's voyeurism.

On the surface, this spectatorship, minimizing the fans' own presence, might not seem an active or autonomous mode of consumption. To take a case in point, female fans rarely want to make themselves visible inside or outside of performances. Online spaces, where an individual can remain anonymous, are the preferred venue for the fan community and fan activities. Although sometimes female fans hand over their performance tickets to others or share snacks or handmade goods (e.g. photo cards) with other fans, they are careful to avoid encountering each other in real life. For example, they may put the tickets or goods in a certain place and alert others online how to find them so that other fans can take them without having to face someone in person.[19] Many prefer watching alone and privately enjoy the culture. This is markedly different from what Stacy Wolf describes of the Broadway musical *Wicked*'s female musical fandom. According to Wolf, *Wicked*'s female fans tend to seek out opportunities to be seen and perform themselves. Wolf says,

> as aspiring performers themselves, they solicit advice for an audition number and describe their dreams of performing on Broadway. Girls' distinctively homosocial fandom extends well beyond spectatorship, as they create their own performances on fan websites, at *Wicked* singing contests, and even in *Wicked* yoga classes.
> (Wolf 2011: 222)

Unlike *Wicked* fans, South Korean fans never perform musical performances themselves or enjoy gathering together.

However, I contend that the female musical fans use different and equally satisfying performative strategies when they join the musical subculture. Fans figure out their own cultural tastes as they watch numerous musicals and broadcast those opinions online. Some people prefer watching as many different performances as they can, while others find their own '*ponjin*' which literally means 'main base' or 'one's favourite'. The process of discovering one's own consuming habits or *ponjin* performance/performer/writer/composer in itself is a self-identifying process that encourages the fans to pursue their own cultural identities. Moreover, their spectatorship, which thoroughly focuses on the stage performance, is the way fans enjoy a private and restful time rather than mere passive viewing. Through spectatorship, South Korean female fans exercise their rights to secure their favourite time, private space and cultural taste. Also, as fans who love the performance, they cooperate in making a better performance by keeping quiet during the show. A deathly silent attentive manner thereby becomes the most active and autonomous way to claim a right to see the fine quality performances in their own way.

Online fan activities

If theatres allow women voyeuristic pleasures, the internet fan forum provides the young female voyeurs a space to speak out. The anonymity of online spaces makes young women feel free to talk about their views, likes and dislikes about performances. In the offline world, young South Korean women are typically discouraged from being outspoken or aggressive. This is partly because directly voicing negative feelings such as dissatisfaction, disapproval, grievance, complaint or refusal in person violates South Korean provisions of etiquette, and partly because the cultural ideal of femininity continues to be a kind, docile, affable, tender, submissive and chaste young woman. This expectation was one of the reasons why female victims of the #MeToo movement were not able to easily say 'no' to their offenders, and why they covered up their suffering. However, when hidden from such public social scrutiny within their online domain, female musical fans are not compelled to adhere to the normative expectations of 'femininity'.

The biggest musical fan community *yŏnmyugael* is notoriously cliquish and bellicose. In the fan forum, all users use the same nickname 'ㅇㅇ' not only to protect individual anonymity but also to enact the ideal democratic system of the community denying the controlling powers of stratified society. In this way, the online fan community deconstructs dominant social rules and norms of the offline world and establishes the community's own rules. The fan forum is also full of many slang terms, abbreviations, nasty words, vulgar language and implicit rules for wording and writing that only *yŏnmyugael* users can understand. *Yŏnmyugael* users call each other *hyŏng* (elder brother), a Korean word that originally men used literally. While every individual's right to express their opinion or personal performance taste is equally respected, irrational, illogical, incoherent, irrelevant and ignorant comments that violate community rules and conversation are strictly disregarded. Members of *yŏnmyugael* never voluntarily let newcomers know information, community rules or insider terms because they think that it disrespects others' accumulated time and experience.

THE RIGHT TO SEE AND NOT BE SEEN

The online female fans also aggressively express their opinions about performances and strongly remonstrate against musical companies or specific people once they find a problematic issue. Since the community members' reviews and critiques significantly influence not only ticket sales but also the reputation of companies, performers or creators, musical companies regularly monitor the Internet fan forum and respond to feedback in real time. Everything about the performance is observed, analysed, reviewed, criticized and shared by community members in *yŏnmyugael*. The female fans discuss the price of tickets, casting choices, the location of a theatre, acting skills, quality of music, legal usage of intellectual property rights, acoustics in the auditorium, believability of story, performer's behaviours, service in the theatres, audiences' attitudes, backstage sightings and more. Whatever topic they discuss, they continuously debate over 'what would be fair, acceptable, reasonable, and better'. This clannish, aggressive and coarse character of the online musical fan community is largely incompatible with the normative feminine images upheld in the offline world. This trained criticism of the *yŏnmyugael* community and female musical fans also set the stage for its 2018 activities as part of the #MeToo movement.

The masked protest

> We [audiences] gain consolation and inspiration from theater performances. We spend our precious time in those performances. Therefore, we will not accept performances that are built on the tears of [#MeToo] victims. We also won't excuse the offenders who completely ruin performances [by continuing to appear in them].
> (Anon. 2018b; Im 2018)

Unlike ordinary political protests in South Korea, the participants in the 2018 feminist protest #WithYou, held in Taehangno by South Korean theatre audiences, took steps to protect their identities. The organizers of the rally distributed pickets and masks to participants before the rally began in order to preserve anonymity. The participants also made clear that they wanted to remain incognito and refused to be photographed without consent. Some requested the press to delete images after some media outlets distributed pictures of the protest with the activists' unblurred faces.[20] Their shielded faces with masks and pickets show how South Korean women have to risk or feel shame when they are involved in or talk about sexuality in public. Although the #MeToo movement contributed to conversations about feminism in Korea, most individual activists chose to remain in the crowd rather than to out themselves in this particular phase of South Korean feminist activism. Interestingly, the #WithYou protest was later followed by consequential feminist protests against 'illegal filming', which condemned hidden cameras filming women without consent for illegal pornography (from May to December 2018). That is, female theatre fans, who enjoy voyeurism, ironically avoid being seen themselves, availing exposure to the male gaze, and actually claiming their right not to be viewed at all.

The ability to hide one's identity or visibility often relates to authority. The capacity to 'see but not be seen' means the power to watch others almost omnisciently and simultaneously to escape the surveillance of others. In theatre tradition, from Shakespeare's *Hamlet* to the contemporary musical *The Phantom of the Opera*, the spectres haunting the stage are not simply immaterial. Rather, those characters possess controlling power. The power of the mask, which conceals or modifies identity, also permits the masked performer to represent any sensitive issues in performance, thereby focusing spectators' sympathetic or emotional response on the character rather than the actor (Roy 2016: 3–4). Cultural anthropologist Elizabeth Tonkin sees that the mask has the symbolic power letting the individual transform and become 'other' (Tonkin 1979). As an illustration, Korean performers in the period of the Chosŏn Dynasty (1392–1910) wore masks in *t'alch'um* performances (the traditional styles of masked dance drama) to satirize the hypocrisy of the upper class. Since the mask exempted *t'alch'um* performers from political animus, the performers could address class conflict and political problems even in front of the ruling class. Arts pedagogue David Roy gives another example in Greek theatre. Roy writes, 'the mask meaning also shielded the performer and spectator from direct identification with any political ramifications from performances, as it did with *Commedia dell'Arte*, allowing the performer and spectator to feel safe and immune from the performance' (Roy 2016: 4). Similarly, the mask empowered the feminist activists in the #WithYou protest. Musical fans were able to raise their voices in public with their shielded individual identities. Here, the mask provides both a feeling of safety and power to perform for the gathered crowds who talk about sexual violence and women's rights. Although the social taboo on their gendered bodies and the issue of sexuality undermined young women's righteous rage and pushed the young women – even the survivors of sexual harassment – to cover their faces, the masked audiences connoted a more powerful feminism representative of young women in today's South Korea.

Conclusion

In this essay, I have attempted to identify a correlation between South Korean musicals and feminism. Importantly, not every artistic form with female audiences or female fandom is labelled as 'women's culture'. Although film, (non- musical) theatre, K-pop music and classical music concerts likewise have young women spectators and female fandom, those genres are not associated so predominantly with women's culture as a whole. Also, not every female fan community goes out into the street for feminist activities. The analogous social status of South Korean women and South Korean musicals, however, reaffirms and rationalizes the denigrated female subculture of musicals. Musical fans provide a natural demographic for young South Korean feminist activism, countering patriarchal capitalist South Korean society and inveterate male-centred conventions that have continuously constrained women's activities in the public sphere. The female performers of the earlier musical theatre genre *yŏsŏng kukkŭk* were labelled deviant, anachronistic or failed. Today, the social stigmatization of sexuality still makes female victims of sexual harassment mask themselves or act in internet spaces to avoid shame and identification.

In the spaces of contemporary South Korean musical culture, young female feminists are still symbolically and physically half-visible. However, I view musical theatre as the space where young South Korean women negotiate a patriarchal capitalist society. In the theatre, female fans reverse the conventional gender role of the 'male voyeur' and 'female spectator'. In the online fan forum, fans display a non-normative model of femininity that aggressively demands fairness and better opportunities. The feminist protest #WithYou held in Taehangno explicitly demonstrated how young female fans express their feminism, asserting their right to the female gaze while avoiding the conventional male gaze. Female musical audience members' practices of spectatorship, online activities and feminist rallies illustrate furthermore how feminist voyeurism empowers women as they navigate the demands of South Korean patriarchy. Even though current South Korean female musical fans and feminists are half-visible in musical theatre subcultures, South Korean musical theatre plays a meaningful role in improving South Korean feminist activism by providing spaces for diverse feminist conversations.

NOTES

1. dcinside.com is a massive online site incorporating numerous subcategories classified according to users' topics of interest. Each subcategory is termed a 'gallery'.
2. '*Yŏnmyugael*' is the abbreviation of '*yŏn'gŭk*, musical gallery', https://www. dcinside.com. The Korean term *Yŏn'gŭk* means 'theatre play'.
3. There is a post that chronicles this scandal in detail, but no one can be sure whether the post was deleted by the site moderator or if the writer redacted it (Anon. 2018c).
4. Commonly Korean names are composed of three syllables, and each syllable contains one initial consonant.

5. Note on transliteration: Except the cases where Korean names and words have conventional spellings in English (e.g. Hyewon Kim), I employed the McCune-Reischauer system for the Romanization of Korean terms and names. Although Koreans write their names with the family name first and the given name last, I put the given name first and the family name last here in accordance with the usual name order in English publications.
6. Tarana Burke (civil rights activist) founded the 'MeToo' movement in 2006. The phrase developed into a social media movement in 2017 when Alyssa Milano (actor) suggested that all the women who have been sexually harassed or assaulted write 'Me too' on Twitter to give people a sense of the magnitude of the problem.
7. This protest is also referred to as '*hyehwayŏk siwi* (which literally means, *hyehwa* station protest)'. The protest title was taken from the subway station name located in Taehangno.
8. For photos and video of the rally, see Sung (2018) or YTN News (2018).
9. The multicast system casts more than two performers for a role. I followed Hyewon Kim's translation of the Korean term '*hoejŏnmun kwan'gaek*". *Hoejŏnmun kwan'gaek* refers to the audiences who revisit a performance over and over again as if they went through a revolving door. See Kim (2018).
10. Although there are numerous reports analysing audience demography of musicals, I mostly considered Jung (2017) for the fans' marital status, educational level and income level (Jung 2017: 10–12); data published by Interpark (2014) for the fans' age and residence (Interpark 2014: 5–7); and the Internet newspaper article published by *Edaily* (2018) for additional information regarding fans' marital status and income level.
11. Although I have observed and heard many relevant discussions about this, fans expressed that they were uncomfortable with the raped female character Aldonza in *Man of La Mancha* (performed in 2018) (Anon. 2018d); with the glamorized infidelity of the male character Victor in *Pulgŭnjŏngwŏn* (performed in 2018) (Anon. 2018e); and with the stereotyped narrative of sacrificing a woman for a man (Elena, the sister of the male character) in *Rachmaninoff* (premiered in 2016) (Pamsikppang 2016).
12. For example, *Hedwig* (premiered in 2005), *Thrill Me* (premiered in 2007) and *P'ungwŏlchu* (premiered in 2012). *P'ungwŏlchu* implies a romantic relationship between the two male characters (Yŏl and Sadam).
13. For example, Mast Entertainment offered a special discount for more than three 'female' audience members in the 2018 performance of *Anna Karenina*. And in another marketing event related to a 2018 performance of the musical *Redbook*, FNC Add Culture limited participants to 'women'.
14. For example, one internet forum post contends that musical fans are abandoned in reality and take comfort from fantasy romances with male actors in theatres (see Anon. 2018f). Some forum users on the post make sarcastic comments about female fans' appearances (see Anon. 2017a, 2017b).

15. Critics and audiences often comment that the South Korean musical theatre is not as specialized an art form as that in the West. For some examples, see Lora Paik (2015) and Seungyeon Choi (2014).
16. By comparison, Koskoff asserts, forager or horticultural societies that have little distinction between domestic and public spheres give men's and women's social activities equal value. Koskoff (2014: 129–30) argues that agrarian societies, or recently developed capitalist societies with an agrarian past that have rigorous distinction between public and domestic spheres, tend to be patrilineal, patriarchal and characterized by a high degree of technology, materialism and class stratification – as contemporary South Korea experiences.
17. Laura Mulvey, in her article, explained Sigmund Freud's theory of scopophilia and brought the psychoanalytic theory to feminist film theory (Mulvey 1975). Also see Rodosthenous (2015: 9).
18. Mulvey (1975) first used the term 'male gaze' to describe phallocentrism in the way of reflecting women in classical Hollywood films.
19. For example, one audience member found a missing reward stamp card in a theatre and gave it back to the person who had lost it through a post on *yŏnmyugael*. They exchanged their e-mail addresses instead of their names to identify each other, and the reward card was supposed to be left at an appointed ticket office with the e-mail address to avoid facing each other. See discussion about this plan at Anon. (2017c). Also, Jungwon Kim provides similar cases of female fan subcultures in K-pop fandom (Kim 2017).
20. As an example, people wrote a lot of comments on the online newspaper article published by *Nesw1* to insist upon deletion of the pictures (Sung 2018).

REFERENCES

Anon. (2017a), 'Nan ch'unggyŏkchŏgŭro yeppŭndŏk pwannŭnde', *dcinside*, 10 December, https://gall.dcinside.com/board/view/?id=theaterM&no=2218167. Accessed 11 December 2017.

Anon. (2017b), 'Yeppŭndŏk pwattanŭn aedŭl, hogŭn ponini yeppŭndŏgiranŭn saram', *dcinside*, 10 December, https://gall.dcinside.com/board/view/?id=theaterM&no=2218190. Accessed 12 December 2017.

Anon. (2017c), 'Yŏbosŏjaegwank'adŭ irhŏbŏrinhyong ch'annŭn sohwan'gŭl ssŭn pabarinde', *dcinside*, 10 December, https://gall.dcinside.com/board/view/?id=theaterM&no=2218209. Accessed 10 December 2017.

Back, Hyun-Mi (2007), '1950yŏndae yŏsŏnggukkŭgŭi sŏngjŏngch'isŏng(2)', *Taejungsŏsayŏn'gu*, 13:2, pp. 73–46.

Choi, Seungyeon (2014), 'musicalŭi ironhwa, kŭ yowŏnhan kwaje', *The Journal of Korean Drama and Theatre*, 47:47, pp. 309–18.

Douglas, Mary (1986), *How Institutions Think*, New York: Syracuse University Press.

Im, Jaeu (2018), 'Yŏn'gŭk musical kwan'gaek #WithYou ch'uakhan sŏngbŏmjoeja mudaesŏ mullŏnara', *The Hankyoreh*, 25 February, http://www.hani.co.kr/arti/society/society_general/833584.html. Accessed 26 February 2018.

Interpark (2014), *'Interpark yŏnmalgyŏlsan' ('Interpark annual settlement of accounts')*, document, Interpark, Seoul.

Jang, Hasung (2015), *Wae punnohaeya hanŭn'ga: Captalism in Korea II*, Bundang: Heybooks.

Joo, Sung-Hye (2008), 'Chŏnt'ong yesullosŏŭi yŏsŏnggukkŭk-chubyŏnjŏk chang nŭrŭlt'ongan jungsimjŏkkach'igwan ilgi', *Nangman Quarterly*, 20:3, pp. 167–77.

Jung, Heamin (2017), 'A study on the audience that watches a performance alone (HonGongJok)', Ph.D. thesis, Seoul: The Korea National University of Arts.

Jung, Jiyoon (2018a), in person interview with the author, Seoul, 11 November.

Jung, Jiyoon (2018b), participant, #WithYou protest, Seoul, 25 February.

Jung, Jiyoon (2018c), 'Yi Myeonghaeng sŏngch'uhaeng kwallyŏn kaelk'aibŭ', *dcinside*, 12 October, https://gall.dcinside.com/board/view/?id=theaterM&no=2424278. Accessed 13 November 2018.

Jung, Jiyoon (2018d), '(ㅎㄱㄱ)20180425 Man of La Mancha (purhojuŭi, sŭp'ojuŭi)', *dcinside*, 26 April, https://gall.dcinside.com/board/view/?id=theaterM&no=2321000. Accessed 29 April 2018.

Jung, Jiyoon (2018e), 'Pulgŭnjŏngwŏn wae pullyunmihwasik'inŭn kŭk katchi', *dcinside*, 29 June, https://gall.dcinside.com/board/view/?id=theaterM&no=2357399. Accessed 29 June 2018.

Jung, Jiyoon (2018f), 'Hyŏnsiresŏn pŏrimbakko kongyŏnjangwasŏ paeuege', *dcinside*, 10 February, https://gall.dcinside.com/board/view/?id=theaterM&no=2259169. Accessed 10 February 2018.

Kim, Ji-Hye (2009), '1950yŏndae yŏsŏnggukkŭgŭigongyŏn'gwasuyongŭisŏngb yŏlchŏngch'ihak', *Han'gukkŭgyesuryŏn'gu*, 30, pp. 247–340.

Kim, Ji-Hye (2011), '1950yŏndae yŏsŏnggukkŭgŭi tanch'ehwaltonggwa soet'oegw- ajŏnge taehan yŏn'gu", *Han'gugyŏsŏngak*, 27:2, pp. 1–33.

Kim, Hyewon (2016), 'Celebrating heteroglossic hybridity: Ready-to-assemble Broadway-style musicals in South Korea', *Studies in Musical Theatre*, 10:3, pp. 343–54.

Kim, Jungwon (2017),'K-popping: Korean women, K-pop, and fandom', Ph.D. thesis, Riverside: University of California.

Kim, Jonhyun (2018a),'A study on the performing arts industry analysis and the evaluation model for Korean original musical commercialization strategy', Ph.D. thesis, Seoul: Sangmyoung University.

Kim, Jonhyun (2018b), 'Domesticating Hedwig: Neoliberal global capitalism and compression in South Korean musical theater', *Journal of Popular Culture*, 51:2, pp. 421–45.

Koskoff, Ellen (2014), *A Feminist Ethnomusicology: Writings on Music and Gender*, Urbana, Chicago and Springfield: University of Illinois Press.

Lee, Hyunjung (2012), '"Broadway" as the superior "other": Situating South Korean theater in the era of globalization', *The Journal of Popular Culture*, 45:2, pp. 320–39.

Lee, Hyunjung (2015), *Performing the Nation in Global Korea: Transnational Theatre*, New York and Basingstoke: Palgrave Macmillan.

Lee, Junghyun (2018), 'Honja sanŭn 20tae yŏsŏngi taehangno ch'oego k'ŭnson', *Edaily*, 7 March, https://m.news.naver.com/read.nhn?mode=LSD&sid1=001&oid=018& aid=0004050532. Accessed 10 September 2018.

McRobbie, Angela (2009), *The Aftermath of Feminism: Gender, Culture and Social Change*, Los Angeles: Sage Publications.

Mulvey, Laura (1975), 'Visual pleasure and narrative cinema', *Screen*, 16:3 pp. 6–18.

Paik, Lora (2015), 'Ch'angjak myujik'ŏrŭi tayangsŏnggwa hŏyakham', *Yŏn'gŭk p'yŏngnon*, 76, pp. 86–90.

Pamsikppang (2016), 'Musical Rachmaninoff', *Naver*, 24 August, https://blog.naver.com/ yellopb/220795809715. Accessed 1 February 2019.

Papaioannou, Spyros (2014), 'Immersion, "smooth" spaces and critical voyeu-rism in the work of Punchdrunk', *Studies in Theatre & Performance*, 34:2, pp. 160–74.

Papalexiou, Eleni (2015), 'The dramaturgies of the gaze: Strategies of vision and optical revelations in the theatre of Romeo Castellucci and Socìetas Raffaello Sanzio', in G. Rodosthenous (ed.), *Theatre as Voyeurism: The Pleasures of Watching*, London: Palgrave Macmillan, pp. 50–68.

Rodosthenous, George (ed.) (2015), *Theatre as Voyeurism: The Pleasures of Watching*, London: Palgrave Macmillan.

Roy, David (2016), 'Masks as a method: Meyerhold to Mnouchkine', *Cogent Arts & Humanities*, 3:1, https://www.tandfonline.com/doi/full/10.1080/23311983.2016.1236436. Accessed 9 April 2019.

Sung, Donghun (2018), 'kongyŏn'gye "MeToo'chijigwan'gaektŭl kŏriro..". sŏngbŏmjoeja paksubadŭl chagyŏgŏpta', *News1*, 25 February, https://news.naver.com/main/read.nhn?mode=LSD&mid=sec&oid=421&aid=0003227523&sid1=001. Accessed 28 February 2018.

Tonkin, Elizabeth (1979), 'Masks and powers', *Man, New Series*, 14:2, pp. 237–48.

Wolf, Stacy (2011), *Changed for Good: A Feminist History of the Broadway Musical*, New York: Oxford University Press.

YTN News (2018), 'Kongyŏn'gye "MeToo" chiji kwan'gaektŭl "WithYou" chiphoe yŏrŏ', *YouTube*, 2 February, https://www.youtube.com/watch?v=ytcgia3te6Q. Accessed 9 April 2020.

Contributors

RYAN DONOVAN is the author of *Broadway Bodies: A Critical History of Conformity* (Oxford University Press, 2023), *Queer Approaches in Musical Theatre* (Bloomsbury/Methuen, 2023) and co-editor of *The Routledge Companion to Musical Theatre* (2022). He is assistant professor of theater studies at Duke University and his articles appear in the *Journal of American Drama and Theatre* and *Studies in Musical Theatre*. He holds a Ph.D. in theatre and performance from The Graduate Center, City University of New York. Website: www.ryan-donovan.com

✯ ✯ ✯ ✯ ✯

MICHELE DVOSKIN (she/her) is an associate professor and the BA Theatre Program Coordinator in Western Kentucky University's Department of Theatre & Dance, where she teaches courses in areas including dramatic literature, theatre and musical theatre history, and the creation of new work as well as regularly directing both plays and musicals. Her current research and creative interests live among the intersections of queer and feminist theatre, musical theatre, historical performance and the development and training of multi-hyphenate theatre artists.

✯ ✯ ✯ ✯ ✯

JORDAN EALEY (they/she) is a Ph.D. candidate in theatre and performance studies at the University of Maryland, College Park. Their work has been published in *The Black Scholar, Girlhood Studies, Frontiers: Augmented*, and *Studies in Musical Theatre*. Jordan's research focuses on the forms and aesthetics of black women-authored musicals from the nineteenth century to the present.

✯ ✯ ✯ ✯ ✯

SHERRILL GOW is the joint head of postgraduate performance at Mountview Academy of Theatre Arts in London, UK. She completed her graduate studies at the Royal Central School of Speech and Drama. Her practice-led research brings together actor training, musical theatre and feminist pedagogies.

* * * * *

JIYOON JUNG is an ethnomusicologist specializing in South Korean contemporary musical culture. Her research interests include tracking omnifarious music cultural formations/transformations, especially in terms of the ways music is perceived in Korean society with issues of postcolonialism, nationalism, Orientalism, identity, cultural subjectivity, modernization and globalization. She received her BA and MA in musicology at Korea National University of Arts, Seoul.

* * * * *

KELLY KESSLER is a professor of media and cinema studies at Chicago's DePaul University. She's the author of *Broadway in the Box: Television's Lasting Love Affair with the Musical* (Oxford, 2020) and *Destabilizing the Hollywood Musical: Music, Masculinity, and Mayhem* (Palgrave, 2010). Her work frequently engages with issues of gender, sexuality and genre in American television, film and theatre and can be found in publications such as *Studies in Musical Theatre*, *Television and New Media* and the *Journal of Popular Music Studies*.

* * * * *

DAVID HALDANE LAWRENCE received his doctorate from Birkbeck College, University of London, in October 2006. He published articles and presented conference papers on the nineteenth- and early twentieth-century theatre and gender issues. His book, *Diverse Performances: Masculinities and the Victorian Stage*, was published by Paradise Press in 2014, five years after his death.

* * * * *

STEPHANIE LIM studies the use of American Sign Language in musical performances on stage and on screen, focusing on the cultural shifts that occur in translation and adaptation. She teaches undergraduate courses in english and theatre at California State University, Northridge, where she received her BA and MA in English. She holds a Ph.D. in drama and theatre from the University of California, Irvine and works as a dramaturg in the Southern California area.

* * * * *

CONTRIBUTORS

DUSTYN MARTINCICH is an associate professor of theatre and dance at Bucknell University, has movement directed, choreographed and performed for concert dance and theatrical stages, and has contributed to *Studies in Musical Theatre, Dueling Grounds: Revolution and Revelation in the Musical Hamilton, Toni Morrison: Forty Years in The Clearing*, the upcoming *Cambridge Companion to West Side Story* and *Leonard* Bernstein: In *Context*. She has a forthcoming, co-edited collection: *Dance in Musical Theatre: A History of the Body in Movement*.

✶ ✶ ✶ ✶ ✶

ADRIENNE GIBBONS OEHLERS is currently a Ph.D. candidate in the Department of Theatre, Film and Media Arts at The Ohio State University and a recipient of the American Fellowship from AAUW for her final year. Her research and creative work intersect both dance and theatre, focusing on gender and race in musical theatre ensembles. She has performed extensively in musical theatre, including in national tours, on Broadway and as a Radio City Rockette.

✶ ✶ ✶ ✶ ✶

DEBORAH PAREDEZ is the author of *Selenidad: Selena, Latinos, and the Performance of Memory* (Duke 2009) and two volumes of poetry. Her work has appeared in the *New York Times*, *Los Angeles Review of Books*, *Boston Review*, *NPR* and elsewhere. Her book of auto-criticism, *American Diva*, is forthcoming from Norton. She is a professor of ethnic studies and creative writing at Columbia University.

✶ ✶ ✶ ✶ ✶

ALEJANDRO POSTIGO is a senior lecturer in musical theatre at the London College of Music, University of West London. His practice-based Ph.D. from The Royal Central School of Speech and Drama (2019) explores the intercultural adaptation of Spanish *copla* songs in international theatre settings. Recent research has led him to address the cultural and linguistic barriers found in Anglophone theatre contexts, and to champion the artistic contributions of audible minorities.

✶ ✶ ✶ ✶ ✶

GEORGE RODOSTHENOUS is a professor of theatre directing and Deputy Head of School at the School of Performance and Cultural Industries, University of Leeds. His research interests include the body in performance, refining improvisational techniques and compositional practices for performance, updating Greek tragedy and the British musical. He has edited the books *Theatre as Voyeurism, Contemporary Approaches to Greek Tragedy, The Disney Musical on Stage and Screen* and *Twenty-First Century Musicals: From Stage to Screen.*

* * * * *

BRYAN M. VANDEVENDER is an assistant professor in the Department of Theatre and Dance at Bucknell University. His scholarship on musical theatre has appeared in *Theatre Annual, New England Theatre Journal, Texas Theatre Journal, Studies in Musical Theatre, The Palgrave Handbook of Musical Theatre Producers, iBroadway: Musical Theatre in the Digital Age* and *The Routledge Handbook to the Contemporary Musical.* His current book project centers the exigencies and ethics of reviving musicals for Broadway, regional theatres and amateur stages

* * * * *

JANET WERTHER is a Ph.D. candidate in theatre and performance at The Graduate Center, CUNY. They have taught theatre/performance and women's/gender/sexuality studies throughout the SUNY and CUNY systems in New York State. Their writing is published in *Studies in Musical Theatre, PAJ: A Journal of Performance and Art* and *TDR: The Drama Review.* Janet also co-convenes the Transfeminisms working group at the American Society for Theatre Research (ASTR) and has performed with The Ballez Company.

* * * * *

STACY WOLF is a professor of theatre and American studies at Princeton University. She is the author of *A Problem Like Maria: Gender and Sexuality in the American Musical; Changed for Good: A Feminist History of the Broadway Musical* and *Beyond Broadway: The Pleasure and Promise of Musical Theatre Across America,* which was selected as a finalist for the Best Book of 2020 Award by the Association for Theatre in Higher Education.

* * * * *

ELIZABETH L. WOLLMAN is a professor of music at Baruch College, CUNY. She is the author of the books *The Theater Will Rock: A History of the Rock Musical, From* Hair *to* Hedwig (2006), *Hard Times: The Adult Musical in*

1970s New York City (2012) and *A Critical Companion to the American Stage Musical* (2017). With Jessica Sternfeld she co-edited *The Routledge Companion to the Contemporary Musical* (2020) and is co-editor of the journal *Studies in Musical Theatre*.